Assessment and management of seafood safety and quality

by
H.H. Huss
Danish Institute for Fisheries Research
Department of Seafood Research
Denmark
L.Ababouch
Fish Utilization and Marketing Service
FAO Fisheries Department
and
L. Gram
Danish Institute for Fisheries Research
Department of Seafood Research
Denmark

Published by arrangement with the
Food and Agriculture Organization of the United Nations
by
Daya Publishing House®
A Division of
Astral International Pvt. Ltd.
New Delhi - 110 002

First Indian Edition, 2007
Reprinted, 2016
ISBN: 978-81-7035-507-6

Published by : **Daya Publishing House®**
A Division of
Astral International Pvt. Ltd.
– ISO 9001:2008 Certified Company –
4760-61/23, Ansari Road, Darya Ganj
New Delhi-110 002
Ph. 011-43549197, 23278134
E-mail: info@astralint.com
Website: www.astralint.com

Printed at : **Salasar Imaging Systems,**
Delhi-110035

PREPARATION OF THIS DOCUMENT

A document entitled "Assurance of Seafood Quality" was published by the Food and Agriculture Organization of the United Nations (FAO) in 1995 (Huss, 1995). This document was based on a series of lecture notes used at workshops and training activities organized by the FAO/Danish International Development Agency (DANIDA) Training Project on Fish Technology and Quality Control (GCP/INT/391/Den).

By the end of 2000 it became clear that this document required updating. New ideas and developments, particularly in the presentation of the Hazard Analysis Critical Control Point (HACCP) concept, needed to be included. In early 2002, I was requested by FAO to prepare an updated and expanded version of the 1995 document including available information on fish safety and quality, especially as it pertains to:

- fish and seafood-borne illnesses: ecology of causative agents and control measures;
- fish safety and quality management systems, including HACCP, monitoring programmes and risk analysis.

Extensive and significant changes have been made compared with the first document. For this reason a new title was chosen: "Assessment and Management of Seafood Safety and Quality". A number of colleagues, all eminent scientists, some with practical experience, have contributed to this new version and I wish to thank them all for their willingness to assist in completing this project within a reasonable time. First of all I wish to thank my co-editors and co-authors, Professor Lone Gram, DIFRES[1] and Professor Lahsen Ababouch, Chief, Fish Utilization and Marketing Service, FAO[2], Rome for their contributions. Very special and sincere thanks to Professor Gram for her skilful and high quality work in editing the text and contributions from a variety of authors.

For valuable contributions, I wish to thank:

Dr John Ryder, Director of FAO/Eastfish[3] Copenhagen, Denmark
Dr Paw Dalgaard, Senior scientist, DIFRES[1], Denmark
Dr Marco Frederiksen, Scientist, DIFRES[1], Denmark
Dr Peter Karim Ben Embarek, WHO[4], Geneva
Mr Alan Reilly, Deputy Chief Executive, Food Safety Authority[5], Ireland

I also wish to thank Dr Maria Rasch from DIFRES for great assistance in editing and proofreading, and Birgitte Rubæk and Valeriu Popesco for providing excellent drawings.

The Danish Institute for Fisheries Research provided secretarial assistance and other resources (stationary, photocopies, etc.) for the project, which was valuable and very appreciated. Special thanks to librarian Søren Tørper Christensen without whom we would not have managed to write the book.

Lyngby 6 January 2003

Hans Henrik Huss (HHH)

Danish Institute for Fisheries Research
Department of Seafood Research

---

[1] DIFRES: Danish Institute for Fisheries Research, Department of Seafood Research, c/o Technical University of Denmark bldg. 221, DK-2800 Lyngby, Denmark
[2] Fish Utilization and Marketing Service, Food and Agriculture Organization of the United Nations (FAO), Viale delle Terme di Caracalla, 00100 Rome, Italy
[3] FAO/Eastfish, Midtermolen 3, DK-2100 København Ø, Denmark
[4] World Health Organization (WHO), Avenue Appia 20, CH - 1211 Geneva 27, Switzerland
[5] Food Safety Authority of Ireland, Abbey Court, Lower Abbey Street, Dublin 1, Ireland

Huss, H.H; Ababouch, L; Gram, L.

Assessment and management of seafood safety and quality
FAO Fisheries Technical Paper. No. 444. Rome, FAO. 2003. 230p.

ABSTRACT

This paper compiles the state of knowledge on fish safety and quality with the view to provide a succinct yet comprehensive resource book to risk and fish quality managers. After an introduction about world fish production and consumption and the developments in safety and quality systems, it provides a detailed review of the hazards causing public health concerns in fish and fish products. It devotes several Chapters to risk mitigation and management tools, with a detailed description of the requirements for the implementation of Good Hygienic and Manufacturing Practices (GHP/GMP), of the Hazard Analysis and Critical Control Point (HACCP) system and of the monitoring programmes to control biotoxins, pathogenic bacteria and viruses and chemical pollutants. Chapters on the use of microbiological criteria, the use of the HACCP approach to target quality aspects other than safety matters, predictive microbiology, traceability and examples of food safety objectives complete the document.

Distribution:
FAO Members and interested organizations
FAO Regional and Subregional Fisheries Officers
FAO Fisheries Department

CONTENTS

page

1 **INTRODUCTION** (Hans Henrik Huss) 1

2 **WORLD SEAFOOD PRODUCTION AND CONSUMPTION** (Lone Gram) 3
2.1 **Fish utilization** 5

3 **DEVELOPMENTS IN FOOD SAFETY AND QUALITY SYSTEMS** 7
3.1 **Traditional quality control** (Hans Henrik Huss/John Ryder) 7
3.1.1 **Principles of sampling** 8
3.1.2 **The concept of probability** 9
3.2 **Modern safety and quality assurance methods and systems** (Hans Henrik Huss/John Ryder) 10
3.2.1 **Methods to manage quality and safety** 10
3.3 **Risk analysis, food safety objectives** (Lone Gram) 13

PART I: ASPECTS OF SEAFOOD RISK ASSESSMENT
4 **IDENTIFICATION OF HAZARDS IN SEAFOOD** 19
4.1 **Statistics on seafood-borne diseases** (Lone Gram) 19
4.2 **Detentions and rejections of seafood in international trade** (Lone Gram/Lahsen Ababouch) 21

5 **CHARACTERIZATION OF HAZARDS IN SEAFOOD** 26
5.1 **Biological hazards** 26
5.1.1 **Pathogenic bacteria** (Hans Henrik Huss/Lone Gram) 26
5.1.2 **Production of biogenic amines** (Lahsen Ababouch/Lone Gram) 52
5.1.3 **Viruses** (Lone Gram) 57
5.1.4 **Parasites** (Hans Henrik Huss/Peter Karim Ben Embarek) 60
5.1.5 **Aquatic biotoxins** (Hans Henrik Huss) 70
5.2 **Chemical hazards** 77
5.2.1 **Industrial and environmental contaminants** (Hans Henrik Huss) 77
5.2.2 **Veterinary drugs** (Allan Reilly) 79
5.3 **Physical hazards** (Hans Henrik Huss) 84

PART II: RISK MANAGEMENT TOOLS
6 **INTERNATIONAL REGULATORY FRAMEWORK FOR FISH SAFETY AND QUALITY** (Lahsen Ababouch) 96
6.1 **The World Trade Organization (WTO) agreement** 96
6.1.1 **The agreement on the Application of Sanitary and Phytosanitary Measures** 96
6.1.2 **The agreement on Technical Barriers to Trade** 97
6.2 **The Food and Agriculture Organization of the United Nations (FAO)** 97
6.2.1 **Codex Alimentarius** 97
6.2.2 **The FAO Code of conduct for responsible fisheries** 98
6.3 **Conclusion** 99

7 **PREREQUISITES TO HACCP** (Hans Henrik Huss/John Ryder) 101
7.1 **The processing plant** 104
7.1.1 **Plant location, physical environment and infrastructure** 104
7.1.2 **Buildings, construction and layout** 104
7.1.3 **Facilities** 106
7.1.4 **Utensils and equipment** 107
7.2 **Operational conditions including GHP** 109
7.2.1 **Safety of water and ice** 109
7.2.2 **Cleanliness of food contact surfaces** 114
7.2.3 **Prevention of cross-contamination** 123
7.2.4 **Maintenance of facilities for personnel hygiene** 125

7.2.5 **Protection of food from adulterants** 126
7.2.6 **Proper labelling, safe storage and use of toxic compounds** 126
7.2.7 **Control of employee health conditions** 127
7.2.8 **Pest control** 127
7.2.9 **Waste management** 128
7.2.10 **Storage and transportation** 129
7.2.11 **Traceability and recall procedures** 129
7.2.12 **Training** 130

8 **THE HACCP SYSTEM** 133
8.1 **Development and adoption of the HACCP principles** (Hans Henrik Huss) 133
8.2 **The basic seven principles of HACCP** (Hans Henrik Huss) 134
8.3 **Application of the HACCP principles** (Hans Henrik Huss) 135
8.4 **HACCP implementation in the fish industry** (Hans Henrik Huss) 145
8.5 **HACCP audit** (Lahsen Ababouch) 146
8.5.1 **Planning and conducting an HACCP audit** 146
8.5.2 **Frequency of audit** 150
8.5.3 **HACCP approval /certification** 150
8.5.4 **Qualifications of HACCP auditors** 150

9 **CONSIDERATIONS IN THE APPLICATION OF THE HACCP PRINCIPLES TO SEAFOOD PRODUCTION** (Hans Henrik Huss) 153
9.1 **Hazard analysis of raw material** 153
9.2 **Molluscan shellfish** 157
9.3 **Raw fish – to be consumed raw** 158
9.4 **Fresh/frozen fish and crustaceans – to be fully cooked before consumption** 159
9.5 **Lightly-preserved fish products** 162
9.6 **Fermented fish** 164
9.7 **Semi-preserved fish** 166
9.8 **Mildly heat-processed fish products** 167
9.9 **Heat-sterilized fish products packed in sealed containers (canned fish)** 170
9.10 **Dried, smoke-dried, heavily-salted fish** 171
9.11 **Seafood risk categories** 173

10 **APPLICATION OF HACCP PRINCIPLES IN THE MANAGEMENT OF OTHER QUALITY ASPECTS** (Lone Gram) 178
10.1 **Microbiological aspects** 178
10.2 **Chemical aspects** 179
10.3 **Physical aspects** 180
10.4 **Example** 180

11. **MONITORING PROGRAMMES** (Hans Henrik Huss) 184
11.1 **Toxic algae** 184
11.2 **Pathogenic bacteria and viruses** 186
11.3 **Chemical contaminants** 187

12. **EXAMPLES OF FSOs FOR BACTERIA OR TOXINS IN SEAFOOD PRODUCTS** (Lone Gram) 189
12.1 ***Listeria monocytogenes*** **in RTE seafoods** 189
12.2 **Staphylococcal enterotoxin in cooked crustaceans** 192

13 **USE OF CRITERIA** (Hans Henrik Huss) 195
13.1 **Microbiological criteria (MC) and testing** 195
13.1.1 **Definitions and components of MC** 195
13.1.2 **Purpose and application of MC** 196
13.1.3 **Principles for establishing MC** 197
13.1.4 **Sampling and microbiological testing** 197

13.1.5 **MC applied by the EU and others** 198
13.1.6 **Concluding remarks** 201
13.2 **Performance and process criteria** 202

14 **PREDICTIVE MICROBIOLOGY** (Paw Dalgaard) 204
14.1 **Development and validation of predictive models** 204
14.2 **Practical use of models and application software** 207

15 **TRACEABILITY** (Marco Frederiksen/Lone Gram) 210
15.1 **Internal versus external (chain) traceability** 211
15.2 **Traceability systems** 211
15.3 **Labelling products** 211
15.4 **Fresh fish quality traceability** 212
15.5 **EU legislation on traceability of fish and fish products** 213

APPENDIXES (Hans Henrik Huss) 216
1 **Assessment of food safety programmes** 216
2 **Hazard analysis worksheet** 222
3 **HACCP plan form** 223
4 **Generic HACCP plan for the production and processing of oysters** 224

Index 227

1 INTRODUCTION (Hans Henrik Huss)

Food quality, including safety, is a major concern facing the food industry today. A number of surveys have shown that consumer awareness about quality of their food is increasing. The extensive coverage in the daily press of food safety issues such as the BSE crisis, concerns about genetically modified foods, use of growth promoters, existence of pesticide and dioxin residues in food, the *Salmonella* problem, transfer between micro organisms of resistance to commonly used antibiotics add to consumers' fear and unease about what they eat.

The situation is further complicated by the fact that many consumers suffer from a serious lack of knowledge on simple food safety issues. Thus, less than one percent of US and Canadian consumers met minimum criteria for acceptable safety practices in a North America audit of food preparation behaviour, in which 106 consumers agreed to be watched while preparing food (Daniels, 1998). In a similar study, only 4.7% of UK consumers fully implemented appropriate food safety control practices (Griffith *et al.,* 1998). Furthermore, most consumers exhibit a general disbelief in the importance of good handling practices and a great resistance to effective protective treatment such as chemical preservation or irradiation. As a consequence, there is an increasing demand for more fresh or even raw food with enhanced natural flavours and produced with less or no use of salt and other preservatives.

A great number of socio-economic changes such as increased urbanization (crowding), migrations and population demographics are further contributing to the safety of foods. The population of highly susceptible persons is expanding worldwide because of ageing, malnutrition, HIV infections and other underlying medical conditions with a weakened immune system.

To meet these challenges, food manufacturing is becoming a highly complex business, particularly since raw material is sourced on a global scale and new processing technologies are used to produce a vast array of products. Much research is needed to evaluate new techniques and to consider food safety issues at all stages, from production of raw materials to sale of final product.

Despite great efforts in research, food-borne diseases continue to present a major problem of both health and economic significance. The cost of food-borne disease is high. Although the full economic impact is not known, preliminary estimates in the United States in 1994 placed the cost between US$ 10-83 billion (FDA, 1997). Some of this huge cost is borne by the food-producing company – and loss of consumer confidence may even cause bankruptcy – but the great majority is borne by the government. It has become overwhelmingly clear that all countries need an adequate food control programme to ensure a safe food supply to protect and promote the health of the consumer.

Yet, food safety is not only a consumer concern, but also at the very root of a properly functioning market. Food safety as a prerequisite for protecting consumer health also serves the interest of producers and those involved in processing and marketing foodstuffs. The production and consumption of food is central to any society and has a wide range of economic, social and in many cases environmental consequences.

Food control includes all activities carried out to ensure the quality and safety of food. Every stage from initial production to processing, storage, marketing and consumption must be included in a food quality and safety programme. The overall goal is to provide a systematic approach to all control and inspection activities through a managed programme based on proper scientific principles and appropriate risk assessment, leading to careful targeting of inspection and control resources. Furthermore, the risk assessment must be transparent, i.e. it must be carefully documented, including any constraints that may have affected the quality of the risk estimate and fully available to independent assessors. Sufficient financial and personnel resources must be made available. However, it must be emphasized that no management system can offer zero risk in terms of consumer health protection.

Fish and fishery products are in the forefront of food safety and quality improvement because they are among the most internationally traded food commodities. In 2001, fish trade amounted to US$ 54 000 million, of which approximately 50 percent originated in developing countries.

The first part of this publication provides some of the information required to make risk assessment for seafood products. It shows that in many situations the essential data needed to perform a formal quantitative risk assessment are currently not available. However, in most cases, semi-quantitative risk assessments are more than sufficient to allow for appropriate control action.

The second part outlines the risk management strategies used in seafood processing today. The prerequisite to use the HACCP system and the HACCP system itself are outlined in detail as examples of risk management programmes.

The management of other quality parameters such as spoilage and shell life of seafood, chemicals and physical quality aspect are discussed in a final Chapter.

The present publication is an update and expansion of an earlier document by Hans Henrik Huss (1994) *Assurance of Seafood Quality*. FAO Fisheries Technical Paper No. 334.

References*

Daniels, R.W. 1998. Home food safety. *Food Technology* 52, 54-56.

FDA (Food and Drug Administration) 1997. *Food Code*. US Department of Health and Human Services, Public Health Service, FDA, Washington DC, USA.

Griffith, C., D. Worsfold & R. Mitchell 1998. Food preparation, risk communication and the consumer. *Food Control* 9, 225-232.

* All references in this Technical Paper have been left in the authors' bibliographic style

2 WORLD SEAFOOD PRODUCTION AND CONSUMPTION (Lone Gram)

World fish production (catches of wild fish plus production in aquaculture) has increased steadily to approximately 120 million tonnes in recent years (Figure 2.1) (FAO, 2000). Declines in captured fish were seen in 1998 (Figure 2.2), mainly due to decreased catches of small pelagic fish in Chile and Peru, caused by the "El Niño". This decline affected mainly fish meal production, while food fish production stayed the same. In 1999 and 2000 fish production recovered and returned to pre-El Niño level. China is the top producer with some 41.6 million tonnes in 2000. Peru was the second major fishing nation with catches of 10.7 million tonnes. The importance of aquaculture continues to expand, especially for freshwater species such as carp, and almost one third of fish used for human consumption are now produced in aquaculture (FAO, 2000).

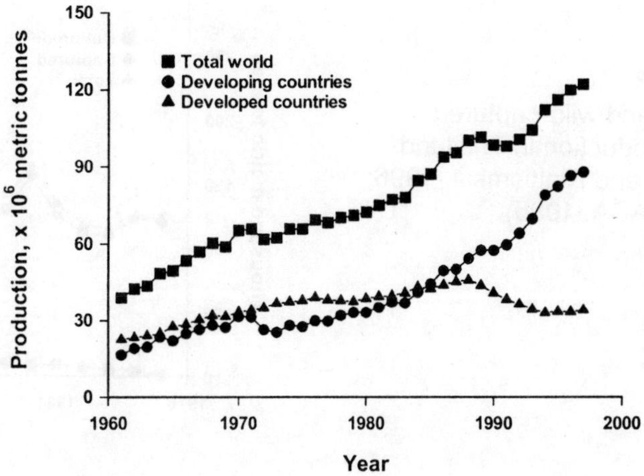

Figure 2.1
Total world fish production from 1961 to 1997 divided between developed and developing countries (FAO, 2000).

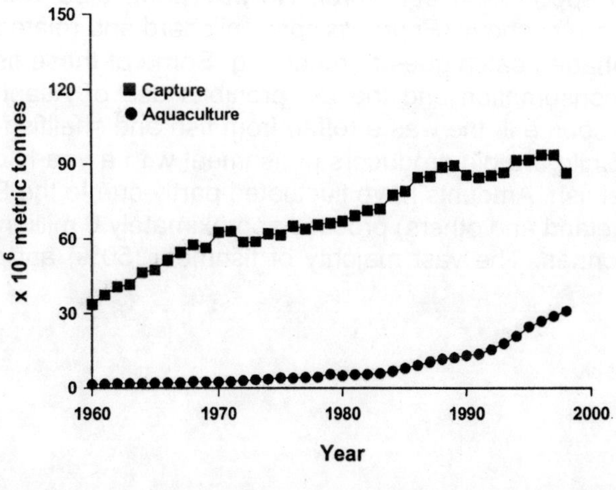

Figure 2.2
Total world fish catches and aquaculture production from 1960 to 1998 (FAO, 2000).

While aquaculture has been increasing for the last 20 years, the increment has dropped during the last five years. The total value of aquaculture and catches by 2000 was approx US$ 130 000 million and total world trade of fish and fishery products increased in 2000 to r each US$ 54 000 million for exports. Thailand is the main exporting country with US$ 4 300 million. China experienced a sharp increase in its export performance. It is now number two among all fish exporting countries with US$ 3 700 million. The Chinese fisheries exporting industry is specializing in re-processing of imported raw material, creating a strong value-addition in this process. Norway, which used to be number two fish exporter in previous years, reported lower export values. This is in part due to lower salmon prices, but also caused by low value of the euro – the currency of the main trading area for Norwegian fish. Almost two thirds of the total world production is produced by or caught in developing countries (Figure 2.1).

Developed countries accounted for more than 80% of total imports of fishery products in 2000 in value terms. Japan was the biggest importer of fishery products, accounting for some 26% of the global total. The European Union (EU) has increased its dependency on imports for its fish supply. The United States, besides being the world's fourth major exporting country, was the second biggest importer. Imports were growing in 2000, mainly due to expanding shrimp imports. Shrimps and prawns are increasingly produced in aquaculture especially in Southeast Asia. A significant increase has been seen in countries such as Thailand (Figure 2.3).

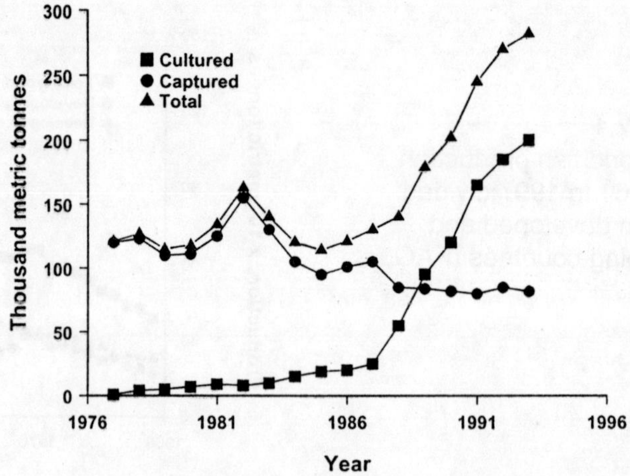

Figure 2.3
Cultured and wild-captured shrimp production in Thailand (Dierberg and Kiattismkul, 1996; cf FAO/NACA, 1995).

Between 20 and 30% of the total world production of fish is used to manufacture animal feeds (Figure 2.4). The greater tonnage comes from processing whole fish that are not suitable for human consumption because they are too bony, too oily, or otherwise unsatisfactory; these fish are sometimes called "industrial fish". Examples of fish used for fishmeal include capelin, menhaden (*Brevoortia* spp.), sand eel, sprat, Norway pout, blue whiting, horse mackerel, Atlantic herring (*Clupea* spp.), anchovy (*Engraulis* spp.), pilchard and related species. In the USA, for example, the entire menhaden catch goes to rendering. Some of these fish, e.g. Atlantic herring, could be used for direct consumption and the EU prohibits use of Atlantic herring for fish meal production. A secondary source is the waste (offal) from fish and shellfish operations. South America, especially Peru and Chile are big producers of fishmeal with a yearly catch between 5 and 15 million tonnes of industrial fish. Amounts have fluctuated partly due to the El Niño. European countries (Denmark, Norway, Iceland and others) process approximately 6 million tonnes per year and the USA process 1 million tonnes. The vast majority of fishmeal (50%) and fish oil (90%) is used for aquaculture feeds.

Figure 2.4
Use of world fish production for human consumption and other use (FAO, 2000).

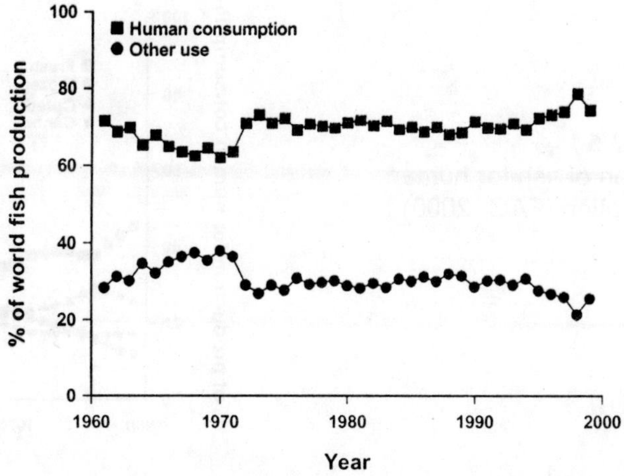

The bovine spongiform encephalopathy (BSE) scare has had an impact on the fish meal market particularly in Europe in 2001. In early 2001 the EU prohibited the use of animal proteins in all animal feeds with the exception of milk powder and fish meal. The use of the latter was prohibited in ruminant's diets only. Fish oil is mostly used for fish feed, although a minor amount is used for human consumption. The demand for fish oil is high and competing vegetable oils seem to be in shorter supply than initially forecast for 2001, and their prices are expected to move up. As a result, a further increase in fish oil prices is likely.

A small – and declining – amount of the fish produced is used for food aid. In 2000, some 7 600 tonnes were donated which compares to 25 800 tonnes in 1989. Canned fish is the main product, while edible fat reported a dramatic decline in recent years. Norway continues to be the main supplier of fish for food aid, and reported a sharp decline in 1998. Developing countries are practically not tapped as a source of fish for food aid.

2.1 Fish utilization

Since 1994, more and more fish has been used for direct human consumption rather than for other purposes (see Figure 2.4). Of the products used for human consumption, fresh fish showed significant growth during the 1990s, and almost 50% of fish used for human consumption is sold fresh (Figure 2.5). This change has been accompanied by a decline in the use of cured and canned fish. Also, the proportion sold as frozen fish is declining. This pattern has largely been driven by growth in consumption.

Fish has a significant capacity for processing and almost two thirds of the catch (in 1998) were used for further processing. A large fraction, approximately 30%, of the fish used for human consumption was frozen, approximately 14% canned and approximately 12% cured. The remaining 45% was sold fresh (Figure 2.5).

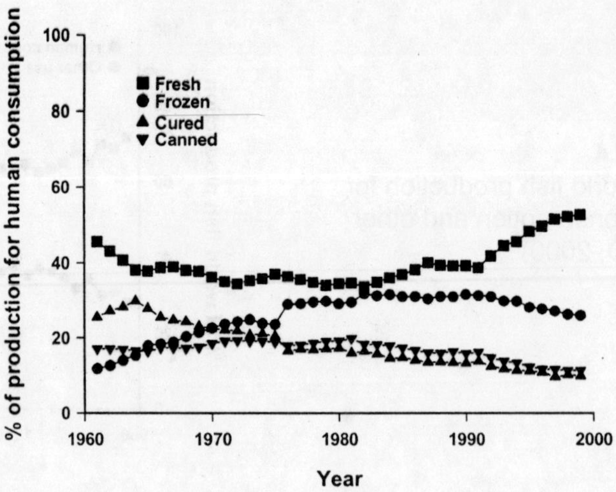

Figure 2.5
Utilization of fish for human consumption (FAO, 2000).

Different regions of the world have very different eating habits with respect to seafoods. Demersal fish such as cod are much preferred in northern Europe and North America, and cephalopods are consumed in several Mediterranean and Asian countries, but to a much lesser extent in other regions. Despite the fast-growing contribution of aquaculture to production, crustaceans are still high-priced commodities and their consumption is mostly concentrated in affluent economies (FAO, 2000).

References

Dierberg, F.E. & Kiattismkul, W. 1996. Issues, impacts and implications of shrimp aquaculture in Thailand. *Environmental Management* 20, 649-666.

FAO (Food and Agriculture Organization). 2000. *The State of World Fisheries and Aquaculture*. FAO, Rome, Italy.

FAO/NACA (Food and Agriculture Organization of the United Nations/Network of Aquaculture Centres in Asia-Pacific). 1995. Regional study and workshop on the environmental assessment and management of aquaculture development (TCP/RAS/2253) *NACA Environment and Aquaculture Series* No. 1. Network of Aquaculture Centres in Asia-Pacific, Bangkok, Thailand.

3 DEVELOPMENTS IN FOOD SAFETY AND QUALITY SYSTEMS

3.1 Traditional quality control (Hans Henrik Huss/John Ryder)

The traditional quality control program was based on establishing effective hygiene control. Confirmation of safety and identification of potential problems was obtained by end-product testing. Control of hygiene was ensured by inspection of facilities to ensure adherence to established and generally accepted Codes of Good Hygiene Practices (GHP) and of Good Manufacturing Practices (GMP).

Traditional Quality Control
Codes of GHP/GMP
Inspection of facilities and operations
End-product testing

Codes of GHP/GMP are still the basis of food hygiene as outlined in Chapter 7. However, codes – although being essential – only provide for the general requirements without considering the specific requirements of the food and the processing of specific foods. Also the requirements are often stated in very imprecise terms such as "satisfactory", "adequate", "acceptable", "suitable", "if necessary", "as soon as possible" etc. This lack of specifics leaves the interpretation to the inspector, who may place too much emphasis on relatively unimportant matters. He may fail in distinguishing between "what is nice and what is necessary" and consequently increase the cost of the programme without reducing the hazards.

Perhaps one of the most common mistakes that many inspection services and some food companies make is to rely on end-product testing. Very often this has been the only quality and safety assurance system applied. Samples have been taken randomly from the day's production, and examined in detail in the laboratory. There are several problems related to this procedure:

- is costly. A well equipped laboratory will be needed as well as trained personnel. The running costs of a laboratory is high. Also, the cost of products "lost" to testing may be very high;
- the results are retrospective, and all cost and expenses have already been incurred if any hazards are identified in the end-product testing programme. What is needed is a preventive system, where safety hazards are anticipated and safety is built into the product right from the start;
- it may take several days before results from end-product testing are available;
- the chances of finding a hazard will be variable, but most often very low (see below). Nevertheless, the hard work of sampling and testing will give a sensation of "being in control" and create a strong but false sense of security.

It is important to understand the ineffectiveness and limitations in using end-product sampling and testing to ensure product safety. In most cases there is no test that give an absolutely accurate result with no false positives and no false negatives. This is certainly the case for all microbiological testing. Furthermore, there are the principles of sampling and the concept of probability to consider.

3.1.1 Principles of sampling

The number, size and nature of the samples taken for analysis greatly influence the results. In some instances it is possible for the analytical sample to be truly representative of the "lot" sampled. This applies to liquids such as milk and water. However, in cases of lots or batches of food this is not the case, and a food lot may easily consist of units with wide differences in (microbiological) quality. Even within the individual unit (i.e. a retail pack) the hazard (i.e. the presence of pathogens) can be very unevenly distributed, and the probability of detecting may be very low (Table 3.1).

Table 3.1 Detection probabilities – end-product testing of milk powder contaminated with *Salmonella* (Mortimore and Wallace, 1998).

	Contamination rate	Number of random samples	Probability of detection[1]
Homogenously contaminated	5 cells/kg	10	71%
	1 cell/kg	10	22%
Heterogeneously contaminated	5 cells/kg in 1% of batch	10	<2%
	10^4 cells/kg in 1% of batch	10	<15%

1. Assuming detection test is 100% effective (most are <90%)

In this example, a contamination rate of *Salmonella* at 5 cells/kg and assuming the contamination is restricted to 1% of the batch, the probability of detecting the hazard by taking 10 samples of 25 g would be lower than 2%. If the contamination with *Salmonella* is homogeneously distributed at the same rate, probability of detection would increase to 71%.

A sampling plan (Attributes plan) can be based on positive or negative indications of a micro organism. Such a plan is described by the two figures "n" (number of sample units drawn) and "c" (maximum allowable number of positive results). In a 2-class attributes sampling plan, each sample unit is then classified into acceptable or non-acceptable. In some cases the presence of an organism (i.e. *Salmonella*) would be unacceptable. In other cases, a boundary is chosen, denoted by "m", which divides an acceptable count from an unacceptable. The 2-class sampling plan will reject a "lot" if more than "c" out of "n" samples tested are unacceptable.

In a 3-class sampling plan "m" separates acceptable counts from marginally acceptable counts and another figure "M" is indicating the boundary between marginally acceptable counts and unacceptable counts as shown in Figure 3.1.

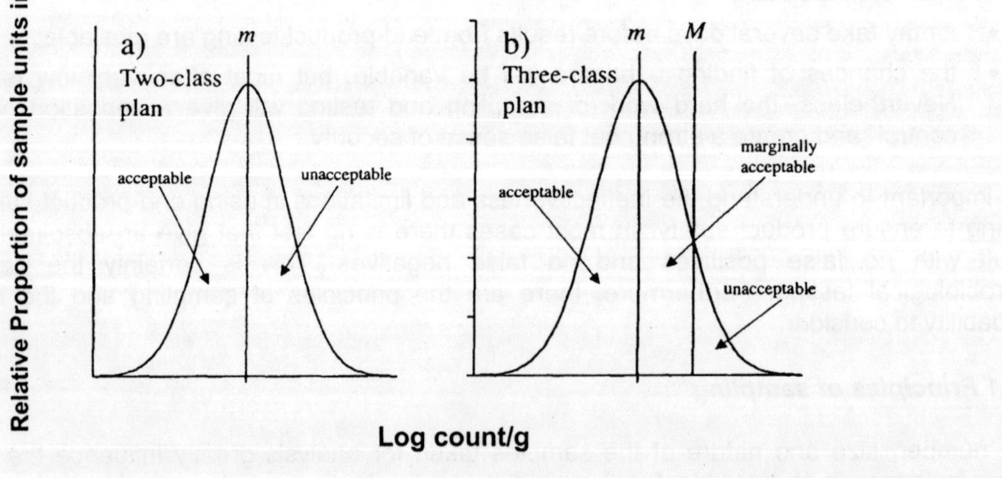

Figure 3.1 Two- and three–class attributes plans (based on ICMSF, 2002).

3.1.2 The concept of probability

The safety which can be obtained with such sampling plans depends on the figures chosen for "c" and "n". This can be illustrated with the so-called operating characteristic curves which are demonstrating the statistical properties of such plans (Figure 3.2).

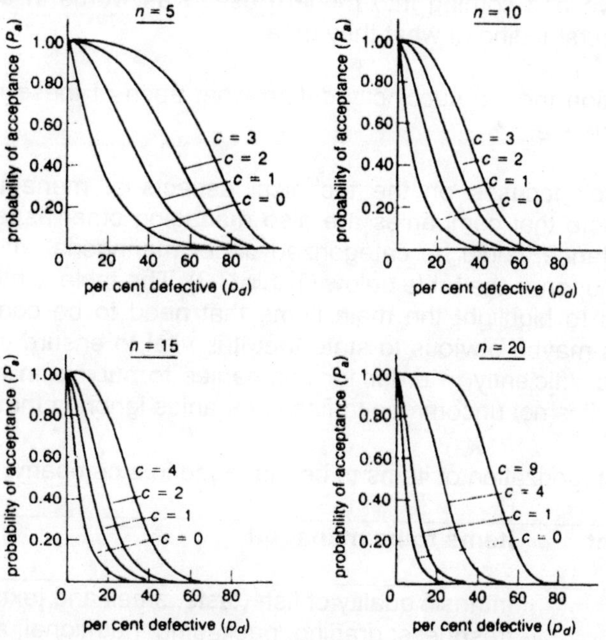

Figure 3.2
Operating characteristic curves for different sample sizes (n) and different criteria of acceptance (c) for 2-class attributes plan (ICMSF, 1986).

The figures show that the greater the number of defective units (P_d), the lower is the probability of acceptance (P_a) of the lot. It is further demonstrated, that high value of "n" and low value of "c" reduces the risk of accepting lots with same number of defective units. It can be seen that testing of foods for the presence of contaminants offers very little protection even when large numbers of samples are examined as also shown in Table 3.2.

Table 3.2 Effect of lot quality (% defective in a lot) on the probability of acceptance (%) for different 2-class sampling plans (based on EC, 1998).

% defective samples in lot	probability of acceptance (%) given sampling plans with a total of "n" samples and allowance of "c" defect samples			
	n=1, c=0	n=5, c=0	n=10, c=0	n=60, c=0
1	99.0	95.1	90.4	54.7
2	98.0	90.4	81.7	30.0
5	95.0	77.4	59.9	4.6
10	90.0	59.1	34.9	0.18
20	80.0	32.8	10.7	0.00015

Table 3.2 clearly shows, that lot testing is not effective when defect rates are low. A product safety defect rate of 1% is absolutely intolerable in many food operations. Potentially, it represents 10 000 unsafe units per one million units manufactured. More than 3 000-5 000 units would need to be sampled and tested in order to detect a 1% defect rate with 95% or 99% probability (Corlett, 1998).

It is evident, that even the most elaborate sampling and testing of end-product cannot guarantee safety of the product. There is no way to avoid some degree of risk and error in each acceptance and each rejection of lots unless the entire lot is tested, in which case no edible food will be left.

3.2 Modern safety and quality assurance methods and systems (Hans Henrik Huss/John Ryder)

To the uninitiated, and also the initiated, there may seem to be a whole host of different options or methods for ensuring the safety and quality of food products. The situation is not helped by the acronyms arising from these methods i.e. ISO, GMP, GHP, HACCP, TQM, etc. seeming to have a life of their own and coming into modern usage as words in themselves, and sometimes used without an understanding of what they mean.

This brief section tries to succinctly define what each of these methods are and what they were designed to achieve.

While this book focuses on the technical aspects of managing quality including safety, it is important to note that companies are also managing other aspects of quality in their companies, which, for instance, could be categorized under managerial and environmental concerns. These are expanded upon in the table below (Table 3.3). The table is more indicative than exhaustive and merely serves to highlight the main items that need to be considered in managing quality in a company. It is maybe obvious to state that it is vital to ensure that all these factors are managed effectively and efficiently in order for companies to survive in today's competitive environments. Unfortunately, it is not uncommon to find companies ignoring these principles.

Table 3.3 Categorization of items to be managed in a company.

Management concern	Items to be managed
Technical	Intrinsic quality of fish (taste, smell and texture); safety; spoilage/ freshness; grading; packaging; nutritional; authenticity; shelf life, etc.
Managerial	Administrative systems; customer relations; promotion; delivery commitments; invoicing and payment, etc.
Environmental	Waste and water management; noise pollution; odeurs; pollutants, etc.

3.2.1 Methods to manage quality and safety

So, what is there in existence to manage quality and safety, and how do they relate to each other?

Below are listed the most well known methods to manage quality and/or safety, and these will be briefly discussed individually and then how they integrate with each other.

- Good Hygienic Practices (GHP) / Good Manufacturing Practice (GMP) or Sanitation Standard Operating Procedures (SSOP) or prerequisite programmes
- Hazard Analysis Critical Control Point (HACCP)
- Quality Control (QC)
- Quality Assurance (QA) / Quality Management (QM) - ISO standards
- Quality Systems
- Total Quality Management (TQM).

The food safety tools and their relationship is shown in Figure 3.3.

Good Hygienic Practices / Good Manufacturing Practices

The terms GHP and GMP basically covers the same ground as discussed in Chapter 7. They refer to measures and requirements which any establishment should meet to produce safe food. These requirements are prerequisites to other and more specific approaches such as HACCP, and are often now called prerequisite programmes. In recent years the term Standard Sanitary Operating

Procedures (SSOP) has also been used in the US to encompass basically the same issues, i.e. best practices.

Hazard Analysis Critical Control Point

Hazard Analysis Critical Control Point (HACCP) is a systematic approach which identifies, evaluates, and controls hazards which are significant for food safety (CAC, 1997). HACCP is discussed in great detail throughout this book. In the context of this section, HACCP ensures food safety through an approach that builds upon foundations provided by good manufacturing practice. It identifies the points in the food production process that require constant control and monitoring to make sure the process stays within identified limits. Statistical Process Control systems are relevant to this operation.

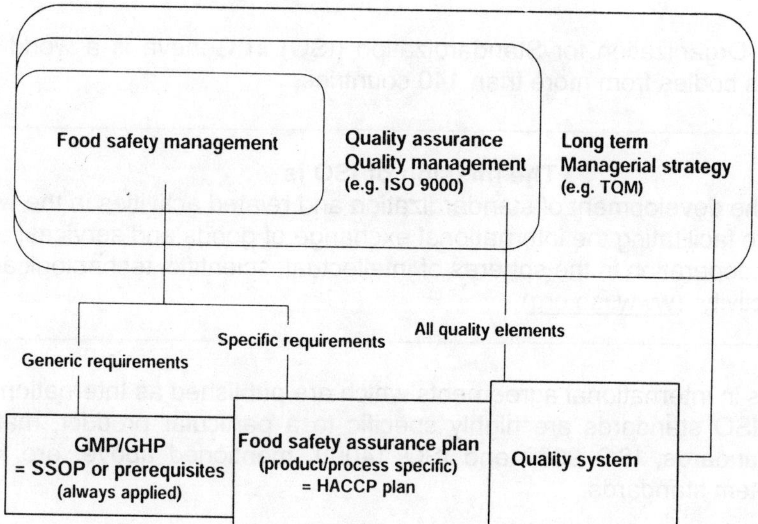

Figure 3.3 Food safety tools: an integrated approach (modified from Jouve *et al.*, 1998).

HACCP is legislated in many countries, including the USA and the European Union. The combination of GHP/GMP and HACCP is particularly beneficial in that the efficient application of GHP/GMP allows HACCP to focus on the true critical determinants of safety.

Quality Control

> **Quality control (QC)**
> Can be defined as the operational techniques and activities that are used to fulfil quality requirements (Jouve *et al.*, 1998)

It is an important subset of any quality assurance system and is an active process that monitors and, if necessary, modifies the production system so as to consistently achieve the required quality.

It can be argued that QC is used as part of the HACCP system, in terms of monitoring the critical control points in the HACCP plan. However, traditional QC is much broader than purely this focus on critical control points for safety systems. The pitfalls of relying on QC procedures, more importantly as end product testing, have been detailed in section 3.1 and will not be expanded upon here.

Quality Assurance / Quality Management

This can be defined as all the activities and functions concerned with the attainment of quality in a company. In a total system, this would include the technical, managerial and environmental aspects as alluded to above. The best known of the quality assurance standards is ISO 9000 and for environmental management, ISO 14000.

The term quality management is often used interchangeably with quality assurance. In the seafood industry, the term quality management has been used to focus mostly on the management of the technical aspects of quality in a company, for instance, the Canadian Quality Management Programme which is based on HACCP but covers other technical issues such as labelling.

ISO Standards

The International Organization for Standardization (ISO) in Geneva is a worldwide federation of national standards bodies from more than 140 countries.

> **The mission of ISO is**
> to promote the development of standardization and related activities in the world with a view to facilitating the international exchange of goods and services, and to developing cooperation in the spheres of intellectual, scientific, technological and economic activity (www.iso.org)

ISO's work results in international agreements which are published as International Standards. The vast majority of ISO standards are highly specific to a particular product, material, or process. However, two standards, ISO 9000 and ISO 14000, mentioned above, are known as generic management system standards.

Over half a million ISO 9000 certificates have been awarded in 161 countries and economies around the world and in 2001 alone over 100 000 certificates were awarded, 43% of which were the new ISO 9001:2000 certificate.

Historically, the ISO 9000 series of standards of relevance to the seafood industry included:

- ISO 9001 Quality systems - Model for quality assurance in design/ development, production, installation and servicing
- ISO 9002 Quality systems - Model for quality assurance in production and installation.

More recently, the new ISO 9001:2000 certificate is the only ISO 9000 standard against whose requirements a quality system can be certified by an external agency and replaces the old ISO 9001, 9002 and 9003 with one standard.

It is important to note that the ISO 9000 standards relate to quality management with customer satisfaction as the end point, and that they do not specifically refer to technical processes only. ISO 9000 gives an assurance to a customer that the company has developed procedures (and adheres to them) for all aspects of the company's business.

ISO 14000 is primarily concerned with environmental management. Introduced much later than the ISO 9000 series, there are now over 35 000 ISO 14000 certificates awarded in 112 countries or economies of the world. During 2001, nearly 14 000 certificates were awarded, around 40% of the total awarded since the introduction of the standard.

In most countries, implementation of ISO 9000 quality management systems or ISO 14000 environmental systems are voluntary.

Quality Systems

This term covers organizational structure, responsibilities, procedures, processes and the resources needed to implement comprehensive quality management (Jouve *et al.* 1998). They are intended to cover all quality elements. Within the framework of a quality system, the prerequisite programme and HACCP provides the approach to food safety.

Total Quality Management (TQM)

TQM is an organization's management approach, centred on quality and based on the participation of all its members and aimed at long-term success through customer satisfaction and benefits to the members of the organization and to society (Jouve *et al.* 1998). Thus TQM represents the organizations' "cultural" approach and together with the quality systems provides the philosophy, culture and discipline necessary to commit everybody in the organization to achieve all the managerial objectives related to quality.

3.3 Risk analysis, food safety objectives (Lone Gram)

The management and control of (sea)food borne diseases is carried out by several groups of people. It involves experts assessing the risk, i.e. providing the epidemiological, microbiological and technological data about the pathogenic agent, the food, the host etc. It involves risk managers who at government level have to decide what level of risk society will tolerate and risk managers in both industry and government that have to implement procedures to control the risk. At industry level this is done using GHP and HACCP procedures as described below.

The term "risk analysis" it the process underlying development of food safety standards (FAO/WHO, 1997). It consists of three separate but integrated parts, namely risk assessment, risk management and risk communication. The risk analysis process must be open and at every step all stakeholders should be allowed to participate and comment. It has been seen as important that there is a separation between the risk management and the risk assessment (FAO/WHO, 1995). The risk assessment is a science based evaluation whereas risk management (at government level) also involves a range of societal issues.

The objective of the rules that govern international trade with food, the WTO/SPS[1] agreement, is to permit countries to set certain safety measures for their population and ask that imported foods allow the same level of public health protection. To justify and compare the levels of public health protection and food safety measures, risks must be analysed using the risk assessment techniques described by Codex (CAC, 1999).

Analysis of risk includes the following steps:

- identification of a food safety problem
- assessment of the risk
- establish a public health goal, e.g. expressed as a food safety objective
- implement risk management decisions
- establish performance criteria
- establish process and product criteria
- establish acceptance criteria
- communication of risk.

[1] *The rules were agreed during the Uruguay Round of Trade Negotiations and apply to members of the World Trade Organization (WTO). Food safety matters are ruled by the Agreement on the Application of Sanitary and Phytosanitary Measures (the SPS agreement).*

Identification of a food safety problem

A food safety problem may be identified either through a sudden change in disease frequency, i.e. epidemiological data indicate a sudden rise in a particular disease, or the hazard analysis carried out as part of the HACCP system may indicate reason for concern. This could be caused by implementation of new processing technologies, or by changes occurring in population composition.

Assessment of the risk

Evaluating the risk associated with the problem involves estimating the severity of the disease and the likelihood of occurrence. Basically, the magnitude of the problem to public health is being determined. This evaluation of risk can be done by just one or two experts, by an expert panel or a so-called quantitative risk assessment may be conducted. Whether one or the other is chosen depends on the urgency of the matter – sometimes a risk management decision has to be made immediately – and of the complexity and its implications for international trade.

The term "quantitative risk assessment" can be a bit misleading, since any evaluation of risk requires considerations of quantitative aspects. However, it has recently been used to describe a lengthier and structured process in which the impact of different factors from farm to fork that contribute to risk are quantified. Typically this process involves the use of mathematical modelling at several steps using Monte Carlo simulations. An example of a quantitative risk assessment is the FAO/WHO work on *Listeria monocytogenes* in ready to eat foods (FAO/WHO, 2001). One result of the risk assessment is the graphical representation of dose-response curve in which the likelihood of disease is presented as a function of levels of *L. monocytogenes* consumed (Figure 3.4).

Figure 3.4
Simulated dose-response function for *Listeria monocytogenes* in ready to eat foods for consumers in the high risk group. Based on FAO/WHO (2001).

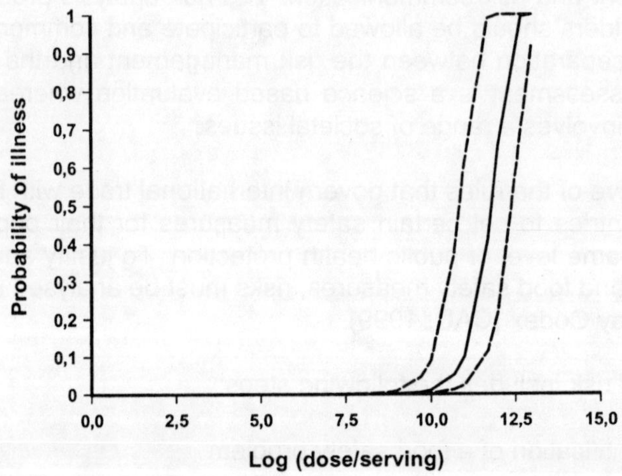

The graph clearly demonstrates that the risk of disease is related to consumption of high numbers of the organism. However, if the risk is expressed as the log value it becomes evident that there is no threshold value below which the risk disappears but even a few cells do carry some, albeit very low, level of risk (Table 3.4). This curve can be used to determine how many cases a particular level of consumption of a pathogen leads to. Based on the consumption pattern and data from the FDA/FSIS risk assessment as well as the risk characterization curve from the same study (FDA/FSIS, 2001), one can predict how many cases are the result of different levels at point of consumption (FAO/WHO, 2001).

The data in Table 3.4 are based on the US situation. The numbers add up to approximately 2 100 comparable to the reported number of cases of approximately 2 500 per year (in a population of a total of 280 million people). Two things are apparent: i) that it is especially the high doses that cause the problem and ii) that even the lowest number of cells carry a low risk of disease.

Establish a public health goal

When determining a public health goal, risk is most often expressed as a number of cases of illness per capita per year. For instance, the level of listeriosis cases in the US is 0.5 per 100 000 of the population per year and recently, the White House announced that this had to be reduced to 0.25 cases per 100 000 of the population per year.

Several terms exist for such public health goals. Ideally, the goal would be to reduce all (sea)food borne diseases to "zero risk", however, this is technically and financially not possible. It is important to understand that there is no such thing as "absence of risk". Therefore, the public health goal is expressed using different terms such as "appropriate level of protection" (ALOP). Realising that no risk is really ever appropriate, the ICMSF (2002) has suggested to use the term "tolerable level of risk" (TLR).

Table 3.4 Baseline number of cases of listeriosis from ready-to-eat foods as predicted by the FDA/FSIS dose-response model (after FAO/WHO 2001).

Maximum log dose at consumption (log CFU/serving)	Number of servings at the specified dose	Number of cases[1] per year attributed to a specified dose level	Comment
-1.5	5.93×10^{10}	0.01	1 case per 100 years
-0.5	2.50×10^{9}	0.005	1 case per 200 years
0.5	1.22×10^{9}	0.02	1 case per 50 years
1.5	5.84×10^{8}	0.1	1 case per 10 years
2.5	2.78×10^{8}	0.5	1 case per 2 years
3.5	1.32×10^{8}	2.4	2.4 cases per year
4.5	6.23×10^{7}	11.5	etc.
5.5	2.94×10^{7}	54.4	
6.5	1.39×10^{7}	25.7	
7.0	3.88×10^{6}	228	
7.5	2.67×10^{6}	1 580	
8.0 and above	very few	227	
	6.41×10^{10}	2 130	Total

1. The number of cases is predicted based on the dose and the number of servings containing that dose.

Food Safety Objective

Levels of disease attack rate are difficult to measure and target by food managers in government and industry and therefore the term **Food Safety Objective** (FSO) has been introduced. The FSO translates risk into a measurable goal and is expressed as the concentration or frequency of a hazard in a food [at point of consumption] that is considered "safe" or meeting the level of protection/risk set by society. The FSO has been used in broad terms by several (Jouve, 1996; Hathaway, 1997) but was explicitly defined by the ICMSF (van Schothorst, 1998).

Food Safety Objective
Concentration or frequency of a hazard in a food [at point of consumption] that is considered safe or meeting the level of protection set by society

If a quantitative risk assessment has been conducted, the FSO is simply the translation for the Y-axis (with disease risk or cases) to the X-axis (with the number or frequency of the pathogen).

FSOs can – and are often – set even when quantitative risk assessments and the risk characterization curve are not available. Investigations of food borne diseases, epidemiological surveillance programmes, industry records and knowledge of the influence of food processing parameters can (and has for decades) provided information about which foods cause adverse health effects, which pathogens are implicated, and, to some extent, which levels of pathogens are involved. In effect, the setting of microbiological criteria for foods has been and is an indirect way of setting an FSO – and thus implies a desired public health goal. Many examples of this are present. One is the standard for *Staphylococcus aureus* in cooked crustaceans (n=5, c=2, m=100/g and M=1000/g). This criteria contains an evaluation of the risk related to the concentration of the hazard (growth and high concentrations are required to produce the amount of enterotoxin causing disease) (FAO/WHO, 2002).

It is important to realise that FSOs are not equivalent to microbiological criteria but that, if appropriate, criteria can be derived from FSOs. An FSO is a public health goal whereas a microbiological criteria defines acceptability of a food product or a lot of foods and should indicate sampling plan, method, number of units that must conform etc. (see Chapter 13). An example of an FSO is a concentration of 100 *L. monocytogenes* per gram at point of consumption for ready-to-eat-foods (van Schothorst, 1998; ICMSF, 1994). Criteria for *L. monocytogenes* at earlier points in the chain will typically be lower than the 100 cfu/gram.

It must be evaluated if the FSO as expressed by risk managers is achievable. If not, it must be decided (i) if changes in the industry has to be enforced, (ii) if the product should be taken off the market or (iii) if the product should be labelled as carrying a risk. Examples of such procedures are (i) the mandatory pasteurisation of milk, (ii) the ban of tetrodotoxin containing fish species for the EU market and (iii) the notice by restaurants in several US states that eating raw oysters may be detrimental to health. Examples of FSOs are shown in Chapter 12.

Implement risk management decisions

When a public health goal has been set, it is the responsibility of risk managers in industry (and government) that measures are taken to control the risk. With respect to food-borne pathogens, the risk can in principle be controlled at three levels:

- the initial level of the pathogen
- reducing the level of the pathogen or
- preventing increase of the pathogen.

The primary tools available to the food industry to control safety risks are GHP and HACCP programmes. Incorporated into these programmes may be various processes and criteria that ensure that the FSO (ultimately) is met.

A *performance criteria* describes the outcome of a process or step. This can for instance be that a canning procedure should ensure a 12D kill of *C. botulinum* spores or that only 3% of freshly produced cold-smoked salmon must contain *L. monocytogenes*.

Process and *product criteria* are statements of values for specific processes, such as time x temperature combinations during hot-smoking, or values such as NaCl-% and pH in the product. For instance, the control of *C. botulinum* in lightly preserved fish is not carried out by sampling and testing for *C. botulinum* but by ensuring that the combination of salt and temperature is sufficient to prevent growth.

Acceptance criteria are measurements or statements of conditions that distinguish acceptable from non-acceptable products. These may be based on sensory evaluations, on chemical measurements and may in some cases be *microbiological criteria*. These should specify the agent to be measured, the number of samples and the method used. As described later (Chapter 13), sampling and microbiological testing is best used for detection of high concentrations or frequencies of microorganisms.

Overall the interaction between government's and industry's roles in food safety activities can be described as below (Figure 3.5).

Risk communication

An integral, and very important step, in all stages of a risk analysis is the communication of risk to stakeholders, including industry and consumers. An important part of the risk communication is using the findings of the risk assessment for training purposes and in the process of setting specifications.

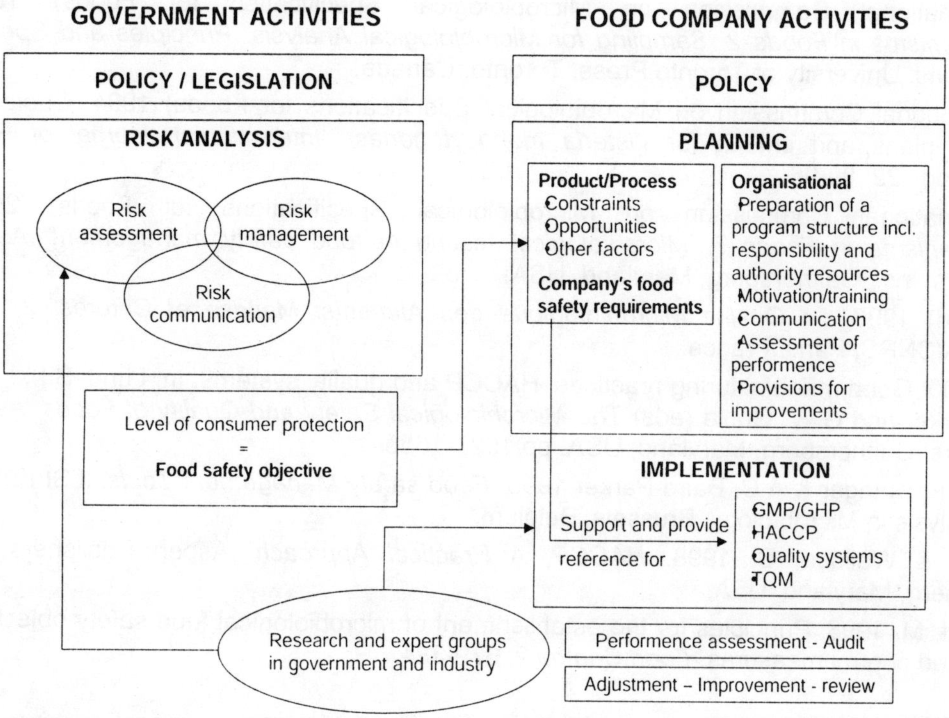

Figure 3.5 Interaction between the government's and industry's food safety activities (modified from Jouve 2000, Jouve *et al.*, 1998).

References

CAC (Codex Alimentarius Commission) 1999. *Principles and Guidelines for the Conduct of Microbiological Risk Assessment*. CAC/GL-30. Food and Agriculture Organization / World Health Organization, Rome, Italy.

CAC (Codex Alimentarius Commission) 2001. *Food Hygiene. Basic Texts*. 2nd ed. Food and Agriculture Organization / World Health Organization, Rome, Italy.

Corlett, Jr. D.A. 1998. *HACCP Users Manual*. An Aspen Publication, Gaithersberg, Maryland, USA.

EC (European Commission) 1998. Food – Science and Techniques. Reports on tasks for scientific cooperation. Microbiological criteria. Collation of scientific and methodological information with a view to the assessment of microbiological risk for certain foodstuffs. EUR 17638.

FAO/WHO (Food and Agriculture Organization/World Health Organization) 1995. Joint FAO/WHO Expert Consultation on the application of risk analysis to food safety standards. 13-17 March, Geneva, Switzerland.

FAO/WHO (Food and Agriculture Organization/World Health Organization) 1997 Joint FAO/WHO Expert Consultation on risk management and food safety. 27-31 January, Rome, Italy.

FAO/WHO (Food and Agriculture Organization/World Health Organization) 2001. Risk Assessment of *Listeria monocytogenes* in ready-to-eat foods. Preliminary report. Authors Buchanan, R., R. Lindqvist, T. Ross, E. Todd, M. Smith and R.C. Whiting. FAO/WHO, Rome, Italy.

FAO/WHO (Food and Agriculture Organization/World Health Organization) 2002. Joint FAO/WHO Expert Consultation on risk the elaboration of Principles and guidelines for incorporating quantitative risk assessment in the development of microbiological food hygiene standards, guidelines and related texts. 18-22 March, Kiel, Germany.

FDA/FSIS (US Food and Drug Administration/Food Safety and Inspection Services) 2001. Draft Assessment of the Relative Risk to Public Health from Foodborne *Listeria monocytogenes* Among Selected Categories of Ready-to-Eat Foods. Washington DC, USA.

Hathaway, S.C. 1997. Development of risk assessment guidelines for foods of animal origin in international trade. *Journal of Food Protection* 60, 1432-1438.

ICMSF (International Commission on Microbiological Specification for Foods) 1986. *Microorganisms in Foods 2. Sampling for Microbiological Analysis: Principles and Specific Applications*. University of Toronto Press, Toronto, Canada.

ICMSF (International Commission on Microbiological Specifications for Foods) 1994. Choice of sampling plans and criteria for *Listeria monocytogenes* *International Journal of Food Microbiology* 22, 89-96.

ICMSF (International Commission on Microbiological Specifications for Foods) 2002. *Microorganisms in Foods 7. Microbiological testing in food safety management*. Aspen Publishers, Inc., Gaithersberg, Maryland, USA.

Jouve, J.L. (ed) 1996. *La Qualité Microbiologique des Aliments: Maitrise et Critéres*. 2nd ed. CNERNA/CNRS, Paris, France.

Jouve, J.L. 2000. Good manufacturing practices, HACCP and quality systems. In: Lund, B.M., T.C. Baird Parker and G.W. Gould (eds) *The Microbiological Safety and Quality of Foods*. Aspen Publishers. Gaithersberg, Maryland, USA. pp.1627-1655.

Jouve, J.L., M.F. Stringer & A.C. Baird-Parker 1998. *Food safety Management Tools*. ILSI Europe Risk Analysis in Microbiology, Brussels, Belgium.

Mortimore, S. & Wallace, C. 1998. *HACCP. A Practical Approach*. Aspen Publishers Inc. Gaithesberg, Maryland. USA.

van Schothorst, M. 1998. Principles for the establishment of microbiological food safety objectives and related control measures. *Food Control* 9, 379-384.

4 IDENTIFICATION OF HAZARDS IN SEAFOOD

4.1 Statistics on seafood-borne diseases (Lone Gram)

The true incidence of diseases transmitted by foods is not known. There are many reasons for this. In most countries there is no obligation to report on food borne diseases to public health authorities. In the few countries which have a reporting system there is severe underreporting. It has been estimated that as few as 1% of the actual cases of food-borne diseases are reported (Mossel, 1982). This is because neither the victim nor the physician are aware of the etiological role of foods. Furthermore, the food responsible is often not available for analysis and the true vehicle for the disease agent is not identified. The statistics presented should therefore be used as indications of trends and areas of concern.

The Centre for Disease Control (CDC) in Atlanta compiles all information on food-borne disease in the US. Between 1993 and 1997, 2 751 outbreaks involving 86 000 people were reported (Table 4.1). In only 1/3 of the outbreaks was a food vehicle identified. Seafoods were often implicated in disease but did not, as opposed to some other foods, result in deaths. As products such as meat and poultry are consumed in much larger amounts, the number of cases traced to seafood is rather alarming.

Table 4.1 Food implicated in food-borne disease in the US 1993-1997 (modified from Olsen *et al.*, 2000).

Food	Outbreaks		Cases		Deaths	
	Number	%	Number	%	Number	%
Meat	66	2.4	3 205	3.7	4	13.8
Pork	28	1.0	988	1.1	1	3.4
Poultry	52	1.9	1 871	2.2	0	0.0
Other meat	22	0.8	645	0.7	2	6.9
Shellfish	47	1.7	1 868	2.2	0	0.0
Fish	140	5.1	696	0.8	0	0.0
Egg	19	0.7	367	0.4	3	10.3
Dairy products	18	0.7	313	0.4	1	3.4
Ice cream	15	0.5	1 194	1.4	0	0.0
Bakery goods	35	1.3	853	1.0	0	0.0
Fruits and vegetables	70	2.5	12 369	14.4	2	6.9
Salads	127	4.6	6 483	7.5	2	6.9
Other	66	2.4	2 428	2.8	0	0.0
Several foods	262	9.5	25 628	29.8	1	3.4
Total known foods	967	35.2	58 908	68.5	16	55.2
Total unknown food	1 784	64.8	27 150	31.5	13	44.8
TOTAL	2 751	100.0	86 058	100.0	29	100.0

In the USA, the etiological agent was identified in approximately 50% of the outbreaks caused by shellfish (both molluscan shellfish and crustaceans) whereas the cause of disease was identified in almost 90% of the outbreaks related to fish (Olsen *et al.*, 2000). It is likely that several of the outbreaks caused by molluscan shellfish for which a cause was not identified were indeed viral. This could, in part, be explained by the lack of methods for detecting foodborne virus.

Outbreak Alert (CSPI, 2001) lists outbreaks/cases in which an etiological agent has been identified. From 1990 to 1998, more than 5 000 cases of seafood borne diseases were linked to a cause.

Molluscan shellfish, although being responsible for a much lower number of outbreaks than fish, caused the double the number of cases.

Table 4.2 Number of outbreaks and cases related to seafood in the US from 1990 to 1998. Listed are only outbreaks for which an etiological agent has been identified (CSPI, 2001).

Seafood group	Outbreaks	Cases
Fish	263	1 661
Molluscan shellfish	66	3 281
Other shellfish	8	146
Total	337	5 088

A total of 1 661 cases were caused by consumption of "fish" (Table 4.2). The majority of cases were caused by scombroid or ciguatera intoxication (Table 4.3). Also, several outbreaks of botulism were recorded as were more than 300 cases of salmonellosis. These outbreaks were, however, not universally distributed. Thus the vast majority of ciguatera outbreak occurred in Hawaii or in Florida where the consumption of tropical reef fish is high. Similarly, three fourth of the botulism cases were registered in Alaska and were attributed to the consumption of various fermented seafood preparations.

Etiological agents were identified in more than 3 000 cases of disease caused by molluscan shellfish (Table 4.4). Bacteria indigenous to the marine environment, e.g. *Vibrio* spp. did cause several cases, but organisms from the human-animal reservoir were the dominant causes. This included the major cause of disease, viral gastroenteritis, in particular Norwalk virus, but also *Salmonella* and *Shigella* were responsible for outbreaks.

Shellfish other than molluscan shellfish also caused disease. Etiological agents were identified in 146 cases of food-borne disease from 1990 to 1998 (CPIS, 2001). These were caused by Norwalk virus ·(one outbreak, 46 cases), *Salmonella* (one outbreak, 45 cases), *Campylobacter* (one outbreak 32 cases), *Vibrio parahaemolyticus* (one outbreak, 7 cases), *Staphylococcus aureus* (one outbreak, two cases) and 3 outbreaks of *V. cholerae* (14 cases).

Table 4.3 Seafood borne diseases traced to "fish" in the USA from 1990 to 1998. Outbreaks and cases for which the etiological agent has been identified (CSPI, 2001).

	Outbreaks					Cases				
Agent	total	%	Hawaii	Florida	Alaska	total	%	Hawaii	Florida	Alaska
Scombroid	131	50	46	10	0	759	47	287	55	0
Ciguatera	98	37	73	16	0	394	24	260	82	0
Botulism	14[1]	5	1	0	10	43	3	3	0	30
Salmonella	11	4				305	18			
Haff disease[2]	2	1				6	-			
S. aureus	1	-				2	-			
E. coli O157	1	-				3	-			
V. cholerae	1	-				26	2			
C. perfringens	1	-				25	2			
Norwalk	1	-				37	2			
Tetrodotoxin	1	-				3	-			
"chemical"	1	-				58	4			
Total	263	100				1 661	100			

1. *One outbreak in New Jersey (salted whitefish) and two in California (both home-canned tuna)*
2. *Haff disease is an unexplained rhabdomyolysis (the breakdown of muscle fibres with leakage of potentially toxic cellular contents into the systemic circulation) in a person who ate fish in the 24 hours before onset of illness.*

Table 4.4 Seafood borne diseases traced to "molluscan shellfish" in the USA from 1990 to 1998. Outbreaks and cases for which the etiological agent has been identified (CSPI, 2001).

Agent	Outbreaks total	Outbreaks %	Cases total	Cases %
V. parahaemolyticus	18	27	733	22
Norwalk / virus	15	23	2 175	66
PSP / toxin	14	20	92	3
Salmonella	6	9	183	6
Scombroid	2	3	4	-
Ciguatera	3	5	5	-
Shigella	2	3	17	0.5
Campylobacter	2	3	6	-
V. vulnificus	1	-	2	-
V. alginolyticus	1	-	4	-
C. perfringens	1	-	57	2
Giardia	1	-	3	-
Total	66	100	3 281	100

Between 1992 and 1999, 1 425 foodborne outbreaks of Infectious Intestinal Disease (IDD) were reported in the UK (Gillespie *et al*,. 2001). This represented one third of all infectious intestinal disease outbreaks reported (Table 4.5). Ten percent of the 1 425 foodborne outbreaks were caused by seafoods. Of the 148 outbreaks traced to seafood, 47% were traced to finfish and most were caused by scombroid toxin. These outbreaks typically occurred in the warm summer months. Molluscan shellfish were responsible for one third (36%) of the outbreaks and these were typically associated with viral infections from live oysters. The last major cluster was outbreaks caused by crustaceans (11%) which typically involved viral pathogens or salmonellae. Salmonellae were also involved in four outbreaks traced to finfish.

Table 4.5 Etiological agents of foodborne outbreaks in UK associated with seafood (Gillespie *et al.*, 2001).

Agent	No. of outbreaks 1992-1999							
	Total[1]	Food-borne	Seafood suspected	Seafood confirmed	Fish	Molluscs	Crustaceans	Other
Scombrotoxin				47	47	0	0	0
DSP				1	0	1	0	0
Virus				26	0	21	3	2
Salmonella				14	7	1	4	2
Campylobacter				3	1	0	1	1
S. aureus				1	0	0	1	0
B. cereus				1	1	0	0	0
C. perfringens				3	1	0	1	1
Unknown				52	12	31	7	2
Total	4 603	1 425	181	148	69	54	17	8

1 Total number of reported intestinal disease outbreaks

4.2 Detentions and rejections of seafood in international trade (Lone Gram/Lahsen Ababouch)

Seafoods constitute a major commodity in international trade and despite the introduction of quality assurance schemes in the sector, various sampling and control analysis of end products are carried out, particularly of imported foods at port of entry. Section 4.1 on seafood borne diseases gives indications of the health consequences of biological hazards, but results from import controls may also point to areas of concern.

In the USA, the Food, Drug and Cosmetic Act authorizes FDA to detain a regulated item that appears to be out of compliance with the act (FDA, 2002). This covers a vast range of commodities: foods, beverages, drugs, cosmetics, animal feed, chemicals, orthopaedic equipment etc. Each month, the import refusal report (IRR) is published based on data generated by the FDA's Operational and Administrative Import Support (OASIS). The data are available by country or by product commodity. Approximately 1/10 of the refused products are seafood products (Table 4.6).

The most common reason for import refusal is "filthy" which describes that the product appears to consist in whole or in part of a filthy, putrid or decomposed substance. Although details are not given for the individual products, it is assumed that microbial spoilage is the major reason for the refusal. Second in terms of rejection reason is the detection of *Salmonella*. Both cooked, ready-to-eat products and raw, frozen products are rejected if *Salmonella* is detected. Although *Salmonella* has its niche in the gastrointestinal tract of birds and mammals, it is a common bacterium in ponds in tropical areas and its detection may not indicate hygienic failure. Whether or not the detection in raw foods constitute a health hazard is debatable.

The category "other" covers a vast range of different reasons such as mis-labelling, lack of description of the process, or lack of verification of a HACCP plan.

Table 4.6 Seafood import refusals by US FDA from July 2001 to June 2002 (FDA, 2002).

Year	Month	No. refused		No. of seafood import refusals according to reason					
		Total	Seafood	Filthy	*Salmonella*	*Listeria*	Histamine	Poison	Other
2001	July	1497	122	74[1]	20	5	2	4	21
	Aug	954	146	79	40	3	3	4	25
	Sep	906	59	27	14	7	0	2	11
	Oct	1082	136	59	50	2	3	4	26
	Nov	1079	121	51	39	4	0	1	26
	Dec	826	83	57	18	2	2	5	7
2002	Jan	1452	177	84	71	2	6	1	42
	Feb	1569	184	84	35	12	4	0	64
	Mar	1630	213	90	38	8	4	4	73
	Apr	1381	126	60	20	0	0	5	43
	May	1621	174	72	41	1	1	5	64
	Jun	1525	143	80	41	3	2	2	34

1. Number of rejections where "filthy" is stated as a reason. Note that for some products several reasons, e.g. both "filthy" and "Salmonella" are given as reason for rejection.

The European Commission is operating a Rapid Alert system for foodstuffs. The system is used to inform Member States about problems or risks concerning foods which do not meet food safety requirements. The legal basis for the system is Council decision 92/59/EEC (EC, 1992) on general product safety. The principal objective is to prevent the placement on or the recall from the community market foodstuffs which pose a serious risk to the health of the consumer. Member States notify the Commission when

- a foodstuff poses a serious risk to the health and safety of consumers, and
- the probability that the foodstuff is on the market in another Member State.

The data from 1999 were compiled by Huss (unpublished) who concluded that in 1999, 107 seafood products were involved in Rapid Alerts (out of 295 in total). The main products and the main reasons for the Alerts were: chilled and frozen fish (or fish products) were implicated in 75 Alerts. The reason was primarily the presence of pathogenic bacteria (*Vibrio* spp., *Salmonella*, *Listeria monocytogenes*, *Staphylococcus*, Enterobacteriaceae, "aerobic mesophiles"), but also a number of chemical dangers were listed (heavy metals, pesticide-residues) shrimp, cray-fish tails, crab-tails (without specification of whether they were raw or cooked) were implicated in 30 Alerts, and the reason was always the presence of pathogenic bacteria (pathogenic *Vibrio* spp., *Salmonella*, *Staphylococcus*) tuna-fish products (canned, frozen or fresh) were involved in 6 Alerts: too high content of histamine (3), mercury (1) or presence of *Salmonella* or "aerobic mesophiles" detection of biotoxins, viruses or indicator bacteria (faecal coliforms, *E.coli*) in bivalve molluscs (8) presence of pathogenic bacteria in a number of un-specified seafood.

In an ongoing study, Ababouch and Gandini (unpublished) analysed the EU Rapid Alert System data of interest to Third Countries, i.e. non EU countries exporting fish and fishery products to the EU member states. The analysis encompassed the period from January 1999 to June 2002 (Table 4.7).

These data indicate that the number of alerts has increased steadily during the period January 1999 – December 2001 and basically exploded in 2002. The initial steady increase and the explosion of alerts in 2002 are due to several concurrent facts:

- The alert system has become generalized and fully operational only during the last 12 or 18 months, indicating some underreporting in the initial phase;
- Several safety concerns have emerged during the period 2001-2002 which triggered several additional controls at the entry point to the EU, e.g. analysis of *Vibrio*, analysis of antibiotic residues and other chemical pollutants (polycyclic aromatic hydrocarbons), following the enacting of recent EU regulations to monitor these residues in fish and fishery products marketed in the EU;

Regarding the cause of rejection/detention (Table 4.7), chemical and drug residues (46.4%), followed by microbial contaminants (39.7%) were the main causes for alert during the period 1999-2002. The majority of alerts because of chemical and veterinary drugs residues (74.4%) occurred recently in 2002, with chloramphenicol and nitrofurans representing respectively 54% and 24.5% of the alerts caused by chemical hazards and 39.6% and 18% of the total. Histamine and parasites caused the lowest rates of alerts, respectively 1.3% and 4%;

For microbial contaminants, there was a decrease (from 59.3 % in 1999 to 41% in 2001) of alerts due to the presence of indicator organisms and an increase (from 40.1 % in 1999 to 59.2 % in 2001) of alerts because of the presence of indigenous organisms, especially *Vibrios*. The former indicates improvement in the sanitary and hygienic conditions in handling and processing fish in their countries, probably as a result of the gradual implementation of GHP/GMP and HACCP. The latter reflects more recent decisions of the EU to analyse for indigenous microorganisms, especially *Vibrio* species while awaiting the results of risk assessments of Vibrios in seafood. In the meantime, the temporary EU decisions have led to rejections and detention of consignments that were probably safe to consume and have led to economic losses by exporters.

In fact, a risk assessment commissioned in 2001 by the European Commission (EC, 2001) concluded that:

i) the practice of judging seafood exclusively based on total Vibrio counts as indicative for the presence of pathogenic Vibrios is not appropriate and should be discontinued.

ii) the practice of judging seafood exclusively based on total *V. Paraheamolyticus* counts without consideration of the virulence factors (TDH/TRH (or *tdh/trh*) is not appropriate and should be discontinued;

iii) currently available scientific data do not support setting specific standards or microbiological criteria for *V. Vulnificus* and *V. Parahaemolyticus* in seafood. Codes of practice should be established to ensure that GHP has been applied.

Table 4.7 Causes of rejection/detention of seafood imported into the EU during the period January 1999 – June 2002 (Ababouch and Gandini, unpublished)

Cause of detention/rejection	No. of rejections / detentions			
	1999	**2000**	**2001**	**2002**
Microbial	59	53	49	47
V. parahaemolyticus	13	10	19	14
V. vulnificus		2	1	3
V. cholerae	9	8	9	5
Other vibrios		1		
Enterobacteria	6	2	4	6
S. aureus	7	0		
Listeria		0		
Salmonella	20	18	10	12
Hepatitis	1	1		
Total plate count	1	8	4	7
Molds		1	1	
Clostridium		2	1	
Chemicals / residues	13	15	34	158
Biotoxins		1		1[1]
Pesticides	2			
Mercury	4	4	9	8
Cadmium	5	2	3	4
Lead				2
Nitrofurans				39
Histamine	1	4	1	1
Chloramphenicol	1		16	86
Phenols				
Policyclic Aromatic Hydrocarbons		4	3	7
Veterinary drug residues				4
Sulfites			2	2
Benzopyran				1
Malachite green				1
Antimicrobial agents				2
Parasites	1	13	11	7[2]
Others	6	13	18	5
Labelling	3	7	8	2
Sanitary certificate	1	1	3	
Shelflife	1		2	
Interrupted cold chain	1	1		
Insects				1
Import prohibited		2	2	1
Mixing of fish species				1
Uncertified establishment		1		
packaging			2	
Not specified		1	1	
Total	79	94	112	217

1. *DSP*
2. *One cestode*

By region, exporting countries from Asia accounted for 69.8% of the alert cases, followed by Africa (17.8%), the Americas (8.8%), Europe (non-EU) (2.7%) and Oceania (0.9%). This does not reflect the volume of exports by region, which amounted in 2000 for Asia to 14.7 % of the total export from third countries, 19.9% for Africa, 22.7% for the Americas (5.5% for North America and 17.2% for Latin America). These data indicate a need for improving further the sanitary conditions in Africa and Asia throughout the food chain from fish harvesting to export. In addition, there is an urgent need to improve sanitary conditions in aquaculture, especially by generalizing the application of

Good Aquaculture Practices and a strict control on the use of banned drugs such chloramphenicol. These drugs banned for use in aquaculture and animal husbandry are becoming a significant health concern in major markets of Europe and the USA. Obviously, Asia, which produces around 89% of the world aquaculture fish is concerned at the highest level.

References

CSPI (Centre for Science in the Public Interest) 2001. Outbreak Alert. Closing the Gaps in our Federal Food-Safety Net. CSPI, Washington DC, USA.

EC (European Commission) 1992. Council Directive 92/59/EEC of 29 June 1992 on general product safety. *Official Journal of the European Communities* L. 228, 11/08/1992, p. 0024-NBNB

EC (European Commission) 2001. Opinion of the Scientific Committee on veterinary measures relating to public health on Vibrio vulnificus and Vibrio parahaemolyticus (in raw and undercooked seafood). Report adopted 20 September 2001. Health and Consumer Protection Directorate General. 64 Pages.

FDA (Food and Drug Administration) 2002. Introduction to FDA's Import Refusal Report (IRR). http://www.fda.gov./ora.oasis/ora_oasis_ref_intro.html

Gillespie, I.A., G.K. Adak, S.J. O-Brien, M.M. Brett and F.J. Bolton 2001. general outbreaks of infectious intestinal disease associated with fish and shellfish, England and Wales, 1992-1999. *Communicable Disease and Public Health* 4, 117-123.

Mossel, D.A.A. 1982. *Microbiology of Foods*. University of Utrecht. Faculty of Veterinary Medicine, Bittshact 172, Utrecht, The Netherlands.

Olsen, S.J., L.C. MacKinnon, J.S. Goulding, N.H. Bean and L. Slutsker 2000. Surveillance for foodborne-disease outbreaks – United States, 1993-1997. Report CDC Surveillance Summary. *Morbidity and Mortality Weekly* 49,1-62.

5 CHARACTERIZATION OF HAZARDS IN SEAFOOD

The aim of this Chapter is to discuss known data on each hazard and provide information useful in the control of seafood-borne diseases. This includes data on frequency or likelihood of contamination of raw material and/or foods by the hazardous agent. Also, the Chapter discusses changes in the level or frequency of the hazard over time depending on processing, preservation parameters and storage conditions.

Hazard
A biological, chemical or physical agent in, or condition of, food with a potential to cause an adverse health effect (CAC, 2001)

The presence, growth, survival or death of microorganisms or destruction of toxins as influenced by processing, packaging and storage conditions will also be considered. The adverse health effects (the disease), the dynamics of infection or intoxication, host susceptibility, healthy carriers and possible spread of disease through secondary transmission are factors included in the characterization of the hazards. Where relevant, each hazard will be described under the following subheadings:

- The disease (adverse health effect) and epidemiological aspects
- The niche or origin of the organism/agent and its prevalence in fish and fishery products
- Growth and survival in fish and fishery products
- Prevention and control (including critical limits)

It should be noted that the information provided in this Chapter are some of the aspects needed in: "Exposure Assessment" and "Hazard Characterization", which are two of the elements in a Risk Assessment project (see section 3.3). However, in a quantitative risk assessment, much more data than presented here will be required.

5.1 Biological hazards

Biological hazards include pathogenic bacteria (infectious or toxin producing), biogenic amines, viruses, parasites and aquatic biotoxins.

5.1.1 Pathogenic bacteria (Hans Henrik Huss/Lone Gram)

Pathogenic bacteria are defined as those bacteria that that may cause illness in humans. Some pathogenic bacteria are transmitted to humans via food. Food-borne pathogenic bacteria are few among the many different types of seafood bacteria, which are causing no harm to humans. Many microorganisms are even beneficial being used in the production of food and drinks. Others are able to spoil food. Bacterial food-borne pathogens may be grouped into those that cause food intoxication and those that can result in food-borne bacterial infection.

In case of bacterial food poisoning or intoxication the causative organism multiplies in the food where it produces its toxins. A food poisoning is therefore characterized by rapid onset of the illness (typically symptoms are nausea, vomiting) as the toxins are already formed in the food before consumption. Thus ingestion of viable bacteria is <u>not</u> a prerequisite for the induction of the disease. Most often intoxications require that the toxin producing bacteria have grown to high numbers (10^5 – 10^8 cfu/g) in the food before it is eaten.

In contrast, the food merely act as a carrier for the causative organism in food-borne infections. The infectious agent may or may not have multiplied in the food, but the ingested viable bacteria continue to grow within the host's body to produce the typical symptoms (fever, diarrhoea). The number of viable bacterial cells necessary to cause disease (the Minimum Infective Dose, MID) varies considerably between bacterial species. Thus the MID is known to be high (>10^5-10^6 cells) for pathogenic *Vibrio* spp. (Twedt, 1989) and very low for some *Salmonella typhi* and *Shigella* species (Kothary and Babu, 2001).

Seafood-borne pathogenic bacteria may conveniently be divided into 3 groups according to their ecology and origin as those who are indigenous to:

- the aquatic environment (Table 5.1)
- the general environment (Table 5.2)
- the animal/human reservoir (Table 5.3).

The level of human pathogenic bacteria in fish is generally quite low as shown in Table 5.1. Highest concentrations are found in molluscs and in the intestines of molluscs' predators. The ambient temperature strongly influences the composition (quantitatively and qualitatively) of the natural micro flora present in the environment and on the fish raw material.

Table 5.1 Pathogenic bacteria indigenous to the aquatic environment and naturally present on fish (based on Huss 1997).

Organism	Primary habitat	Quantitative levels
Clostridium botulinum; non-proteolytic types B, E, F	Temperate and Arctic aquatic environment; multiplication in aquatic carrion (type E)	Generally low (<0.1 spores/g fish) but up to 5.3 spores/g fish has been recorded
Pathogenic *Vibrio* spp. incl. *V. cholerae* *V. parahaemolyticus* *V. vulnificus*	Ubiquitous in warm (>15°C) seawater environment	Up to 10^2-10^3 cfu/g in shellfish; up to 10^4-10^8 cfu/g in intestines of shellfish-eating fish
Plesiomonas shigelloides	Warm aquatic environment; Freshwater fish (animals)	
Aeromonas spp.[1]	Aquatic environment	Generally low, but up to 10^4 cfu/ml in seawater; 10^7 cfu/ml in sewage and 10^6 cfu/g in raw seafood

1. The role of Aeromonas spp. in food-borne disease is not resolved

The presence of pathogenic bacteria in the general environment is also low (Table 5.2). Furthermore it should be emphasized that all the genera of pathogenic bacteria listed in Tables 5.1 and 5.2 contain non-pathogenic environmental strains. Thus *V. cholerae* non-01 was detected in six samples (out of 752 samples examined) of warm-water shrimps imported to Denmark, but none of these strains contained plasmids or genes encoding cholera toxins (CT) or heat-stable enterotoxin (NAG-ST) suggesting that these organisms do not constitute a public health problem (Dalsgaard *et al.*, 1996). However, for some organisms, such as *Listeria monocytogenes*, there is no known method available to distinguish between pathogenic and non-pathogenic strains.

Table 5.2 Pathogenic bacteria indigenous to the general environment and frequently present on fish (based on Huss, 1997).

Organism	Primary habitat	Quantitative levels
Listeria monocytogenes	Soil, decaying vegetation ubiquitous in general (temperate) environments	<100 cfu/g in freshly produced fish products
Clostridium botulinum proteolytic type A, B	Soil	Generally low (<0.01 spore/g soil)
Clostridium perfringens	Soil (type A); animals (type B, C, D and E)	10^3-10^4 cfu/g soil
Bacillus spp.	Ubiquitous in general environment (soil, natural waters, vegetation)	10^1-10^3 cfu/g or ml raw, processed food

The pathogenic bacteria found in the animal/human reservoir are shown in Table 5.3. They are found on outer and inner surfaces of diseased or asymptomatic carriers. Contamination of fish products is almost always due to poor hygiene (poor personal hygiene, poor processing hygiene or poor water quality).

It must be emphasized that it is nearly always possible to detect a range of human pathogenic bacteria on any fish or fish product that has not received any bactericidal treatment. Some of these pathogens may constitute part of the natural flora on the fish (pathogens from the aquatic environment) or be there as a result of unavoidable contamination (pathogens from the general environment). It is common for these pathogens that some growth in the fish products is required to produce disease in humans. This applies naturally for the intoxicating types, but as the MID for the infective environmental pathogens is high (- or higher than the natural level found in fish products), some growth is also required for these types. This means that the preventive measure for all these pathogens is prevention of growth of the organisms in the products (see Table 5.4).

Table 5.3 Pathogenic bacteria in the animal/human reservoir.

Organism	Primary habitat	Quantitative levels
Salmonella spp. *Shigella* spp. *Escherichia coli*	Intestines of warm blooded animals/humans	Levels in symptomatic and asymptomatic carriers vary; levels in seafood assumed to be sporadic and low. May accumulate in molluscan shellfish
Campylobacter jejuni and other mesophilic campylobacter	Birds, intestines of warm blooded animals	Sporadic, low levels. Possibly accumulation in molluscan shellfish
Staphylococcus aureus	Outer surface (skin) and mucus membranes (nose)	Transient, but present on 50% of population. Generally <100 cfu/cm² skin

The MID for pathogens originating in the animal/human reservoir may be high or as low as < 10 organisms for some *Shigella* and for *E. coli* O157 (Kothary and Babu, 2001). As these bacteria are not normally present in fish and fish products, the main preventive measure is to avoid contamination by applying good hygienic practices (GHP) and good manufacturing practices (GMP) (Table 5.4). However, for some of these bacteria, including *Staphylococcus aureus*, which is a toxin producing pathogen, growth in the products is required to produce disease.

Table 5.4 Seafood-borne pathogenic bacteria and disease.

Natural habitat of pathogen	Mode of action of disease: Infection		Intoxication
	High MID	Low MID	
Aquatic environment	*Vibrio* spp. *(Aeromonas)* *(Plesiomonas)*		*Clostridium botulinum* Type E (non-proteolytic)
General environment	*Listeria monocytogenes*		*Clostridium botulinum* Type A, B (proteolytic) *C. perfringens* *Bacillus cereus*
Animal-human reservoir	*Salmonella* *E. coli* (EPEC, ETEC)[1]	*S. typhi* *Shigella* *E. coli* (EHEC)[1] *Campylobacter*	*Staphylococcus aureus*
Preventive measure	Prevention of growth	Hygiene; GHP/GMP	Prevention of growth

1. *EPEC: Enteropathogenic E. coli; ETEC: Enterotoxigenic E. coli; EHEC: Enterohaemorragic E. coli.*

The safety concerns related to pathogenic bacteria in seafood is demonstrated in Table 5.5. The mere presence (in low numbers) of pathogens from the aquatic and general environment is of no safety concern, not even in ready-to-eat (RTE) products.

In contrast, the presence of pathogens from the animal/human reservoir is a serious safety concern for products to be eaten without (further) cooking. Growth of pathogens is likewise a serious safety concern for most RTE products. For raw fish products to be eaten raw the safety concern is limited. Growth of these pathogens is only possible at elevated temperatures (>5°C) (Table 5.16), and at this condition spoilage will proceed very rapidly and the fish will probably be rejected due to off-odours and off-flavours long before being either toxic or infective organisms reach high numbers.

Table 5.5 Safety concerns related to pathogenic bacteria in seafood.

Natural habitat of pathogen	State of pathogen	Safety concern[1]: Fresh fish to be eaten cooked	raw	RTE[2]
Aquatic environment	Presence	-	-	-
	Growth	-	(+)	+
General environment	Presence	-	-	-
	Growth	-	(+)	+
Animal-human reservoir	Presence	-	+	+
	Growth	(+)	+	+

1. *"+" definitely a safety concern; "(+)" limited safety concern; "-" no safety concern*
2. *Ready-to-eat products see Table 9.5.*

Growth of pathogens in raw fish to be cooked is similarly of little safety concern. Only limited growth is possible before spoilage is causing rejection and in borderline cases, cooking will destroy the pathogen. Growth of pathogens from animal/human reservoir is of no direct safety concern in raw fish to be cooked before consumption as described above, but it may constitute a secondary hazard due to increased spread and contamination of the processing or kitchen environment with these pathogens.

5.1.1.1 Bacteria indigenous to the aquatic and general environment

Control of disease from human pathogenic bacteria occurring in the aquatic or general environment is very often ensured by preventing their growth – or destroying any organisms present. Tables 5.6 and 5.7 give overviews of growth limiting factors and heat resistance of these organisms. The D-value used to determine heat-resistance indicates the length of time (seconds, minutes) which is required at a given temperature to reduce the population to 10% of its initial count (decimal reduction).

Table 5.6 Growth limiting factors of pathogenic bacteria indigenous to the aquatic and the general environment (adapted from Huss, 1994; ICMSF, 1996).

Pathogenic bacteria	Temperature, °C		pH	a_w	NaCl (%)
	minimum	Optimum	minimum	minimum	maximum
Clostridium botulinum					
Proteolytic, type A, B, F	10	35-40	4.6	0.94	10
non-proteolytic, type B, E, F	3.3	25-28	5.0	0.97	3-5
Vibrio spp.					
V. cholerae	10	37	5.0	0.97	< 8
V. parahaemolyticus	5	37	4.8	0.93	8-10
V. vulnificus	8	37	5.0	0.96	5
Plesiomonas shigelloides	8	37	4.0		4-5
motile *Aeromonas* spp.	0-4	28-35	4.0	0.97	4-5
Listeria monocytogenes	0-2	30-37	4.6	0.92	10
Bacillus cereus	4[1]	30-40	5.0	0.93	10
Clostridium perfringens	12	43-47	5.5	0.93	10

1. Most strains of B. cereus are mesophilic with minimum temperature of approximately 8-10°C, however, psychrotrophic variants have been isolated

Table 5.7 Heat resistance of pathogenic bacteria indigenous to the aquatic and the general environment (adapted from Huss, 1994; ICMSF, 1996; Ababouch 1987).

Pathogenic bacteria	Heat resistance
Clostridium botulinum	
proteolytic, type A, B, F	D_{121} (spores) = 0.1 – 0.25 min D_{119} (spores) = 7.44 min in products with high fat content
non-proteolytic, type B, E, F	D_{100} (spores) < 0.1 min; $D_{82.2}$ = 0.5 – 2.0 min (broth); D_{80} (spores) = 4.5 – 10.5 min in products with high fat content
Vibrio spp.	
V. cholerae	D_{55} = 0.24 min
V. parahaemolyticus	D_{60} = 0.71 min
V. vulnificus	D_{50} = 1.15 min (buffer); 0.66 min (oysters)
Plesiomonas shigelloides	All cells killed after 30 min at 60°C
motile *Aeromonas* spp.	D_{55} = 0.17 min
Listeria monocytogenes	D_{60} = 2.4 – 16.7 min in meat products; 1.95 – 4.48 min in fish
Bacillus cereus	D_{121} (spores) = 0.03 – 2.35 min (buffer) D_{95} (spores) = 3.0 – 19 min (milk)
Clostridium perfringens	D_{90} (spores) = 0.015 – 4.93 min (buffer) D_{100} (spores) = 0.31-13.0 min (broth)

Clostridium botulinum (Hans Henrik Huss)

Clostridium botulinum is classified into toxin types from A to G. The types pathogenic to humans (types A, B, E and F) can conveniently be divided into two groups:

- the proteolytic types A, B and F, which are also heat resistant, mesophilic, NaCl-tolerant and have the general environment as the natural habitat
- the non-proteolytic types B, E and F, which are heat sensitive, psychrotolerant, NaCl-sensitive and have the aquatic environment as the natural habitat.

a) The disease and some epidemiological aspects

Toxins produced by *C. botulinum* types A, B, E and F are the cause of human botulism. The disease can vary from a mild illness, which may be disregarded or misdiagnosed, to a serious disease, which may be fatal within 24 hours. In most cases, the symptoms develop within 12 to 36 hours. These are generally nausea and vomiting followed by neurological symptoms such as visual impairment (blurred or double vision), loss of normal mouth and throat function (difficulty in speaking and swallowing, dry mouth), lack of muscle coordination and respiratory impairment, which is usually the immediate cause of death.

Type E botulism tends to have most rapid onset of symptoms, while type A botulism tend to be the most severe. Early fatality rates in the first half of the 20th century were about 50% or higher for botulism, but with the availability today of antisera and modern respiratory support systems, they have decreased to about 10% (Austin and Dodds, 2001).

The majority of botulism outbreaks in the northern and temperate regions are associated with fish, and in general type E was the responsible type. Type A and B botulism has generally been associated with meat or meat products, but fish and fish products have also been vehicle for those types. All types of fish products except raw fish to be cooked immediately before consumption have been involved in outbreaks of botulism, but the majority of outbreaks has been associated with fermented fish (Huss, 1981).

Botulinum toxin is one of the most potent of all poisons, and the amount needed to cause death in humans has been estimated to be as low as 30-100 ng (Lund and Peck, 2000). The toxin is sensitive to heat and pH above 7. For safe inactivation of any botulinum toxin at concentrations up to 10^5 LD/g in foods, time/temperature combinations of 20 min. at 79°C or 5 min. at 85°C has been recommended (Hauschild 1989). Normal household cooking and frying of raw fish products are therefore sufficient to destroy any pre-formed toxin. This may be one of the reasons for the excellent safety record of unprocessed fish with respect to problems from *C. botulinum*.

While botulinum toxin is rapidly destroyed in fish products with pH>7.5, such as spoiling cod, it is extremely stable in a salty and acid environment. Thus botulinum toxin formed in the raw material will be found again or even increase in situ in the final products such as heavily salted, marinated or fermented fish (Huss and Rye Petersen, 1980). This is illustrated by the fact that many outbreaks of botulism have been traced to products, which do not support the growth of *C. botulinum*.

b) Prevalence in fish and fishery products

The spores of the non-proteolytic *C. botulinum* types, particularly type E are widely distributed in the aquatic (marine and fresh water) environment in the temperate and arctic zones. Thus, up to 100% of sediment samples from coastal areas, particularly in closed, shallow fjords and from aquaculture ponds may contain the organisms (Huss, 1980; Dodds, 1993). The distribution patterns of *C. botulinum* type E suggest that this is a true aquatic organism and that multiplication occurs, in situ, particularly in carrion. A much lower prevalence is found in live fish although up to 100% of fish from aquaculture and coastal waters may carry this organism. Fish caught in the high seas are generally free from *C. botulinum*. In warm tropical waters and in fish from these areas, other types than type E are frequently found, see Figure 5.1.

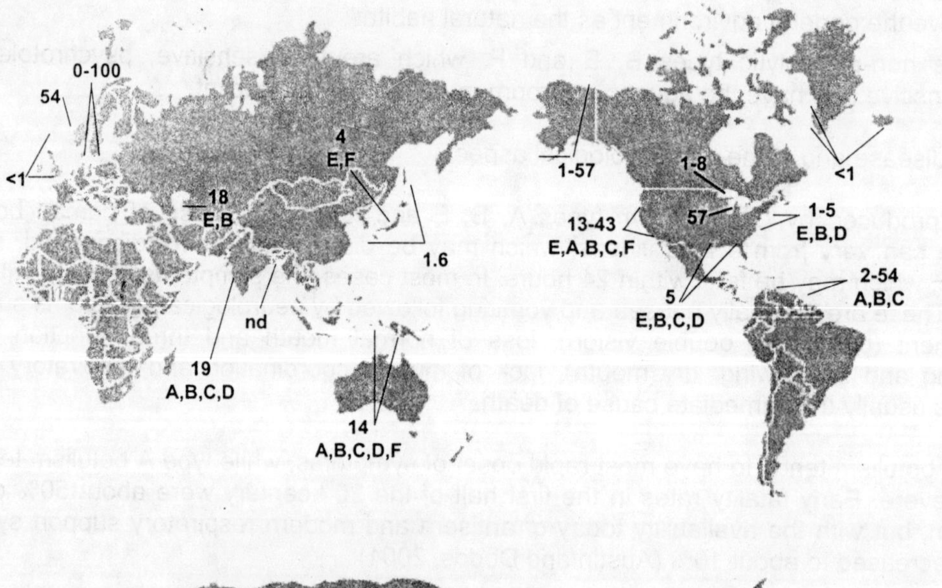

Figure 5.1 Prevalence (%-values) of *Clostridium botulinum* in fish. Numbers with no letter attached refer to type E; otherwise letters indicate *C. botulinum* types detected. ND = Not detected. For references to surveys, see Huss (1980). Cochin data from Lalitha and Surendran (2002).

The proteolytic *C. botulinum* are frequently found in soil and the terrestrial environment (Huss, 1980; Hauschild, 1989; Dodds, 1993). Animals, both vertebrates and invertebrates, have an important role in both the distribution and build up of botulinum spores. Spread of spores from the terrestrial environment to the aquatic environment (coastal waters and fresh waters systems) including the fish in these areas is therefore a distinct possibility as well as spread of spores to the fish processing environment. Being mesophilic, the proteolytic types do not have the same possibilities for multiplication in nature as type E.

c) Growth and survival in fish and fishery products

The main factors that control growth of *C. botulinum* in foods are temperature, pH, water activity (a_w), salt, redox potential and added preservatives. Maximum and minimum limits for these parameters, which would permit growth are shown in Table 5.6.

The figures quoted in Table 5.6 are used in many regulations worldwide. These figures have mostly been established at near optimal conditions in challenge studies, where *C. botulinum* spores have been inoculated in large numbers and as a single organism. There are at least three factors adding to the safety of fish products using the figures from Table 5.6 in the control of *C. botulinum*:

- the natural level of *C. botulinum* in fish is much lower than levels used in most challenge studies. Initiating growth and toxin production will therefore be much delayed at comparable conditions
- the associate flora in fish products may cause spoilage before the product becomes toxic. Some microorganisms may also inhibit *C. botulinum*
- *C. botulinum* is an anaerobic organism preferring a low redox potential (Eh) for growth. The Eh for fish and fish products is high (Huss and Larsen, 1979, 1980) and this may cause delay in growth and toxin production at otherwise comparable condition in bacteriological media.

The presence of an associate (spoilage) micro flora may, however, also add to the risk, as this micro flora may use oxygen and facilitate the growth and toxin production by *C. botulinum* type E. It is clear therefore, that using the figures in Table 5.6 in control of *C. botulinum* does provide considerable safety margin. It should also be emphasized, that those factors seldom function independently. Usually they act in concert often having synergetic and accumulative effects. A few examples are shown in Table 5.8.

Table 5.8 Toxin production in smoked fish inoculated with 10^2 *C. botulinum* type E spores per gram (cold smoked) or using naturally contaminated fish (hot-smoked).

Product	Salt WPS[1]	Storage Temp.	Time to Toxicity	Reference
Cold-smoked salmon	1.7%	8°C	>28d.	Dufresne *et al.*, 2000
Hot smoked trout	3%	10°C	>30d.	Cann and Taylor, 1979

1. *WPS = water phase salt*

The data in Table 5.8 clearly demonstrate, that a combination of salt and low temperature very effectively inhibits toxin production (and growth) of *C. botulinum*. A very detailed review of the effect of growth limiting factors can be found in Lund and Peck (2000) and in Eklund (1993).

Thermal inactivation of *C. botulinum* spores have been extensively studied. The D-value varies considerably among *C. botulinum* types and even among strains within the same type. The spores of the non-proteolytic types are considerably less resistant than the proteolytic types as shown in Table 5.7. The heat resistance of non-proteolytic types is particularly important for mildly heat treated, pasteurised products, where conditions for growth are excellent for surviving spores. The D-values at 82°C for these product may vary from 0.5 to 2 min as shown in Table 5.7. A minimum heat treatment of 90°C for 10 min should provide a safety factor of 10^6 (a 6-D process or a 6-log reduction of spore count) for non-proteolytic *C. botulinum* as recommended by a number of advisory committees (Martens, 1999).

The spores from proteolytic *C. botulinum* are much more heat resistant. In general, D_{121} values are in the range of 0.1-0.25 min. These spores are a particular concern in the sterilisation of low acid canned foods, and the canning industry has adopted a D-value of 0.2 min at 121°C as a standard for calculating thermal processes. For the most resistant strains, z-values (the temperature change necessary to bring about a 10-fold change in D-value) are approximately 10°C, which has also been adopted as a standard (Austin and Dodds, 2001).

d) Prevention and control

Control of *C. botulinum* in fishery products can be achieved by inactivation of spores or by inhibition of growth. Current guidelines regarding safety with respect to *C. botulinum* includes one of the following procedures (listed by Martens, 1999):

- storage at all times at <3.3°C
- storage at 5-10°C and a shelf life of <5 days
- a heat treatment of 90°C for 10 min combined with chill storage (<10°C)
- a pH ≤ 5.0 throughout the food combined with chilled storage (<10°C)
- a salt-on-water concentration ≥ 3.5% or $a_w \leq 0.97$ throughout the food combined with chill storage (<10°C).

It should be noted that products where growth of non-proteolytic *C. botulinum* is completely inhibited (by salt or low pH) or inactivated still has a requirement for chilled storage. The reason is that the proteolytic *C. botulinum* may still be able to grow if temperatures are >10°C. It is a US-requirement, that vacuum packed cold smoked fish contain 3.5% NaCl (water phase salt = WPS) or 3% if combined with 100-200 ppm nitrite. For air packaged fish not less than 2.5% NaCl (WPS) in the loin muscle is required (FDA, 1998).

The canning industry has adopted a 12-D process as a minimum heat process applied to commercial canned low acid foods. The heat required to provide this "botulinum cook" or a 12-decimal reduction in proteolytic *C. botulinum* spores (also called F-value) is therefore equal to 12 x D_{121}-value or 12 x 0.2 = 2.4 min at 121°C. The highest know D_{121}-values is 0.25 min which gives a F-value of 12 x 0.25 = 3. Using F-values between 2.4-3 has led to safe production of canned low acid food for many decades. Often higher F values (e.g. 5) are used in commercial practice.

Refrigeration is often regarded as the primary method of preservation of fresh foods, including seafoods. At temperatures below 10°C there is no risk of toxin production by proteolytic *C. botulinum* types A and B. At higher storage temperature additional preservation or treatment is required to produce safe food as summarised in Table 5.9.

Table 5.9 Control of *Clostridium botulinum* in food.

Storage temperature		Preservation				Heat treatment
t < 3.5°C						
3.5°C < t < 10°C	AND	(pH < 5.0	OR	WPS[1] > 3.5%	OR	90°C,10 min)
t > 10°C	AND	(pH < 4.5	OR	WPS > 10%	OR	121°C, 2.4-3 min)

1. WPS = Water phase salt

***Vibrio* species** (Lone Gram)

Vibrio species belong to the Vibrionaceae family. All species are typical of marine and/or estuarine environments and most require NaCl (2-3%) to grow. Since the marine environment is their natural niche, *Vibrio* species are commonly isolated from fish and crustaceans. Most of the species are mesophilic and their numbers tend to increase during the warm seasons. The genus comprises 34 species of which 13 species can cause human disease, including wound infections, septicemia and gastroenteritis (Kaysner, 2000; FAO/WHO, 2001). Seafood-borne diseases are primarily caused by *Vibrio parahaemolyticus*, *Vibrio vulnificus* and *Vibrio cholerae* (Oliver and Kaper, 1997). *V. parahaemolyticus* and *V. cholerae* both cause gastrointestinal disease whilst *V. vulnificus* causes a septicemic condition.

Vibrio species are indigenous to the aquatic environment and their presence and numbers are influenced by factors such as temperature, salinity and algal density. There is no correlation between their occurrence or numbers and faecal human pathogens or indicators of faecal human pathogens.

***Vibrio parahaemolyticus** (Lone Gram)*

a) The disease and some epidemiological aspects

V. parahaemolyticus may cause gastroenteritis in humans and the disease has exclusively been linked to consumption of seafood, in particular raw or inadequately cooked seafoods. The incubation period ranges from 8 to 72 hours and the onset of disease is very sudden with explosive diarrhoea. Other symptoms include nausea, vomiting, headache, fever and chills (Kaysner 2000). Symptoms typically subside within 48 to 72 hours but may last up to a week and treatment of most cases primarily include rehydration. Volunteer feeding trials suggest that ingestion of 2×10^5 to 3×10^7 cells is required to cause disease. In these feeding trials, antacid treatment was administered to the volunteers and this probably protected the bacteria. Recent US data using epidemiological evidence indicate that doses of approximately 10 times more are required (FDA, 2000). The genus is one of the leading cause of gastroenteritis in Japan and eastern Asian countries whereas the occurrence in other countries is much lower (Table 5.10). This difference could be linked to seafood consumption patterns as the disease is mainly associated with consumption of raw seafoods.

Table 5.10 European and Japanese gastroenteritis cases caused by *Vibrio parahaemolyticus* (EC, 2001; CAC, 2002)

Country	Period	Cases
UK and Wales	1995-1999	115
Northern Ireland	1997	44
Scotland	1994-1999	6
Spain	1995-1998	19
France	1995-1998	6
	1997	44[1]
Sweden	1992-1997	350[2]
Norway	1999	4
Denmark	1980-2000	2
Japan	1991-2000	64 000

1. Associated with seafood imported from Asia
2. Associated with crayfish imported from China

The exact virulence mechanisms of *V. parahaemolyticus* are not known. However, at least four haemolytic components are produced. Of these, two components: a thermostable direct hemolysin (TDH) and a TDH-related hemolysin (TRH) are strongly correlated with virulence. TDH positive strains causes hemolysis of human red blood-cells and this phenomenon is known as the Kanagawa reaction. Some strains, which are TDH-negative but TRH-positive have been reported to cause gastroenteritis (EC, 2001). An elaborate serotyping system has been developed relying on O-antigens (12 types) and K-antigens (65 types) and this system is widely used in Japan. It is important to realise that the majority of environmental strains (approximately 95-99%) are not pathogenic whilst 99% of strains isolated from human cases are Kanagawa positive. Due to its mesophilic nature, incidents of *V. parahaemolyticus* are clearly correlated with temperature and the vast amount of cases/outbreaks occurs during the warmer months (Figure 5.2).

b) Prevalence in fish and fishery products

V. parahaemolyticus is commonly isolated from seafood products, especially in bivalve molluscs. Levels fluctuate with temperature, especially in the temperate zones, with the higher numbers being isolated in the warmer months. During colder months, the organism probably survives in sediments and is then released into the water with zooplankton when the temperature rises (EC, 2001). Also, salinity affects occurrence and the highest numbers are seen at 20-25 ppt salinity (FAO/WHO, 2001). The incidence seems to be highest in molluscan shellfish, followed by crustaceans, and lowest in finfish (Sumner *et al.*, 2001). Numbers in oysters may range from less than one per gram to 10^4 cfu/g but is typically less than 10 cfu/g. *V. parahaemolyticus* occurs less frequently in European fish and shellfish probably due to the relatively low water temperatures. During summer months, e.g. from August to October, 25 of 91 Dutch shellfish samples were positive for *V. parahaemolyticus* (Tilburg *et al.*, 2000).

Figure 5.2
Number of *Vibrio parahaemolyticus* incidents per month in Japan (CAC, 2002).

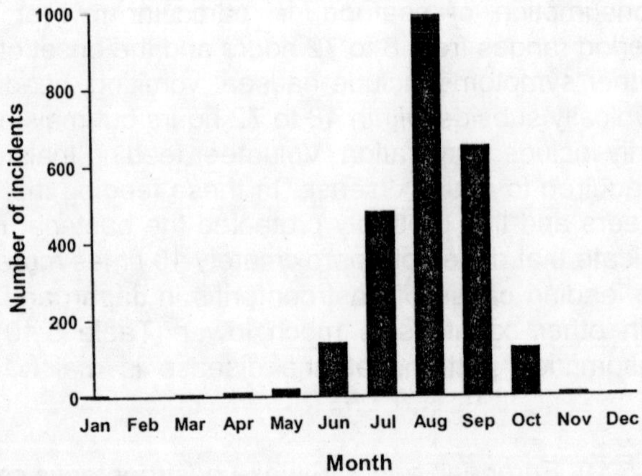

c) Growth and survival in fish and fishery products

Being a mesophilic, halotolerant bacteria, *V. parahaemolyticus* will grow well in seafoods stored at ambient temperature. The very low generation time at high temperatures (e.g. 12-18 minutes at 30°C) allows the organism to proliferate rapidly. The bacteria is also capable of proliferation in <u>live</u> oysters during storage. Thus numbers increased 50 fold when oysters were stored at 26°C for 10 hours and almost 800 fold after 24 hours storage. Subsequent cooling to 3°C reduced numbers by almost 10-fold during 14 days of storage (Gooch *et al.*, 2002). In general, low temperature storage will cause numbers to decrease, however, the extent of decrease depends on food matrix, salinity and other factors.

V. parahaemolyticus is very heat sensitive and easily destroyed by cooking. D-values at 50-60°C are in the range of 0.3-0.8 min (Kaysner, 2000). Growth limits with respect to NaCl-%, temperature and pH are indicated in Table 5.6.

d) Prevention and control

Numbers of *V. parahaemolyticus* may be high in some live bivalves during warm months and a recent US risk assessment (FDA, 2000) demonstrated that the (initial) level in raw oysters was the most significant risk factor. However, the high infectious dose indicates that mostly growth has to take place in the product for the organism to reach hazardous levels. Thus, it is the high levels (growth) of *V. parahaemolyticus* and not its mere presence (in low numbers) that is the hazard. Rapid and efficient cooling (time x temperature control) is one of the most important control parameters in prevention of *V. parahaemolyticus* gastroenteritis. Cooling to 5°C will prevent growth. High NaCl-concentrations (>10% NaCl in water phase) or acidification as used in several semi-preserved products can prevent growth. Good Hygienic Practices (GHP) programmes should ensure that cooked products are not cross-contaminated. Depuration of molluscan shellfish has no significant effect on the level of *Vibrio* that may even multiply in depurating shellfish (FDA, 2000; Eyles and Davey, 1984).

Vibrio vulnificus

a) The disease and some epidemiological aspects

V. vulnificus can cause wound infections in humans and a range of fish diseases, however, it may also cause a very serious infection transmitted by seafood. As opposed to the other seafood-borne *Vibrio* diseases, this is a bacteremia and a septicemia not a gastrointestinal disease. Seafood-borne *V. vulnificus* infections are almost exclusively caused by consumption of raw bivalve molluscs such as oysters. Infections with *V. vulnificus* are not common in Europe but have for some years been a safety issue in the Gulf Coast area of the USA. The disease is an invasive disease causing primary septicemia, i.e. with no infectious focus. Common symptoms are fever, chills, and nausea. Symptoms occur approximately 38 hours after consumption. The disease primarily affects people in specific risk groups with underlying medical conditions such as chronic cirrhosis, hepatitis or a history of alcohol abuse (EC, 2001). Liver dysfunction is typical of several of these conditions and iron overload (typical in liver conditions) appears to facilitate infection. In particular males above 40 that have a history of alcohol consumption (and eat live oysters) are at risk (Kaysner, 2000). Mortality in risk groups may be as high as 60%.

V. vulnificus produce an extracellular cytotoxin and a battery of hydrolytic enzymes. These are probably responsible for the rapid degradation of muscle tissue seen during infection. The presence of a polysaccharide capsule is essential for infection.

Three different biotypes of *V. vulnificus* have been identified. Approximately 85% of strains isolated from human clinical cases are biotype 1 whereas biotype 2 mainly causes infections in eels. Biotype 3 was identified recently (Bisharat *et al.*, 1999) and was associated with seafood mediated bacteremia.

Disease – and numbers of *V. vulnificus* – fluctuate with the water temperature. Most cases occur during the warm summer months. The infectious dose is not known, but shellfish with levels of 10^3 *V. vulnificus* per gram have been implicated in disease. Using data on numbers in oysters, modelling growth between harvest and consumption, estimating number of servings based on landings and comparing this to the reported number of cases per months (Table 5.11) it becomes clear that especially high levels are likely to result in disease (FDA, 2000).

b) Prevalence in fish and fishery products

Isolation of *V. vulnificus* from the environment can be difficult, however, it is frequently isolated from warmer marine or estuarine waters. It appears to be associated with the Gulf Coast of the USA, although it has been isolated from other areas such as the East coast of the USA (Oliver *et al.*, 1983) and from the Italian Adriatic coast (Barbieri *et al.*, 1999). *V. vulnificus* accumulates in oysters up to 10^4 cfu/g and can be found in levels of up to 10^6 cfu/g in intestines of fish feeding on oysters. Just as *V. parahaemolyticus,* the occurrence in both water and oysters follows a seasonal pattern with high numbers (and disease) being detected in the summer-months – and 90% of the cases in the US occurring between April and October. Motes *et al.* (1998) found that the density in oysters was approximately 10^4 per gram when the water was 25-30°C but dropped to below 100 per gram when the temperature decreased below 15°C. Also salinity affects its occurrence with optimal salinity at 17 ppt. *V. vulnificus* may multiply within the live animal and each oyster may shed up to 10^6 bacteria per day (Tamplin and Capers, 1992).

Table 5.11 Environmental and epidemiological data for *Vibrio vulnificus* in the USA (modified from FDA, 2000)

Month	Water-temp. °C	Mean log Vv/g at harvest[1]	Mean log Vv/g at consumption	Servings for at risk individuals	Log of mean Vv per serving dose	Average # cases in month
Jan	12.5	-0.03	-0.34	62 000	2.45	0
Feb	15	0.76	0.61	63 000	3.40	0
Mar	17.5	1.45	1.51	73 000	4.30	0.2
Apr	22.5	2.52	2.96	63 000	5.75	1
May	26	3.04	3.75	53 000	6.54	3
Jun	28.5	3.28	4.19	51 000	6.98	2.5
Jul	30	3.38	4.41	47 000	7.20	2.5
Aug	30	3.38	4.41	42 000	7.20	3.5
Sep	28	3.24	4.11	48 000	6.90	3
Oct	23	2.61	3.12	61 000	5.91	3
Nov	18	1.57	1.68	70 000	4.46	1.5
Dec	15	0.76	0.61	72 000	3.40	2

1. Vv = *Vibrio vulnificus*

c) Growth and survival in fish and fishery products

V. vulnificus is a mesophilic bacterium and grows poorly below 15°C (minimum temperature approximately 13°C) and disease seems to be correlated to temperatures above 20°C. In seafood products stored at ambient temperature it grows rapidly and numbers can in live oysters increase with a factor 100 (2 log units) during 14 hours of storage at 24 to 33°C. Growth limiting parameters are indicated in Table 5.6.

d) Prevention and control

V. vulnificus is very sensitive to a range of food-relevant treatments. It dies rapidly during heating with D-values of approximately 78 sec at 47°C. The EU directive (EC, 1991) requires that shellfish from so-called Class C areas are heat treated at 90°C for 90 sec (or equivalent). Class C areas are areas where there is a microbiological limit on the shellfish of < 60 000 faecal coliforms/100g and the shellfish must be relayed for at least 2 months (see Chapter 11). It is more sensitive to cold-storage than *V. parahaemolyticus* and declines with approximately 0.04 log units per day under "normal" cold storage (FAO/WHO, 2001). The bacterium is relatively sensitive to low pH and does not grow below pH 5 (Little *et al.*, 1997). Thus products such as pickled fish do not constitute a risk. Storage at refrigerated temperatures or below 0°C results in reduction of counts of *V. vulnificus*. This is either attributed to a die-off of the organism or to entrance into a so-called viable-but-non-culturable state. Frozen storage (-40°C) can result in a 4-5 log reduction over a 3 week period.

The bacterium is not removed from oysters by normal depuration and the bacterium may, as *V. parahaemolyticus*, actually multiply in depurating animals. In contrast, relaying in waters of high salinity does decrease numbers. Heat treatment is a very efficient way of reducing numbers. For animals with an initial low number of *V. vulnificus*, rapid and efficient cold-storage is crucial in preventing proliferation.

Vibrio cholerae

a) The disease and some epidemiological aspects

V. cholerae may be sub-typed into more than 130 serotypes. Of these only serotype O1 and O139 are associated with epidemic and pandemic cholera. Both produce the cholera toxin. The O1 may be further subdivided into the serogroups Ogawa or Inaba or Hikojima which is an uncommon type. O1 types may also be subdivided into two biotypes: classical and El Tor of which the latter is hemolytic. O139 strains resemble the El Tor types being also hemolytic (Kaysner, 2000).

Cholera affects only humans and the main source of the bacteria during epidemics are the faeces of acutely infected people. However, the bacteria persists in the environment and is often found attached to plankton (Chiavelli *et al.,* 2001). *V. cholerae* non-O1 and non-O139 are as the other *Vibrio* species, ubiquitous in marine and estuarine waters. Some non-O1 and non-O139 may be pathogenic to man, causing mainly gastroenteritis, but they are not associated with the epidemic diseases. Water contaminated with sewage is the main cause of spread of cholerae but also seafood products being contaminated with cholera-containing waters have been the cause of disease. The largest recent out-break of cholera, the pandemic South American outbreak in the early 1990s was partially caused by ceviche, a raw, marinated fish product, for which contaminated water or fish was used in the preparation. This was a O1-outbreak and caused more than 400 000 cases.

Cholera is a gastrointestinal disease characterized by diarrhoea and passage of watery, voluminous (so-called rice-water) stools leaving the patient dehydrated. Treatment with salt- and sugar-water is required. One of the major virulence factors is the production of the cholerae toxin secreted by O1 and O139 serotypes. The infective dose is believed to be approximately 10^6 cells (Kaysner, 2000) although some authors state that ingestion of as much as 10^{11} cells are required to make up for the rapid reduction by gastric acids (Stewart-Tull, 2001).

b) Prevalence in fish and fishery products

As mentioned, an association between phyto- or zoo-plankton and numbers of *V. cholerae* has been observed. Water temperature and salinity also affect the occurrence and persistence of *V. cholerae.* Thus the highest numbers are observed at lower salinities of 2-5 ppt (Kaysner, 2000) and the natural niche of *V. cholerae* is estuarine waters (Oliver and Kaper, 1997). *V. cholerae* survives for long periods of time in river waters (FAO/WHO, 2001). Toxigenic *V. cholerae* have been isolated from the hindgut of crab (Huq *et al.* 1996) and it is believed that their chitinolytic activity, which also explains their preference for plankton aggregates, is the cause of this adherence. *V. cholera* is not common on fresh fish, thus none of 748 samples of warm water shrimp imported into Denmark were positive (Dalsgaard *et al.* 1996), nor were 131 fresh and brackish water prawn samples from Bangladesh (Balakrish Nair *et al.,* 1991). However, in some areas of the world it may be more prevalent. *V. cholerae* O1 has been isolated from 3.5-18.3% of fresh fish in Mexico (Torres-Vitela *et al.,* 1997).

c) Growth and survival in fish and fishery products

V. cholerae is very sensitive to heat, acid and cooling. Therefore, it is either eliminated by food processing treatments or its growth in foods is prevented. The majority of cases in which cholera has been linked to seafoods have involved raw products, often molluscs. Due to the involvement of ceviche in the South American epidemic, its survival in slightly acidified products has been studied and a 2-3 log reduction is seen over a 24 hour period. Limits for growth are given in Table 5.6.

d) Prevention and control

Inadequate sanitation and lack of safe water are the major causes of cholera epidemics. Therefore, cholera can only be reliably prevented by ensuring that all populations have access to adequate excreta disposal systems and safe drinking water. WHO has issued recommendations for water supply and sanitation (Table 5.12).

Table 5.12 WHO recommendations for water supply and sanitation with respect to cholera control (WHO, 1992).

<table>
<tr><th colspan="2">Recommendation</th></tr>
<tr><th>Water supply</th><th>Sanitation</th></tr>
<tr><td>• Drinking water should be adequately disinfected, procedures for disinfection in distribution systems and rural water systems should be improved
• Tablets releasing chlorine or iodine may be distributed to the population with instructions on their use
• Where chemical treatment of water is not possible, health educators should stress that water for drinking (as well as for washing of hands and utensils) should be boiled before use
• Water quality control should be strengthened by intensifying the surveillance and control of residual chlorine, and the conduct and analysis of bacteriological tests, in different points in production and distribution systems</td><td>• Quality control in sewage treatment plants should be strengthened
• The use of treated waste water for irrigation should be carefully controlled, following national and international guidelines
• Large-scale chemical treatment of waste water is very rarely justified, even in emergencies, because of the high cost, uncertain effect, and possible adverse impact on the environment and health
• Health education should emphasize the safe disposal of human faeces:
o All family members should use a latrine or toilet that is regularly cleaned and disinfected
o Faeces of infants and children should be disposed of rapidly in a latrine or toilet, or by burying them</td></tr>
</table>

Low temperature storage may reduce numbers of *V. cholerae* (Mitcherlich and Marth 1984, Table 5.13) but must never be relied on as a preventive measure.

Table 5.13 Survival of *Vibrio cholerae* (culturable cells) (Mitcherlich and Marth, 1984).

Food	Survival times, days
Fish stored at 3-8°C	14-25
Ice stored at –20°C	8
Shrimp, frozen	180
Vegetables, 20°C	10
Carrots	10
Cauliflower	20
River water	210

Listeria monocytogenes (Lone Gram)

Listeria monocytogenes is a Gram-positive, motile bacteria that grows well at 37°C at human body temperature but which at the same time is psychrotolerant and halotolerant (Table 5.6). Seven species of *Listeria* are known and of these only *L. monocytogenes* is pathogenic to humans (Farber and Peterkin, 2000). *Listeria* species are closely related to the lactic acid bacteria. *L. monocytogenes* is divided into 13 serovars on the basis of somatic (O) and flagellar (H) antigens, however, most isolates involved in human disease belong to three serotypes. From an epidemiological point of view, DNA-based methods such as random amplification of polymorphic DNA (RAPD), ribotyping or amplified fragment-length polymorphism (AFLP) are more discriminatory and have allowed tracing of outbreaks and contamination sources in the food industry.

a) The disease and some epidemiological aspects

Listeriosis is in its most known form an invasive disease transmitted by food products. Listeriosis is a rare disease and mostly affects people in particular risk groups where the immune defence system is reduced. This is typically elderly people, people with HIV infection, transplant patients but also pregnant women (where the immune defence is reduced to avoid rejection of the foetus). The disease infects the central nervous system and often manifests itself as meningitis. The bacterium multiplies within the macrophages and "shoots" itself from cell to cell using a tail of actin polymers. The fatality rate in the risk group is high; typically 20-40%. In infected pregnant women, listeriosis typically results in abortion. The incubation period is very variable ranging from one to 91 days and since most people do not remember their food consumption three months ago, it is often difficult to trace the food that was the source of the pathogen. If diagnosed, the disease can be treated with standard antibiotics. The incidence of listeriosis is approximately 0.5 cases per 100 000 inhabitants in the western countries. Neonates are infected since *L. monocytogenes* can cross the placenta and whilst the pregnant women suffer only a mild flu-like disease, the foetus is seriously affected. Recently, it has been documented that *L. monocytogenes* may also cause a non-invasive febrile gastroenteritis in otherwise healthy people that have eaten smoked trout (Miettinen *et al.*, 1999). The incidence of this type of listeriosis is not known.

Listeriosis is typically caused by processed, industrialized foods that have extended shelf lives at chill temperatures and that are ready-to-eat (RTE). Thus there is no final heat treatment by the consumer. Due to its widespread occurrence, *L. monocytogenes* is easily isolated from several types of RTE foods. The disease was noticed initially from soft cheeses made from raw milk but has since been caused by a range of products such as paté, frankfurters, salads and RTE fish products (cold-smoked trout). Several risk assessments (Buchanan *et al.*, 1997; FAO/WHO, 2001a; FDA, 2001) have concluded that although even low number of cells carry some risk of infection, the majority of cases (>99%) are caused by food products with high levels of the bacterium (Figure 5.3). Thus, the real risk is the growth of the organism in the product rather than its mere presence. Despite this knowledge and the understanding that low levels are unlikely to cause disease, several countries, including the United States, have regulation asking so-called zero tolerance, i.e. that the organism must not be detected in 25 grams of food.

Figure 5.3
Simulated dose-response function for *Listeria monocytogenes* in ready to eat foods for consumers in the high risk group. Based on FAO/WHO (2001).

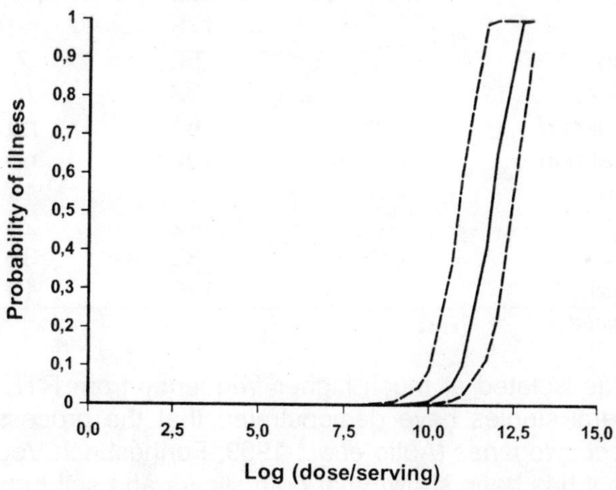

Epidemiological evidence suggests that listeriosis has been associated with smoked mussels (Brett *et al.*, 1998), "gravad" trout (Ericsson *et al.*, 1997), and smoked trout (Miettinen *et al.*, 1999). In the latter case the outbreak was not the classical invasive listeriosis, but cold-smoked trout was associated with febrile gastroenteritis in five healthy people.

b) The niche and prevalence in fish and fishery products

As indicated, *L. monocytogenes* is an organism indigenous to the general environment where it is typical of decaying plant material. Also, it occurs in the gastrointestinal tract and 2-6% of humans are healthy carriers. It is not typical of aquatic and marine environments. Thus the organism cannot be isolated from free open waters nor from fish caught or cultured in such waters (Table 5.14) . In contrast, water close to agricultural run-off harbour the organism and in principle the bacterium must be assumed to be present, albeit in low levels on raw fish (Gram, 2001; Huss *et al.*, 1995). In contrast to the low levels or absence on raw fish, *L. monocytogenes* can easily be isolated from processed fish products. Thus 3-40% of RTE seafoods are positive for *L. monocytogenes* (Table 5.15), but in some smoke houses as much as 80% of the samples are positive.

Table 5.14 Prevalence of *Listeria* spp. and *Listeria monocytogenes* in live or newly slaughtered fish (modified from Gram (2001)).

Sampling location	No. of samples	% positive for *Listeria* spp.	% positive for *L. monocytogenes*
Freshwater			
skin of live trout (Switzerland)	45	33	11
channel catfish (USA)	4	100	nd
slaughtered trout (Switzerland)	27	22	15
Seawater			
salmon, at harvest (Norway)	10	0	0
salmon, at processing plant (Norway)	18	0	0
salmon (Faroe islands)	18	nd[1]	1
frozen salmon (received at plant) (USA)	65	nd	34
salmon (USA, Chile, Norway, Canada, Scotland)	32	nd	10

1. nd = not determined

Table 5.15 Prevalence of *Listeria* spp. *and Listeria monocytogenes* seafood products (modified from Farber and Peterkin (2000) and Gram (2001)).

Product	No. of samples	% positive for *Listeria* spp.	% positive for *L. monocytogenes*
Fresh shrimp	74	nd[1]	11
Fresh shrimp	178	nd	17
Slaughtered fish	50	2	0
Ceviche	32	75	9
Cold-smoked salmon	61	nd	0
Cold-smoked salmon	100	nd	24
Smoked salmon	65	11	11
Hot-smoked fish	142	25	5
Seafood salads	37	32	16
Cooked blue crab	126	10	8

1. nd = not determined

The bacterium is isolated at much higher frequency from RTE seafood products than from raw materials. Several studies have demonstrated that the processing environment is an important niche for *L. monocytogenes* (Autio *et al.*, 1999; Fonnesbech Vogel *et al.*, 2001). Thus using DNA-typing methods it has been shown that both slicers and salt brine harbours the types found in the product. Also, Table 5.15 shows that the bacterium is detected in heat processed products subjected to a listericidal process. Post-process contamination is the likely cause of this contamination. Cleaning and disinfection may temporarily remove the organism which is often found in more permanent niches in drains or floor mats.

c) Growth and survival in fish and fishery products

Listeria monocytogenes is halo- and psychrotolerant and can grow well in refrigerated foods. It is difficult to control it in RTE seafood products where there is no listericidal processing step and where *L. monocytogenes* can grow at the temperature / a_w / atmosphere conditions prevailing in the products. Several studies have demonstrated that it grows (rapidly) in brined shrimp and cold-smoked fish. Most – if not all – of these experiments were conducted with inoculated samples and growth in naturally contaminated products appear much slower. This may partly be explained by the so-called Jameson effect where the presence of a competitive associate micro flora depresses the maximum cell density of the bacterium (Figure 5.4).

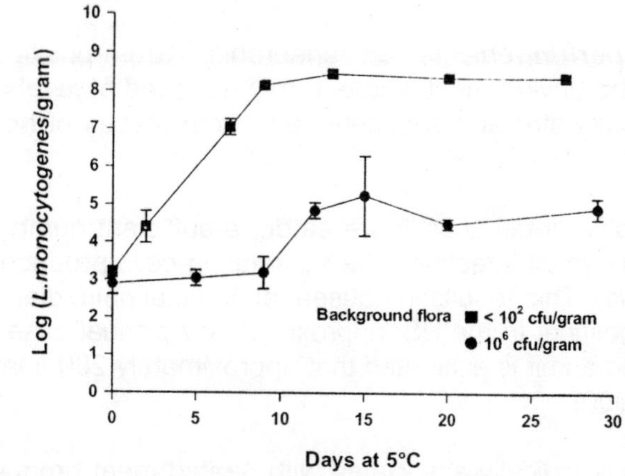

Figure 5.4
Growth of *Listeria monocytogenes* (mixture of 6 strains) on vacuum-packed cold-smoked salmon (5°C) when initial background flora is low or high (Huss *et al.*, 2000).

The NaCl concentration is critical when evaluating growth potential, as the bacterium may grow rapidly at 3-4% NaCl but much slower with 7-8% NaCl. *L. monocytogenes* is of little importance in semi-preserved seafood products where 2.5% acetic acid is used. Also, use of citric acid can be used to clean floors and drains and eliminate the organism from processing environments. Nitrate, lactate, di-acetate and bacteriocins inhibit or delay growth. The limited growth illustrated in Figure 5.4 can be used deliberately as preservation by adding a bio protective competitive lactic acid bacterial flora that inhibits *L. monocytogenes* (Nilsson *et al.*, 1999).

Listericidal processing consists primarily of heat treatment. The heat resistance of *L. monocytogenes* has been extensively studied in milk and dairy products (ICMSF, 1996). The thermal death time curve for *L. monocytogenes* in cod and salmon was studied by Ben Embarek and Huss (1993). The heat resistance of the bacterium is higher in salmon than in cod with D_{60} values being 4.5 min and 1.8 min, respectively. It is assumed that the higher lipid content (approximately 13%) of salmon protected the bacterium.

d) Prevention and control

Control of listeriosis can be achieved using HACCP and GHP. A critical control point occurs when processing can include a step where *L. monocytogenes* is eliminated. This can only be guaranteed in products that after packaging are subjected to a listericidal process, typically a heat treatment. In many products, low levels of *L. monocytogenes* will occur regularly or sporadically. Control of growth in products where a listericidal process is not used can be done in several ways. Freezing of products will eliminate growth, and sufficient levels of acid and NaCl will also prevent growth. Sorbate (0.05-0.1%) or the combination of lactate (2%) and di-acetate (0.1%) has been shown to eliminate growth in frankfurters (Tompkin, 2001). As mentioned, the addition of live lactic acid bacteria may inhibit growth in some products.

Critical control points cannot be identified in the processing of a number of RTE seafood products. Therefore, control of level of contamination using GHP is of outmost importance. *L. monocytogenes* is sensitive to common cleaning and disinfecting agents and both chlorine, iodine, acid, anionic and quaternary ammonium-type sanitizers are effective against *L. monocytogenes* at concentrations of 100 ppm, 25-45 ppm, 200 ppm and 100-200 ppm, respectively. *L. monocytogenes* often hides in niches in the processing environment and great care must be taken to clean such niches. The processing plant must have a *Listeria* surveillance programme installed and procedures to be implemented when the organism is detected.

As several risk assessments have shown that low levels of *L. monocytogenes* are consumed daily with no adverse effect, a limit of 100 cfu/g has been suggested as a food safety objective (van

Schothorst, 1998). A microbiological criteria involving 20 samples with m = 100 cfu/g and c = 0 is used has been suggested for RTE products where there is a potential for growth of the organism (van Schothorst, 1996).

Other clostridia and bacilli *(Lone Gram)*

Clostridium perfringens is an anaerobic, Gram-positive mesophilic spore-former widely distributed in the environment where it may be found at levels of 10^3-10^4 per gram soil. It can also be isolated from water and sediments and from faeces of healthy individuals (Adams and Moss, 2000).

If high levels of vegetative cells are eaten, a sufficient number may survive the gut passage and sporulate in the small intestine. The sporulating cells produce an enterotoxin of approximately 35 kilo Dalton (kDa). This results in nausea, abdominal pain, diarrhoea and, sometimes, vomiting 8-24 hours after ingestion. In the US, approximately 7 annual cases of *C. perfringens* are reported with links to seafood and it is estimated that approximately 200 seafood-caused cases occur every year (Feldhusen, 2000).

C. perfringens is typically associated with heated meat products or dishes which are temperature abused or heated slowly for long time. Due to its anaerobic nature, it prefers food with low redox potential.

C. perfringens does not grow at chill temperatures and grows only slowly below 20°C. The vegetative cells are sensitive to acid (minimum pH of 5), salt (maximum 6%) and do not grow at water activities below 0.95. Therefore controlling proliferation in seafoods is not complicated. Observing proper time-temperature conditions and avoiding cross-contamination to heated foods is essential.

Bacillus cereus strains are aerobic, Gram-positive spore-forming bacteria. As *C. perfringens* they are widely distributed in the environment. The spores are resistant to drying and are easily spread with dust. *B. cereus* can easily be isolated from many foods but typically occurs only in low numbers especially in raw foods (Granum and Baird-Parker, 2000). Heat processing will select for the spore formers.

B. cereus causes two types of disease, both caused by toxin formation. One is characterized by abdominal pain and profuse watery diarrhoea and symptoms occur 8-16 hours after ingestion. This type resembles the *C. perfringens* intoxication described above. The other, the so-called emetic type, has a shorter incubation period (½ to 5 hours) and nausea and vomiting are typical effects. This resembles the *S. aureus* gastroenteritis. The diarrhoeal type is associated with toxin formation in the gut whereas the emetic type is caused by a toxin preformed in the food. The toxin is produced in the late exponential to stationary phase and thus high numbers of *B. cereus* are a prerequisite for disease. The emetic type is typically related to rice, dough or other starchy products.

Most strains of *B. cereus* are mesophilic and do not grow below 10-15°C. However, psychrotrophic, toxin-producing strains have been isolated from foods stored at 4-6°C. Such strains must be considered for instance in the production of *sous-vide* products, where a mild heat-treatment is combined with subsequent cold-temperature storage. Although vacuum-packed, *Bacillus* species have been isolated in high numbers from *sous-vide* cod fillets stored at 5°C (Ben Embarek, 1994). Except for the few psychrotrophic strains, control of *B. cereus* is efficiently obtained by chilling.

Plesiomonas shigelloides *(Lone Gram)*

a) The disease and some epidemiological aspects

The genus *Plesiomonas* belongs to the Vibrionaceae family and consists of a single species, *P. shigelloides*. The species can be sub-typed and contain many serovars (Kirov, 1997). *P. shigelloides* can cause wound infections and septicemia but has also been suspected as cause of gastroenteritis. Thus the same serotype was found in tap water and in patients suffering diarrhoea (Tsukamoto *et al.,* 1978) and the organism has been isolated from patients with watery (mild) diarrhoea. In the USA, *P. shigelloides* has mainly been linked to consumption of raw oysters. There appears to be seasonal variation, with the peak occurring during the warm summer months. The role of *P. shigelloides* in the described cases may be doubtful since volunteers participating in feeding studies have failed to develop diarrhoea after ingestion of 10^9 organisms. Mild diarrhoea has, however, been induced in piglets (Kirov, 1997).

b) Prevalence in fish and fishery products

P. shigelloides is an environmental organism but is mostly associated with aquatic environments, both freshwater and marine waters (Farmer *et al.,* 1997). The organism is mesophilic and typically growth does not occur below 8°C, however, it has been isolated from freshwater environments in cold climates (Krovacek *et al.*, 2000). The bacterium can be isolated from different food products but is typically found in fish and seafood.

c) Growth and survival in fish and fishery products

As mentioned, *P. shigelloides* is a mesophilic bacteria and does not grow at chill temperatures. The organism does survive freezing. The organism is sensitive to low pH and growth is slowed at moderate salt-concentrations (> 3.5% WPS).

d) Prevention and control

The evidence of *P. shigelloides* as a human food-borne pathogen is not completely convincing. As an organism indigenous to the aquatic environment, it must be expected to be present on fish and shellfish. Bearing in mind the volunteer studies, it must be anticipated that some growth to high concentrations is needed for any (potential) disease to occur. Thus its control in foods is straight forward since chill storage or moderate salting/acidifying conditions will prevent growth of the organism.

Aeromonas *(Lone Gram)*

a) The disease and some epidemiological aspects

The genus *Aeromonas* is a member of the Aeromonodaceae family which was created in 1986. Formerly the genus belonged to the Vibrionaceae family. It contains species pathogenic to animals (fish) and man. In humans, *Aeromonas* species may cause several adverse conditions including skin or soft tissue infection through invasion via burn injury. Such infections are most commonly associated with immunosuppression (Monteil and Harf-Monteil, 1997). The taxonomy of *Aeromonas* is rather confusing, but the species *A. hydrophila, A. sobria* and *A. caviae* which are motile and often (but not always) mesophilic have been linked to human gastroenteritis. They are, even more commonly than *P. shigelloides*, isolated from patients with mild diarrhoea, often as the sole potential human pathogen. Several classical virulence factors (extracellular enzymes, exotoxins (including enterotoxins), siderophores) have been identified in these *Aeromonas* species. There is no evidence that toxins preformed in the food play any role (Ahmed, 1991). As for *P. shigelloides*, feeding high levels to human volunteers have failed to cause disease (Morgan *et al.,* 1985) and the association between eating fish and shellfish and *Aeromonas*-gastroenteritis is at best circumstantial.

b) Prevalence in fish and fishery products

The *Aeromonas* species is a common, natural member of freshwater environments and between 33 and 100% of water samples contain the bacterium (Palumbo *et al.*, 2000). These organisms can also be isolated from marine and estuarine environments (Knøchel, 1989). The *A. hydrophila* group is very commonly found in fish and fish products at levels between 10^2 and 10^6 cfu/g but is also readily isolated from meat, milk, poultry and vegetable products (Palumbo *et al.*, 2000). Several studies have implicated *Aeromonas* species as spoilage organisms of raw meat (Dainty *et al.*, 1983), raw packed salmon (Gibson, 1992), fish from warm tropical waters (Gram *et al.*, 1990) and milk (Eneroth *et al.*, 1998). In such products the organisms may grow to 10^7-10^9 cfu/g.

c) Growth and survival in fish and fishery products

Although the motile aeromonads as a group are mesophilic, several studies have demonstrated that many environmental (food derived) strains grow well at chill temperatures (Knøchel, 1990; Eneroth *et al.*, 1998). Growth is inhibited by approximately 5% NaCl (Gram, 1991) and at pH 5. The organisms are able to grow in both vacuum and modified atmosphere packed products (Palumbo *et al.*, 2000).

d) Prevention and control

Aeromonas species are readily isolated from water, fish and shellfish and must be expected to be present. Limitation of growth requires a combination of chilling, salting and/or acidification. Growth of aeromonads will not be a problem in foods with pH below 6.5 and NaCl > 3% WPS.

5.1.1.2 Bacteria indigenous to the human/animal reservoir (Lone Gram)

Bacteria from the human/animal reservoir may, as presented in the tables in section 4.1 on statistics, cause seafood-borne diseases. Thus cases of staphylococcal enterotoxin gastroenteritis have been reported from cooked crustaceans, and oysters and other ready-to-eat products have caused salmonellosis or shigellosis. Several of these diseases are zoonotic since the major source of human illness is infected animals. The tolerance of these organisms to food-relevant preservation parameters is presented in Table 5.16.

Table 5.16 Growth limiting factors of pathogenic bacteria indigenous to the human and animal reservoir (adapted from Huss, 1994; ICMSF, 1996)

Pathogenic bacteria	Temperature, °C		pH	a_w	NaCl (%)
	minimum	optimum	minimum	minimum	maximum
Salmonella	5[1]	35-43	3.8	0.94	6
Shigella	6	35-40	4.9	0.96	5
Escherichia coli	7	35-40	4.4	0.95	8
Yersinia enterocolitica	-1.3	25-37	4.2	0.96	7
Campylobacter	30	42	4.9	0.99	1.5
Staphylococcus aureus	7	37	4	0.83	20-25[2]
toxin production	10	40-45	4.5	0.87	10-15[2]

1. *Some authors report growth at temperatures as low as 2°C (D'Aoust 2000)*
2. *Different maximum limits are reported in the literature*

Salmonella species or Serovars

The genus *Salmonella* is a member of the Enterobacteriaceae family. Salmonellosis is a leading cause of bacterial enteric disease in both humans and animals (Brenner *et al.*, 2000). The nomenclature is complex and causes confusion. At the Centre for Disease Control (CDC) in USA, the following scheme is used: only two species of *Salmonella* are recognised; the *S. enterica* and the *S. bongori*. The former occurs in 6 sub-species. Within each of these, several serotypes exists. Thus *S. enterica* subsp. *enterica* as the largest group covers approximately 1500 serotypes. Examples of such serotypes are Enteritidis, Typhimurium or Typhi (Brenner *et al.*, 2000). The serotypes of the other sub-species are not named but identified by antigenic formula (D'Aoust, 2000).

a) The disease (adverse health effect) and some epidemiological aspects

Salmonellosis manifests itself clinically either as the enteric fever syndrome caused by typhoid or paratyphoid strains or as the nontyphoid dependent gastroenteritis. The latter may progress to a more severe systemic infection. Symptoms of the non-typhoid salmonellosis include nausea, abdominal cramps, diarrhoea with watery and possibly mucoid stools, fever and vomiting appearing 8-72 hours after exposure to the pathogen (D'Aoust, 2000). Systemic spread may occur leading to cardiac and circulatory problems. Poultry, pork and beef products are important sources of salmonellosis and eggs have, especially due to transovarian infection of the egg with *S.* Enteritidis, been involved in many outbreaks. Recently, also a variety of ready to eat vegetables, including bean-sprouts, have caused salmonellosis. Seafoods are relatively uncommon as causes of salmonellosis, however, the number of cases seems to be increasing. The infectious dose of salmonellae is, in general, high – typically around 10^6 cells, however, much lower infectious doses (10-100 cells) are reported if the organism is protected against stomach acidity e.g. by fat and if the product is eaten by more susceptible groups such as children.

b) Prevalence in fish and fishery products

Salmonellae are typically mesophilic bacteria with a global distribution. However, their main reservoir is the gastrointestinal tract of man and animals, including birds. Also, environments, such as water reservoirs, contaminated with human or animal excreta may harbour *Salmonella*. In particular shellfish growing in contaminated waters may accumulate *Salmonella* and raw oysters have been the cause of salmonellosis outbreaks (Ahmed, 1991).

Open marine waters are free from *Salmonella* but estuaries and contaminated coastal waters may harbour the pathogen. Also, poor personal hygiene may transmit the organism. *Salmonella* is rarely detected in fish from temperate waters but may occur in tropical waters and on fish and shellfish from such waters. Up to 10-15% of fish samples from India and Mexico were positive of *Salmonella* which has also been detected in several crustacean and molluscan products from India and Malaysia (D'Aoust, 2000). There is evidence that specific serotypes of *Salmonella* are common in fish farms and become part of the indigenous micro flora (Feldhusen, 2000).

The integrated fish farming in some areas of South-East Asia and Asia where poultry manure and/or so-called "night soils" are sometimes used as fertilisers for the ponds may add to the *Salmonella* contamination. However, the use of chicken manure does not *per se* lead to *Salmonella* detection as demonstrated by Dalsgaard *et al.* (1995) who did not find a single positive sample out of 158 samples from shrimp production in Thailand. To further complicate the situation, *Salmonella* may also, in these warm climates, originate from the environment itself (Reilly *et al.*, 1992; Bhaskar *et al.*, 1995) and does not necessarily indicate poor hygiene. In a Japanese study, *Salmonella* was detected in approximately one fifth of eel culture ponds (Saheki *et al.*, 1989).

Cooked shrimp may be post-process contaminated from the raw crustaceans or by employees and since no competing micro flora is present, it may constitute a high risk product if the bacterium is allowed to grow e.g. following temperature abuse.

c) Growth and survival in fish and fishery products

The vast majority of salmonellae are mesophilic bacteria growing from just above 5°C to approximately 45°C with an optimum at 37°C. Vegetative, unstressed cells are heat-sensitive and are easily destroyed at pasteurisation (hot-smoking) temperatures. D-values at 60°C are typically 1-3 minutes. Although *Salmonella* does not grow well at low water activity, it has been found to survive well in dry environments and (re)-contaminate products such as fish meal. *Salmonella* does not grow below pH 4.5.

Shigella

Four species of *Shigella* are known all of which are human pathogenic. The genus *Shigella* is very closely related to another Enterobacteriaceae genus, *Escherichia*.

a) The disease and some epidemiological aspects

Sh. dysenteriae causes the most severe condition of bacilliary dysentery whereas *Sh. sonnei* causes the mildest of the diseases. The infectious dose is low, approximately 10-100 cells and from 7 hours to 7 days may lapse before symptoms present themselves. These include abdominal pain, vomiting, fever and diarrhoea which may contain bloody stools. The disease is an infectious disease. *Sh. dysenteriae* occurs on the Indian subcontinent, in Africa and Asia whereas the mildest of the species, *Sh. sonnei* is the most common in the western countries (Lampel *et al.*, 2000). In children, particularly in developing countries, the disease may be severe and *Shigella* diarrhoea accounts for hundreds of thousands deaths every year.

The primary route of infection is the faecal-oral route with person-to-person being the most common route of transmission. Shigellosis outbreaks follow a seasonal pattern with the largest number of outbreaks in the warm (summer) months.

b) Prevalence in fish and fishery products

Unlike *Salmonella*, Shigella is not associated with particular food raw materials but its presence is exclusively a question of poor hygienic handling and humans are its natural reservoir. Outbreaks have been caused by a multitude of food products, including shrimp and clams (Lampel *et al.*, 2000). *Shigella* are not naturally present in water but may survive for up to 6 months in water (Wachsmuth and Morris, 1989) and may survive for long time in clams and oysters (Feldhusen, 2000). Outbreaks have typically involved contamination of raw or previously cooked foods during preparation by an infected, asymptomatic carrier with poor personal hygiene.

In the US, FDA in 1994 and 1995 reported 7 cases of shigellosis caused by seafood and estimate that the annual total number of seafood-related shigellosis cases is approximately 200 cases (Feldhusen, 2000).

c) Growth and survival in fish and fishery products

Shigella species are truly mesophilic and do not grow below 6-7°C. They are sensitive to salting and heating. As mentioned, they may survive for long periods of time in bivalves.

Escherichia coli

The genus *Escherichia* is a member of the Enterobacteriaceae family and *E. coli* is the most common aerobic organism in the intestinal tract of man and warm-blooded animals. Most of the *E. coli* strains are harmless commensals that colonise the intestinal tract and probably play important roles in maintaining intestinal physiology. However, some strains of *E. coli* are pathogenic and can cause diarrhoeal disease. *E. coli* strains are differentiated based on a serotyping scheme involving O (somatic), H (flagellar) and K (capsular) antigens. Pathogenic *E. coli* are divided into specific groups depending on virulence, clinical symptoms and distinct O:H antigens. The important groups are (Doyle *et al.*, 1997):

- enteropathogenic *E. coli* (EPEC)
- enterotoxigenic *E. coli* (ETEC)
- enteroinvasive *E. coli* (EIEC)

- diffuse-adhering *E. coli* (DAEC)
- enteroaggregative *E. coli* (EAggEC) and
- enterohemorrhagic *E. coli* (EHEC) or verotoxic *E. coli* (VTEC).

a) The disease and some epidemiological aspects.

EPEC causes a watery type of diarrhoea accompanied by vomiting and fever. It typically occurs in infants and young children. The EIEC produced a diarrhoeal disease similar to *Shigella* whereas ETEC causes diarrhoea resembling *V. cholerae* diarrhoea. ETEC are a major cause of diarrhoea in children in developing countries and also a cause of so-called travellers' diarrhoea in adults. ETEC strains produce two types of toxin of which one resembles the cholera toxin. Also, the DAEC and EAggEC cause various variants of diarrhoea.

Due to recent outbreaks of EHEC in developed countries, much research has been directed against these organisms. By the early 1980ies it was realised that some *E. coli* strains caused hemorrhagic colitis (HC) and hemolytic uremic syndrome (HUS). Following diarrhoea and a sub-set of symptoms, EHEC may result in renal failure; the HUS condition. Whilst the disease may affect all age groups, in particular children are susceptible (Willshaw *et al.*, 2000). *E. coli* O157:H7 is the most common EHEC serotype. The attachment capability appear to be important virulence factors for EHEC strains which produce two Shiga-like toxins capable of killing Vero (African Green Monkey Kidney) cells. The infectious dose is low and levels of 2 – 2 000 cells have been recorded as ingested concentrations in outbreaks.

b) Prevalence in fish and fishery products

The main source of *E. coli* infections have been (faecally) contaminated water and contaminated food handlers. Outbreaks by EHEC have mostly involved undercooked ground beef and raw milk. Also vegetables, such as alfalfa sprouts, washed or cultured in contaminated water have caused outbreaks. A number of famous outbreaks have been related to unpasteurised apple juice. Due to the relatively low pH, these juices were considered safe, however EHEC strains have an unusual acid tolerance and thus survived in the product.

Neither of the *E. coli* strains are typical of water or of aquatic products. However, poor hygiene, cross contamination by food handlers or dirty water may transfer the organism. Also, such strains may accumulate in filter feeding bivalves cultured in contaminated waters.

Whilst *E. coli* is not indigenous to the aquatic environment, it may survive and even multiply in warm tropical waters (Rhodes and Kator, 1988; Jiménez *et al.*, 1989) and thus also be isolated from presumed unpolluted waters. There are no reports of isolation of O157:H7 strains from seafood products.

c) Growth and survival in fish and fishery products

All *E. coli* strains are mesophilic organisms with optimum growth at 37°C. They do not grow at chill temperatures and are readily destroyed by mild heating. Most isolation procedures rely on incubation at 44°C, however, EHEC strains do not grow on selective media at 44°C. In general, the organisms are sensitive to salting and acidifying. A notable exception is the acid tolerance seen in EHEC strains.

Prevention and control of mesophilic Enterobacteriaceae

Although both *Salmonella* and *E. coli* can be isolated from non-contaminated tropical waters, the main source of these organisms and *Shigella* are human and animal (faecal) contamination. Therefore adherence to Good Hygienic Practices with emphasis on clean water and personnel hygiene will control the organisms. As all are sensitive to heating, the GHP-programme must be particularly strict when ready-to-eat foods are processed.

Proper treatment (e.g. chlorination) of water and sanitary disposal of sewage are essential parts in a control programme.

The infectious dose of *Shigella* and *E. coli* is low and thus it is their mere presence that must be avoided. In contrast, most Salmonellae have a higher infectious dose if they are not consumed in very fatty (protective) products. Therefore their growth in the product must be avoided. Growth will be inhibited at chill temperatures and by salting.

Current levels of *Salmonella* in various foods and its importance in human food-borne infections underline that bacteriological testing and stringent bacteriological standards (e.g. absence) of most foods are insufficient measures in the control of salmonellosis. Even the microbiological quality of harvest water (for live bivalves) appears not to be a good predictor for *Salmonella* contamination, because oysters removed from closed and open beds had the same level of contamination (4%) and no correlation was observed between the presence of *E. coli* and *Salmonella* (D'Aoust *et al.*, 1980).

Yersinia enterocolitica

As *Salmonella, Shigella* and *E. coli*, *Yersinia enterocolitica* is a member of the Enterobacteriaceae. It is discussed separately from the above as it is psychrotrophic and thus capable of growth at chill temperatures. The species is divided into sero- and phage types and only certain sub-types are pathogenic.

a) The disease and some epidemiological aspects

Y. enterocolitica causes a gastrointestinal disease characterized by abdominal pain, diarrhoea and mild fever. Whilst the diarrhoeal disease is self-limiting, sequela may occur resulting in arthritis and red skin lesions. These post-infection conditions may last several months. *Y. enterocolitica* produces an enterotoxin but its exact role in disease is not known.

b) Prevalence in fish and fishery products

Y. enterocolitica is associated with pigs which are chronic carriers of the serotypes involved in human infection. Food products washed in contaminated water or contaminated milk also causes yersiniosis. The bacterium has only sporadically been detected in seafoods.

c) Growth and survival in fish and fishery products

Although seldomly occurring in seafoods, *Y. enterocolitica* should be considered when evaluating the risks of seafood products with long, chilled shelf lives. In particular ready-to-eat products may become hazardous if contaminated with the organisms. Jeppesen and Huss (1993) demonstrated that *Y. enterocolitica* serotype O3 may grow well in brined (salted) shrimp stored at 5°C.

d) Prevention and control

Proper hygienic conditions may prevent cross-contamination from agricultural sources. Due to its psychrotrophic nature, chill storage may not be sufficient to prevent growth of the bacterium in products where the competing Gram-negative spoilage flora has been eliminated. Heating (cooking) will destroy the organism as will the salting and acidifying procedures used in semi-preserved seafood products.

Campylobacter

The genus *Campylobacter* is the most prominent species of the family Campylobacteriaceae. The genus contains several species of which especially one, *C. jejuni* causes gastrointestinal disease in humans. The disease is zoonotic with several animals serving as reservoirs. Although very sensitive to a range of environmental conditions, *Campylobacter* can commonly be isolated from waters close to agricultural run-off and waste waters.

a) The disease and some epidemiological aspects

Campylobacter jejuni and in some cases *C. coli,* cause diarrhoeal disease. Symptoms develop between one and 11 days after ingestion and abdominal pain, fever and diarrhoea are the main ones. The disease is self-limiting, but in a few instances, *Campylobacter* has been the cause of the neurological disease, Guillain-Barrè syndrome. Although the bacteria are sensitive to acid (and thus low stomach pH), the infective dose appears to be low (< 1 000 cfu) (Nachamkin, 1997).

b) Prevalence in fish and fishery products

Although poultry appears to be the main source of *Campylobacter* it may be isolated from several other food products. Milk has been linked to outbreaks. Up to 14% of oyster flesh samples have been found to contain campylobacters and an outbreak in the US has been ascribed to raw clams (Adams and Moss, 2000). Campylobacters are frequently isolated from water and water supplies (Nachamkin, 1997). Whilst the bacteria die quickly in open marine waters, they may accumulate in shellfish where they appear to be protected. One study has reported that up to 42% of (Irish) shellfish were positive for mesophilic *Campylobacter* (cf Feldhusen, 2000).

c) Growth and survival in fish and fishery products

Campylobacter species have a narrow growth spectrum and do not grow at temperatures below 28-30°C and are sensitive to oxygen. Thus they will not grow in chill stored products but may survive under chill temperatures. The organism is sensitive to heating (D_{55} of approximately 1 minute).

d) Prevention and control

Due to its sensitivity to food-relevant parameters, the control of *Campylobacter* in seafood appears simple. Avoidance of seafood from contaminated waters will control the hazard. This applies in particular to live bivalves.

Staphylococcus aureus

The *Staphylococcus* genus comprises several species of which especially *S. aureus* is associated with food-borne disease. The staphylococci are Gram-positive cocci with their primary habitat in the skin, glands and mucous membranes of warm-blooded animals including humans. Infected sores and scratches are often harbourage sites for *S. aureus.* The bacteria survive well in the environment and may also be isolated from a range of sources that come into contact with man and animals.

a) The disease and some epidemiological aspects

The disease caused by *S. aureus* is intoxication. The bacteria produce enterotoxin that upon ingestion causes nausea, vomiting, stomach cramps and, sometimes, diarrhoea. The enterotoxins are preformed in the food – thus growth of the organisms is a prerequisite for disease – and the incubation period is short, typically 2-4 hours. Seven antigenically different proteins cause the disease. All the enterotoxins have molecular weight of approximately 27 kD. The primary effect of the toxins is really a neurological (and not an enterotoxic) effect stimulating the vomiting centre in the brain. The disease is self-limiting and typically lasts only 24-48 hours, however, it may be extremely unpleasant. Due to the relatively short-lived nature of the disease, it is believed that only a small fraction (1-5%) of cases are reported. A higher frequency is seen during the warmer months and in November and December. The latter peak is probably correlated to left over holiday foods and buffets (Jablonski and Bohach, 1997).

b) Prevalence in fish and fishery products

Staphylococci may be isolated from newly caught fish, especially in warm waters (Gram and Huss, 2000). However, enterotoxigenic strains are typically transferred from food handlers with hand infections or with a cold or a sore throat. *S. aureus* has been isolated at levels of 2-10% in fish and bivalves but much more commonly in cooked, handled crustaceans where as much as 24-52% of samples may be positive (Jablonski and Bohach, 1997).

c) Growth and survival in fish and fishery products

Growth (to levels above 10^6 cfu/gram) is required for toxin formation and since *S. aureus* is a mesophilic organism some degree of temperature abuse typically precedes intoxication. Staphylococci are poor competitors and do not grow well in the presence of other microorganisms. Although they may be detected on raw fish (and meat), they will not be able to grow to toxigenic levels. The bacterium is tolerant to high levels of salt and toxin may be produced in up to 10-15% NaCl. Growth and toxin production may occur in products such as cooked crustaceans where the heat processed meat is virtually sterile and where the hand peeling operations provides ample opportunity for contamination with staphylococci.

d) Prevention and control

Growth and toxin formation may easily be prevented by proper chilling of products. Avoidance of cross contamination of heat treated (cooked) products is also important. The toxins are compact molecules and are not degraded by gut proteases. Also, they are resistant to heat and will resist boiling for some time. Toxins have not been detected in canned foods.

EU has set a microbiological criteria for *S. aureus* in cooked crustaceans where none of five samples may exceed 1000 cfu/g and only two samples may exceed 100 cfu/g (EC 2001a).

5.1.2 Production of biogenic amines (Lahsen Ababouch/Lone Gram)

a) the disease and some epidemiological aspects

Histamine poisoning is a food-borne chemical intoxication occurring few minutes to several hours following the ingestion of foods that contain unusually high levels of histamine (Taylor 1983, 1986).

It is usually a mild disorder with a variety of symptoms. The primary symptoms are cutaneous (rash, urticaria, oedema, localized inflammation), gastrointestinal (nausea, vomiting, diarrhoea), haemodynamic (hypotension) and neurological (headache, tingling, oral burning and blistering sensation, flushing and perspiration, itching). More serious complications such as cardiac palpitations are rare. The toxicity of histamine is probably potentiated by other biogenic amines (Taylor, 1986; Lehane and Olley, 2000).

Histamine poisoning occurs throughout the world and is perhaps the most common form of toxicity caused by the ingestion of fish (see Tables 4.3 and 4.5). However, good statistics about its incidence do not exist because the poisoning incidents are often unreported due to the mild nature of the illness, to lack of adequate system for reporting food-borne diseases or ignorance by medical personnel who misdiagnose histamine poisoning as a food allergy (Taylor, 1986; Lehane and Olley, 2000). Japan, the USA and the UK are the countries with the highest number of reported incidents, although this possibly implies better reporting on their part. Less frequent incidents have been reported elsewhere in Europe, Asia, Africa, Canada, New Zealand and Australia (Ababouch, 1991; Lehane and Olley, 2000).

Despite its toxicity, histamine is not a substance foreign to the human body. It is stored in specialized cells where its release is regulated. In small physiological doses, histamine is a necessary and desirable substance involved in the regulation of such critical functions as the release of stomach acid. But in large doses, histamine becomes toxic and can precipitate poisoning symptoms.

Although compelling evidence exists for the involvement of histamine as the causative agent of histamine food poisoning, it has been virtually impossible to reproduce the illness in oral challenge studies with human volunteers. The paradox between the lack of toxicity of pure histamine and the apparent toxicity of even smaller doses of histamine in spoiled fish has been attributed to the possible occurrence of histamine toxicity potentiators in the spoiled fish. Other biogenic amines (agmatine, putrescine, cadaverine, anserine, spermine and spermidine) trimethylamine or trimethylamine oxide have been suggested as potentiators (Taylor, 1986). Three theories have been advanced to explain the mechanism of histamine toxicity potentiation.

- the potentiators inhibit histamine-metabolizing enzymes (diamine oxidase (DAO) or histaminase and histamine N-methyltransferase (HMT)) which are present in the intestinal tract
- the potentiators interfere with the possible protective action of intestinal mucin which prevents histamine absorption by binding it (Lehane and Olley, 2000). Taylor (1986) estimates, however, that inhibition of histamine binding to mucin in the gastrointestinal tract would play only a secondary role in the potentiation of histamine toxicity
- the potentiators cause release of endogenous (mast cell) histamine (Clifford *et al.,* 1991; Ijomah *et al.,* 1991,1992; Bartholomew *et al.,* 1987; Gessner *et al.,* 1996). Clifford *et al.* (1993) even suggested that saxitoxins, which were found at low levels in the mackerel used during the feeding experiment may be responsible for the release of endogenous histamine. However, this theory and the role of endogenous histamine release, if any, remain uncertain and unproven (Lehane and Olley, 2000).

There is uncertainty regarding the threshold toxic concentration because potentiators of toxicity may be present in fish and lower the effective dosage compared with pure histamine. Different fish could contain different potentiators, and the levels of potentiators could also vary considerably from one fish to another.

Simidu and Hibiki (1955) estimated the threshold toxic dose for histamine in fish at approximately 60 mg/100g (600 ppm). Shalaby (1996) reviewed the oral toxicity to humans of histamine and other biogenic amines in foods. He considered that histamine-induced poisoning is, in general, slight at 8–40 mg/100g, moderate at > 40 mg/100g and severe at >100 mg/100g. Based on an analysis of recent poisoning episodes, Shalaby (1996) suggested the following guideline levels for histamine content of fish:

- < 5 mg/100 g (safe for consumption)
- 5–20 mg/100 g (possibly toxic)
- 20–100 mg/100 g (probably toxic), and
- >100 mg/100 g (toxic and unsafe for human consumption).

b) prevalence in fish and fishery products

Biogenic amines are produced in foods by decarboxylation of the corresponding free amino acid (Table 5.17). This decarboxylation reaction is catalyzed by bacterial amino acid decarboxylases. Figure 5.5 represents the decarboxylation of histidine into histamine.

Table 5.17
Amino acid precursors and biogenic amines formed in food products.

Amino acid precursor	Biogenic amine
Histidine	Histamine
Ornithine	Putrescine
Putrescine[1]	Spermidine
Lysine	Cadaverine
Tyrosine	Tyramine
Arginine	Agmatine

1. Not an amino acid

Histamine poisoning is often referred to as scombrotoxin poisoning because of the frequent association of the illness with the consumption of spoiled scombroid fish such as tuna (*Thunnus* spp.), skipjack (*Katsuwonus pelamis*), saury (*Kololabis saira*), bonito (*Sarda* spp.) and mackerel (*Scomber* spp.). However, non-scombroid fish such as sardines (*Sardinella* spp.), herring (*Clupea* spp.), pilchards (*Sardina pilchardus*), anchovies (*Engraulis* spp.), marlin (*Makaira* spp.), bluefish (*Pomatomus* spp.) and mahi-mahi (*Coryphaena* spp.) have also been implicated in outbreaks of this illness (Taylor, 1986; Lehane and Olley, 2000). More recent reports indicate the implication of salmon (*Arripis truttaceus*, *Oncorrhynchus nerka*) as well (Lehane and Olley, 2000).

Figure 5.5
Formation of histamine.

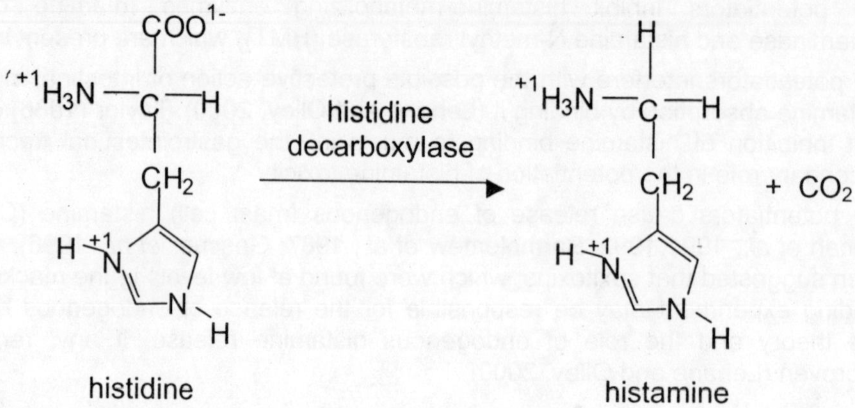

Many of these fish species have significant amounts of histidine in their muscle tissues that serves as a substrate for bacterial histidine decarboxylase. Free histidine is generally found in large amounts in the muscle of fatty, red-meat active and migratory species as compared to its amount in the white meat of slower species. The level of other amino acids, precursors of biogenic amines (Table 5.17) has not been sufficiently studied.

c) growth of biogenic amine forming bacteria and stability of toxin in fish products

Most studies have investigated histidine decarboxylation into histamine, whereas fewer reports exists on production of other biogenic amines (Flick *et al.*, 2001).

In some studies (Taylor, 1986; Middlebrooks *et al,*. 1988), the potential for histamine and biogenic amines formation was evaluated by measuring the decarboxylase activity. This is not always appropriate as it ignores the role of histaminase for example, which has been found in some bacterial species (Taylor, 1986). Therefore, measurement of the actual amines must be done.

In general, the amino acid decarboxylase enzymes, especially histidine decarboxylase, can be found in species of Enterobacteriaceae, *Clostridium, Lactobacillus, Vibrio, Pseudomonas and Photobacterium* (Ababouch, 1991; Taylor, 1986; Lehane and Olley, 2000; Flick *et al.*, 2001). *Vibrio, Pseudomonas* and *Photobacterium* species are indigenous bacteria found naturally in the marine environment and on fish whereas the mesophilic Enterobacteriaceae and *C. perfringens* typically occur as a result of post-harvest contamination. The enteric bacteria (especially *Morganella morganii*) tend to prevail during the summer season, whereas the indigenous bacteria may predominate during the winter (Okuzumi *et al.*,1984). The group of psychrophilic and halophilic bacteria named "N-group bacteria" were later identified as *Photobacterium phosphoreum* by Fujii *et al.* (1997).

Enterobacteriaceae species are the most important biogenic amines forming bacteria in fish. These include *Morganella morganii, K. pneumoniae, Proteus vulgaris* and *Hafnia alvei* (Frank, 1985). Since the most prolific histamine forming bacteria are mesophilic enteric bacteria, the formation of histamine, and probably of other biogenic amines, takes place at high rates at high temperatures (> 15 - 20°C) (Ababouch, 1991; Lehane and Olley, 2000; Flick *et al.*, 2001). However, several other studies have also demonstrated that histamine and other biogenic amines can accumulate in fish to reach toxic levels even at low temperatures (Ababouch *et al.*, 1991; Flick *et al.*, 2001). Thus Jørgensen *et al.* (2000, 2000a) demonstrated that several biogenic amines were formed in vacuum-packed cold-smoked salmon stored at 5°C. Psychrotrophic lactic acid bacteria, Enterobacteriaceae and, especially, *P. phosphoreum* were the producing organisms. Whilst biogenic amines clearly may be formed in some fish at low temperatures, this is not common (Lehane and Olley, 2000; Flick *et al.*, 2001) indicating that several factors, other than time and temperature play a major role.

Klausen and Huss (1987) reported that large amounts of histamine were formed by *M. morganii* at low temperatures (0 – 5°C) following storage at higher temperatures (10-25°C) even though bacterial growth did not take place at 5°C or below. It was argued that the enzyme histidine decarboxylase generated during storage at high temperature was responsible for subsequent histamine production at 5°C or below. Similar findings were reported by van Spreekens (1986). Biogenic amines are very heat stable and once formed, they will not be destroyed even by dramatic heat treatment such as autoclaving (Figure 5.6).

d) prevention and control

Histamine poisoning following the consumption of fish requires that:

- The fish muscle contains the amino acid(s) precursor of histamine and other biogenic amines
- the fish contains and/or gets contaminated with bacteria capable of decarboxylating the amino acid(s)
- the handling and storage conditions (especially hygiene and time –temperature conditions) are conducive to the growth of these bacteria
- consumers eat fish with high levels of histamine and other biogenic amines.

Control of histamine poisoning can be achieved by eliminating one or more of these steps. It is worthy to recall that histamine is thermostable and once it is in the fish, there is no treatment capable of removing it. The most used methods for the control of histamine and biogenic amines formation in the fish industry are (FDA, 2001a):

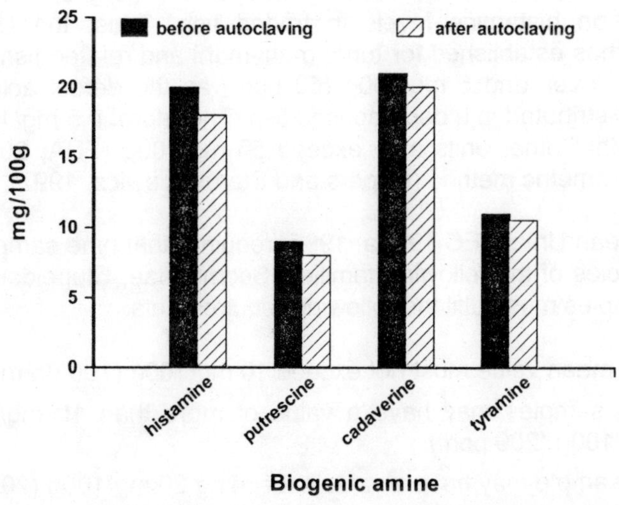

Figure 5.6
Effect of heating on mackerel spiked with biogenic amines before autoclaving (Luten *et al.*, 1992).

1) Rapid chilling of fish immediately after death. This is particularly important for fish that are exposed to warmer waters or air, and for large tuna that generate heat in the tissues of the fish following death. It is recommended that:

- Generally, fish should be placed in ice or in refrigerated seawater, in chilled sea water or brine at 4.5°C or less within 12 hours of death, or placed in refrigerated seawater, chilled sea water or brine at 10°C or less within 9 hours of death
- Fish exposed to air or water temperatures above 28°C, or large tuna (i.e. above 20 lbs.) that are eviscerated before on-board chilling, should be placed in ice (including packing the belly cavity of large tuna with ice) or in refrigerated seawater or brine at 4.5°C or less within 6 hours of death
- Large tuna (i.e., above 20 lbs.) that are not eviscerated before on-board chilling should be chilled to an internal temperature of 10°C or less within 6 hours of death.

This will prevent the rapid formation of the decarboxylase enzymes. Once histidine decarboxylase is formed, control of the hazard is unlikely. Further chilling towards the freezing point is also desirable to safe-guard against longer-term, low temperature development of histamine. Additionally, the shelf-life of the fish is significantly compromised when product temperature is not rapidly dropped to near freezing.

2) Good hygienic practices on-board, at landing and during processing to avoid contamination or recontamination of the fish by bacteria capable of amino acid decarboxylation.

Freezing of the fish can significantly reduce the bacterial load, but will not limit the activity of decarboxylase enzymes that may have been produced prior to freezing. Therefore, it is important to know the temperature history of the frozen fish since outbreaks of histamine poisoning can be caused by the ingestion of thawed- frozen fish containing biogenic amines if the fish was previously temperature-abused (Flick *et al.,* 2001).

Conflicting results have been reported on the effect of salting on biogenic accumulation (Flick *et al.,* 2001). This reflects the diversity of the bacteria that are involved and their adaptation to different levels of salts. Likewise, bacteria producing biogenic amines are not equally affected by smoking and vacuum packaging and these procedures cannot therefore be relied upon to control biogenic amine accumulation. They have to be combined with refrigeration and limits on storage time to be efficient.

Because of the recurrence of histamine poisoning in many parts of the world and the importance of international trade of the concerned fish species, many countries have enacted maximal limits or guidelines on histamine levels in traded fish. Thus, the US Food and Drug Administration guidelines has established for tuna, mahi-mahi and related fish specify 50 mg/100 g (500 ppm) as the toxicity level, and 5 mg/100g (50 ppm) as the defect action level because histamine is not uniformly distributed in a decomposed fish. Therefore, if 5 mg/100g found in one section, there is a possibility that other units may exceed 50 mg/100g (FDA, 2001a). FDA requires the use of the AOAC fluorometric method (Rogers and Staruszkiewicz, 1997).

The European Union (EC 1991a, 1995) requires that nine samples must be taken from each batch of fish species of the following families: Scombridae, Clupeidae, Engraulidae and Coryphaenidae. These samples must fulfil the following requirements

- the mean value must not exceed 10 mg/100g (100 ppm)
- two samples may have a value of more than 10 mg/100g (100 ppm) but less than 20 mg/100g (200 ppm)
- no sample may have a value exceeding 20 mg/100g (200 ppm).

However, fish belonging to these families which have undergone enzyme ripening treatment in brine may have higher histamine levels but not more than twice the above values, i.e. in preserved anchovies, it can be as high 200 and 400 ppm instead of 100 and 200 ppm. Examinations must be carried out in accordance with reliable, scientifically recognized methods, such as high-performance liquid chromatography (HPLC) (EC 1991a, 1995).

In Australia and New Zealand, the level of histamine in a composite sample of fish or fish products, other than crustaceans and molluscs must not exceed 10 mg/100g (100 ppm). A 'composite sample' is a sample, taken from each lot, consisting of five portions of equal size taken from five representative samples. This clause, which came into force in October 1994, is currently under review, with a proposal to increase the maximum allowable level of histamine in fish and fish products to 20 mg/100g (200 ppm) (Lehane and Olley, 2000).

5.1.3 Viruses (Lone Gram)

Viruses are very small microorganisms (typically 25-70 nm) which consist of genetic material (RNA or DNA) and a protein cover. Viruses are obligatory intracellular pathogens and cannot, as bacteria, yeasts and filamentous fungi, multiply outside host cells. Thus virus particles *per se* are totally inert. The marine environment is full of viruses which represent the most abundant life form in the sea, typically numbering ten billion per litre, however, none of these are pathogenic to man (Lees, 2000). Viruses being implicated in seafood-borne diseases all have their niche in the human gastro-intestinal (GI) tract and their presence in water and seafood is a consequence of poor hygiene; either water being contaminated with sewage or products being contaminated by food handlers.

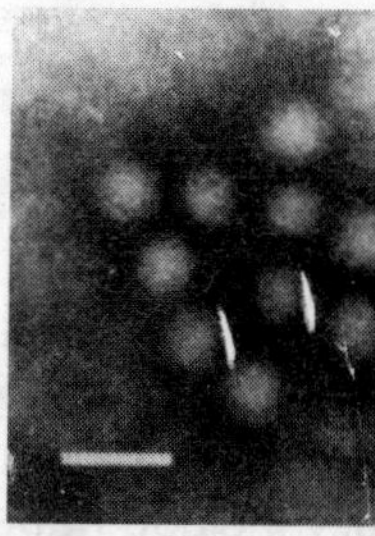

Figure 5.7
Norwalk virus as observed by Transmission Electron Microscopy; Bar represents 100 µm. By F.P. Williams, US Environmental Protection Agency.

The diseases caused by human enteric viruses fall into two major categories: viral gastroenteritis and viral hepatitis (Caul, 2000). As is evident from data in section 4.2, viruses are responsible for the largest number of cases of seafood-borne diseases and is in particular associated with raw (under-cooked) molluscan shellfish. Notably, the largest outbreak of food-borne disease ever to be recorded was an outbreak of Hepatitis A in Shanghai, China, in 1988 where more than 290 000 people were infected by eating clams harvested in a sewage polluted area (Lees, 2000; Halliday *et al.*, 1991; Tang *et al.*, 1991).

Viruses may cause a range of diseases in humans and are the cause of mild diseases as flu and cold as well as more serious diseases as AIDS. Viruses traced to seafood-borne diseases are primarily so-called Norwalk-like virus and Hepatitis A virus.

Viruses are divided into groups depending on the organization and transcription of the genetic material (Table 5.18). The genetic material is DNA or RNA and they carry a single or a double stranded strand of genetic information. Many viral orders and families exist. Norwalk virus belongs to the viral family, Caliciviridae, which also includes three other genera, including the Sapporo-like virus. Norwalk-like virus are sometimes also called small-round-structured virus (SRSV). Hepatitis A belongs to the Picornaviridae family. Taxonomy of virus was for a long time dependent on electron microscopically classification (Caul, 2000) but has been greatly facilitated by molecular techniques allowing sequencing and molecular phylogenetic studies.

Studies of viral (seafood-borne) diseases have been and are greatly hampered by lack of methods for culturing and enumeration. Several viruses, including the Norwalk-like virus cannot be cultured on cell lines and enumeration relies on molecular (e.g. PCR-based) detection. Some laboratory adapted strains of hepatitis A can be cultured but most wild type strains escape culturing.

Table 5.18 Groups of viruses causing gastrointestinal diseases from seafood. Based on Lees (2000) and Caul (2000).

Virus	Type	Family	Associated with seafood-borne disease	Comment
Norwalk-like	SS[1] RNA	Caliciviridae	Frequently	
Hepatitis A	SS RNA	Picornaviridae	Frequently	
Hepatitis E	SS RNA	Caliciviridae ?	not documented	cause of enteric non-A and non-B hepatitis. Outbreaks associated with drinking water
Astrovirus	SS RNA	Astroviridae	astrovirus from oysters were suspected in <u>one</u> outbreak	few food-borne cases
Rotavirus	DS[2] RNA	Reoviridae	not documented	isolated from sewage
Adenovirus	DS DNA	Adenoviridae	not documented	isolated from sewage and seafood

1. *SS = Single Stranded*
2. *DS = Double Stranded*

a) The disease and some epidemiological aspects

Norwalk-like virus (NLV) forms a distinct group of viruses which includes the "classical" Norwalk virus as well as Snow mountain virus, the Hawaii agent and the Montgomery agent. Disease is caused by ingesting viruses and symptoms appear after approximately 24 hours. These are sudden in onset and typically include nausea, vomiting, low-grade fever and diarrhoea. In general, NLV infections are mild and self-limiting and cease after 1-4 days. Due to the short duration and the self limiting disease, the number of NLV cases (from all sources) is probably underreported (EC, 2002). The infective dose of NLV – and most other viruses – is not known but several studies with human volunteers ingesting enteric virus point to low MIDs; probably less than 50 plaque forming units (PFU) (Gerba and Haas, 1988).

NLV is highly transmissible and the attack rate, i.e. the number of people becoming ill following ingestion, is high, typically between 50 and 90%. NLV is transmitted by perosn-to-person contact, by contaminated environments and by water and food (EC, 2002). Food-borne NLV gastroenteritis is especially caused by consuming contaminated molluscan shellfish. The link between molluscan shellfish and NLV was made in the UK where electron microscopy of faecal material from "winter vomiting disease" patients revealed virus particles.

Hepatitis A virus (HAV) causes a food- and water-borne infectious viral disease which lasts for several weeks. The liver is typically infected and jaundice, anorexia, vomiting and profound malaise are characteristic symptoms. The incubation period range from 15 to 50 days. The patient develops immunity but relapses and sequela may appear. Vaccines are available in both Europe and the United States and it has been suggested that food handlers should be immunized (Cliver, 1997).

b) The niche and prevalence in fish and fishery products

Like all viral diseases transmitted by seafood, NLV and HAV are associated with the gastrointestinal tract of humans and are shed in large quantities on faeces of infected persons. NLV are shedded from infected people, and food handlers must not work with foods for at least two days after symptoms have disappeared. In contrast, HAV is often shed in faeces from infected people 10-14 days before onset of disease and continues 1-2 weeks after onset.

The most common cause of viral gastroenteritis is live molluscan shellfish in which viral particles from the surrounding (contaminated) water are filtered and accumulated in the animals. However, a range of other foods have been implicated in viral diseases. Hepatitis A has been caused by orange juice, salads, bakery goods and lettuce. NLV has cause outbreaks involving butter cream, cool drinks and fresh cut fruits.

c) Growth and survival in fish and fishery products

Viruses do not multiply outside the host, and thus their numbers will not increase after the initial contamination event. Subsequent processing will affect the survival of the viruses, although little is known about the effect of food processing parameters on NLV and HAV. In general, viruses are more resistant to préservation parameters and processing steps than vegetative bacteria. Virus particles are stable at refrigeration temperatures when they are not de-stabilised by other factors, and frozen storage will only cause a slight increase in rate of inactivation (ICMSF, 1996). Heat inactivates viruses and D-values are typically measured in seconds at temperatures > 60°C but in minutes at temperatures in the range of 50 to 60°C. This means that household cooking / steaming often is not sufficient to inactivate viruses.

HAV is more resistant to heat and drying than other enterovirus but heating to 85-90°C caused a 4 log reduction in PFUs (Millard *et al.,* 1987). HAV is resistant to short exposures to acid (pH 2). Due to the lack of culture methods for NLV, studies on the influence of food relevant parameters on virus survival are almost impossible to conduct. Based on studies of food-borne outbreaks it can be concluded that infectivity persists for 3 h at pH 2.7 at room temperature and for 60 min at neutral pH at 60°C.

Temperature has a major impact on survival of virus in seawater. At 4°C, it took 671 days to reduce HAV with 90% whereas the same reduction was obtained in 25 days at 25°C (Gantzer *et al.,* 1998). UV-light inactivates virus and HAV was reduced with 90% in 2.6 minutes at 42 mW s /cm (Gantzer *et al.,* 1998).

d) Prevention and control

Control of seafood-borne viral disease is, in principle, simple since the source of disease is indirect or direct faecal contamination. Thus, measures that prevent this contamination control the disease. Bivalve shellfish are suited for human consumption if harvested from waters free from sewage and pollution. Alternatively, the processing can include a virucidal treatment such as heat treatment at high temperatures (e.g. canning), or the viruses can be removed from the shellfish before consumption.

Depuration. Molluscan shellfish are filter feeding animals and the viruses – and other pathogenic agents accumulated – may be removed by depuration. This involves the transfer of the animals to clean water enabling them to shed the virus and other agents. The process is very difficult to control and there is no simple test to indicate that a shellfish has been depurated effectively. Several studies have shown that viruses are retained in the animals longer than bacteria. Epidemiological evidence indicate strongly that depuration may fail to eliminate enteric viruses from contaminated shellfish and that compliance with bacterial standards do not guarantee absence of viruses (Lees, 2000) (Figure 5.8). Several studies have suggested the use of a viral indicator such as the F+ RNA bacteriophage. This enteric virus is culturable and numbers correlates with the presence of NLV and the outbreaks of diseases (Doré *et al.,* 2000).

Figure 5.8
Depuration of *Escherichia coli* and F+ bacteriophage from oysters following the exposure to crude sewage discharge (redrawn from Lees (1995).

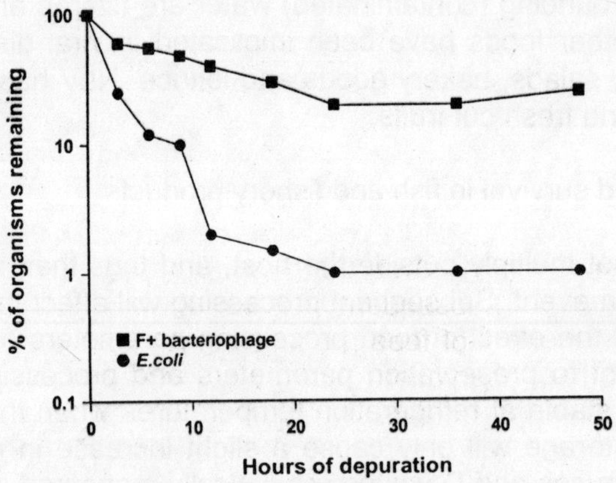

However, since such viral indicators are not widely accepted and most viruses like NLV cannot be cultured, waters in which bivalves are harvested are monitored using bacterial counts. The EU and the US both have several guidelines and standards relating to bacteriological quality of live bivalves or shellfish growing waters. Due to the lack of correlation between water quality and presence of pathogens in the animals, EU has set standards for the animals (EC, 1991) while US standards refer to the quality of the water in harvesting areas (see section 11.2).

Hygienic practices. Contamination by food handlers can be prevented by good personal hygiene and education. As mentioned, food handlers must not handle foods for 2 days following an outbreak of NLV. Disposable gloves may be worn since viruses are difficult to remove by hand washing. Viruses are relatively resistant to disinfectants (e.g. phenolics, quaternary ammonium compounds, ethanol) while halogens (chlorine, iodine) inactivate viruses in water and on clean surfaces. The sensitivity to halogens is, however, lower than that of vegetative bacterial cells. Levels of > 10 mg chlorine / litre for 30 min are sufficient to inactivate the viruses.

5.1.4 Parasites *(Hans Henrik Huss/Peter Karim Ben Embarek)*

The presence of parasites in fish is very common, but most of them are of little concern with regard to economics or public health. Reviews have been published by Higashi (1985), Olson (1987) and Cross (2001) and recently a scientific status summary was prepared by Orlandi *et al.*, (2002).

More than 50 species of helminth parasites from fish and shellfish are known to cause diseases in man. Most are rare and involve only slight to moderate injury but some pose serious potential health risks. The most important are listed in Table 5.19.

Table 5.19 Pathogenic parasites transmitted by seafood.

Parasite	Geographical distribution
Nematodes or round worms	
Anisakis spp.	Worldwide
Gnathostoma spp.	Worldwide
Capillaria philippensis	The Philippines
Angiostrongylus spp.	Worldwide
Cestodes or tape worms	
Diphyllobothrium spp.	Worldwide
Trematodes or flukes	
Clonorchis spp.	South East Asia
Opisthorchis spp.	South East Asia, Eastern Europe
Heterophyes spp.	Worldwide
Paragonimus spp.	Worldwide
Metagonimus yokagawai	Asia, Egypt

All the parasitic helminths have complicated life cycles. They do not spread directly from fish to fish but must pass through a number of intermediate hosts in their development. Very often sea-snails or crustaceans are involved as first intermediate host and marine fish as second intermediate host, while the sexually mature parasite is found in mammals as the final host. In between these hosts, one or more free living stages may occur. Infection of humans may be part of this life cycle or it may be a side track causing disruption of the life cycle as shown in Figure 5.9. In most cases, infections of man are acquired by eating intermediate hosts that are raw or incompletely cooked, partially pickled or smoked or poorly preserved. The infections are preventable if the food is prepared sufficiently to destroy the infective stages of the parasite. However, it is extremely difficult to change cultural and eating habits, and therefore these parasites will continue to prevail.

Anisakis species

a) The disease and epidemiological aspects

Anisakiasis is a gastrointestinal parasitosis caused by the larval stages of anisakid nematodes. Humans acquire the disease by eating raw or improperly cooked or preserved seafood. Surviving worms will then penetrate the gut wall and enter the peritoneal cavity. Symptoms are often non-specific with abdominal pain, nausea and vomiting. Vague abdominal pain and possibly fewer may persist for weeks. Anisakiasis is common in Europe (the Netherlands), Japan and the US. The complete life cycle of *Anisakis* species is shown in Figure 5.9. Humans become infected by eating fish containing life third stage larvae. However, humans are accidental hosts, since transfer of parasites to humans cannot result in a complete life cycle for the parasite.

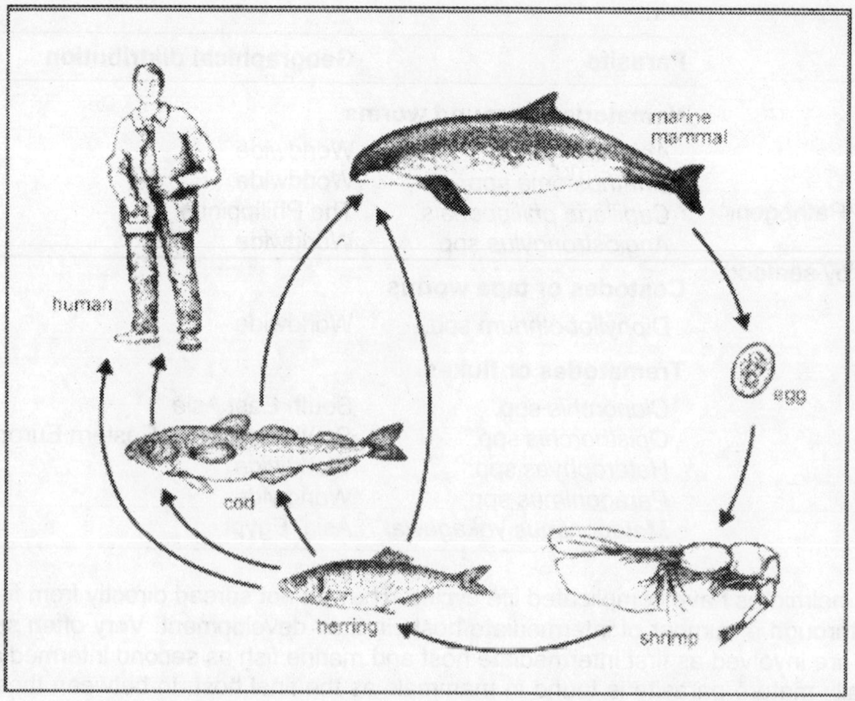

Figure 5.9. Life-cycle of *Anisakis* species.

The species of anisakidae most often associated with disease are *Anisakis simplex* (the herring worm) and *Pseudoterranova dicipiens* (the cod worm). The infective larval stage of the parasites can be found in the viscera and in the musculature of a variety of fish (see Figure 5.10). It is easy to distinguish between the two species as seen in Table 5.20.

Table 5.20 Characteristics of *Anisakis* species.

Species	Size	Colour	Common name	Common feature	Common host
Anisakis simplex	18-36 mm long 0.3-0.7 mm wide	White	Herring worm	Curled up in a spiral	Herring
Pseudoterranova dicipiens	25-60 mm long 0.3-1.2 mm wide	Yellowish, brownish or reddish	Cod worm	Straight or in S-shape	Cod

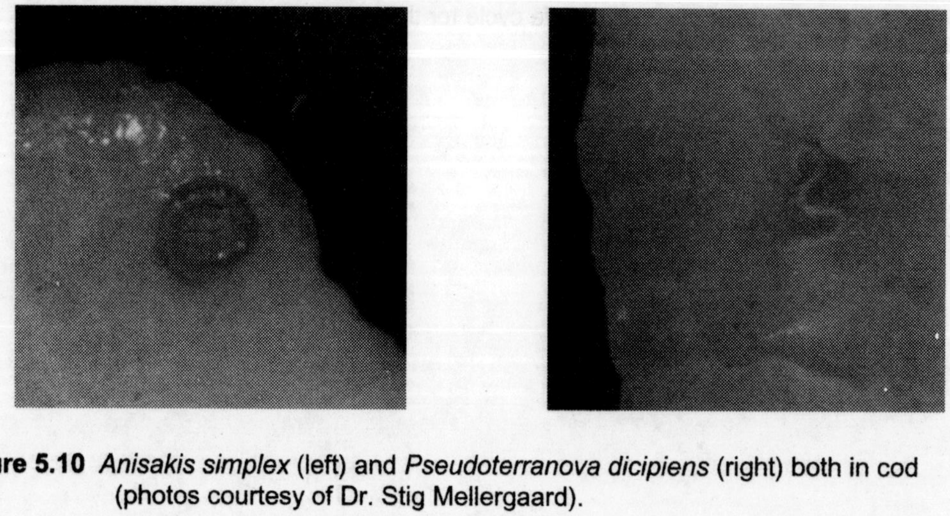

Figure 5.10 *Anisakis simplex* (left) and *Pseudoterranova dicipiens* (right) both in cod (photos courtesy of Dr. Stig Mellergaard).

b) Prevalence in fish and fishery products

Anisakis spp. are widely distributed geographically as well as within numerous fish hosts (cod, herring, squid, salmon a.o.). Thus prevalence reached more than 75% in fresh US commercial salmon (Deardoff and Overstreet, 1991) and nearly 100% in herring from the North Sea (Roepstorff *et al.,* 1993). In areas with no presence of sea-mammals, the prevalence of *Anisakis* will naturally also be very low. It should also be noted, that the parasite has never been detected in a large number of aquaculture salmon examined as shown in Table 5.21 (Angot and Brasseur, 1993; Deardoff and Kent, 1989; Bristow and Berland, 1991).

Table 5.21. Prevalence of *Anisakis simplex* in reared and wild caught marine fish species (after ICMSF,2003).

Fish	Origin	Number of samples	% positive
Farmed salmon,	Washington	50	0
Farmed salmon	Norway	2 832	0
Farmed salmon	Scotland	867	0
Farmed coho salmon	Japan	249	0
Farmed rainbow trout	Japan	40	0
Wild salmon	Washington	237	100
Wild salmon	North Atlantic	62	65
Wild salmon	West Atlantic	334	80-100
Wild salmon	East Atlantic	34	82
Wild coho salmon	Japan	40	100
Sardines	Mediterranean	7	14
Herring	Mediterranean	4 948	86
Herring	Pacific Ocean	127	88
Cod	Pacific Ocean	509	84

c) Survival in fishery products

Low or high temperatures or high salt concentrations may be used to kill or inactivate nematodes in fish (Table 5.22). In contrast, acid conditions are not affecting the nematodes.

Table 5.22 Conditions to kill or inactive nematodes in fish

Condition	Value	Time to inactivation	Reference
Temperature	- 20°C	24 h	Howgate 1998
	55°C	1 min	Huss unpublished data
NaCl, % WPS	4-5	>17 weeks	Karl *et al.* 1995
	6-7	10-12 weeks	
	8-9	5-6 weeks	

d) Prevention and control

In the EU, conditions concerning control of parasites are laid down in Council Directive no. 91/493/EEC (EC, 1991a). All fish and fish products must be subject to a visual inspection during processing for the purpose of detecting and removing any visible parasite. Further, all fish that are to be consumed raw or almost raw must be subjected to a freezing process (-20° for at least 24 h in all parts of the fish). This also applies to fish products that are heated (e.g. hot smoked) to a temperature of less than 60°C. As far as salted fish is concerned, the process must be sufficient to destroy the larvae of nematodes. The US regulations stipulate that the freezing process to destroy parasites should be -20°C for 7 days or -35°C for 15 h (FDA, 2001a).

Thus, the best prevention and control of anisakiasis is eating well-cooked or well-frozen fish only. A number of well-known fish products can be unsafe. This applies to all lightly preserved fish products (< 5% NaCl in water phase) such as cold smoked fish, gravad fish, matjes herring, lightly salted caviar, ceviche and several other local traditional products. A short period of freezing – either of the raw material or the final product – must be included in the processing as a mean to control parasites.

Gnathostoma

This nematode has carnivores (dogs, cats, wild animals) as the natural definitive hosts. *Gnathostoma* is acquired by eating raw or under-cooked freshwater fish or by drinking contaminated water. Clinical manifestation of gnathomiasis is caused by migrating larval. The larval can reach 10 mm. Acute pain is experienced as the larval penetrate and migrate through abdominal and thoracic organs and eventually makes its way to the subcutaneous tissues causing swellings ("creeping eruption"). In serious cases the larval may reach the eye or central nervous system.

***Capillaria* species**

These nematodes are of great public health importance although with restricted focus. Infection with *C. phililppensis* causes serious illness and usually leads to death if not treated in time.

The adult parasite inhabits the intestinal tract, causing severe diarrhoea and death attributed to fluid loss. Eggs of the parasite are passed with faeces into soil or water, and the larval are found in intestines of freshwater fish having ingested embryonated eggs. The adult worm is most likely a parasite of piscivorous of birds with humans being accidental host.

***Angiostrongylus* species**

Angiostrongylus is a 25-30 mm long nematode having rats as the final host (Figure 5.11).

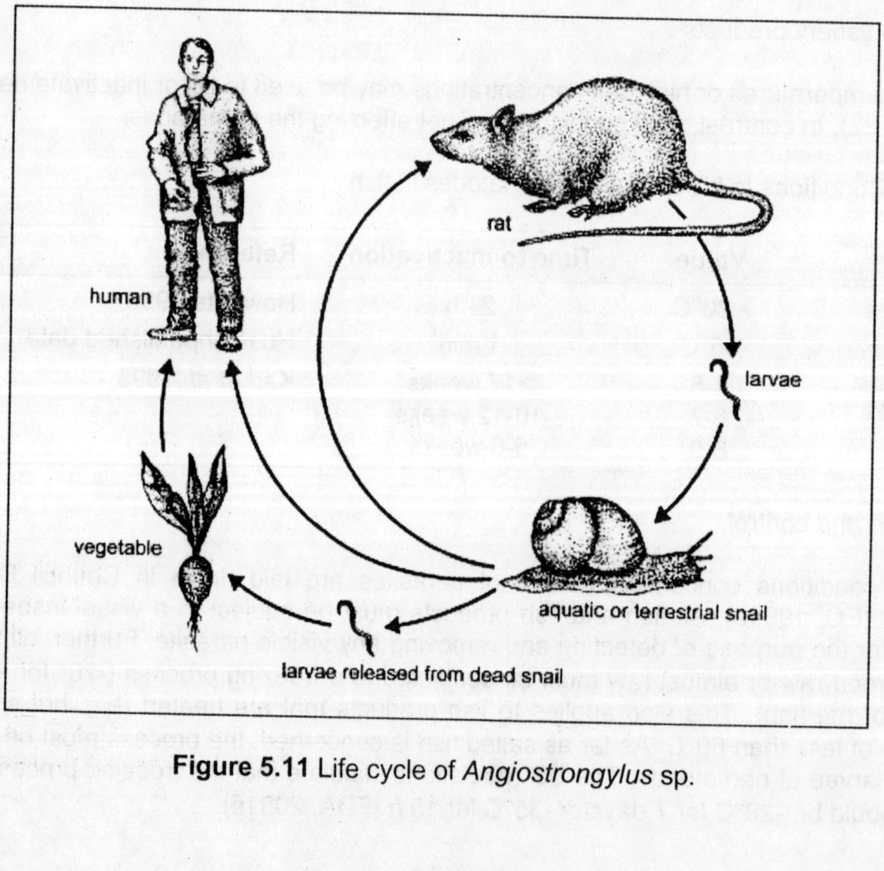

Figure 5.11 Life cycle of *Angiostrongylus* sp.

Humans become infected by eating infected snails or molluscs. The worms migrate to the brain causing life-threatening meningo-encephalitis. The parasite was originally seen in certain parts of Asia, but parasitosis caused by this worm continues to be reported from new areas of the world. This could possibly be attributed to stow away rats.

Diphyllobothrium species

Diphyllobothrium are cestodes or tape worms. *D. latum* is the largest human tape worm and can reach more than 10 m in length. It resides in the small intestines of fish.

Diphyllobothriasis is a long lasting infection (decades). Most infections are asymptomatic but manifestations may include abdominal discomfort, diarrhoea, vomiting and weight loss. The distribution of the tape worm is widespread in the temperate and sub-Arctic regions of the Northern Hemisphere where freshwater fish are eaten (Figure 5.12).

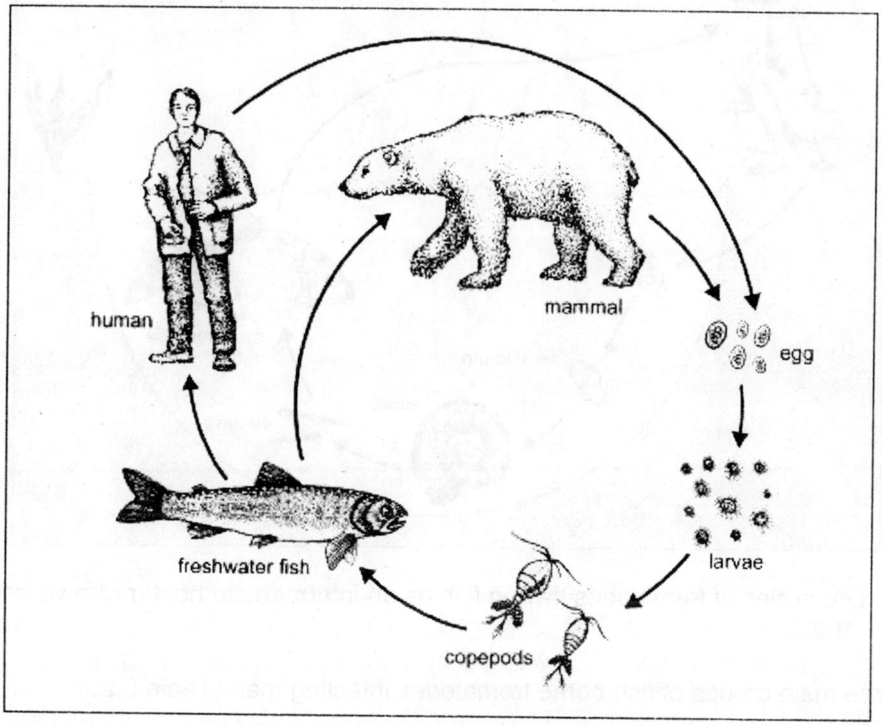

Figure 5.12 Life cycle of the broad fish tapeworm, *Diphyllobothrium* sp.

A recent mass occurrence of human infection with *Diplogonoporus grandis,* which is a cestode belonging to Diphyllobothridae, has been recorded in Japan (Kino *et al.,* 2002). It was suggested that the transmission was due to consumption of raw, juvenile Japanese anchovies. The tapeworms recovered from patients had a mean length of 230 cm and a mean with of 9 mm. The life cycle of *D. grandis* has not been established.

Trematodes

While more than 750 million people around the world are at risk for food-borne trematode infections (FBT), an estimated 40 million people are infected with one or more of these parasites (WHO. 1995). The majority of these infections (around 38 million) are fish-borne infections and are mainly occurring in some 20 countries where the parasites are endemic. Although seldom fatal, trematode diseases can cause morbidity and complications leading to death. The cause of infection is the ingestion of viable trematode metacercariae, which can be present in the flesh of, raw, inadequately cooked or minimally processed freshwater fish, molluscans and crabs. Infections are prevalent in several countries and among communities where eating raw, fermented or inadequately cooked fish is a cultural habit.

To control a disease, it is important to know where it is endemic. In trematode disease it is also necessary to have a complete understanding of the biology of the parasite, the life cycle and each stage of the life cycle must be known from the egg via the miracidium to the cercaria to the metacercaria to the adult parasite. All hosts must be determined: the snail (first intermediate), the animal host or vegetation (second intermediate) upon which metacercaria may encyst.

The adult worms are small, flat, slender and measures from a few up to 20 mm in length and 3-5 mm at the widest area. The general life cycle of trematodes, having fish as the second intermediate host is shown in Figure 5.13.

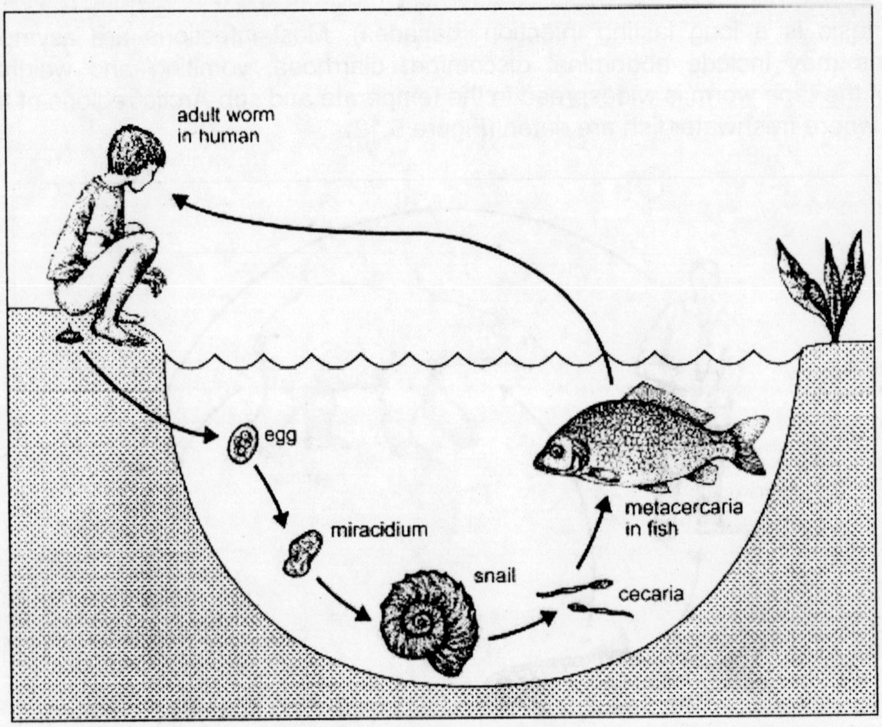

Figure 5.13 Life cycles of trematodes having fish as an intermediate host (redrawn from Strauss 1996).

There are three main groups of fish-borne trematodes infecting man (Table 5.23):

- the liver flukes
- the lung flukes
- the intestinal flukes.

Table 5.23 Trematode parasites transmitted by fish

Parasite	Second intermediate host	Geographical area[1]	Estimated no. of infections (millions)
Liver flukes:			
Opisthorchis viverini	> 35 species of freshwater fish	SEA	8
Opisthorchis felineus	> 35 species of freshwater fish	EE, R, V	2
Clonorchis sinensis	> 100 species of freshwater fish, mainly carp	C, RK, J, R, V	7-13
Lung flukes:			
Paragonimus spp.	crustaceans – freshwater crab	SEA, P, E, W+CA	21
Intestinal flukes:			
Metagonimus yokagawai	freshwater fish	A, (EU)	1.3
Heterophyes heterophies	brackish water fish, bivalves, molluscs	EU, ME, A	

1. Geographical area: SEA: South East Asia, EE: East Europe, R: Russia, U: Ukraine, C: China, RK: Republic of Korea, J: Japan, P: Peru, E: Ecuador, W+CA: West- and Central Africa, EU: Europe, ME: Middle East

Liver flukes

These parasites are named as liver flukes due to their preference for migrating to the bile ducts and the liver. Small amounts of adult trematodes can be present without causing any disease or symptoms of disease. Large numbers of trematodes (up to 20 000 have been counted at autopsy of a patient) causes obstruction of bile ducts and possibly secondary bacterial infections followed by hepatitis. Also, the incidence of liver carcinoma is high in patients with liver flukes. The clinical symptoms are fever, epigastric pain, anorexia, diarrhoea, jaundice and abdominal pain.

Lung flukes

The adult lung fluke is located in the lungs of man and a number of domestic and wild animals (dogs, cats, pigs, tigers, leopards). The eggs from the parasite are passed into the bronchioles and expectorated from the body or swallowed and passed with the faeces.

The first intermediate host is a snail and the second intermediate host is crustaceans or freshwater crab. Humans become infected by eating raw or undercooked crustaceans or crab. The immature worms will penetrate the intestinal tissue, enter the body cavity and penetrate the diaphragm into the pulmonary cavity and the lungs.

The pathology associated with lung flukes depends on the number of worms ingested. A few worms are harmless, but large numbers cause chronic pulmonary disease. A complicating factor is the tendency of lung worms to enter the central nervous system (CNS). Invasion of the brain may result in mental disorder and meningitis.

The clinical symptoms may be diarrhoea and abdominal pain. Once the worms are established in the lungs, there might be general malaise and cough. In severe cases, and when other organs are involved, the outcome of infection may be fatal.

Intestinal flukes

In recent years various species of fish-borne intestinal trematodes have gained epidemiological significance. An estimated 1.3 million people suffer from metagonimiasis, heterophyasis and echinostomiasis caused by approximately 70 species of intestinal flukes of which the *Heterophyidae* and *Echinostomatidae* are the main families. The two most important species are *Metagonimus yokagawai* and *Heterophyes heterophies*. They are very small flukes (1-2 mm) living in the intestines of the final host, causing inflammation, symptoms of diarrhoea and abdominal pain. The primary intermediate hosts are snails. Freshwater fish act as the second intermediate host for the metacercarial stage of *Metagonimus* sp. and brackish water fish for the *Heterophyes* sp.; while brackish water bivalves, molluscs and oysters serves as secondary intermediate hosts to a range of other species of intestinal flukes (Chai and Lee, 2002). Raw or improperly cooked freshwater-, brackish water fish and bivalves including oysters are the major sources of infections. Clinical symptoms differ depending on the parasites involved and include acute abdominal pain, diarrhoea, lethargy, weight loss, fever and malabsorption. In some cases, eggs of the parasite mature deep in the intestinal tissues and may enter the circulatory system and cause cardiac damage. Light infections are asymptomatic.

Control of diseases caused by trematodes

Fish-borne trematode infections are a major public health problem that has largely gone unrecognised by the health sector and the fish inspection services in recent years. All parasites of concern are transmitted to man by eating raw or uncooked fish products. Transmission of fish-borne trematodes is associated with behavioural patterns determined by socio-economic and cultural conditions in endemic areas. Consumption of trematode-borne fish and shellfish occurs most often around lakes, streams and ponds. Korean men will eat raw fish while drinking sake at social gatherings acquiring clonorchiasis. In South China people like to eat congee (rice gruel) with slices of raw fish. In Hong Kong freshwater fish is imported from the mainland and therefore expensive resulting in the more affluent groups acquiring clonorchiasis and possibility cholangiocarcinoma. Paragonimiasis is acquired by eating wine soaked "drunken" crabs in parts of China and in Thailand and the Philippines crab juice is used for medicinal purposes as well as using it in food preparations. Opisthorchiasis is acquired in Thailand by eating raw fish salads or low-salt fermented fish. Echinostome infections are from eating snails and raw fish in Northern Luzon in the Philippines and in Korea.

Eating habits are deeply rooted in a culture and are resistant to changes. In some cultures raw animals and plants are eaten for medicinal as well as nutritional purposes. Raw crayfish is used to treat measles and transmits paragonimiasis. In the Cameroon, raw crab is thought to increase fertility and in Ecuador macerated crab supernatant is given to sick children. Raw foods are often eaten out of necessity because of the lack of cooking fuel. The use of human and animal faeces (night soil) for fertiliser and indiscriminate defecation contaminates the environment and water bodies. In some areas toilets are built over fishponds, thereby perpetuating the infectious cycle in rural aquaculture. The relative contributions of farmed fish and wild caught fish to the burden of these diseases are yet unclear. In countries such as China and Vietnam, aquaculture fish in small traditional ponds are heavily infected with *C. sisensis* and play an important role in the spread of the disease.

Although there are effective drugs for treatment of most fish-borne trematode disease, it is more important to prevent infections. Control of trematode infections is difficult and the measures that have been employed have not been successful.

The parasites involved in FBT infections have complex life cycles involving one or two intermediate hosts. Effective control strategies are therefore difficult to implement.

The WHO Technical Report on trematode infections (WHO, 1995) details the basis of strategies for the control of fish-borne trematode infections. Many sectors are important and collaboration between all of them is necessary: i.e. public health, agriculture, aquaculture, food industry, food control and education. Methods for controlling food-borne trematodes in freshwater fish have shown promising results in countries like Korea and Thailand. These involve case detection and treatment, health education, improved sanitation, legislation of food safety measures and management of human faeces. Application of preventive approaches based on HACCP (Hazard Analysis and Critical Control Points) could also contribute to provide a high degree of food safety. Control of snail populations could also be envisaged together with the promotion of infestation resistant fish species for aquaculture purpose in endemic areas.

So far very little have been done to control the infections in the food, i.e. the fish products. Most preservative parameters (temperature, pH, salt) used in processing fish, shellfish and aquatic animals have been only the subject of limited studies for their potential to control trematodes (Table 5.24).

Heat inactivation of parasites is an effective method for eliminating the risk of parasitic infections. (Adams *et al.,* 1997). The only data available for trematodes would seem to indicate a higher heat resistance of trematodes compared to nematodes. For nematodes, a recommended min of 63°C for 15 sec should be enough to inactivate the parasites (FDA, 2001a). Obviously, more work should be undertaken to gain a better knowledge of the necessary heat treatment needed to inactivate trematodes in the fish. Freezing provides an effective mean of inactivating parasites in raw fish. Again, for nematodes, 15 h at –35°C or 7 days at –20°C will be effective (FDA, 2001a) while data on trematodes (Fan 1998) indicates that 7 days at –20°C had no inhibitory effect on the viability of metacercariae of *C. sinensis* in naturally infected fish. Based on the work of Fattakhov (1989), the Ministry of Health of the USSR recommended in 1990, holding fish at –28°C for 32 h or at –40°C for 7h to inactivate the trematode *O. felinus* in fish (Table 5.24). Storage at refrigeration temperatures does not seem to affect trematodes. *O. vevirrini* was virtually unaffected when stored in saline solution at 4°C for 5 weeks (Sithithaworn *et al.,* 1991). The large differences observed in the experiments reported in Table 5.24 reflect the differences in the methodology applied and in the way the viability of metacercariae are determined (visually or by artificial infection in laboratory animals).

Table 5.24 Preservative parameters necessary to inactivate trematodes. Adapted from WHO (1995).

Preservative parameter	Parasite	Process variable	Time	Reference
Salting	*Opisthorchis* metacercariae in fermented fish	13.6%	24 h	Kruatrachue *et al.* 1982
	C. sinensis in naturally infected fish.	30% (wt based)	8 days	Fan 1998
	O. viverrini metacercariae in fermented fish	20% (wt based)	5 h[1]	Tesana *et al.* 1986
Freezing	*C. sinensis* in naturally infected fish	-12°C	20 days[2]	Fan 1998
	C. sinensis in naturally infected fish	-20°C	3-4 days[3]	Fan 1998
	O. felinus in fish	-28°C	32 h	Recommendation, Ministry of Health, USSR, 1990.
	O. felinus in fish	-40°C	7 h	-"-
	O. felinus in fish	-28°C	20 h	Fattakhov 1989
		-35°C	8 h	-"-
		-40°C	2 h	-"-

1. *Viability was markedly reduced but not completely inhibited*
2. *10 days had no inactivating effect and 18 days had only marginal inactivating effect*
3. *7 days at –20°C had no inhibitory effect on 10 rats infected but 3 days storage at –20C, followed by thawing and re-freezing for 4 days had 100% inhibitory effect on 10 infected rats.*

Protozoan

A large number (nearly 40) of parasitic protozoans are known to be infectious to humans. The most important of those being transmitted primarily via water are shown in Table 5.25.

Table 5.25
Protozoans transmitted via water.

Name	Reservoir host
Cryptosporidium sp.	>130 species of mammals
Entamoeba histolytica	Human
Giardia sp.	Human and animals
Cyclospora sp.	Human

All of these protozoan parasites are excreted in the faeces of the host. The protozoan can enter water and be transmitted directly by drinking the water or indirectly via contaminations of food, utensils, hands of food handlers or flies and other pests. Direct person to person contact is also possible as no intermediate host is required for protozoan parasites.

Infections can range from asymptomatic or mild bowel discomfort to diarrhoea or dysentery with or without blood in the stools and can last several months (amoebiasis). Cryptosporiasis often begins with an influenza-like illness and with possible development of diarrhoea, abdominal pain, nausea, vomiting and fever. Infections with *Giardia* can range from asymptomatic to fatal following months with severe symptoms of discomfort in the upper intestines.

The important steps in preventing protozoan infections are good personal hygiene, proper sanitation of toilet seats, avoid eating raw fruit and vegetables and treatment of drinking water. Slow sand filtration combined with chemical flocculation has been recommended as the best method (Fayer 2001). A review of water purification methods has been given by Ives (1990).

5.1.5 Aquatic biotoxins (Hans Henrik Huss)

The possible presence of natural toxins in fish and shellfish has been known for a long time. Most of these toxins are produced by species of naturally occurring marine algae (phytoplankton). There are over 4,000 species of marine algae, but only 70-80 species (~2%) are known to produce toxins (Scoging, 1998).

A proportion of the toxic phytoplankton has a red-brown pigmentation, giving rise to the naming of algal blooms as "red tides". However, it should be emphasised that not all coloured algae are toxic, and incidence of poisoning have occurred in the absence of red tides. Visible red tides may contain from 20 000 to > 50 000 algal cells per ml. Concentrations as low as 200 cells/ml may produce toxic shellfish. During a bloom, bivalves can accumulate sufficient toxin to cause human illness after filter feeding for only 24h (Scoging, 1998) (see Figure 5.14).

Molluscan shellfish are filter feeders and continually pump water through their gills where particulate matters is removed and ingested. Mussels ingest food particles of any type of 2 to 90 µm in size with a rate of ingestion dependent on water temperature and environment. Optimally, they can filter 2.5 l/h extracting 98% of the available algae. Consequently, any toxin associated with the phytoplankton ingested can rapidly accumulate and hence become concentrated in the bivalve mollusc. The consumption of these toxic shellfish by humans causes illness with symptoms ranging from mild diarrhoea and vomiting to memory loss, paralysis and death.

Toxins associated with phytoplankton are known as phycotoxins. These toxins have been responsible for incidents of wide-scale death of sea-life and are increasingly responsible for human intoxication. There are a number of different seafood poisoning syndromes associated with toxic marine algae and these include paralytic shellfish poisoning (PSP), amnesic shellfish poisoning (ASP), diarrhetic shellfish poisoning (DSP), neurotoxic shellfish poisoning (NSP) and azaspiracid shellfish poisoning (AZP). There are also different types of food poisoning associated with finfish and these include ciguatera poisoning and puffer fish poisoning. Consumption of raw molluscan shellfish poses well-known risks of food poisoning, however, intoxication from finfish is not so well known. Most of the algal toxins associated with seafood poisoning are heat stable and are not inactivated by cooking. It is also not possible to visually distinguish toxic from non-toxic fish and shellfish. Many countries rely on biotoxin monitoring programmes to protect public health and close harvesting areas when toxic algal blooms or toxic shellfish are detected. In non-industrialized countries, particularly in rural areas, monitoring for harmful algal blooms does not routinely occur and death due to "red tide toxins" commonly occurs.

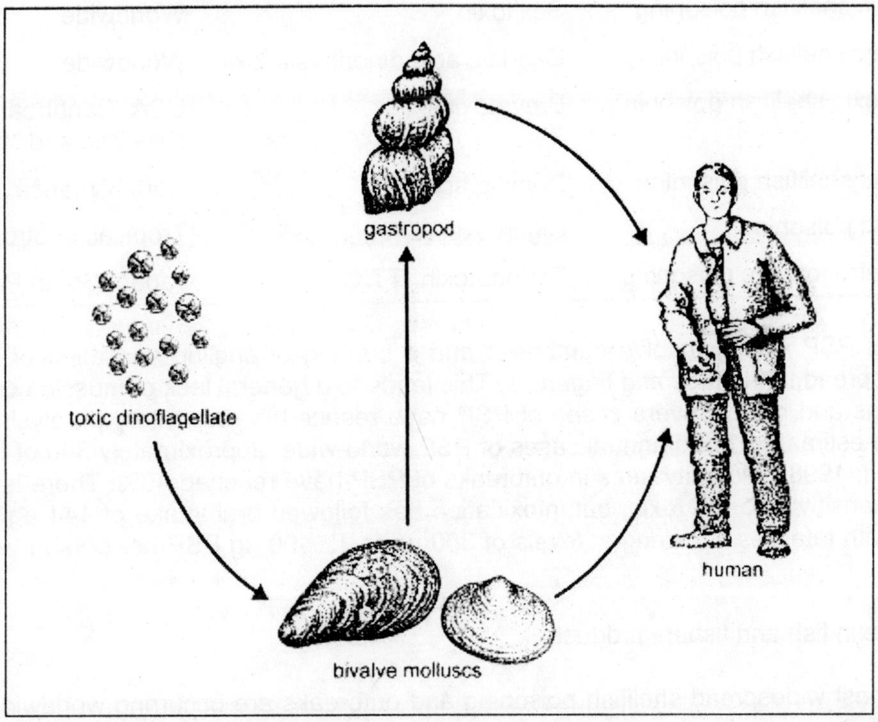

Figure 5.14 Generalized pathways of human intoxication with molluscan shellfish toxins via filter feeding bivalves and carnivorous and scavenging gastropods. (from Anderson *et al.*, 2001).

The toxins are accumulated in the digestive gland of the shellfish (hepatopancreas) and do not affect the shellfish themselves. The shellfish may reduce toxicity in clean water, but depuration times vary greatly according to the bivalve specie involved, the pumping activity of the bivalve and the hygrographic conditions.

Fish may also consume toxic algae and cause disease in humans (ciguatera). Also, there are toxins in some fish species that do not involve marine algae (puffer fish poisoning), see Table 5.26.

Paralytic shellfish poisoning (PSP)

a) The disease and epidemiological aspects

Intoxication after consumption of shellfish is a syndrome that has been known for centuries, the most common being PSP. It is caused by a group of toxins (saxitoxins and derivates) produced by dinoflagellates of the genera *Alexandrium*, *Gymnodium* and *Pyrodinium*.

Table 5.26 Marine biotoxins and the associated poisonings.

The disease	Toxins	Occurrence
PSP-Paralytic shellfish poisoning	Saxitoxin	Worldwide
DSP-Diarrheic shellfish poisoning	Okadaic acid dinophysis toxin	Worldwide
NSP-Neurotoxic shellfish poisoning	Brevetoxins	USA, Caribbean, New Zealand
ASP-Amnesic shellfish poisoning	Domoic acid	North America
Ciguatera fish poisoning	Ciguatoxin (CTX)	Tropical, subtropical
Puffer fish (tetrodotoxin) poisoning	Tetrodotoxin (TTX)	Japan, South Pacific

Symptoms of PSP initially involve numbness and a burning or tingling sensation of the lips and tongue that spread to the face and fingertips. This leads to a general lack of muscle coordination in the arms, legs and neck. Severe cases of PSP have resulted in respiratory paralysis and death. There are an estimated 1 600 annual cases of PSP world-wide, approximately 300 of these will be fatal (Scoging, 1998). Mortality rates in outbreaks of PSP have reached 40%. There is an extreme variation in sensitivity to the toxin, but intoxication has followed oral intake of 144 μg to 1,660 μg per person with fatalities occurring at levels of 300 μg to 12 400 μg PSP per person (van Egmond *et al.*, 1993).

b) Prevalence in fish and fishery products

PSP is the most widespread shellfish poisoning and outbreaks are occurring worldwide as shown in Figure 5.15.

Blooms of toxic algae – and outbreaks of PSP – occur regularly throughout Europe, and the EU-monitoring programmes regularly detect high toxin levels (van Egmond *et al.*, 1993). The dinoflagellates bloom as a function of water temperature, light, salinity, presence of nutrients and other environmental conditions. Blooms of toxic algae have recently become more prevalent, and many experts believe coastal pollution and shipping practices have contributed to this expansion (Anderson 1994). Water temperature must be ≥ 5-8°C for blooms to occur. If temperature decreases to below +4°C, the dinoflagellates will survive as cysts buried in the upper layer of the sediments.

Shellfish that have fed on toxic dinoflagellates retain the toxin for varying periods of time depending on the shellfish. Some clear the toxin very quickly and are only toxic during the actual bloom. Others retain the toxin for a long time, even years (Schantz, 1984).

c) Stability of toxin

The toxic compounds are water-soluble and heat stable. A 5-minute cook will reduce toxicity by only 30% and increasing this to 20 min. will only effect a 40% denaturation (Scoging, 1998).

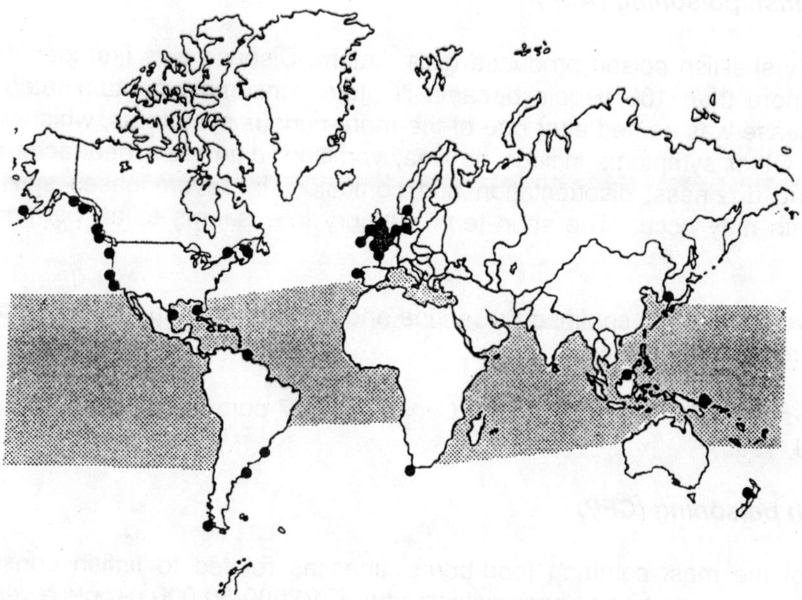

Figure 5.15 World distribution of outbreaks of paralytic shellfish poisoning (black spots) and ciguatera (shaded area). See Huss (1994) for references.

Diarrheic shellfish poisoning (DSP)

Thousands of cases of gastrointestinal disorders caused by DSP have been reported in Europe, Japan, South East Asia, North- and South-America (Sechet *et al.,* 1990). The causative dinoflagellates, which produce the toxins are within the genera *Dinophysis* and *Prorocentrum*. These dinoflagellates are widespread, which means that this illness could also occur in any other parts of the world. A great number of toxins has been identified including okadaic acid (OA) and associated toxins (DTX 1-4). Levels producing diarrhoea in adults are estimated at $\geq$ 40 µg for OA and $\geq$ 35 µg for DTX 1 (Scoging, 1998).

Onset of disease is within half an hour to a few hours following consumption of shellfish, which have been feeding on toxic algae. Symptoms are gastrointestinal disorder (diarrhoea, vomiting, abdominal pain) and victims recover within 3-4 days with or without treatment. No fatalities have ever been observed.

The toxins are heat stable and survive normal cooking.

Neurotoxic shellfish poisoning (NSP)

The occurrence of NSP has historically been limited to the west coast of Florida, where blooms of the dinoflagellate *Gymnodinium breve* occurs regularly offshore and is carried inshore by wind and current conditions. However, also shellfish harvested on the southern Atlantic coast may be toxic and there have been reports of outbreaks of NSP in New Zealand.

The responsible toxins are a family of brevetoxins. The toxins are extraordinarily stable (survive heat up to 300°C) and the oral LD_{50} value in rats being in the order of 520-6 600 µg/kg (Llewellyn 2001). Pathogenic dose for human is in the order of 42-72 mouse units (MU).

Typical symptoms of NSP are tingling in the face, throat and digits, dizziness, fever, chills, muscle pains, abdominal pains, nausea, vomiting, headache and reduced heart rate. There have been no recorded human deaths from NSP, but the toxin is fatal to fish and can cause massive fish kill.

Amnesic shellfish poisoning (ASP)

ASP is the only shellfish poison produced by a diatom. Disease was first identified in Canada in 1987, where more than 100 people became ill often consuming contaminated shellfish (Todd, 1993). The disease was named after one of the more curious symptoms, which was loss of short-term memory. Other symptoms include nausea, vomiting, diarrhoea, headache and neurological effects including dizziness, disorientation and confusion. In severe cases seizures followed by coma and death may occur. The short-term memory loss seems to be permanent in surviving victims.

Outbreaks have so far been confined to Canada and the USA, although the responsible algae has been found in many other areas.

The causative agent is domoic acid. In the Canadian 1987 outbreak, human toxicity occurred at 1-5 mg/kg (Todd, 1993).

Ciguatera fish poisoning (CFP)

CFP is one of the most common food-borne illnesses related to finfish consumption. Its true incidence is not known, but it has been estimated that 10 000-50 000 people a year suffer from this disease. It is caused by consumption of fish that have become toxic by feeding on toxic dinoflagellates or toxic herbivore fish. The principal source is the benthic dinoflagellates *Gambierdicus toxicus*, which is found primarily in the tropics where it lives in association with macro algae, usually attached to dead corals. More than 400 species of fish are known to be vectors of ciguatoxins. Toxins can be detected in the gut, liver and muscle tissue by means of mouse assay. Some fish may be able to clear the toxins from their systems (Taylor, 1988). The toxic fish may be found in tropical and subtropical Pacific and Indian Ocean regions and in the tropical Caribbean as shown in Figure 5.15.

Ciguatoxins arise from bio-transformation in the fish of precursor toxins produced in the dinoflagellates and it causes disease when present in $\geq$ 1 ppb (0.1 µg/kg) in the flesh of the fish (Lehane and Lewis, 2000).

Clinical symptoms vary widely but are characterized by gastrointestinal, neurological and cardiovascular disturbances often within 10 min but also up to 24 h after ingestion of toxic fish. The initial gastrointestinal symptoms are similar to any other food poisoning (abdominal pain, nausea, vomiting, diarrhea). The neurological symptoms most often encountered are tingling and numbness in the mouth, hand and feet, muscle cramping and weakness, temperature reversal, superficial hyperesthasia with a sensation of burning. Headache, vertigo, stiffness, convulsions, hallucinations, transient blindness, salivation, perspiration are symptoms that may occur. A slow, irregular pulse and law arterial pressure may follow. Cardiovascular disorders usually disappear within 48-72 h while neurological effects may persist for weeks, even years in severe cases. Death from CFP is rare (<1% worldwide).

Puffer fish (Tetrodotoxic) poisoning (PFP)

Tetrodotoxin (TTX) is one of the most potent non-proteinacous toxins known and responsible for numerous fish poisonings. The toxin is named after the order Tetraodontidae (common names: puffer fish, balloon fish, globe fish, fugu, toad fish, blow fish), since many of these fish often carry the toxin. Apart from Tetraodontidae toxin has been found in goby, blue-ringed octopus, various gastropods, newts and houseshoe crab.

PFP has frequently occurred in Japan, where these fish are a traditional food. Nearly 300 cases (nearly 500 patients) were recorded in the 10-year period 1987-1996 with an average mortality rate of 6.6% (Yoshikawa-Ebesu *et al.,* 2001). Sporadic cases of PFP are seen in other Asian and Pacific countries incl. USA. Symptoms of PFP occur within minutes and rarely more than 6 h after ingestion of toxic fish. Nausea and vomiting may or may not occur, but the most common symptoms are tingling or pricking sensation and dizziness. Disease may progress to muscle and respiratory paralysis. Where death occurs it is usually within 6 h and sometimes as rapidly as 20 min following toxin ingestion. Persons who have not died within 24 h generally recover completely.

The distribution of the toxin in the fish is mainly in the ovaries (eggs), liver and skin. The muscle tissue is normally free of toxin. The origin of the toxin has historically been much debated (Figure 5.16). The question has been whether it is endogenous or exogenous. It is now assumed that TTX in fish comes directly from its feed. The toxin is produced by bacteria, absorbed on or precipitated with plankton, transmitted to TTX-bearing animals such as small gastropods, starfish, flatworks etc. and from here transmitted to fish and large gastropods. Fish, except those processing tetrodotoxin such as puffers and tropical goby, do not accumulate tetrodotoxin even where toxin-containing diets are fed to them at sub-lethal doses (Yoshikawa-Ebesu *et al.*, 2001).

TTX is a potent toxin with a LD_{50} of 2 mg for man. The minimum dose necessary to cause symptoms has been estimated to 0.2 mg (Yoshikawa-Ebesu *et al.*, 2001).

Control and prevention of natural toxins

Natural toxins are very heat stable. Normal household cooking (e.g. boiling, steaming, frying) has no or very little effect on toxin levels. Also a heat treatment of 70°C in 20 min was insufficient to reduce the toxin level significantly and even after retorting (120°C for 60 min) some toxicity remained (Nagashima *et al.*, 1991). The normal industrial canning process may significantly decrease the toxin levels present in shellfish, but it is only sufficient when the initial toxin level is relatively low. Thus in the European Union it is acceptable to utilise bivalve molluscs when the initial level of

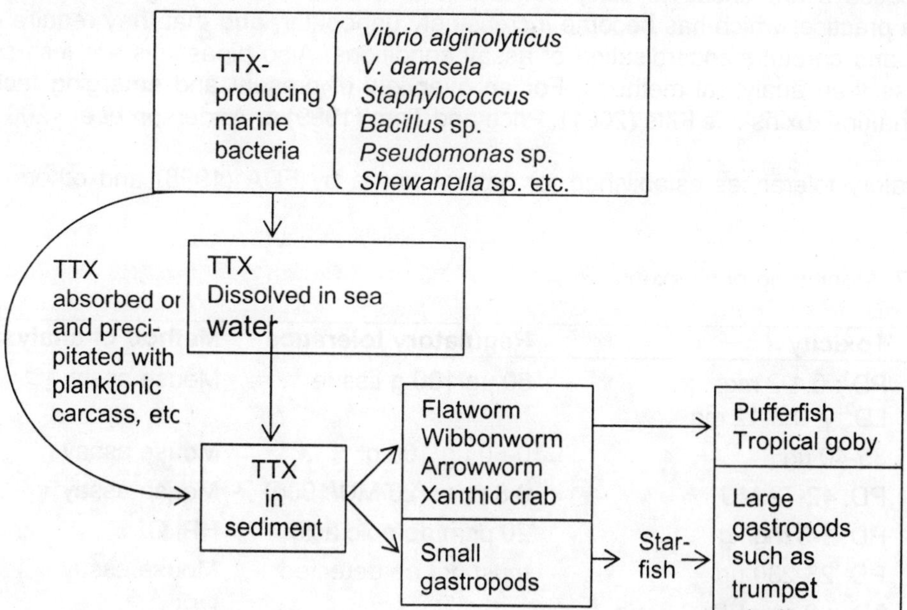

Figure 5.16 Assumed mechanism of toxification of tetrodotoxin-bearing animals (after Yoshikawa-Ebesu *et al.*, 2001).

contamination with PSP exceeds the limit of 80 µg/100 g laid down in Council Directive 91/492/EEC but is below 300 µg/100 g (EC, 1996). However, the molluscs have to undergo the following operations sequentially:

1. Preliminary cleaning in fresh water for a minimum of two minutes at a temperature of 20°C, plus or minus 2°C

2. Pre-cooking in fresh water for a minimum of three minutes at a temperature of 95°C, plus or minus 5°C
3. The separation of flesh and shells
4. Second cleaning in running fresh water for a minimum of 30 seconds at a temperature of 20°C, plus or minus 2°C
5. Cooking in fresh water for a minimum of nine minutes at a temperature of 98°C, plus or minus 3°C
6. Cooling in running cold fresh water for approximately 90 seconds
7. The separation of the edible parts (foot) from the non-edible parts (gills, viscera and mantle) mechanically with water pressure
8. Conditioning in containers closed hermetically in a non-acidified liquid medium
9. Sterilisation in autoclave at a minimum temperature of 116°C for a time calculated according to the dimension of the containers used but which cannot be lower than 15 minutes.

A new chemical method for decontamination of PSP toxins in shellfish was recently developed by Lagos *et al.* (2001). The method involves one or two alkaline treatment (pH $\approx$ 9) followed by boiling and washing. The method was reported to yield 99% decontamination.

Detection of natural toxins is mainly based on mouse-bioassays, while analytical methods may be used for confirmatory analysis of toxic compounds. Only in one case (analysis for domoic acid) is an analytical method – high-performance liquid chromatography (HPLC) – approved as a certified method.

Mouse-bioassays are cheap to carry out, but it is to their disadvantage that they involve live animals, a practice, which has become increasingly unpopular, and that they require experienced personnel and careful standardisation of assay conditions. Also bioassays are less sensitive and less precise than analytical methods. For an overview of present and emerging technologies in detecting natural toxins see Kitts (2001), Price and Tom (1999) or Anderson *et al.* (2001).

The regulatory tolerances established for natural toxins by FDA (1998) and others are listed in Table 5.27.

Table 5.27 Monitoring of biotoxins

Toxin	Toxicity	Regulatory tolerance	Method of analysis
PSP	PD[1]: 0.1-2 mg; LD[2]: ≧ 0.3-12 mg	80 µg/100 g tissue	Mouse assay
DSP	35-40 µg	0-60 µg/100 g	Mouse assay
NSP	PD: 42-72 MU	0.8 ppm (20 MU/100g)	Mouse assay
ASP	PD: 1-5 mg/kg	20 ppm domoic acid	HPLC
CFP	PD: 23-230 µg	must not be detected	Mouse assay
PFP	LD_{50}: 2 mg; PD: 0.2 mg		HPLC

1. *PD = Pathogenic dose for humans*
2. *LD = Lethal dose for humans.*

The primary preventive tool for intoxications with natural toxins is the monitoring of toxin levels in algae in the harvesting areas (see Chapter 9). Based on the presence of toxins, waters can be classified and harvesting of shellfish forbidden if levels of toxin are too high. Other elements of a control programme will include (FDA, 1998):

- a requirement that containers of in-shell molluscan shellfish bear a tag that identifies the type and quality of shellfish, harvester, harvest location and date of harvest
- a requirement that molluscan shellfish harvesters be licensed

- a requirement that processes that chuck molluscan shellfish or ship, repack the chucked product be certified
- a requirement that containers of chucked shellfish bear a label with the processor's name, address and certification number.

Depuration and ozonation are not effective and are not used in reducing toxins in shellfish (Anderson *et al.*, 2001).

5.2 Chemical hazards

There are no toxic chemicals, but there are toxic concentrations of all chemicals. Very few chemicals are present in high enough concentrations to pose a threat to human health. Mass toxication has occurred in connection with accidental exposure to high concentrations but in reality the risk of acute chemical intoxication is very low. However, long-term low level exposure to some chemical contaminants may be associated with serious diseases such as neurological damage, birth defects and cancer.

The chemical contaminants with some potential for toxicity are (Ahmed, 1991):

- Inorganic chemicals: arsenic, cadmium, lead, mercury, selenium, sulphites (used in shrimp processing)
- Organic compounds: polychlorinated biphenyls, dioxins, insecticides (chlorinated hydrocarbons). This is a very diverse group with a wide range of industrial users. Unfortunately the chemical stability allow them to accumulate and persist in the environment
- Processing related compounds: nitrosamines and contaminants related to aquaculture (antibiotics, hormones).

5.2.1 Industrial and environmental contaminants (Hans Henrik Huss)

A modest concentration of contaminants is ubiquitous in the clean aquatic environment. A few metals such as copper, selenium, iron and zinc are essential nutrients for fish and shellfish. Contamination occurs when there is a statistically significant increase in the mean levels in the comparable organisms.

Problems related to chemical contamination of the environment are nearly all man-made. The ocean dumping of hundreds of millions tons of material from industrial processing, sludge from sewage treatment plants, draining into the sea of chemicals used in agriculture and raw untreated sewage from large urban populations all participate in contaminating the coastal marine environments or freshwater environments. From here the chemicals find their way into fish and other aquatic organisms. Increasing amounts of chemicals may be found in predatory species as a result of biomagnification, which is the concentration of the chemicals in the higher levels of the food chain. Or they may be there as a result of bioaccumulation, when increasing concentrations of chemicals in the body tissues accumulated over the life span of the individual. In this case, a large (i.e. an older) fish will have a higher content of the chemical concerned than a small (younger) fish of the same species. The presence of chemical contaminants in seafood is therefore highly dependent on geographic location, species and fish size, feeding patterns, solubility of chemicals and their persistence in the environment.

In a review on chemical residue concerns in seafood, Price (1992) concluded that risk from chemical contaminants in commercially harvested fish and shellfish is low and not a problem. Risk from chemical residues (mercury, selenium, dioxins, PCPs, kepone, chlordane, dieldrine and DDT) are primarily a concern with recreational fish and shellfish, caught in coastal waters and (possibly) in highly polluted waters.

In a more recent review, Smith and Gangolli (2002) similarly concluded that organochlorine levels in fish intended for human consumption are low and probably below levels likely to adversely affect human health. However, they are of potential concern for two groups: populations for whom seafoods form a major part of the diet and infants and young children who consume substantial quantities of oily fish.

A large section of a committee report concerned with Seafood Safety in U.S. (Ahmed, 1991) has been devoted to occurrence of chemical contamination and related health risks. Some of the general conclusions and recommendations from this report are cited below:

- From both natural and human sources, a small proportion of seafood is contaminated with appreciable concentrations of potentially hazardous organic and inorganic chemicals. Some of the risks that may be significant include reproductive effects from PCBs and methylmercury, and carcinogenesis from selected PCB congeners, dioxins, and some chlorinated hydrocarbon pesticides
- Consumption of some types of contaminated seafood poses enough risk that efforts toward evaluation, education and control of that risk must be improved
- Present quantitative risk assessment procedures used by government agencies can and should be improved and extended to non-cancer effects
- Current monitoring and surveillance programs provide an inadequate representation of the presence of contaminants in edible portions of domestic and imported seafood, resulting in serious difficulties in assessing both risks and specific opportunities for control
- Because of the unevenness of contamination among species and geographic areas, it is feasible to narrowly target control efforts and still achieve meaningful reductions in exposures
- The data base for evaluating the safety of certain chemicals that find their way into seafood via aquaculture and processing is too weak to support a conclusion that these products are being effectively controlled.

The principal recommendations of the committee are as follows:

- Existing regulations to minimize chemical and biological contamination of the aquatic environment should be strengthened and enforced
- Existing FDA and state regulations should be strengthened and enforced to reduce the human consumption of aquatic organisms with relatively high contaminant levels (e.g. certain species from the Great Lakes with high levels of PCBs, swordfish and other species with high methylmercury levels)
- Federal agencies should actively support further research to determine the actual risks from the consumption of contaminants associated with seafood and to develop specific approaches for decreasing these risks
- Increased environmental monitoring should be initiated at the state level, as part of an overall federal exposure management system
- States should continue to be responsible for site closures, and for issuing health and contamination advisories tailored to be specific consumption habits, reproductive or other special risks, and information sources of specific groups of consumers
- There should be an expanded program of public education on specific chemical contaminant hazards via governmental agencies and the health professions.

The conclusions from the Committee report (Ahmed, 1991) are still valid (2002), although some of the recommendations have been put into practice. Environmental monitoring at state level is done by many countries, and government agencies are responsible for closures of harvesting areas and management of risks related to chemical contaminants. Most countries have laws and regulations defining the conditions for use of agrochemicals. Usually, a holding period is required between the use of such chemicals and harvest or slaughter (aquaculture). Maximum levels have been established for a number of compounds. Examples are shown in Table 5.28. Results from a large number of surveys have shown, that residues of chemical contamination normally are lower than the limits shown in Table 5.28, and do not give rise to any concerns regarding health of the consumer.

A class of compounds made up of the polychlorinated dibenzo-p-dioxins (PCDD) and polychlorinated dibenzofurans (PCDF), collectively known as dioxins has recently received widespread attention.

Table 5.28 Environmental chemical contaminants. Tolerances and critical limits in fish and fish products (EC, 2001a; FDA, 1998).

Substance	Maximum levels		Food commodity
	US (ppm)	EU (mg/kg wet weight)	
Arsenic	76-86		molluscs, crustaceans
Cadmium	3-4	0.05-1.0	fish, molluscs
Lead	1.5-1.7	0.2-1.0	fish, molluscs
Methyl mercury	1.0	1.0	all fish
PCB	2.0		all fish
DDT, TDE	5.0		all fish
Diedrin	0.0		all fish
Dioxin		0.000004	

Dioxins are commonly formed when organic substances smoulder or burn in the presence of chlorine. This may happen in industrial operations within metallurgy, paper mills, chemical industries (the Seveso case) and others. Due to the high persistence of dioxins these compounds are relatively stable once released into the environment. Due to the chemical nature of dioxins, the compounds will accumulate in the fat deposits of fish and animals and amounts will increase in higher levels of the food chain. The WHO has recently re-evaluated the toxicity of dioxins and is recommending a Tolerable Daily Intake (TDI) of max. 1-4 picogram TEQ (toxic equivalent)/kg body weight. Examples of dioxin amounts in food are shown in Table 5.29.

Table 5.29 Dioxin amounts in common foods (Compilation of EU dioxin exposure and health data, October 1999)

Food commodity	Picogram TEQ/g fat	
	Min	Max
Milk products	0.5	3.8
Meat and meat products	0.1	16.7
Poultry	0.7	2.2
Fish	2.4	214.3
Eggs	1.2	4.6
Fat and oils	0.2	2.6
Bread and cereals	0.1	2.4

5.2.2 *Veterinary drugs* (Allan Reilly)

As aquaculture has developed, a range of fish and shellfish diseases have been encountered that have led to major economic losses and the failure of the industry in some parts of the world. This has led to the increased use of veterinary drugs and vaccines in intensive production systems to combat diseases in farmed fish. Antibiotics are commonly used in aquaculture worldwide to treat infections caused by a variety of bacterial pathogens of fish including *Aeromonas hydrophila*, *Aeromonas salmonicida*, *Edwardsiella tarda*, *Pasteurella piscidida*, *Vibrio anguillarum*, *Vibrio salmonicida* and *Yersinia ruckeri*. They are commonly used as in-feed medications or surface coated onto feed pellets and dispersed in water. There is a wide range of antimicrobial agents used in aquaculture (Alderman and Hastings, 1998; GESAMP, 1997; ACMSF, 1999). Where antibiotics are approved for use, specific doses and withdrawal periods are specified by manufactures. Since fish are poikilotherms, their metabolic rate is determined by environmental temperatures. Withdrawal periods are specified as degree days, for example, 10 days at 5°C equals 50 degree-days. Some of the antibiotics in common use are shown in Table 5.30.

The use of antibiotics in fish farming is associated with new hazards in fishery products that are not encountered in wild captured species. The main hazards are antibiotic residues and the development of antimicrobial resistance in bacteria that may be transferred to consumers of farmed fish.

5.2.2.1 Antibiotic residues

With the increased use of veterinary drugs in food production, there is global concern about the consumption of low levels of antimicrobial residues in aquatic foods and the effects of these residues on human health. This concern is not limited to only aquaculture products but to all foods of animal origin where the use of antibiotics has become an integral part of intensive animal husbandry.

The potential hazards associated with the presence of antimicrobial drug residues in edible tissues of products from aquaculture include allergies, toxic effects, changes in the colonisation patterns of human-gut flora and acquisition of drug resistance in pathogens in the human body (WHO, 1999).

Table 5.30 Examples of antibiotics used in aquaculture.

Group	Compound	Comments
Sulphonamides	Sulphamerazine Sulphaimidine Sulfadimethoxine[1]	Bacteriostatic agents with broad-spectrum activity against furunculosis in salmonids (trout and salmon).
Potentiated Sulphonamide	Co-trimazine/Sulfatrim[1,2,3] (combination of trimetho-prim and sulfadiazine)	Used for treating diseases in salmon and trout (furunculosis, vibriosis and enteric red mouth).
Tetracyclines	Chlortetracycline Oxytetracycline[1,2,3,4]	Wide use in aquaculture. Effective against several fish pathogens and is relatively cheap. Used in salmon, trout, turbot and shrimp farming. Approved for prevention of "red tail" in lobsters in Canada.
Penicillins (Beta-lactams)	Ampicillin[4] Amoxycillin[2,4]	Used to treat furunculosis in salmon and rainbow trout fry syndrome (RTFS) in Europe.
	Benzyl penicillin[3]	Used for yellowtail and sea bream in Japan
Quinolones	Ciprofloxacin Enrofloxacin Norfloxacin Oxolinic acid[2,3,4] Perfloxacin Flumequine[3,4] Sarafloxacin[2]	Used in shrimp farms in Asia Used in shrimp farms in Asia Used in shrimp farms in Asia EU MRL 150ug/kg fish muscle
Nitrofurans	Furazolidone	Broad-spectrum antimicrobial agent. Used in shrimp farms in Asia. Use discouraged as it is a potential carcinogen.
Macrolides	Erthromycin[4] Spiramycin	
Aminoglycosides	Gentamycin	
Other antibiotics	Chloramphenicol	Residues in foods may cause aplastic anaemia in man[5]. Use banned in the European Union.
	Florfenicol[1,3,4]	Used to treat RTFS and furunculosis in salmon.
	Thiamephenicol[4] Tiamulin Nalidixic acid Milozacin	

1. *Use permitted in Canada (http://www.syndel.com/msds/canada_approved.htm)*
2. *Licensed for use in the UK (Alderman and Hastings 1998)*
3. *Use permitted in Norway (Alderman and Hastings 1998)*
4. *Use permitted in Japan (Okamoto 1992)*
5. *Tan (1999).*

Antibiotics are used in aquaculture as prophylactics, as growth promoters and in the treatment of diseases. Prophylactic use of antibiotics is defined as the administration of antibiotics in advance of disease occurrence and this is a common practice in shrimp hatcheries in Asia to reduce the incidence of diseases (GESAMP, 1997). A recent review (Graslund and Bengtsson, 2001) report the widespread prophylactic use of antibiotics in both shrimp hatcheries and in shrimp ponds in Southeast Asia. Antibiotics are usually administered in aquatic feeds and most commercial shrimp feeds contain antibiotics (Flaherty *et al.*, 2000). In contrast, antibiotics are not used either as prophylactic agents or as growth promoters in temperate water aquaculture production in Europe and North America (Alderman and Hastings, 1998). In recent years the use of antibiotics has fallen dramatically in the farmed salmon industry in Norway form about 50 tonnes to less than one tonne annually (Figure 5.17). This is largely as a result of the successful development and use of vaccines against the principle fish pathogens (Alderman and Hastings, 1998).

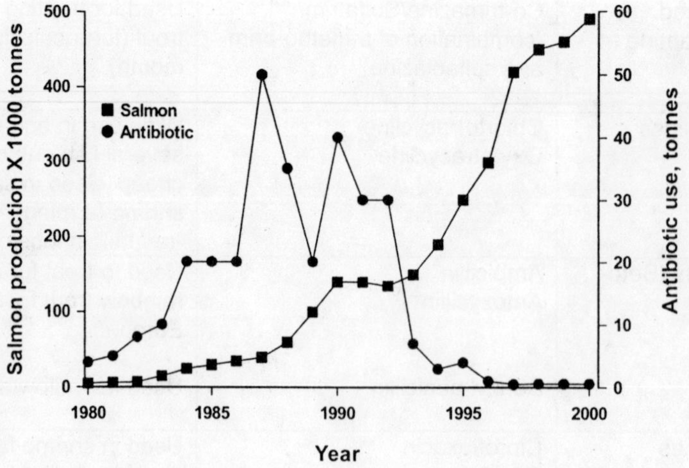

Figure 5.17
Increase in production of farmed salmon and decrease in use of antibiotics in Norway from 1984 to 2000 (modified from Buchmann and Larsen (2001)).

While vaccines have been developed for finfish, the same success story has not be true for farmed shrimp. Vaccines are of little use in shrimp culture because of the nature of the shrimp host defence system is such that no long term specific immune memory has been demonstrated to exist. Control over the sale and use of antibiotics in some shrimp producing countries is limited which has led to problems in overseas markets. The occurrence of antibiotic residues in cultured shrimp from Asia has led to the rejection of products in export markets (Saitanu *et al.*, 1994) and more recently, the European Union has introduced new legislation requiring the testing of all shipments of farmed shrimp from China, Vietnam and Indonesia for residues of chloramphenicol (EC, 2001b,c).

5.2.2.2 Antimicrobial resistance

There are a number of ways in which bacteria become resistant to antibiotics. When a population of sensitive bacteria is exposed to an effective antibiotic, the majority will be killed or their growth will be inhibited. However, within a population there may be a few relatively resistant organisms that are capable of survival and growth. These have a selective advantage over the sensitive organisms and are able to survive and grow. Bacteria develop resistance through random mutations in bacterial genes or they can acquire resistance from another bacterium. There are three ways in which genes can be transferred between cells:

- by transformation where naked DNA released by a bacterium is taken up and incorporated into the chromosome of the host cell
- by transduction, which involves a bacteriophage transferring DNA into the hosts' chromosome
- by conjugation, which involves direct transfer between cells and where genes are carried on plasmids or conjugative transposons.

Conjugation is thought to be the principal way in which transfer of antibiotic resistant genes occurs between bacteria. Large plasmids that encode resistance to several different antibiotics have been found in human pathogens such as *Salmonella* Typhimurium DT 104.

The emergence of antimicrobial resistance following the use of antimicrobial agents in aquaculture has been identified in fish pathogens. (WHO, 1999; Midvedt and Lingass, 1992). For instance, plasmid-mediated resistance to antimicrobials have been identified in a number of bacterial fish pathogens including *Aeromonas salmonicida*, *A. hydrophila*, *Vibrio anguillarum*, *Pseudomonas fluorescens*, *Pasteurella piscicida*, *Edwardsiella tarda* (Aoki, 1988) and *Yersinia ruckeri* (DeGrandis and Stevenson, 1985). Transferable R-plasmids have been found in *A. salmonicida* encoding resistance to chloramphenicol, sulphonamide and streptomycin in Japan, and to combinations of sulphonamide, streptomycin, spectinomycin, trimethoprim and/or tetracycline in Ireland (Aoki, 1997). In Scotland, transferable R-plasmids were found in 11 out of 40 oxytetracycline-resistant *A. salmonicida* isolates (Inglis *et al*., 1993). Transferable resistance was detected to combinations of oxytetracycline, streptomycin, sulphamethoxine and/or trimethoprim. These are all examples of the emergence of antimicrobial resistance in fish pathogens following the use of antimicrobial agents in fish farming.

Use of antimicrobial agents in aquaculture also selects for resistance in bacteria in fish in the local environment and in sediments close to fish farms. Medicated feeds that are not eaten by fish fall to the bottom of ponds or through the bottom of cages. Additionally, some of the antimicrobials in medicated feed that is consumed by fish will be excreted in faeces into the local environment. Uneaten feeds may be consumed by other fish in the vicinity of a fish farm. Samuelson *et al.* (1992) reported residues of oxolinic acid in wild fish, crabs and mussels in the vicinity of a Norwegian fish farm up to 13 days post-treatment. A number of authors have reported oxytetracycline in sediments in the vicinity of salmon farms (Coyne *et al*., 1994; Bjorklund *et al*., 1991; Samuelson *et al*.,1992a).

Potential risks to consumer health exist in that antimicrobial resistance arising from the use of antibiotics in aquaculture can be transferred to human pathogens, such as *Vibrio parahaemolyticus* (Hayashi *et al*., 1982) and *Vibrio cholerae* (Nakjima *et al*., 1983). The strain of *Vibrio cholerae* O1 that caused the epidemic of cholera in South America in 1991 was multidrug-resistant and the epidemic in Ecuador began among persons working on shrimp farms (Weber *et al*., 1994). Similar multi-drug resistance was found in non-cholera *Vibrio* that were pathogenic to shrimp which may have been transferred to the *V. cholera* O1 (Weber *et al*., 1994). Bacteria on farmed fish and shrimp can be transmitted to humans when these are eaten or when such bacteria are transferred to food that are subsequently eaten. *Vibrio parahaemolyticus* is a common cause of food-borne illness in Japan and *Salmonella* species have been isolated from farmed fish and shrimp (Reilly and Twiddy, 1992). Other bacteria that are human pathogens, such as *Streptococcus iniae* and *Vibrio vulnificus,* have been associated with wound infections in fish handlers and can cause serious illness (Weinstein *et al*., 1997; Bisharat and Raz, 1996). Another route for the transfer of antimicrobial resistant bacteria to man is by ornamental fish. Multi-drug resistant strains of *Mycobacterium marinum* have been isolated from ornamental fish and are the cause of "fish tank granuloma" in man. There is also a potential for resistance development in bacteria in integrated fish/poultry/animal production systems in parts of Asia where the waste from animals is used to fertilize fish ponds. Antibiotics administered to poultry and animals are inadvertently dose the fish ponds in faeces and urine with subsequent selective pressure for resistance development.

5.2.2.3 Control Strategies

There can be little doubt that the use of antibiotics in aquaculture selects for antimicrobial resistance among bacteria in farmed fish and in the environment surrounding fish farms. It is well established that antibiotics given to animals have resulted in the emergence of some resistant germs that can infect humans via the food chain. Additionally, illegal residues have been reported in aquaculture products in export markets.

Antibiotics should never be used as an easy alternative to good fish farming practices. National governments need to put in place control programmes for residues of antimicrobials in aquaculture production. Such control programmes should control the approval or licensing of antimicrobials and should control their sale and use in fish farming. What is required at national level is up-to-date legislation and standards that are based on sound science, a monitoring programme and adequate resources for enforcement of the legislation.

Consumers can protect themselves against antibiotic resistant bacteria as these are just as susceptible to heat and hygiene as their non-resistant counterparts. Thorough cooking, frequent hand washing, prevention of cross-contamination by separating raw seafoods from other foods and proper chilled storage will minimise the incidence of seafood poisoning.

5.3 Physical Hazards (Hans Henrik Huss)

Physical hazards include any potentially harmful extraneous matter not normally found in food. The extraneous matter found in fish products can be divided or classified as:

- non-food safety hazards (e.g. filth)
- food safety hazards (e.g. glass, metal, wood, bones, stones, hard plastic).

The adverse health effect of physical hazards may be choking, injury incl. laceration and perforation of tissues in the mouth, throat, stomach or intestines. Broken teeth and damage to gums may also be the result. The FDA Health Hazard Board has found that foreign objects that are less than 7 mm maximum dimensions rarely cause trauma or serious injury except in special risk groups such as infants, elderly or surgery patients (FDA, 1998)

Although physical hazards rarely cause serious injury, they are among the most commonly reported consumer complaints, because the injury occurs immediately or soon after eating, and the source of the hazard is often easy to identify.

Control measures for physical hazards can include:

- for metal inclusions:
  periodically checking all equipment for damage or missing parts
  passing the product through metal detection or separation equipment
- for non-metallic objects:
  passing the product through an X-ray detector.

References

Ababouch, L. 1987. Effect of thermal treatments in oils on bacterial spore survival. *Jpurnal of Applied Bacteriology* 62, 491-502.

Ababouch, L. 1991. Histamine food poisoning: An update. *Fish Tech News* 11, 3-5,9.

Ababouch, L., M.E. Afilal, H. Benabdeljelil & F.F. Busta 1991. Quantitative changes in bacteria, amino acids and biogenic amines in sardines *(Sardina pilchardus)* stored at ambient temperature (25–28°C) and in ice. *International Journal of Food Science and Technology* 26, 297– 306.

ACMSF (Advisory Committee on the Microbiological Safety of Food) 1999. Report on Microbial Antibiotic Resistance in relation to Food Safety. HMSO, London, UK.

Adams, A.M., K.D. Murrell & J.H. Cross 1997. Parasites of fish and risks to public health. *Revue Scientifique et Technique Office International des Epizooties* 16, 652-660.

Adams, M. & M.O. Moss 2000. *Food Microbiology*. 2nd edition The Royal Society of Chemistry, UK.

Ahmed, F.E. (ed) 1991. *Seafood Safety*. National Academy Press. Washington DC, USA.

Alderman, D.J. & T.S. Hastings 1998. Antibiotic use in aquaculture. *International Journal of Food Science and Technology* 33, 139-155.

Anderson, D.M. 1994. Red Tides. *Scientific American*, August. pp. 52-58.

Anderson, D.M., P. Andersen, V.M. Briceli, J.J. Cullen & J.E. Rensel 2001. Monitoring and management strategies for Harmful Algal Blooms in Coastal Waters, APEC # 201-MR-01.1, Asia Pacific Economic Program, Singapore and Intergovernmental Oceanographic Commission Technical Series No. 59, Paris, France.

Angot, V. & P. Brasseur 1993. European farmed Atlantic salmon (*Salmo salar*) are safe from anisakid larvae. *Aquaculture* 118, 339-344.

Aoki, T. 1988. Drug resistant plasmids from fish pathogens. *Microbiological Sciences* 5, 219-223.

Aoki, T. 1997. Resistant plasmids and the risks of transfer. In: Bernoth, E.M. (ed) *Furunculosis, Multidisciplinary Fish Disease Research*. Academic Press, San Diego, USA. pp. 433-440.

Austin, J.W. & K.L. Dodds 2001. *Clostridium botulinum*. In: Hui, Y.H., M.D. Pierson & J.R. Gorham (eds) *Food borne Disease Handbook*. 2nd ed., vol.1 *Bacterial Pathogens*. Marcel Dekker, Inc., New York-Basel. pp. 2-38.

Autio T., S. Hielm, M. Miettinen, A.-M. Sjoberg, K. Aarnisalo, J. Bjorkroth, T. Mattila-Sandholm & H. Korkeala 1999. Sources of *Listeria monocytogenes* contamination in a cold-smoked rainbow trout processing plant detected by pulsed-field gel electrophoresis typing. *Applied and Environmental Microbiology* 65, 150-155.

Balakrish Nair, G., R. K. Bhadra, T. Ramamurthy, A. Ramesh & S.C. Pal 1991. *Vibrio cholerae* and other vibrios associated with paddy field cultured prawns. *Food Microbiology* 8, 203-208.

Barbieri, E., L. Falzano, C. Fiorentini, A. Pianetti, W. Baffone, A. Fabbri, P. Matarrese, A. Casiere, M. Katouli, I. Kuhn, R. Molby, F. Bruscolini & G. Donelli 1999. Occurrence, diversity and pathogenecity of halophilic *Vibrio* spp. a non-O1 *Vibrio cholerae* from estuarine waters along the Italian Adriatic coast. *Applied and Environmental Microbiology* 65, 2748-2753.

Bartholomew, B.A., P.R. Berry, J.C. Rodhouse & R.J. Gilbert 1987. Scombrotoxic fish poisoning in Britain: Features of over 250 suspected incidents from 1976 to 1986. *Epidemiology and Infection* 99, 775–782.

Ben Embarek, P.K. 1994. *Microbial safety and spoilage of sous vide fish products*. Ph.D. thesis, Technological Laboratory of the Danish Ministry of Agriculture and Fisheries & the Royal Veterinary and Agricultural University, Denmark.

Ben Embarek, P.K. & H.H. Huss 1993. Heat resistance of *Listeria monocytogenes* in vacuum packaged pasteurized fish fillets. *International Journal of Food Microbiology* 20, 85-95.

Bhaskar, N., T.M.R. Setty, G.V.S. Reddy, Y.B. Manoj, C.S. Anantha, B.S. Raghunath & J.M. Antony 1995. Incidence of *Salmonella* in cultured shrimp *Penaeus monodon*. *Aquaculture* 138, 257-266.

Bisharat, N. & R. Raz 1996. *Vibrio* infection in Israel due to changes in fish marketing. *Lancet* 348, 1585-1586.

Bisharat, N., V. Agmon, R. Finkelstein, R. Raz, G. Ben-Dror, L. Lerner, S. Soboh, R. Colodner, D.N. Cameron, D.L. Wykstra, D.L. Swerdlow, & J.J. Farmer III. 1999. Clinical, epidemiological and microbiological features of *Vibrio vulnificus* biogroup 3 causing outbreaks of wound infection and bacterimia in Israel. *Lancet* 354, 1421-1424.

Bjorklund, H.V., C.M.I. Raberg & G. Bylund 1991. Residues of oxolinic acid and oxytetratcycline in fish and sediments from fish farms. *Aquaculture* 97, 85-96.

Brenner, F.W., R.G. Villar, F.J. Angulo, R. Tauxe & B. Swaminathan 2000. *Salmonalla* nomenclature. *Journal of Clinical Microbiology* 38, 2465-2467.

Brett, M.S.Y., P. Short & J. McLauchlin 1998. A small outbreak of listeriosis associated with smoked mussels. *International Journal of Food Microbiology* 43, 223-229.

Bristow, G.A. & B. Berland 1991. A report of some metazoan parasites of wild marine salmon (*Salmo salar* L.) from the west coast of Norway with comments on their interactions with farmed salmon. *Aquaculture* 98, 223-229.

Buchanan R.L., W.G. Damert, R.C. Whiting & M. van Schothorst 1997. Use of epidemiologic and food survey data to estimate a purposefully conservative dose-response relationship for *Listeria monocytogenes* levels and incidence of listeriosis. *Jcurnal of Food Protection* 60, 918-922.

Buchman, K. & J.L. Larsen 2001. Vaccination secures production of healty salmon (in Danish). Royal Veterinary and Agricultural University. Mosaik No. 6 December.

CAC (Codex Alimentarius Commission) 2001. *Food Hygiene Basic Texts*. 2nd ed. Food and Agriculture Organization / World Health Organization, Rome, Italy.

CAC (Codes Alimentarius Commission) 2002. *Discussion Paper on Risk Management Strategies for Vibrio spp. in Seafood.* DRAFT 6/28/02. CX/FH 03/5 Add 5. Food and Agriculture Organization / World Health Organization, Rome, Italy.

Cann, D.C. & L. Taylor 1979. The control of botulinum hazard in hot smoked trout and mackerel. *Journal of Food Technology* 14, 123-129.

Caul, E.O. 2000. Foodborne Viruses. In: Lund, B.M., T.C. Baird-Parker & G.W. Gould (eds) *The Microbiological Safety and Quality of Foods.* Aspen Publishers, Inc. Gaithersberg, Maryland, USA. pp. 1457-1489.

Chai, J.-Y. & S.-H. Lee 2002. Food-borne intestinal trematode infections in the republic of Korea. *Parasitology International* 51, 129-154.

Chiavelli, D.A., J.W. Marsh & R.K. Taylor 2001. The mannose-sensitive hemagglutinin of *Vibrio cholerae* promotes adherence to zooplankton. *Applied and Environmental Microbiology* 67, 3220-3225.

Clifford, M.N., R. Walker, P. Ijomah, J. Wright, C.K, Murray & R. Hardy 1991. Is there a role for amines other than histamines in the aetiology of scombrotoxicosis? *Food Additives and Contaminants* 8, 641–652.

Clifford, M.N., R. Walker, P. Ijomah, J. Wright, C.K, Murray, R. Hardy, E.P, Martbauer, E. Usleber and G. Terplan 1993. Do saxitoxin-like substances have a role in scombrotoxicosis? *Food Additives and Contaminants* 6, 657–667.

Cliver, D.O. 1997. Foodborne virus. In: Doyle, M.P., L.R. Beuchat & T.J. Montville (eds) *Food Microbiology. Fundamentals and Frontiers.* ASM Press, Washington, USA. pp. 437-446.

Coyne, R., M. Hiney, B. O'Connor, J. Kerry, D. Cazabon & P. Smith 1994. Concentration and persistence of oxytetracycline in sediments under a marine salmon farm. *Aquaculture* 123, 31-42.

Cross, J.H. 2001. Fish and Invertebrate-borne helminths. In: Hui, Y.H. S.A. Sattar, K.D. Murell, W.K. Nip & P.S. Stanfield (eds) *Foodborne Disease Handbook.* 2nd ed. vol. 2. Marcel Dekker, Inc. N.Y. and Basel. pp. 249-288.

D'Aoust, J.-Y. 2000. *Salmonella.* In: Lund, B.M, T.C. Baird-Parker & G.W. Gould (eds). *The Microbiological Safety and Quality of Foods.* Aspen, Gaithersberg, Maryland, USA. pp. 1233-1299.

D'Aoust, J.-Y., R. Gelinas & C. Maishment 1980. Presence of indicator organisms and recovery of *Salmonella* in fish and shellfish. *Journal of Food Protection* 43, 769-782.

Dainty, R., B.G. Shaw & T.A. Roberts 1983. Microbial and chemical changes in chill-stored red meats. In: Roberts, T.A. & F.A. Skinner (eds) *Food Microbiology, Advances and Prospects.* Academic Press, pp. 151-178.

Dalsgaard, A., H.H. Huss, A.H. Kittikun & J.L. Larsen 1995. Prevalence of *Vibrio cholerae* and *Salmonella* in a major shrimp production area in Thailand. *International Journal of Food Microbiology* 28, 101-113.

Dalsgaard, A., T. Bjergskov, V. From Jeppesen, L.B. Jørgensen, P. Echeverria & I. Dalsgaard 1996. Prevalence and characterization of *Vibrio cholerae* isolated from shrimp products imported into Denmark. *Journal of Food Protection* 59, 694-697.

Deardoff, T.L. & M.L. Kent 1989. Prevalence of larval *Anisakis simplex* in pen-reared and wild-caught salmon (*Salmonidal*) from Puget Sound, Washington. *Journal of Wildlife Disease* 25, 416-419.

Deardoff, T.L. & R.M. Overstreet 1991. Seafood transmitted zoonosis in the United States: the fishes, the dishes and the worms. In: Ward, D.R. & C.R. Hackney (eds) *Microbiology of Marine Food Products.* Van Nostrand Reinhold, New York, USA. pp. 211-265.

DeGrandis, S.A. & R.M.W. Stevenson 1985. Antimicrobial susceptibility patterns and R plasmid-mediated resistance in the fish pathogens *Yersinia ruckeri. Antimicrobial Agents and Chemotherapy* 27, 938-942.

Dodds, K.L. 1993. *Clostridium botulinum* in the environment. In: Hauchild, A.H.W. & K.L. Dodds (eds) *Clostridium botulinum. Ecology and Control in Foods.* Marcel Dekker Inc., New York, USA. pp. 21-25.

Doré, W.J., K. Henshilwood & D.N. Lees 2000. Evaluation of F-specific RNA bacteriophage as a candidate human enteric virus inducator for bivalve molluscan shellfish. *Applied and Environmental Microbiology* 66, 1280-1285.

Doyle, M.P., T. Zhao, J. Meng & S. Zhao 1997. *Escherichia coli* O157:H7. In: Doyle, M.P., L.R. Beuchat & T.J. Montville (eds). *Food Microbiology. Fundamentals and Frontiers.* ASM Press, Washington DC, USA. pp.171-191.

Dufresne, I., J.P. Smith, J.N. Liu, I. Tarte, B. Blanchfield & J.W. Austin. 2000. Effect of films of different oxygen transmission rate on toxin production by *Clostridium botulinum* type E in vacuum packaged cold and hot smoked trout fillets. *Journal of Food Safety* 20, 251-68.

EC (European Commission) 1991. Council Directive 91/492/EEC of 15 July 1991 laying down the health conditions for the production and the placing on the market of live bivalve molluscs. *Official Journal of the European Communities* L 268, 24/09/1991 pp. 0001-0014.

EC (European Commission) 1991a. Council Directive 91/493/EEC of 22 July 1991 laying down the health conditions for the production and the placing on the market of fishery products *Official Journal of the European Communities* L 268 , 24/09/1991 pp. 0015 – 0034.

EC (European Commission) 1995. Council Directive 95/71/EC of 22 December 1995 amending the Annex to Directive 91/493/EEC laying down the health conditions for the production and the placing on the market of fishery products. *Official Journal cf the European Communitites* L 332 , 30/12/1995 pp. 0040 – 0041.

EC (European Commission) 1996. Commission Directive 96/77/EC of 2 December 1996 laying down specific purity criteria on food additives other than colours and sweeteners. *Official Journal of the European Communities* L 339, 30/12/1996 pp. 0001.

EC (European Commission) 2001. Opinion of the Scientific Committee on Veterinary Measures relating to Public Health on *Vibrio vulnificus* and *Vibrio parahaemolyticus* in raw and undercooked seafood. Brussels, Belgium.

EC (European Commission) 2001a. Commission Regulation (EC) No. 466/2001 setting maximum levels of certain contaminants of foodstuffs. *Official Journal of the European Communitites* L77, pp. 1-14.

EC (European Commission) 2001b. Commission Decision 2001/699/EC concerning certain protective measures with regard to certain fishery and aquaculture products intended for human consumption and originating in China and Vietnam. *Official Journal of the European Communities* L125, pp. 11-12.

EC (European Commission) 2001c. Commission Decision 2001/705/EC concerning certain protective measures with regard to certain fishery and aquaculture products intended for human consumption and originating in Indonesia. *Official Journal of the European Communities* L 260, pp. 35-36.

EC (European Commission) 2002. Opinion of the Scientific Committee on Veterinary Measures relating to Public Health on Norwalk-like viruses. Brussels, Belgium.

Eklund, M.W. 1993. Control [of *C. botulinum*] in Fishery Products. In: Hauchild, A.H.W. & K.L. Dodds (eds) *Clostridium botulinum. Ecology and Control in Foods.* Marcel Dekker Inc., New York, USA. pp. 209-232.

Eneroth, A., A. Christiansson, J. Brendehaug & G. Molin 1998. Critical contamination sites in the production line of pasteurised milk, with reference to the psychrotrophic spoilage flora. *International Dairy Journal* 8, 829-834.

Ericsson, H., A. Eklow, M.L. Danielsson-Tham, S. Loncarevic, L.O. Mentzing, I. Persson, H. Unnerstad & W. Tham 1997. An outbreak of listeriosis suspected to have been caused by rainbow trout. *Journal of Clinical Microbiology* 35, 2904-2907.

Eyles, M.J. & G.R. Davey 1984. Microbiology of commercial depuration of the Sydney rock oyster, *Crassostrea commercialis. Journal of Food Protection* 47, 703-706.

Fan, P.C. 1998. Viability of metacercariae of *Clonorchis sinensis* in frozen or salted freshwater fish. *International Journal of Parasitology* 28, 603-605.

FAO/WHO (Food and Agriculture Organization/World Health Organization) 2001. Joint FAO/WHO Expert consultation on risk characterization of *Salmonella* spp. in eggs and broiler chickens and of *Listeria monocytogenes* in ready-to-eat foods. FAO Food and Nutrition Paper 72. FAO/WHO, FAO, Rome, Italy.

FAO/WHO (Food and Agriculture Organization/World Health Organization) 2001a. Hazard identification, exposure assessment and hazard characterization of *Vibrio* spp. in seafood. FAO/WHO, MRA 01/03, FAO, Rome, Italy.

Farber, J.M. & P.I. Peterkin 2000. *Listeria monocytogenes*. In: Lund, B.M., T.C. Baird-Parker & G.W. Gould (eds). *The Microbiological Safety and Quality of Foods*. Aspen Publishers, Inc. Gaithersberg, Maryland, USA. pp. 1178-1232.

Farmer, J.J., III, M.J. Arduino & F.W. Hickman-Brenner 1997. The genera *Aeromonas* and *Plesiomonas*, In: Balows, A., H.G. Trüper, M. Dworkin, W. Harder & K.-H. Schleifer (eds) *The Procaryotes*. 2nd ed. Springer Verlag, Heidelberg, Germany. pp. 3012-3028.

Fattakhov, R.G. 1989. [Low-temperature regimes for the decontamination of fish of the larvae *Opisthorchis*] *Med. Parazitol (Mosk)* 5, 63-64.

Fayer, R. 2001. Waterborne and Foodborne Protozoa. In: Hui, Y.H., S.A. Sattar, K.D. Murell, W.K. Nip & P.S. Stanfield (eds) *Foodborne Disease Handbook*. 2nd ed. vol 2. Marcel Dekker, Inc. N.Y. and Basel. pp. 289-321.

FDA (US Food and Drug Administration) 1998. *Fish and Fishery Products Hazard and Control Guide*, 2nd ed. FDA, Center for Food Safety and Applied Nutrition, Office of Seafood, Washington DC, USA.

FDA (US Food and Drug Administration) 2000. Draft risk assessment on the public health impact of *Vibrio parahaemolyticus* in raw molluscan shellfish. Center for Food Safety and Applied Nutrition, FDA, US Department of Health and Human Services.

FDA (US Food and Drug Administration) 2001. Draft Assessment of the Relative Risk to Public Health from Foodborne *Listeria monocytogenes* Among Selected Categories of Ready-to-Eat Foods. Center for Food Safety and Applied Nutrition (CFSAN) and Food Safety and Inspection Services (FSIS), Washington DC, USA.

FDA (US Food and Drug Administration) 2001a. *Fish and Fishery Products Hazards and Controls Guide*. 3rd edition. FDA, Center for Food Safety and Applied Nutrition, Office of Seafood, Washington DC, USA. www.cfsan.fda.gov/~comm/haccpsea.html.

Feldhusen, F. 2000 The role of seafood in bacterial foodborne diseases. *Microbes and Infection* 2, 1651-1660.

Flaherty, M., B. Szuster & P. Miller 2000. Low salinity inland shrimp farming in Thailand. *Ambio* 29, 174-179.

Flick, G.J. M.P. Oria, & L. Douglas 2001. Potential hazards in cold-smoked fish: Biogenic Amines . *Journal of Food Science – Supplement* 66, S1088-S1099.

Fonnesbech Vogel, B., B. Ojeniyi, P. Ahrens, L. Due Skov, H.H. Huss & L. Gram 2001. Elucidation of *Listeria monocytogenes* contamination routes in cold-smoked salmon processing plants detected by DNA-based typing methods. *Applied and Environmental Microbiology* 67, 2586-2595.

Frank, H.A.1985. VI. 1. Use of normographs to estimate histamine formation in tuna, In *Histamine formation in marine products: Production by bacteria, measurement and prediction of formation.* FAO Fisheries Technical Paper No. 252. Food and Agriculture Organization of the United Nations, Rome, Italy. pp. 18–20.

Fujii, T., A. Hiraishi, T. Kobayashi, R. Yoguchi, & M. Okuzumi 1997. Identification of the psychrotrophic hitamine-producing marine bacteria previously referred to as the N-group bacteria. *Fisheries Science* 63, 807-810.

Gantzer, C., E. Dubois, J.M. Crance, S. Billaudel, H. Kopecka, L. Schwarzbrod, M. Pommepuy & F. Le Guyader 1998. Influence of environmental factors on the survival of enteric viruses in seawater. *Oceanologica Acta* 21, 983-992.

Gerba, C.P. & C.N. Haas 1988. Assessment of risks associated with enteric viruses in contaminated drinking water. American Society for testing and materials, Technical publication 976. Philadelphia, USA.

GESAMP (Joint Group of Experts on the Scientific Aspects of Marine Environmental Protection

(IMO/FAO/UNESCO/WMO/IAEA/UN/UNEP)). 1997. *Towards the safe and effective use of of chemicals in coastal aquaculture.* Reports and Studies GESAMP No 65. FAO, Rome, Italy.

Gessner, B. Y. Hokama & S. Isto 1996. Scombrotoxicosis-like illness following the ingestion of smoked salmon that demonstrated low histamine levels and high toxicity on mouse bioassay. *Clinical and Infectious Disease* 23, 1316–1318.

Gibson, D. 1992. Personal communication. Torry Research Station, Aberdeen, Scotland.

Gooch, J.A., A. DePaola, J. Bowers & D.L. Marshall 2002. Growth and survival of *Vibrio parahaemolyticus* in post-harvest American oysters. *Journal of Food Protection* 65, 970-974.

Gram, L. 1991. Inhibition of mesophilic *Aeromonas* spp. by salt, potassium sorbate, smoke extract and chilling. *Journal of Food Protection* 54, 436-442.

Gram, L. 2001. Potential hazard in cold-smoked fish: *Listeria monocytogenes.* Special supplement to *Journal of Food Science* 66, S1072-S1081.

Gram, L. & H.H. Huss 2000. Fish and shellfish products. In: Lund, B.M, T.C. Baird-Parker & G.W. Gould (eds) *The Microbiological Safety and Quality of Foods.* Aspen Publishers Inc., Gaithersberg, Maryland, USA. pp. 472-506.

Gram, L., G. Trolle & H.H. Huss 1990. The bacteriology of fresh and spoiling Lake Victorian Nile perch (*Lates niloticus*). *International Journal of Food Microbiology* 10, 303-316.

Granum, P.E. & T.C. Baird-Parker 2000. *Bacillus* species. In: Lund, B.M., T.C. Baird-Parker & G.W. Gould (eds) *The Microbiological Safety and Quality of Foods.* Aspen Publishers, Inc. Gaithersberg, Maryland, USA. pp. 1029-1039.

Graslund, S. & B.E. Bengtsson 2001. Chemicals and biological products used in Southeast Asian shrimp farming and their potential impact on the environment – a review. *The Science of the Total Environment* 280, 93-131.

Halliday, M.L., L.-Y. Kang, T.-K. Zhou *et al.* 1991. An epidemic of hepatitis A attributable to the ingestion of raw clams in Shanghai, China. *Journal of Infectious Disease* 164, 362-364.

Hauschild, A.H.W. 1989. *Clostridium botulinum.* In Doyle, M.P. (ed) *Foodborne Bacterial Pathogens.* Marcel Dekker, Inc., New York and Basel. pp. 111-190.

Hayashi, R., K. Harada, S. Mitsuhashi & M. Inoue 1982. Conjugation of drug resistance plasmids from *Vibrio anguillarum* to *Vibrio parahemolyticus*. *Microbiology and Immunology* 26, 479-485

Higashi, G.H. 1985. Foodborne parasites transmitted to man from fish and other aquatic foods. *Food Techonology* 39, 69-111.

Howgate, P. 1998. Review of the public health safety of products from aquaculture. *International Journal of Food Science and Technology* 33, 99-125.

Huq, A., S.A. Huq, D.J. Grimes, M. O'Brien, K.H. Chu, J. McDowell Capuzzo & R.R. Colwell 1996. Colonisation of the gut of the blue crab (*Callinectes sapidus*) by *Vibrio cholerae. Applied and Environmental Microbiology* 52, 586-588.

Huss, H.H. 1980. Distribution of *Clostridium botulinum*. *Applied and Environmental Microbiology* 39, 764-769.

Huss, H.H. 1981. *Clostridium botulinum* type E and botulism. D Sc. thesis. Technological Laboratory of the Danish Ministry for Fisheries and The Royal Veterinary and Agricultural University, Copenhagen, Denmark.

Huss, H.H. 1994. *Assurance of Seafood Quality*. FAO Fishery Technical Paper No. 334. FAO, Rome, Italy.

Huss, H.H. 1997. Control of indigenous pathogenic bacteria in seafood. *Food Control* 8, 91-98.

Huss, H.H. & L.A. Larsen 1979. The post mortem changes in the oxidation-reduction potential of fish muscles and internal organs. In: Sobolewska-Ceronik, K. & S. Zaleski (eds) *Food as an Ecological Environment for Pathogenic and Index Microorganisms*. Ars Polona, Poland. pp. 265-279.

Huss, H.H. & A. Larsen 1980. Changes in the oxidation reduction potential (Eh) of smoked and salted fish during storage. *Lebensmittel – Wissenshaft und Technologie* 13, 40-43.

Huss, H.H. & E. Rye Petersen 1980. The stability of *C. botulinum* type E toxin in salty and/or acid environment. *Journal of Food Technology* 15, 619-627.

Huss, H.H., P.K. Ben Embarek & V. F. Jeppesen 1995. Control of biological hazards in cold smoked salmon production. *Food Control* 6, 335-340.

Huss, H.H., L.V. Jørgensen & B. Fonnesbech Vogel 2000. Control options for *Listeria monocytogenes* in seafoods. *International Journal of Food Microbiology* 62, 276-274.

ICMSF (International Commission on Microbiological Specifications for Foods) 1996. *Microorganisms in Foods 5. Characteristics of Microbial Pathogens*. Blackie Academic & Professional, UK.

ICMSF (International Commission on Microbiological Specifications for Foods) 2003. *Microorganisms in Foods 6. Microbial Ecology of Foods*. 2nd ed. In preparation.

Ijomah, P. I., M.N. Clifford, R. Walker, J. Wright, R. Hardy & C.K. Murray 1992. Further volunteer studies on scombrotoxicosis. In: Burt, J.R., R. Hardy & K.J. Whittle (eds) *Pelagic fish: The resource and its exploitation*. Fishing News Books, Oxford, UK. pp. 194-199.

Ijomah, P., M.N. Clifford, R. Walker, J. Wright, R. Hardy & C.K. Murray 1991. The importance of endogenous histamine relative to dietary histamine in the aetiology of scombrotoxicosis. *Food Additives and Contaminants* 8, 531–542.

Inglis, V., E. Yimer, E.J. Bacon & S. Ferguson 1993. Plasmid-mediated antibiotic resistance in *Aermonas salmonicidia* isolated from Atlantic salmon, *Salmo salar* L. in Scotland. *Journal of Fish Diseases* 16, 593-600.

Ives, K. 1990. *Cryptosporidium* and water supplies: Treatment process and oocyst removal. In: *Cryptosporidium in water supplies*. Report of a group of experts. HMSO, London, UK. pp. 154-184.

Jablonski, L.M. & G.A. Bohach 1997. *Staphylococcus aureus*. In: Doyle, M.P., L.R. Beuchat & T.J. Montville (eds). *Food Microbiology. Fundamentals and Frontiers*. ASM Press, Washington DC, USA. pp. 353-375.

Jeppesen, V.F. & H.H. Huss 1993. Antagonistic activity of two strains af lactic acid bacteria against *Listeria monocytogenes* and *Yersinia enterocolitica* in a model fish product at 5°C. *International Journal of Food Microbiology* 19, 179-186.

Jiménez, L., J. Munir, G.G. Toranzos & T.C. Hazen 1989. Survival and activity of *Salmonella typhimurium* and *Escherichia coli* in tropical fresh water. *Journal of Applied Bacteriology*, 67, 61-69.

Jørgensen, L.V., P. Dalgaard, & H.H. Huss 2000. Multiple compound quality index for cold-smoked salmon (*Salmo salar*) developed by multivariate regression of biogenic amines and pH. *Journal of Agriculture and Food Chemistry* 48, 2448-2453.

Jørgensen, L.V., H.H. Huss, & P. Dalgaard 2000a. The effect of biogenic amine production by single bacterial cultures and metabiosis on cold-smoked salmon. *Journal of Applied Microbiology* 89, 920-934.

Karl, H., A. Roepstorff, H.H. Huss & B. Bloemsma 1995. Survival of *Anisakis* larval in marinated herring fillets. *International Journal of Food Science and Technology* 29, 661-670.

Kaysner, C.A. 2000. *Vibrio* species. In: Lund, B.M., T.C. Baird-Parker & Gould, G.W. (eds) *The Microbiological Safety and Quality of Foods*. Aspen Publishers Inc., Gaithersberg, Maryland, USA. pp. 1336-1362.

Kino, H., W. Hori, H. Kobayashi, N. Nakamura & K. Nagasawa 2002. A mass occurrence of human infection with *Diplogonoporus grandis* (Cestoda: Diphyllobothriidae) in Shizuoka prefecture, central Japan. *Parasitology International* 51, 73-79.

Kirov, S.M. 1997. *Aermonas* and *Plesiomonas* species. In: Doyle, M., L.R. Beuchat & T.J. Montville (eds) *Food Microbiology. Fundamentals and Frontiers*. ASM Press, Washington DC, USA. pp. 265-287.

Kitts, D. 2001. Laboratory Methodology for Shellfish Toxins. In: Hui, Y.H., D. Kitts, P.S. Stanfield (eds) *Foodborne Disease Handbook*. 2nd ed., vol. 4. Marcel Dekker Inc., N.Y. Basel. pp. 183-207.

Klausen, N.K. & H.H. Huss 1987. Growth and histamine production by *Morganella morganii* under various temperature conditions. *International Journal of Food Microbiology* 5, 147-156.

Knøchel, S. 1989. *Aeromononas* spp. – ecology and significance in food and water hygiene. PhD thesis. Technological Laboratory of the Danish Ministry for Fisheries & The Royal Veterinary and Agricultural University, Denmark.

Knøchel, S. 1990. Growth characteristics of motile *Aeromonas* spp. isolated from different environments. *International Journal of Food Microbiology* 10, 235-244.

Kothary, M.H. & U. Babu 2001. Infectious dose of foodborne pathogens in volunteers: A review. *Journal of Food Safety* 21, 49-73.

Krovacek, K., L.M. Eriksson, C. Gonzalez-Rey, J. Rosinksy & I. Ciznar 2000. Isolation, biochemical and serological characterization of *Plesiomonas shigelloides* from freshwater in Northern Europe. *Comparative Immunology Microbiology and Infectious Diseases* 23, 45-51.

Kruatrachue, M., Y.P. Chitramvong, E.S. Upatham, S. Vichari & V. Viyanant 1982. Effects of physico-chemical factors on the infection of hamsters by metacercariae of *Opisthorchis viverrini*. *Southeast Asian Journal of Tropical Medicine and Public Health* 13, 614-617.

Lagos, N., M. Rutman, J. Blamey, M.P. Ocaranza, M. Chiong, J.P. Hinrichsen & C. Lopez, (inventors) 2001. Jan. 9. Procedure for detoxification of shellfish contaminated with paralytic shellfish toxins. US Patent No. 6, 171, 626 B1.

Lalitha, K.V. & P.K. Surendran 2002. Occurrence of *Clostridium botulinum* in fresh and cured fish in retail trade in Cochin (India). *International Journal of Food Microbiology* 72, 169-174.

Lampel, K.A., J.M. Madden & I.K. Wachsmuth 2000. *Shigella* species. In Lund, B.M., T.C. Baird-Parker & G.W. Gould (eds) *The Microbiological Safety and Quality of Foods*. Aspen Publishers Inc., Gaithersberg, Maryland, USA. pp. 1200-1216.

Lees, D. 1995. Control measures in seafood. In: ACMSF (Advisory Committee on Microbiological Safety of Foods) *Workshop on Foodborne Viral Infections*.Crown, HMSO, London, UK. pp. 61-71.

Lees, D. 2000. Viruses and bivalve shellfish. *International Journal of Food Microbiology* 59, 81-116.

Lehane, L. & J. Olley 2000. Histamine fish poisoning revisited. *International Journal of Food Microbiology* 58, 1-37.

Lehane, L. & R.J. Lewis 2000. Review. Ciguatera: Recent advances but the risk remains. *International Journal of Food Microbiology* 61, 91-125.

Little, C.L., H.A. Monsey, G.L. Nichols & J. de Louvois 1997. The microbiological quality of cooked, ready-to-eat, out-of-the shell molluscs – a report of the results of a study by the LACOT/PHLS co-ordinated food Liaison Group Microbiological Sampling Group. *PHLS Microbiological Digest* 14, 196-201.

Llewellyn, L.E. 2001. Shellfish Chemical Poisoning. In: Hui, Y.H., D. Kitts & P.S. Stanfield (eds) *Foodborne disease handbook*. 2nd ed. vol. 4, Marcel Dekker, Inc., NY, Basel. pp. 77-108.

Lund, B.M. & M.W. Peck 2000. *Clostridium botulinum*. In: Lund, B.M., T.C. Baird-Parker & G.W. Gould (eds) *The Microbiological Safety and Quality of Food*. Aspen Publishers, Inc. Gaithersberg, Maryland, USA. pp. 1057-1110.

Luten, J.B., W. Bouquet, L.A.J. Seuren, M.M. Burggraaf, G. Riekwel-Booy, P. Durand, M. Etienne, J.P. Gouyou, A. Landrein, A. Ritchie, M. Leclerq & R. Guinet 1992. Biogenic amines in fishery products. Standardization methods within EC. In: Huss, H.H., M. Jakobsen & J. Liston (eds) *Quality Assurance in the Fish Industry*. Elsevier Science Publishers, The Netherlands. pp. 427-440.

Martens, T. 1999. Harmonisation of safety criteria for minimally processed foods. FAIR-concerted Action. FAIR CT 96-1020. European Commission DE XII.

Middlebrooks B.L., P.M. Toom, W.L. Douglas, R.E. Harrison & S. McDowell 1988. Effects of storage time and temperature on the microflora and amine development in Spanish mackerel (*Scomberomorus maculatus*). *Journal of Food Science* 53, 1024–1029.

Midvedt, T. & E. Lingass 1992. Putative public health risks of antibiotic resistance development in aquatic bacteria. In: Michael, C. & D.J. Alderman (eds) *Chemotherapy in aquaculture: from theory to reality*. Office International de Epizooties, Paris, France. pp. 302-314.

Miettinen, M.K., A. Siitonen, P. Heiskanen, H. Haajanen, K.J. Bjorkroth, H.J. Korkeala 1999. Molecular epidemiology of an outbreak of febrile gastroenteritis caused by *Listeria monocytogenes* in cold-smoked rainbow trout. *Journal of Clinical Microbiology* 37, 2358-60.

Millard, J., H. Appleton & J.V. Parry 1987. Studies on heat inactivation of hepatitis A virus with special reference to shellfish. *Epidemiology and Infection* 98, 397-414.

Mitcherlich, E. & E.H. Marth 1984. *Microbial Survival in the Environment*. Springer Verlag, Heidelberg, Germany.

Monteil, H. & C. Harf-Monteil 1997. Les infections á *Aeromonas*. *Presse Medicale* 26, 1790-1798.

Morgan, D.R., P.C. Johnson, H.L Dupont, T.K. Satterwhite & L.V. Wood 1985. Lack of correlation between known virulence properties of *Aeromonas hydrophila* and enteropathogenicity for humans. *Infection and Immunity* 50, 62-65.

Motes, M.L., A. DePaola, D.W Cook, J.E. Veazey, J.C. Hunsucker, W.E. Garthright, R.J. Blodgett & S.J. Chirtel 1998. Influence of water temperature and salinity on *Vibrio vulnificus* in Northern Gulf and Atlantic Coast oysters (*Crassostrea virginica*). *Applied and Environmental Microbiology* 64, 3874-3877.

Nachamkin, I. 1997. *Campylobacter jejuni* In: Doyle, M.P., L.R. Beuchat & T.J. Montville (eds) *Food Microbiology. Fundamentals and Frontiers*. ASM Press, Washington DC, USA. pp. 159-170.

Nagashima, Y., T. Noguchi, M. Tanaka & K. Hashimoto 1991. Thermal degradation of paralytic shellfish poison. *Journal of Food Science* 56, 1572-1575.

Nakjima, T., M. Suzuki, K. Harada, M. Inoue & S. Mitsuhashi 1983. Transmission of R plasmids in *Vibrio anguillarum* to *Vibrio cholerae*. *Microbiology Immunology* 27, 195-198.

Nilsson, L., L. Gram & H.H. Huss. 1999. Growth control of *Listeria monocytogenes* on cold-smoked salmon using a competitive lactic acid bacterial flora. *Journal of Food Protection* 62, 336-342.

Okamoto, A. 1992. Restrictions on the use of drugs in aquaculture in Japan. In: Michel, C. & D.J. Alderman (eds) *Chemotheraphy in Aquaculture. From Theory to Reality.* Office International de Epizooties, Paris, France. pp. 109-114.

Okuzumi M, H. Yamanaka & T. Kubozuka , 1984. Occurrence of various histamine-forming bacteria on/in fresh fishes. *Bulletin of the Japanese Society of Scientific Fisheries* 50, 161–167.

Oliver, J.D. & J.B. Kaper 1997. *Vibrio* species. In: Doyle, M.P., L.R. Beuchat & T.J. Montville (eds) *Food Microbiology. Fundamentals and Frontiers*. ASM Press, Washington DC, USA. pp. 228-264.

Oliver, J.D., R.A. Warner & D.R Cleland 1983. Distribution of *Vibrio vulnificus* and other lactose fermenting vibrios in the marine environment. *Applied and Environmental Microbiology* 45, 985-998.

Olson, R.E. 1987. Marine fish parasites of public health importance. In: Kramer, D.E. & J. Liston (eds) *Seafood Quality Determination*. Elsevier Science Publishers, The Netherlands. pp. 339-355.

Orlandi, P.A., D.M.T. Chu, J.W. Bier & G.J. Jackson 2002. Parasites and the food supply. *Food Technology* 56, 72-81.

Palumbo, S., G.N. Stelma Jr. & C. Abeyta 2000. The *Aeromonas hydrophila* group. In: Lund, B.M., T.C. Baird-Parker & G.W. Gould (eds) *The Microbiological Safety and Quality of Foods.* Aspen Publishers, Inc. Gaithersberg, Maryland, USA. pp. 1011-1028.

Price, R.J. 1992. Residue concerns in seafoods. *Dairy, Food and Environmental Sanitation* 12, 139-143.

Price, R.J. & P.D. Tom 1999. *Compendium of Fish and Fishery Product Processes, Hazards and Controls*, National Seafood HACCP Alliance for Training and Education. Food Science and Technol. University of California, Davis, CA, USA.

Reilly, P.J.A. & D.R. Twiddy 1992. *Salmonella* and *Vibrio cholerae* in brackish water tropical prawns. *International Journal of Food Microbiology* 16, 293-301.

Reilly, P.J.A., D.R. Twiddy & R.S. Fuchs 1992. Review of the occurrence of *Salmonella* in cultured tropical shrimp. FAO Fish. Circ. No. 851. FAO, Rome, Italy.

Rhodes, M.W. & H. Kator 1988. Survival of *Escherichia coli* and *Salmonella* spp. in estuarine environments. *Applied and Environmental Microbiology* 54, 2902-2907.

Roepstorff, A., H. Karl, B. Bloemsma & H.H. Huss 1993. Catch handling and the possible migration of *Anisakis* larval in herring, *Clupea harengus*. *Journal of Food Protection* 56, 783-787.

Rogers, P.L. & W.F. Staruszkiewicz 1997. Gas chromatographic method for putrescine and cadaverine in canned tuna and mahimahi and fluorometric method for histamine (minor modification of AOAC official method 977.13): collaborative study. *Journal of American Organization of Analytical Chemistry International* 80, 591-602.

Saheki, K., S. Kobayashi & T. Kawanishi 1989. *Salmonella* contamination of eel culture ponds. *Nippon Suisan Gakkaishi* 55, 675-679.

Saitanu, K., A. Amornsin, F. Kondo & C.E. Tsai 1994. Antibiotic residues in tiger shrimp (*Penaeus monodon*). *Asian Fisheries Science* 7, 47-52.

Samuelson, O.B., T. Lunestad, B. Husevag, T. Holleland & A. Ervik 1992. Residues of oxolinic in wild fauna following medication in fish farms. *Diseases of Aquatic Organisms* 12, 111-119.

Samuelson, O.B., V. Torsvik & A. Ervik 1992a. Long range changes in oxytetracycline concentration and bacterial resistance towards oxytetracycline in a fish farm sediment after medication. *Science of the Total Environment* 114, 25-36.

Schanz, E.J. 1984. Historical perspective on paralytical shellfish poisoning. In: Ragelis (ed) *Seafood Toxins*, ACS – Symposium Series 262, 99-111.

Scoging, A.C. 1998. Marine biotoxins. *Journal of Applied Microbiology Symposium Supplement* 84, 41S-50S.

Sechet, V., P. Safran, P. Hougaard & T. Yasumoto 1990. Causative species of diarrhoeic shellfish poisoning. *Marine Biology* 105, 269-274.

Shalaby A.R. 1996. Significance of biogenic amines to food safety and human health. *Food Research International* 29, 675–690.

Simidu, W. & S. Hibiki 1955. Studies on putrefaction of aquatic products. 23. On the critical concentration of poisoning for histamine. *Bulletin of the Japanese Society of Scientific Fisheries* 21, 365–367.

Sithithaworn, P., S. Phinlor, S. Tesana, S. Keawkes & T. Srisawangwonk 1991. Infectivity of *Opisthorchis viverrini* metacercariae stored at 4° C. *Journal of Tropical Medicine and Parasitology* 14, 14-20.

Smith, A.G. & S.D. Gangolli 2002. Organochlorine chemicals in seafood: occurrence and health concerns. *Food and Chemical Toxicology* 40, 767-779.

Stewart-Tull, D.E.S. 2001. Vaba, Haiza, Kolera, Foklune or Cholera: in any language stille the disease of seven pandemics. *Journal of Applied Microbiology* 91, 580-591.

Strauss, M. 1996. Health (Pathogen) Considerations Regarding the Use of Human Waste in Aquaculture. In: Recycling the Resource - Ecological Engineering for Wastewater Treatment, *Environmental Research Forum*, **5-6**. *Proceedings, 2nd International Conference on Ecological Engineering for Wastewater Treatment* 18-22 Sept. 1995., Wädenswil, Switzerland.

Sumner, J., T. Ross, K. Sanderson & T. McMeekin 2001. *Identification and characterization of food-borne hazards in the Australian seafood industry*. Draft report. Seafood Services Australia.

Tamplin, M.L. & G.M. Capers 1992. Persistence of *Vibrio vulnificus* in tissues of Gulf Coast oysters, *Crassostrea virginica*, exposed to seawater disinfected with UV light. *Applied and Environmental Microbiology* 58, 1506-1510.

Tan, L.K. 1999. Chloramphenicol-induced Aplastic Anaemia- Should Its Topical Use Be Abandoned? *Singapore Medical Journal* 40(07) http://www.sma.org.sg/smj/4007/articles/4007e3.html

Tang, Y.W., J.X. Wang, Z.Y. Xu, Y.F. Guo, W.H. Qian & J.X. Xu 1991. A serologically confirmed case-control study of a large outbreak of hepatitis A in China associated with consumption of clams. *Epidemiology and Infection* 107, 651-658.

Taylor S.L. 1983. Monograph on histamine poisoning. Paper presented at the Codex Committee on Food Hygiene, 19th session. Washington DC, 26-30 September.

Taylor, S.L. 1986. Histamine food poisoning: Toxicology and clinical aspects. *Critical Reviews in Toxicology* 17, 91-128.

Taylor, S.L. 1988. Marine toxins of microbial origin. *Food Technology* 42, 94-98.

Tesana, S., S. Kaewkes & S. Phinlaor 1986. Infectivity and survivorship of *Opisthorchis viverrini* metacercariae in fermented fish. *Journal of Parasitology of the Tropical Medical Association Thailand* 9, 21-30.

Tilburg, J.J.H.C., J.T.M. Zwartkruis-Nahuis, D. van den Berkmortel, J. Rombout, K.M. Jonker & E. de Boer 2000. *Presence of Vibrio species in shellfish*. Report of the Inspectorate for Health Protection and Veterinary Public Health. de Stoven 22, 7206 AX, Zutphen, Netherlands.

Todd, E. 1993. Domoic acid and amnesic shellfish poisoning, a review. *Journal of Food Protection* 56, 69-83.

Tompkin, B.R. 2001. Control of *Listeria monocytogenes* in meat and poultry processing environments. Paper presented at "Control of *Listeria monocytogenes* in the food industry". 13th November Århus, Denmark

Torres-Vitela, M.R., A. Castillo, G. Finne, M.O. Rodriguez-Garcia, N.E. Martinez-Gonzales & V. Navarro Hidalgo 1997. Incidence of *Vibrio cholera* in fresh fish and ceviche in Guadalajara, Mexico. *Journal of Food Protection* 60, 237-241.

Tsukamoto, T., Y. Kinoshita, T. Shimada & R. Sakazaki 1978. Two epidemics of diarrhoeal disease possibly caused by *Plesiomonas shigelloides*. *Journal of Hygeine (Cambridge)* 80, 275-280.

Twedt, R.M. 1989. *Vibro parahaemolyticus*, In: Doyle, M. (ed) *Food-borne Bacterial Pathogens*. Marcel Dekker Inc., NY, USA. pp. 543-568.

van Egmond, H.P., T. Anne, P. Lassus, G.J.A. Speijers & M. Waldock 1993. Paralytic and Diarrhoeic Shellfish Poisons: Occurrence in Europe, Toxicity, Analysis and Regulation. *Journal of Natural Toxins* 2, 41-64.

van Schothorst, M. (International Commission on Microbiological Specifications for Foods (ICMSF)) 1998. Principles for the establishment of microbiological food safety objectives and related control measures. *Food Control* 9, 379-384.

van Schothorst, M. 1996. Sampling plans for *L. monocytogenes*. *Food Control* 7, 203-208.

van Spreekens, K. 1986. Histamine production by the psychrophilic flora. In: Kramer, D.E. & J. Liston (eds) *Seafood quality determination.* Elsevier Science Publishers, Amsterdam, The Netherlands. pp. 309-318.

Wachsmuth, K. & G.K. Morris 1989. *Shigella*. In: Doyle, M.P. (ed) *Foodborne Bacterial Pathogens*. Marcel Dekker Inc. pp. 447-462.

Weber, J.T., E.D. Mintz, R. Canizares, A. Semiglia, I. Gomez, R. Sempertegui, A. Davila, K.D. Greene, N.D. Puhr, D.N. Cameron, F.C. Tenover, T.J. Barrett, N.H. Bean, C. Ivey, R.V. Tauxe & P.A. Blake, 1994. Epidemic cholera in Ecuador: multidrug-resistance and transmission by water and seafood. *Epidemiology and Infection* 112, 1-11.

Weinstein, M.R., M. Litt, D.A. Kertesz, P. Wyper, D. Ross, M. Coulter, A. McGreer, R. Facklam, C. Ostach, B.M. Willey, A. Borczyk, D.E. Low & the Investigative Team. 1997 Invasive infection due to a fish pathogen; *Streptococcus iniae*. *New England Journal of Medicine* 337, 589-594.

WHO (World Health Organization) 1992. WHO Guide on Formulation of national Policy on the Control of Cholera. WHO ICDD/SER/80.4. Rev. 3. WHO, Geneva, Switzerland.

WHO (World Health Organization) 1995. Control of foodborne trematode infections : Report of a WHO study group. WHO, Geneva, Switzerland. WHO Technical Report Series No. 849.

WHO (World Health Organization) 1999. Joint FAO/NACA/WHO Study Group on food safety issues associated with products from aquaculture. WHO Technical Report Series No. 883. World Health Organization, Geneva, Switzerland.

Willshaw, G.A., T. Cheasty & H.R. Smith 2000. In: Lund, B.M., T.C. Baird-Parker & G.W. Gould (eds) *The Microbiological Safety and Quality of Foods*. Aspen Publishers, Gaithersberg, Maryland, USA. pp. 1136-1177.

Yoshikawa-Ebesu, J.S.M., Y. Hokama & T. Nogushi 2001. Tetrodotoxin. In: Hui, Y.H., D. Kitts, P.S. Stanfield (eds) *Foodborne Disease H& book*. 2nd ed, vol. 4. Marcel Dekker Inc, N.Y. and Basel. pp. 253-286.

Part II: Risk Management Tools

6 INTERNATIONAL REGULATORY FRAMEWORK FOR FISH SAFETY AND QUALITY (Lahsen Ababouch)

The increasing demand for fish and fishery products and the development in international fish trade have raised major concerns about the overexploitation of aquatic resources and the quality and safety of the products internationally traded. Globalisation of the economy and the development of regional economic groupings have highlighted the need for harmonizing fish safety and quality assurance approaches, with the view to ensure fish safety and fair trade practices.

Following is a description of the international regulatory framework for fish safety and quality assurance.

6.1 The World Trade Organization (WTO) agreement

The Final Act of the Uruguay Round of multilateral trade negotiations, which began in Punta del Este, Uruguay in September 1986 and concluded in Marrakesh, Morocco in April 1994, established the World Trade Organization (WTO) to succeed the General Agreement on Tariffs and Trade (GATT). The Uruguay Round negotiations were the first to deal with the liberalization of trade in agricultural products, an area excluded from previous rounds of negotiations.

Significant implications for food safety and quality arise from the Final Act of the Uruguay Round, especially from two binding agreements: the Agreement on the Application of Sanitary and Phytosanitary (SPS) Measures and the Agreement on Technical Barriers to Trade (TBT Agreement).

6.1.1 The agreement on the Application of Sanitary and Phytosanitary Measures (SPS)

The SPS agreement confirms the right of WTO member countries to apply measures necessary to protect human, animal and plant life and health. This right was included in the original 1947 GATT as a general exclusion from the provisions of the agreement provided that "such measures are not applied in a manner which would constitute a means of arbitrary or unjustifiable discrimination between countries where the same conditions prevail, or a disguised restriction on international trade". Despite this general condition for the application of national measures to protect human, animal and plant life and health, it had become, whether by design or accident, effective trade barriers.

The purpose of the SPS Agreement is to ensure that measures established by governments to protect human, animal and plant life and health, in the agricultural sector, including fisheries, are consistent with obligations prohibiting arbitrary or unjustifiable discrimination on trade between countries where the same conditions prevail and are not disguised restrictions on international trade. It requires that, with regard to food safety measures, WTO members base their national measures on international standards, guidelines and other recommendations adopted by the *Codex Alimentarius* Commission (CAC) where they exist. This does not prevent a member country from adopting stricter measures if there is a scientific justification for doing so, or if the level of protection afforded by the *Codex* standards is inconsistent with the level of protection generally applied and deemed appropriate by the country concerned.

The SPS Agreement states that any measures taken that conform to international Codex standards, guidelines or recommendations are deemed to be appropriate, necessary and not discriminatory. Furthermore, the SPS Agreement calls for a programme of harmonization based on international standards. This work is guided by the WTO Committee on SPS measures, to which representatives of the CAC, the International Office of Epizootics (OIE) which deals with animal (including fish) health, and the International Plant Protection Convention (IPPC) which deals with plant protection are invited.

Finally, the SPS Agreement requires that SPS measures are to be based on an assessment of the risks to humans, animal and plant life and health using internationally accepted risk assessment techniques. Risk assessment should take into account the available scientific evidence, the relevant processes and production methods, the inspection/sampling/testing methods, the prevalence of specific illnesses and other matters of relevance.

6.1.2 The agreement on Technical Barriers to Trade (TBT)

The Agreement on TBT is a revision of the agreement of the same name first developed under the Tokyo round of negotiations (1973 – 1979). The objective of the TBT Agreement is to prevent the use of national or regional technical requirements, or standards in general, as unjustified technical barriers to trade. The agreement covers standards relating to all types of products including industrial products and quality requirements for foods (except requirements related to SPS measures). It includes numerous measures designed to protect the consumer against deception and economic fraud.

The TBT Agreement basically provides that all technical standards and regulations must have a legitimate purpose and that the impact or cost of implementing the standard must be proportional to the purpose of the standard. It also states that if there are two or more ways of achieving the same objective, the least trade restrictive alternative should be followed. The agreement also places emphasis on international standards, WTO members being obliged to use international standards or parts of them except where the international standard would be ineffective or inappropriate in the national situation.

Both the SPS and TBT Agreements call on Member countries to facilitate the provision of technical assistance, especially to developing countries, either bilaterally or through the appropriate international organizations. Also, special and differential treatment provisions call for the consideration of the needs of developing countries and especially the least developed countries when preparing and implementing SPS and quality measures. Such consideration include providing longer time frames for compliance on products of interest to developing countries

The aspects of food standards that TBT requirements cover specifically are quality provisions, nutritional requirements, labelling, packaging and product content regulations, and methods of analysis. Unlike the SPS Agreement, the TBT Agreement does not specifically name international standard setting bodies, whose standards are to be used as benchmarks for judging compliance with the provisions of the Agreement.

6.2 The Food and Agriculture Organization of the United Nations (FAO)

6.2.1 Codex Alimentarius

Since 1962, the *Codex Alimentarius* Commission (CAC) has been responsible for implementing the Joint FAO/WHO Food Standards Programme. The Commission's primary objectives are the protection of the health of consumers, the assurance of fair practices in food trade and the coordination of the work on food standards.

The CAC is an intergovernmental body with a membership of 165 Member governments. In addition, observers from international scientific organizations, food industry, food trade and consumer associations may attend sessions of the Commission and of its subsidiary bodies. An Executive Committee, six Regional Coordinating Committees and a Secretariat assist the Commission in administering its work programme and other activities.

The work of the *Codex Alimentarius* is divided between two basic types of committees:

- nine general subject matter(s) Committees that deal with general principles, hygiene, veterinary drugs, pesticides, food additives, labelling, methods of analysis, nutrition and import/export inspection and certification systems and

- 12 Commodity Committees which deal with a specific type of food class or group, such as dairy and dairy products, fats and oils, or fish and fish products.

The work of the Committees on hygiene, fish and fishery products, veterinary drugs and import/export inspection and certification systems are of paramount interest to the safety and quality of internationally traded fish and fishery products.

In the environment of the Uruguay round agreements, the work of the CAC has taken on unprecedented importance with respect to consumer protection and international food trade. The specific Codex food safety provisions, which are recognized by the SPS Agreement, include the maximum residue limits for pesticides and veterinary drugs, the maximum level of use of food additives, the maximum levels of contaminants, and food hygiene requirements of Codex standards.

In the specific area of Food Hygiene, the CAC has revised its main document on food hygiene (CAC 2001) to incorporate risk assessment principles and to include specific references to the Hazard Analysis and Critical Control Point (HACCP) System.

The *Codex* standards are meant to be voluntary and adopted by consensus. But under the new SPS/TBT agreements, the *Codex* standards can not be called voluntary, nor are they fully mandatory, falling in an area in between which looks like voluntarism under duress. This is changing the *Codex* deliberations into a highly charged political exercise, because countries know that the standards they are debating might subsequently be the subject of WTO dispute settlement, and act therefore accordingly.

Another major issue increasingly faced by the *Codex* is the critical problem of scientific uncertainty. It can only operate on the hypothesis that best fits the facts available at any given time. To deal with the uncertainty, some countries advocate the precautionary principle: "*Where there are threats, lack of full scientific certainty should not be used as a reason for postponing cost-effective measures to prevent the damage*". However, any precautionary measure taken should be accompanied by a search for greater scientific certainty, and periodic evaluation of the measures in light of new evidence.

6.2.2 The FAO Code of conduct for responsible fisheries

During the recent decades, world fisheries have become a market-driven, dynamically developing sector of the food industry and coastal States have striven to take advantage of their new opportunities by investing in modern fishing fleets and processing factories in response to growing international demand for fish and fishery products. By the late 1980s it became clear, however, that fisheries resources could no longer sustain such rapid and often uncontrolled exploitation and development, and new approaches to fisheries management embracing conservation and environmental considerations were urgently needed.

The FAO Committee on Fisheries (COFI) at its Nineteenth Session in March 1991 called for the development of new concepts which would lead to responsible, sustained fisheries. Subsequently, the International Conference on Responsible Fishing, held in 1992 in Cancûn (Mexico) further requested FAO to prepare an international Code of Conduct to address these concerns. The outcome of this Conference, particularly the Declaration of Cancûn, was an important contribution to the 1992 United Nations Conference on Environment and Development (UNCED), in particular its Agenda 21.

Noting these and other important developments in world fisheries, the FAO Governing Bodies recommended the formulation of a global Code of Conduct for Responsible Fisheries which would be consistent with these instruments and, in a non-mandatory manner, establish principles and standards applicable to the conservation, management and development of all fisheries. The Code, which was unanimously adopted on 31 October 1995 by the 28th Session of the FAO Conference, provides a necessary framework for national and international efforts to ensure sustainable exploitation of aquatic living resources in harmony with the environment (FAO, 1995). Article 6 (General principles, provisions 6.7 and 6.140) and article 11 (Post-harvest practices and trade) are of particular relevance to fish trade, safety and quality. Provisions 11.1.2, 11.1.3 and 11.1.4 encourage States to establish and maintain effective national safety and quality assurance systems, to promote the implementation of the CAC standards and codes of practice and cooperate to achieve harmonization or mutual recognition, or both, of national sanitary measures and certification programmes.

The same 28th FAO Conference requested the elaboration of technical guidelines in support of the implementation of the Code of Conduct in collaboration with member states and relevant organizations. Volume No 7 provides technical guidelines for responsible fish utilization (FAO, 1998).

6.3 Conclusion

The globalization and further liberalization of world fish trade, while offering several benefits and opportunities, also presents new safety and quality challenges. Fish safety and quality assurance in the new millennium will require enhanced levels of international co-operation in setting up standards and regulations. The SPS/TBT agreements of the WTO and the benchmarking role of the Codex provide an international platform in this respect. Consequently, the major fish producing, exporting or importing countries have launched in the early 90's an overhaul of fish inspection regulations to set up the foundations for the implementation of the HACCP-based quality and safety systems, in conformity with the guidelines of the CAC. Regulations enacted by the EU (EC, 1991, 1994, 2000) and the USA (FDA, 1997) have set up the pace and the trend for many other countries, especially the major commercial partners of the EU or the USA, highlighting the need for better harmonization and recognition schemes. More recently, several countries have initiated national works on microbiological risk assessments. But several gaps and differences subsist. These differences entail questions such as:

- Should HACCP address fish safety (USA) only or safety and spoilage (European Union)?
- Where does the clear demarcation between GHP/GMP and HACCP lie?
- Should the control authority assist the industry in developing HACCP programs or should it confine its role to assessment and verification?
- Is HACCP always needed regardless of the product and process?
- In international trade, who should be responsible for verification of HACCP implementation?. Is it the importer, the exporter, the control authority of the importing country, of the exporting authority, a third party?
- How do we reconcile between the precautionary principle and science-based risk assessments
- How can we achieve common understanding of equivalency and of recognition/equivalency schemes?
- Why is the progressive implementation of HACCP not leading to a gradual decrease in end-product sampling and inspection?
- Is it realistic to expect a global harmonization of microbiological standards for fish and fishery products? Even at the European Union level, only one microbiological standard has been developed in 1993 for cooked crustaceans and shellfish. For all the other fish products, different national microbiological standards are applied.

On many of these issues, developing countries are at a disadvantage because of insufficient/inadequate national capacities and resources.

References

CAC (Codex Alimentarius Commission) 2001. *Food Hygiene. Basic Texts*. 2nd ed. Food and Agriculture Organization / World Health Organization, Rome, Italy.

EC (European Committee) 1991. Council Directive 91/493/EEC of 22 July laying down the health conditions for the production and placing on the market of fishery products. *Official Journal of the European Communities*. No. L268. pp.15-34.

EC (European Committee) 1994. Commission Decision of 20 May 1994 laying down detailed rules for the appiication of Council Directive 91/493/EEC, as regards own health checks on fishery products .*Official Journal of the European Communities* L 156. pp. 50 - 57

EC (European Committee) 2000. Proposal for a Regulation of the European Parliament and of the Council on the hygiene of foodstuffs, Brussels, Belgium. pp.17-42.

FAO (Food and Agriculture Organization) 1995. *Code of Conduct for Responsible Fisheries*. FAO, Rome.

FAO (Food and Agriculture Organization) 1998. *FAO Technical Guidelines for Responsible Fisheries*. No. 7. FAO, Rome.

FDA (Food and Drug Administration) 1995. *Procedures for the Safe and Sanitary Processing and Importing of Fish and Fishery Products*; Final Rule. Code of Federal Regulations, Parts 123 and 1240. Volume 60, No 242, 65095-65202.

7 PREREQUISITES TO HACCP (Hans Henrik Huss/John Ryder)

Hygiene standards and procedures usually described as Good Hygienic Practices (GHP) or Good Manufacturing Practices (GMP), have been in place for many years and constituted an essential tool in traditional food control. These concepts are still essential in a modern food control system by providing the basic environmental and operating conditions for production of safe food and thus being a requisite or foundation for HACCP in an overall food safety management programme (Figure 7.1). What is new is the concept of formalising the prerequisite programme alongside HACCP and the legal requirement in some countries (USA) of documented monitoring of certain sanitation areas.

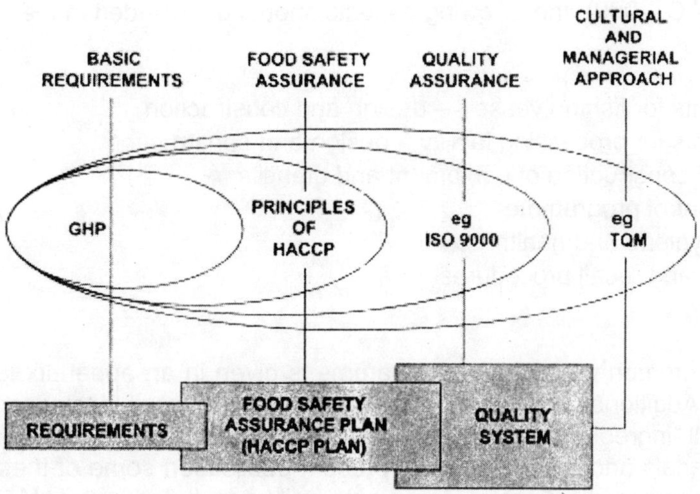

Figure 7.1 Food Safety and quality, an integrated approach (from Jouve, 1998).

In the Code of Federal Regulation (FDA, 2001) it is outlined what is covered by current GMP regulations. These include basically all procedures and practices necessary to produce safe foods.

> **Good Manufacturing Practices (GMP)**
> Those procedures for a particular manufacturing operation which practitioners of, and experts in, that operation consider to be the best available using current knowledge

There is no clear definition of the term Good Hygienic Practices (GHP). However, "food hygiene" has been defined by Codex (CAC, 2001) as "all conditions and measures necessary to ensure the safety and suitability of food at all stages of the food chain" and GHP can therefore be regarded as:

> **Good Hygienic Practices (GHP)**
> all practices regarding the conditions and measures necessary to ensure the safety and suitability of food at all stages of the food chain

The terms GMP and GHP therefore basically cover the same ground and for the purpose of this book, the term GHP will mainly be used.

Various definitions of GHP or prerequisite programmes have been proposed by national and international organizations as shown:

Prerequisite programme = Good Hygienic Practices (GHP)

Prior to the application of HACCP to any sector of the food chain that sector should be operating according to the Codex General Principles of Food Hygiene, the appropriate Codex Codes of Practices, and appropriate food safety legislation (CAC, 2001)	Practices and conditions needed prior to and during the implementation of HACCP and which are essential for food safety (WHO, 1999)	Procedures, including GMP that address operational conditions providing the foundation for the HACCP system (NACMCF, 1998)

According to the Draft Revision of the Recommended International Code of Practice for Fish and Fishery Products (CAC, 2000), the following aspects should be included in the prerequisite programme:

- requirements for fishing vessels – design and construction
- requirements for processing facility – design and construction
- design and construction of equipment and utensils
- hygiene control programme
- personal hygiene and health
- traceability and recall procedures
- training.

An example of the common prerequisite programme is given in an appendix to the publication by NACMCF (1998). Additional to the points listed by Codex it includes: Supplier control, specifications for all ingredients, chemical control and conditions for receiving, storage and shipping of raw materials and products. In the present publication some of these additional points, i.e. supplier control and specifications of ingredients, will be included in the HACCP plan and not in the prerequisite programme.

According to the US-FDA's seafood HACCP regulation (FDA, 1995), processors are required to have key sanitary conditions written into Sanitation Standard Operating Procedures (SSOPs). As outlined, SSOP are equivalent to GHP.

SSOP – Sanitation Standard Operating Procedures
the documented GMP for hygiene and sanitation required to meet the regulatory requirements for food control in the USA

They are also required to monitor these conditions and practices, correct unsanitary conditions and practices in a timely manner and maintain sanitation control records. Thus the sanitation control procedures are an integrated part of the seafood HACCP regulations, but not of the HACCP-programme. The SSOP should address at least the following conditions and practices:

- safety of water and ice
- condition and cleanliness of food contact surfaces
- prevention of cross contamination from unsanitary objects to food
- maintenance of facilities for personal hygiene
- protection of food and food contact surfaces from adulteration
- proper labelling, storage and use of toxic compounds
- control of employee health conditions
- exclusion of pests.

The written SSOP plan should explain the sanitation concerns, controls, in-plant procedures and monitoring requirements. This will demonstrate commitment to buyers and inspectors and also ensure that everyone from management to production workers understands the basics of sanitation.

In the European Union (EU, the prerequisite requirements are included in both 'horizontal' legislation such as the Hygiene Directive (EC, 1993) and 'vertical' or commodity-specific legislation such as the Directive specifying the requirement for fish processing (EC, 1991).

Many activities can be considered part of a prerequisite programme depending on the product and the actual processing conditions. For this reason, it is unlikely that two processing facilities have identical prerequisite programmes.

Although definitions of prerequisites and/or SSOPs refer mostly to operational conditions, there are also basic requirements to the processing plant and the processing environment. Thus the SSOPs are specifying the quality of the water, maintenance of hygiene facilities etc., but it is equally important that the plant has access to enough water and hygiene facilities (quantitative aspects). Below is a list of key points and activities that need to be addressed in any prerequisite programme:

The Processing Plant:

- conditions of premises
- facilities: water, ice, steam (quantitative conditions)
water treatment system (chlorination plant, waste water treatment)
sanitary facilities and installations
- equipment: boxes, containers, and machinery.

Operational conditions and procedures (GHP):

- safety of water and ice (qualitative conditions)
- cleanliness of food contact surfaces
- prevention of cross contamination from insanitary objects to food
- maintenance of facilities for personal hygiene
- protection of food from adulterants
- safe storage and use of toxic compounds
- control of employee health conditions
- pest control
- waste management
- transportation
- traceability and recall procedure
- training.

A proper and well designed prerequisite programme allows the HACCP team to focus and concentrate on the hazards directly applicable to the product and the processing procedures without undue considerations and repetition of protection from hazards from the surrounding environment. It is important to point out that the prerequisite programme certainly relates to safety and therefore is an essential part of the total quality assurance programme. Thus part of the prerequisite programme (e.g. sanitation controls) must lend itself to all aspects of a Critical Control Point (CCP) such as establishing critical limits, monitoring, corrective actions, record keeping and verification procedures. However, occasional deviation from a prerequisite programme requirement would not by itself be expected to create a food safety hazard of concern. Therefore deviations from compliance in a prerequisite programme usually do not result in reaction against the product. This is in contrast to a CCP, where any deviation from the established critical limits always leads to reaction against the product.

The prerequisite programme is a good starting point for companies who have a long way to go to implement a HACCP system. Practical experience has shown that if the general issues related to the prerequisite programme are dealt with first, the HACCP study will be much more straightforward and the resulting HACCP plan easier to manage. All issues related to GMP, hygiene and the environment will be dealt with in the prerequisite programme and only truly 'critical' control points, essential to safety of the product will be included in the HACCP plan.

7.1 The processing plant

7.1.1 Plant location, physical environment and infrastructure

Early considerations in building a new plant are the identification of a suitable location. A number of factors should be considered such as physical and geographical factors and infrastructure available.

Some of the physical needs for a plant location is a plot of adequate size (for present needs and future developments), with easy access by road, rail or water. An adequate supply of potable water and energy must be available throughout the year at a reasonable cost. Special considerations must be given to waste disposal. The plant should have proper sanitary sewers. Seafood processing plants usually contain significant amounts of organic matter which must be removed before waste water is discharged into rivers or the sea. Also solid waste handling needs careful planning, and suitable space – away from the plant – must be allocated or be available.

Assessment of pollution risk from adjacent areas must also be considered. Contaminants such as smoke, dust, ash, foul odours (e.g. neighbouring fish meal plant using poor raw material) are obvious, but even bacteria may have to be considered as airborne contaminants (e.g. proximity of a poultry rearing plant upwind may be a source of *Salmonella* spp).

The immediate physical surroundings of a seafood factory should be landscaped and present attractive appearance to the visitor (or potential buyer of products). However, this should be done in a way that rodents and birds are not attracted. Shrubbery should be at least 10 m away from buildings and a grass free strip covered with a layer of gravel or concrete should follow the outer wall of buildings. This allows for thorough inspection of walls and control of rodents. Ground immediately in front of doors and entrances should be paved to minimize dust. All areas around the plant and facilities should be well drained to prevent any standing water, where flies and microorganisms could breed and develop.

Figure 7.2
Surroundings of seafood processing plants should be clean and well kept (courtesy of Royal Greenland).

7.1.2 Buildings, construction and layout

A food processing plant shall provide (quoted from Troller, 1993):

- adequate space for equipment, installations and storage of materials
- separation of operations to avoid cross contamination
- adequate lightning and ventilation
- protection against pests.

External walls, roofs, doors and windows should be water-, insect- and rodent-proof. Internal walls, on the other hand, should be smooth, flat, resistant to wear and corrosion, impervious, easily cleanable and white or light coloured. Also the floors should ideally be impervious to spillage of product, water and disinfectants, durable to impact, resistant to disinfectants and chemicals used, slip resistant, non-toxic, non-tainting and of good appearance and easy repairable. Floors should be provided with a slope to drains to prevent formation of puddles. All openings (doors, windows, skylights, ventilators) must be adequately screened or otherwise constructed and fitted so as to prevent the entrance of any pests (flies or rodents).

Lighting should be adequate to carry out plant operations and protected so that broken glass will not be a potential hazard.

Proper ventilation is basic to good food plant sanitation. This will control condensation and help to eliminate any mould growth. Intake air should be filtered and positive air pressure maintained in the finished product area. The technical requirements, choice of materials, costs, etc. to obtain these goals may be found in a number of publications such as Shapton and Shapton (1991), Imholte (1984), Troller (1993).

The general layout and arrangement of rooms within a processing establishment is important in order to minimise the risk of contamination of the final product. A large number of bacteria (pathogens and spoilage bacteria) enter with the raw material. To avoid cross contamination it is therefore essential that raw material is received in a separate area and stored in a separate chill room. From here the sequence of processing operations should be as direct as possible – and a "straight line" process flow is regarded as most efficient (Hayes, 1992). This layout minimises the risk of recontamination of a semi-processed product.

Clear physical (e.g. a wall) segregation between "clean" and "unclean" areas is of prime importance. "Unclean" areas are those where raw material is handled and often a cleaning operation (wash) or for example a heat treatment (cooking of shrimp) is marking the point, where the process flow goes from "unclean" to "clean" areas. Thus a "clean" area is defined:

Clean area
An area where any contaminant added to the product will carry over to the final product (ICMSF, 1988)

i.e. there is no subsequent processing step that will reduce or destroy contaminating microbes.

Also cooled rooms must be separated from hot rooms where cooking, smoking, retorting etc. are taking place. Dry rooms must be separated from wet rooms and separate rooms must be provided for waste material, chemicals (cleaning and disinfection compounds, insecticides, all toxic materials), packaging materials and wood (for smoking).

The separation between the clean and unclean areas must be complete. There should be no human traffic between these areas, and equipment and utensils used in the unclean areas should never be used in the clean area. This means that there should also be separate wash and hygiene facilities for equipment and personnel in these areas. For easy identification the personnel should wear different coloured protective clothing for different operations (e.g. white in the clean and blue in the unclean).

Equally important in layout and design of food factories is to ensure that there are no interruptions and no "dead ends" in the product flow, where semiprocessed material can accumulate and remain for a long time at ambient temperature. Time/temperature conditions for products during processing are extremely important critical control points (CCPs) in order to prevent bacterial growth. This means that a steady and uninterrupted flow of **all** products is necessary in order to have full control of this critical factor. If any delays in product flow are necessary, the products should be kept chilled.

In addition, to facilitate product flow the factory layout and practices should ensure that:

- all functions should proceed with no criss-crossing and backtracking
- visitors should move from clean to unclean areas
- ingredients should move from "dirty" to "clean" areas as they become incorporated into food products
- conditioned (e.g. chilled) air and drainage should flow from "clean" to "dirty" areas
- the flow of discarded outer packing material should not cross the flow of products
- there is sufficient space for plant operations including processing, cleaning and maintenance. Space is also required for movement of materials and pedestrians
- operations are separated as necessary. There are clear advantages in minimizing the number of interior walls since this simplifies the movement of materials and employees, makes supervision easier, and reduces the area of wall that needs cleaning and maintenance (the list is partly after Shapton and Shapton, 1991).

Some of the principal requirements to an ideal establishment are outlined in Figure 7.3.

7.1.3 Facilities

Essential facilities in a seafood processing plant are:

- adequate supply of energy
- adequate supply of potable cold water. Hot water and steam must be available for cleaning and sanitation when necessary
- a suitable water treatment system where appropriate (chlorination plant, waste water treatment)
- adequate facilities for washing and disinfecting equipment
- adequate staff amenities (washing facilities, toilets, staff rooms).

Necessary hand-washing facilities must be located at the entrance to the processing areas and in all processing areas where GHP require employees to wash and disinfect their hands. They must be equipped with hand-cleaning and effective disinfection preparations and single use towels or other suitable hand-drying devices. Adequate and readily accessible toilet facilities must be available, properly located (no direct access to processing areas) and maintained in a hygienic condition and good repair.

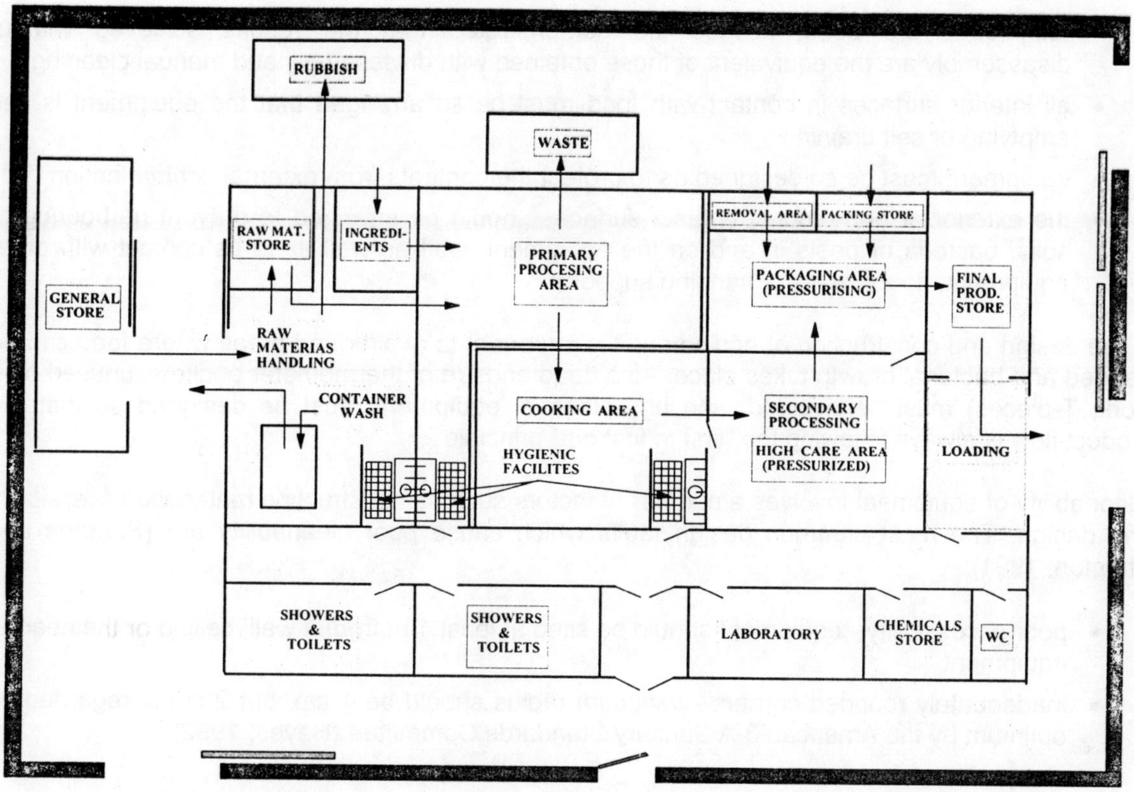

Figure 7.3. Example of a simplified factory layout (drawing by V. Popescu).

7.1.4 Utensils and equipment

A great variety of utensils and equipment is used in the fish industry. There is an abundance of advice and regulations available concerning the requirements for equipment. All of them agree that the food equipment should be non-contaminating and easy to clean. In particular, all food contact surfaces (utensils, knives, tables, cutting boards, boxes and containers, conveyer belts, gloves, aprons etc.) must be designed and of such material as to be easily cleanable. Such surfaces shall be constructed of non-toxic, non-absorbent material that is resistant to the environment, the food, cleaning and disinfecting agents. Food contact materials that should be avoided are: wood, ferrous metals, brass and galvanised metals. However, the degree of stringency in hygienic requirements must be related to the product being processed. Raw fish, for example, do not require the same standard of hygiene as cooked and peeled shrimp. Criteria for hygienic design are particularly important for equipment used in the later stages of processing and particularly after a bacteria-eliminating processing step. There are seven basic principles for hygienic design agreed upon by a working party appointed by the Food Manufacturers Federation (FMF) and Food Machinery Association FMA (FMF/FMA, 1967) as quoted by Hayes (1992):

- All surfaces in contact with food must be inert to the food under the conditions of use and must not migrate to or be absorbed by the food
- all surfaces in contact with food must be smooth and non-porous so that tiny particles of food, bacteria, or insect eggs are not caught in microscopic surface crevices and become difficult to dislodge thus becoming a potential source of contamination
- all surfaces in contact with the food must be visible for inspection or the equipment must be readily disassembled for inspection, or it must be demonstrated that routine cleaning procedures eliminate possibility of contamination from bacteria or insects
- all surfaces in contact with food must be readily accessible for manual cleaning, or if not readily accessible, then readily disassembled for manual cleaning, or if clean-in-place

techniques are used, it must be demonstrated that the results achieved without disassembly are the equivalent of those obtained with disassembly and manual cleaning

- all interior surfaces in contact with food must be so arranged that the equipment is self emptying or self draining
- equipment must be so designed as to protect the contents from external contamination
- the exterior or non-product contact surfaces should be arranged to prevent harbouring of soils, bacteria or pests in and on the equipment itself as well as in its contact with other equipment, floors, walls or hanging supports.

In the design and construction of equipment it is important to avoid dead areas where food can be trapped and bacterial growth takes place. Also dead ends (e.g. thermometer pockets, unused pipe work, T-pieces) must be avoided, and any piece of equipment must be designed so that the product flow is always following the "first in first out" principle

Cleanability of equipment involves a number of factors such as construction materials, accessibility and design. The most common design faults which cause poor cleanability are (Shapton and Shapton, 1991):

- poor accessibility - equipment should be sited at least 1 m from a wall, ceiling or the nearest equipment
- inadequately rounded corners - minimum radius should be 1 cm, but 2 cm is regarded as optimum by the American 3-A Sanitary Standards Committee (Hayes, 1992)
- sharp angles
- dead ends - including poorly designed seals.

One general problem of food processing involves the extremes of temperature, abundant use of water, development of condensations and contamination of food from overhead pipes and surfaces. Equipment design must consider this and include proper protection.

Equipment design is one of the major problems in modern food hygiene. A great number of new machines and equipment are designed and constructed without proper attention to the fact that these tools have to be cleaned and sanitised. The EC (1992) addresses machinery safety and hygiene regulations. Some of the highlights are:

- machinery containing materials intended to come in contact with food must be designed and constructed so that these materials can be cleaned before each use
- all surfaces and their joinings must be smooth, with no ridges or crevices that could harbour organic materials
- assemblies must be designed to minimise projections, edges and recesses. They should be constructed by welding or continuous bonding, with screws, screwheads and rivets used only where technically unavoidable
- contact surfaces must be readily cleaned and disinfected, and built with easily dismantled parts. Inside surfaces must be curved in a way to allow thorough cleaning
- liquid derived from foods, as well as cleaning, disinfecting and rinsing fluids should be readily discharged from machinery
- machinery must be designed and constructed to prevent liquids or living creatures – primarily insects – from entering and accumulating in areas that cannot be cleaned
- machinery must be designed and constructed so that ancillary substances, such as lubricants, do not come in contact with food.

The directive also sets out a certification system where machinery is checked for compliance and tagged with an EC mark if found to be satisfactory. Certification is not retrospective and manufacturers have two years to bring new machinery into compliance.

Apart from literature already cited, additional useful material and information on hygienic design are found in Milledge (1981) and Gould (1994).

A great variability exists in the size, of and extent of handling in, fish processing establishments. Accordingly, the hygienic requirements in, and the design of, fish handling areas may vary considerably. Quite obviously the requirements that a small establishment which is only repacking fish in ice and catering for a local market, must meet are different from the hygienic requirements of a large establishment that is processing a variety of sophisticated products including heat treated and composite products and exporting to countries all over the world. Also the requirements commonly listed in legislation and codes of practice are not equally important. The more important factors include: facilities for water supply, waste disposal and cooling and cold storage facilities and –capacity. Of less importance are buildings, ventilation, factory location, clothes changing facilities, lightning and roadways (ICMSF, 1988).

The forms shown in Appendix 1 have been utilized in assessing fish factories using the HACCP principles. Only the most important factors are evaluated and given a rating from A to C, where A and B are expressions of degrees of excellence and niceties, while a rating of C is given to a condition which is unacceptable and needs immediate correction before further operations can take place. Thus it is an attempt to "distinguish between the nice and the necessary" which is the same approach as applied in the HACCP principles.

7.2 Operational conditions including GHP

A range of operational conditions must be in place prior to the implementation of HACCP in order to control the risks or safety concerns related to the environment and the personnel. The existence and the performance of such a programme must be well documented with written procedures, assigned responsibilities, measurable acceptance criteria, defined record keeping activities and procedures to be followed when acceptance criteria are not met. A written standard format as shown below using 5 of the 7 HACCP principles is useful as a guideline or checklist and to ensure that all essential points have been considered.

Standard format

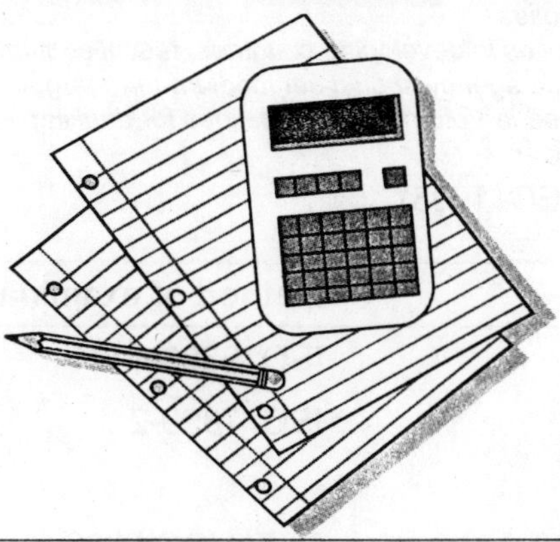

- Criteria
  what is required
- Monitoring
  what, how, when and who
- Corrective actions
  if something goes wrong
- Records
  physical evidence
- Verification
  check that it works

Figure 7.4 Standard format in assessing the prerequisite programme.

7.2.1 Safety of water and ice

Criteria for potable water

Water is used in food processing both as an ingredient and for cleaning and sanitation. Thus the quality of the water is of great importance. WHO (1993) and EC (1998) have published extensive guidelines on drinking water quality where standards for more than 60 parameters have been elaborated. The microbiological criteria suggested are shown in Tables 7.1 and 7.2.

Very often water needs to go through some form of treatment and disinfection before being suitable for use in food processing.

Water treatment

Water treatments vary from region to region depending on the water sources available. While groundwater from sedimentary aquifers has undergone extensive filtration the water from hard rock aquifers or surface water sources should be filtered as part of the water treatment in order to decrease the content of particulates, microorganisms, organic and inorganic matter.

Table 7.1 Bacteriological quality of drinking water (WHO, 1996)[1].

Organisms	Guideline value
All water intended for drinking	
E. coli or thermotolerant coliform bacteria[2,3]	Not detectable in any 100-ml sample
Treated water entering the distribution system	
E. coli or thermotolerant coliform bacteria[2]	Not detectable in any 100-ml sample
Total coliform bacteria	Not detectable in any 100-ml sample
Treated water in the distribution system	
E. coli or thermotolerant coliform bacteria[2]	Not detectable in any 100-ml sample
Total coliform bacteria	Not detectable in any 100-ml sample. In the case of large supplies, where sufficient samples are examined: Not detectable in 95% of samples taken during any 12-months period

1. *Immediate investigative action must be taken if either E. coli or total coliform bacteria are detected. The minimum action in the case of total coliform bacteria is repeat sampling; if these bacteria are detected in the repeat sample, the cause must be determined by immediate further investigation.*
2. *Although E. coli is the more precise indicator of faecal pollution, the count of thermotolerant coliform bacteria is an acceptable alternative. If necessary, proper confirmatory tests must be carried out. Total coliform bacteria are not acceptable indicators of the sanitary quality of rural water supplies, particularly in tropical areas where many bacteria of no sanitary significance occur in almost all untreated supplies.*
3. *It is recognized that, in the great majority of rural water supplies in developing countries, faecal contamination is widespread. Under these conditions, the national surveillance agency should set medium-term targets for the progressive improvement of water supplies, as recommended in Volume 3 of Guidelines for drinking-water quality.*

Table 7.2 Microbiological criteria for drinking water (EC, 1998).

Parameter	Parametric value	Method of examination
E. coli	0/100 ml	ISO, 9308-1
Enterococci Indicator	0/100 ml	ISO, 7899-2
Colony count, 22°C	[No abnormal change][1]	Pr EN ISO 6222
Coliform bacteria	0/100 ml	ISO, 9308-1

1. *Former directive 80/778/EC (EC 1980) used 100 cfu/ml as guidelines.*

Parasites are removed to a large extent by filtration. The levels of bacteria and virus also decrease markedly and the removal mechanisms are both filtration and adsorption. The cation concentration influences adsorption, i.e. increasing concentrations give rise to increased adsorption. Ca^{2+} and Mg^{2+} seem to be especially efficient. These small cations will decrease the repulsive forces between the soil particles and the microorganisms. Iron oxides also have a high affinity for viruses as well as bacteria. Ferric hydroxide impregnated lignite has even been suggested as a local filtration/adsorption media (Prasad and Chaudhuri, 1989).

The disinfection efficiency is greatly affected by

- type of disinfectant,
- type and state of microorganism,
- water quality parameters such as turbidity (or suspended solids),
- organic matter,
- some inorganic compounds,
- pH
- temperature.

The "hardness" of the water may indirectly influence disinfection since deposits may harbour microorganisms and protect them from cleaning agents and disinfectants.

By far the most widespread disinfectant is chlorine but also chloramines, chlorine dioxide, ozone and UV are being used in some instances. **Chlorine** is cheap and available in most places and monitoring the free residual levels is simple. For disinfection WHO (1996) is recommending 5 mg chlorine/litre and for effective disinfection there should be a residual concentration of free chlorine of ≥0.5 mg/l after at least 30 minutes contact time at pH <8.0. For disinfection of clean equipment up to 200 mg/l is used. To avoid corrosion a lower concentration of 50-100 mg/l and longer contact times (10-20 minutes) are often used. Current guidelines are shown in Table 7.3.

Table 7.3 Concentrations of chlorine used in fish processing.

Type of water	Residual levels	Recommendation by
Drinking water	0.5 mg/l	WHO 1996
Water for clean-up	100 mg/l	Reilly 2000
Water in contact with fish	10 mg/l	Reilly 2000
Seawater for cooking of shrimp	20 mg/l	Watson and Prout 1996

Chloramines are more stable but less microbiocidal and much less efficient in killing parasites and virus than chlorine. **Chlorine dioxide** is, if anything, more microbiocidal than chlorine, especially at high pH, but there is concern with regards to the by-products. In the case of **ozone** and **UV** there is no residual matter to monitor. Ozone seems to be very efficient in killing protozoa. The efficiency of UV disinfection decreases markedly if there is any turbidity or dispersed organic matter and problems are often encountered due to a lack of lamp maintenance. The resistance of the various microbiological organisms varies a lot. In the case of most disinfectants the order of sensitivity in decreasing order is:

vegetative bacteria > viruses > bacterial spores, acid-fast bacteria and protozoan cysts.

The sensitivity varies within groups and even within species. Indicator bacteria are unfortunately among the more sensitive microorganisms and the presence of, for example, faecal coliforms in treated, disinfected water is therefore a very clear indication that the water contains potentially pathogenic microorganisms while the absence of such indicator bacteria does not guarantee pathogen-free water.

Bacteria from nutrient-poor media as well as otherwise stressed bacteria may also exhibit greatly increased resistance. Some of the effects mentioned on the efficiency of free chlorine are illustrated in Table 7.4.

Table 7.4 Inactivation of microorganisms by free chlorine.

Organism	Water	Cl_2 residues mg/l	Temp. °C	pH	Time, min.	Reduction %	C•t[1]
E. coli	BDF[2]	0.2	25	7.0	15	99.997	ND[3]
E. coli	CDF[4]	1.5	4	?	60	99.9	2.5
E. coli + GAC[5]	CDF	1.5	4	?	60	<<10	>>60
L. pneumophila (water grown)	Tap	0.25	20	7.7	58	99	15
L. pneumophila (media grown)	Tap	0.25	20	7.7	4	99	1.1
Acid-fast							
Mycobacterium chelonei	BDF	0.3	25	7.0	60	40	>>60
Virus							
Hepatitis A	BDF	0.5	5	10.0	49.6	99.99	12.3
Hepatitis A	BDF	0.5	5	6.0	6.5	99.99	1.8
Parasites							
G. lamblia	BDF	0.2-0.3	5	6.0	-	99	54-87
G. lamblia	BDF	0.2-0.3	5	7.0	-	99	83-133
G. lamblia	BDF	0.2-0.3	5	8.0	-	99	119-192

1. *C•t product of disinfectant concentration (C) in mg/l and contact time (t) in minutes for 99% inactivation (modified after Sobsey (1989))*
2. *BDF = buffered demand free*
3. *ND = no data*
4. *CDF = chlorine demand free*
5. *GAC = granular activated carbon*

If microbes are associated with **granular material or other surfaces** the effect of a disinfectant such as chlorine decreases drastically. Attachment of *Klebsiella pneumonia* to glass surfaces may, for example, increase the resistance to free chlorine by 150-fold (Sobsey, 1989).

Organic matter may react and "consume" disinfectants such as chlorine and ozone and the presence will also interfere with UV light. The chloramines are less susceptible to organic matter.

pH is important in disinfection with chlorine and chlorine dioxide. There is greater inactivation of microorganisms at low pH in the case of chlorine and greater inactivation at high pH in the case of chlorine dioxide (Sobsey, 1989). In general, higher **temperatures** result in increased inactivation rates.

Use of non-potable water

The use of non-potable water may be necessary for water conservation purposes or desirable because of cost. Non-potable water may, for example, be surface water, sea water or chlorinated water from can cooling. Relatively clean water such as chlorinated water from can cooling operations may be used for washing cans after closing and before heat treatment, for transporting raw materials before processing (after the water has cooled off), for initial washing of boxes, for cooling of compressors, for use in fire protection lines in non-food areas and for fluming of waste material.

Separation of potable and non-potable water
It is absolutely necessary that potable and non-potable water should be in separate distribution systems which should be clearly identifiable

If potable water is used to supplement a non-potable supply the potable source must be protected against valve leakage, or back-pressure, for example, by adequate air-gaps. Back-flow, due to sudden pressure differentials or blockage of pipes, has unfortunately occurred in many systems.

Potentially contaminated water such as coastal water or surface water, should not be used at the production premises but may, if aesthetically acceptable, be used for removing waste material in places where no contact to food is possible.

Monitoring water quality
The responsible person should have continuously updated reference drawings of the pipe system and the authority to remove dead-ends. Especially in cases where a plant has undergone many changes, the piperuns, may become more and more complicated over the years. The person should also be in contact with the local waterworks and the authorities in order to be informed of special events (repairs, pollution accidents or other changes).

Water may be contaminated due to bad location of source (close to septic tanks, agriculture drainage systems), cracked or improperly sealed off piping systems or even floods and heavy rains. In the plant, contamination of the water may be due to cross-connections or backflow (back pressure or back siphonage). Where necessary, backflow should be controlled by air-gaps, vacuum breakers or check valves.

A quality monitoring scheme could consist of a plan of all the sampling points and a checklist describing what to examine and why, the frequency, who takes the sample, who does the analysis, what is the limit (value, tolerance) and what to do in case of deviation (Poretti 1990). If the water is obviously polluted there is of course no reason to wait for analytical results. The sampling frequency and the range of parameters will vary with the circumstances and a special monitoring program may be needed after repairs, or when using new water supplies, for example. A minimum monitoring program for water quality could be:

- measurement of free chlorine daily
- measurement of total viable count and coliforms on a weekly basis.

The technical procedures describing the analyses for the common indicator organisms are given in standard textbooks. The EC Directive (EC, 1998) specifies some methods and equipment to be used. The values used by the company should refer to the specific method employed and the recommendations should include how to sample (tap flow, volume, sampling vessel, labelling, etc.) and how to handle and examine the sample. Even though the commonly used methods for detecting, for example, faecal coliforms are standard analyses, faulty handling of the samples often occurs. Samples should be processed within 24 hours or less, be kept cool but not frozen (preferably below 5°C), and be kept in the dark. The impact of sunlight can be very dramatic, causing false negative results (Knøchel, 1990).

Model prerequisite programme: Safety of water and ice	
Goal:	Water that comes into contact with food or food contact surfaces or is used in the manufacturing of ice is from a safe and sanitary source or is treated to make it safe
Criteria:	Water must pass potability standards (e.g. to *E. coli*, Enterococci, Coliform 0/100 mL Aerobic Plate Count (22°C) 10^2 cfu/ml (guide level) residual free chlorine 0.2-0.5 mg/l in water distribution system max 10 mg chlorine/l in water, that comes in contact with fish products
Monitoring:	When public water supply is used, the official records from the water works suffice. Water from own water supply: Check for residual chlorine: daily Check for microbiological contamination: A water sampling schedule must be worked out. Sampling must follow standard microbiological procedures. Responsible person is: chief, Q.A.
Corrective action:	Actions to be taken when criteria is exceeded must be outlined, e.g. adjusting water treatment, stop of production if water is contaminated, search for source of contamination
Records:	Records of all sampling, testing and actions must be kept for two years. Daily hygiene record form (chlorine)
Verification:	Once every year, water samples are tested by certified laboratory

If chlorination is used for disinfection monitoring of the free chlorine level is the simplest way of checking the water treatment and should be performed most often (e.g. on a daily basis). Simple laboratory methods and commercial dip-sticks are now available for on-the-spot measurements (e.g. Merchoquant Chlor 100 from Merck). The microbiological indicator parameters may be checked less frequently. If disinfection systems that leave no residuals are being used, then checking of equipment should be done regularly. The performance of the systems may be monitored at weekly intervals using indicator bacteria measurements. Above is a model of a control programme for this particular requirement.

7.2.2 Cleanliness of food contact surfaces

All food contact surfaces should be adequately and routinely cleaned and disinfected. Cleaning and disinfection belong to the most important operations in today's food industries. In the US, the term sanitation is sometimes used to describe the disinfection process. In some cases, sanitation may refer to the whole cleaning and disinfection process.

> **Food contact surfaces are**
>
> - Those surfaces that contact human food and those surfaces from which drainage onto the food or onto surfaces that contact the food ordinarily occurs during the normal course of operations
> - Typical food contact surfaces include utensils, knives, tables, cutting boards, fish boxes, conveyor belts, ice makers, ice storage bins, gloves, aprons, etc.

The cleaning and disinfection process can be divided into clearly distinct operations. However, these are linked firmly together in that the final result will not be acceptable unless all processes are carried out correctly.

Sanitation
means adequately treating food contact surfaces by a process that is effective in destroying vegetative cells of microorganisms of public health significance, and substantially reducing numbers of other undesirable microorganisms, but without adversely affecting the product or its safety for the consumer (FDA, 2001)

The various steps included in a complete cycle are outlined below.

- remove food products, clear the area of bins, containers, etc.
- dismantle equipment to expose surfaces to be cleaned
- remove small equipment, parts and fittings to be cleaned into a specified area. Cover sensitive installations to protect them against water etc.
- clear the area, machines and equipment of food residues by flushing with water (cold or hot) and by using brushes, brooms, etc.
- apply the cleaning agent and use mechanical energy (e.g. pressure or brushes) as required
- rinse thoroughly with water to completely remove the cleaning agent after the appropriate contact time (residues may completely inhibit the effect of disinfection)
- control of cleaning
- disinfect with chemical disinfectants or heat
- rinse the disinfection chemicals off with water after the appropriate contact time. This final rinse is not needed for some compounds e.g. H_2O_2 based formulations that decompose rapidly
- after the final rinse, reassemble equipment and allow to dry
- control of cleaning and disinfection
- in some cases it would be good practice to re-disinfect (e.g. with hot water or low levels of chlorine) just before production starts.

Cleaning
In the preparatory phase, the processing area is cleared of remaining products, spills, containers and other loose items. Machines, conveyors, etc. are dismantled so that all locations where microorganisms can accumulate become accessible for cleaning and disinfection. Electrical installations and other sensitive systems should be protected against water and the chemicals used.

AVOID starting the cleaning operation by splashing water (using the pressure hose) on floors and machinery before all food products are removed.

Before use of the cleaning agent, a gross food debris removal procedure should be carried out by brushing, scraping or similar action. All surfaces should be further prepared for the use of cleaning agents by a pre-rinse activity, preferably with cold water so as not to coagulate the proteins. Hot water may be used to remove fat or sugars in cases where protein is not present in significant amounts.

Completion of the preparatory work should be checked and recorded, as with any other process to ensure the quality of the complete cycle of cleaning and disinfection.

Cleaning is undertaken to remove all undesirable materials (food residues, microorganisms, scales, grease, etc.) from the surfaces of the plant and the process equipment, leaving surfaces clean, as determined by sight and touch and with no residues from cleaning agents.

Microorganisms present will either be incorporated in the various materials or attached to the surfaces as biofilms. The latter will not be removed completely by cleaning, but experience has shown that a majority of the microorganisms will be removed. However, there will still be some left to be inactivated during the disinfection. Bacteria in biofilm can be up to 1,000 times more resistant to common disinfectants compared to when in the free state.

The effectiveness of a cleaning procedure in general depends upon:

- the type and amounts of debris to be removed
- the chemical and physio-chemical properties of the cleaning agent (such as acid or alkali strength, surface activity, etc.) at the concentration, temperature and exposure time used
- the mechanical energy applied e.g. turbulence of cleaning solutions in pipes, stirring effect, impact of water jet "elbow-grease", etc.
- the condition of the surface to be cleaned.

Some surfaces, e.g. corroded steel and aluminium galvanised metal can not be cleaned easily which means that disinfection also becomes very inefficient. The same applies to other surfaces, e.g. wood, rubber, etc. The preferred material is high quality stainless steel.

The types of residues to be removed in food plants, will mainly be the following:

- organic matter, such as protein, fat and carbohydrate. These are most effectively removed by strong alkaline detergents (especially caustic soda, NaOH)
- inorganic matter, such as salts of calcium and other metals. In beer stone, milk stone, etc. salts are encrusted with protein residues. These are most effectively removed by an acid cleaning agent
- biofilms, formed by bacteria, moulds, yeast and algae can be removed by cleaning agents that are effective against organic matter.

Most cleaning agents work faster and more effectively at higher temperatures, so it can be profitable to clean at a high temperature. Cleaning is often carried out at 60-80°C in areas where it pays, energy-wise, to use such high temperatures.

Water is used as a solvent for all cleaning and sterilising agents and also for intermediate rinses and the final rinse of equipment. The chemical and microbiological quality of the water is important for the efficiency of the cleaning procedures as already described in a previous section of this Chapter. In principle, water used for cleaning must be potable.

Hard water contains a large amount of calcium and magnesium ions. When the water is heated, any calcium and magnesium salts will precipitate as insoluble salts. Also, some cleaning agents, especially alkalis, can precipitate calcium and magnesium salts.

Apart from reducing the effectiveness of detergents hard water leads to the formation of deposits or scales. Scales are not only unsightly but objectionable for several reasons:

- they harbour and protect microorganisms
- they reduce the rate of heat exchange on heat exchange surfaces. This could lead to under-processing, under-pasteurisation or under-sterilisation
- presence of scales tends to increase corrosion.

The formation of scales can be reduced by addition of chelating and sequestering agents, which bind calcium and magnesium in insoluble complexes. However, it is advisable to prevent precipitations by softening the water before it is used for cleaning. Softening can be effectively achieved by ion exchange, in which the calcium and magnesium ions are replaced by sodium ions, the salts of which are soluble. A modern, and more costly, method of softening water is by means of reverse osmosis.

To be effective, a suitable **detergent** or **cleaning agent** must be applied. The ideal detergent would be characterized by the following properties:

- it possesses sufficient chemical power to dissolve the material to be removed
- it has a surface tension low enough to penetrate into cracks and crevices; it should be able to disperse the loosened debris and hold it in suspension
- if used with hard water, it should possess water softening and calcium salt dissolving properties to prevent precipitation and build-up of scale on surfaces
- it rinses freely from the plant, leaving this clean and free from residues, which could harm the products and affect sterilisation negatively
- it does not cause corrosion or other deterioration of the plant. It is recommended always to check by consulting the supplier of machines, etc.
- it is not hazardous for the operator
- it is compatible with the cleaning procedure being used, whether manual or mechanical
- if solid, it should be easily soluble in water and its concentration easily checked
- it complies with legal requirements concerning safety and health as well as biodegradability
- it is reasonably economical to use.

A detergent with all these characteristics does not exist. So one must, for each individual cleaning operation, select a compromise by choosing a usable cleaning agent and water treatment additives so that the combined detergent has the properties that are most important for the procedure concerned.

All cleaning methods, including foams and soaks, require sufficient contact time to fully loosen and suspend soils. A moderately alkaline detergent, which is normally used in plants processing high protein foods such as fish, will typically require 10-15 minutes to fully loosen most processing soils.

Disinfection

Traditionally, the terms "disinfection" and "disinfectants" are used to describe procedures and agents used in food industries to ensure a microbiologically acceptable standard of hygiene. It is realised that the procedures and agents described will rarely introduce "sterility" i.e. total absence of viable microorganisms.

Disinfection can be effected by physical treatments such as heat, U.V. irradiation, or by means of chemical compounds.

Use of heat in the form of steam or hot water is a very safe method and a widely used method of disinfection. The most commonly used chemicals for disinfection are shown in Table 7.5.

With the use of chemical disinfectants, the death rate for microorganisms depends, among other things, upon the agent's microbiocidal properties, concentration, temperature and pH as well as the degree of contact between disinfectant and microorganisms. Good contact is obtained by stirring, turbulence, smooth surfaces and low surface tension. As with heat disinfection, different microorganisms show different resistance to chemical sterilants. Contamination by inorganic or organic matter can reduce the death rate considerably.

Cleaning precedes disinfection
An effective disinfection can only be obtained after an effective cleaning

The desirable plant disinfectant would be characterized by the following properties:

- it has sufficient anti-microbial effect to kill the microorganisms present in the available time and should have a sufficiently low surface tension to ensure good penetration into pores and cracks
- it rinses freely from the plant, leaving this clean and free from residues which could harm the products
- it does not lead to development of resistant strains or any surviving microorganisms
- it does not cause corrosion or other deterioration of the plant. It is recommended that the suppliers, of machines etc. be asked before chlorine or other aggressive disinfectant are used
- it is not hazardous to the operator
- it is compatible with the disinfection procedure being used, whether manual or mechanical
- if solid, it should be easily soluble in water
- its concentration is easily checked
- it is stable for extended storage periods
- it complies with legal requirements concerning safety and health as well as biodegradability
- it is reasonably economical in use.

It will often be necessary to combine disinfectants with additives in order to obtain the required properties. The following are among the most widely used disinfectants and shall be described briefly.

Chlorine is one of the most effective and widely used disinfectants. It is available in several forms, for instance sodium hypochlorite solutions, chloramines and other chlorine containing organic compounds. Gaseous chlorine and chlorine dioxide are also used. Chlorinated disinfectants at a concentration of 200 ppm free chlorine are very active and have a cleaning effect. The disinfectant effect is considerably decreased when organic residues are present. The compounds dissolved in water will produce hypochlorous acid, HOCl, which is the active disinfecting agent, acting by oxidation. In solution it is very unstable, particularly in acid solution where toxic chlorine gas will be liberated. Furthermore, solutions are more corrosive at low pH.

Unfortunately, the germicidal activity is considerably better in acid than in alkaline solution, thus the working pH should be chosen as a compromise between efficiency and stability. Organic chlorinated disinfectants are generally more stable but require longer contact times. When used in the proper range of values (200 ppm free chlorine), chlorinated disinfectants in solutions at ambient temperatures are non-corrosive to high quality stainless steel, but they are corrosive to other less resistant materials.

Table 7.5 Types of disinfectants (based on anon. 2000).

Disinfectant	Forms/ Description	Advantages	Disadvantages
Chlorine	Hypochlorites Chlorine gas Organic chorine, e.g., chloramines	- Kills most types of microorganisms - Less affected by hard water than some - Does not form films - Effective at low temperatures - Relatively inexpensive - Concentration easily determined by test strips	- May corrode metals and weaken rubber - Irritating to skin, eyes and throat - Unstable, dissipates quickly - Liquid chlorine loses strength in storage - pH sensitive
Iodophors	Iodine dissolved in surfactant and acid	- Kills most types of microorganisms - Less affected by organic matter than some - Less pH sensitive than chlorine - Concentration determined by test strips - Solution colour indicates active sanitiser	- May stain plastics and porous materials - Inactivated above 50°C - Reduced effectiveness at alkaline pH - More expensive than hypochlorites - May be unsuitable for CIP[1] due to foaming
Quaternary Ammonium Compounds	Benzalkonium chloride and related compounds, sometimes called quats or QACs	- Non corrosive - Less affected by organic matter than some - Residual antimicrobial activity if not rinsed - Can be applied as foam for visual control - Effective against *Listeria monocytogenes* - Effective for odour control Concentration determined by test strips	- Inactivated by most detergents - May be ineffective against certain organisms - May be inactivated by hard water - Effectiveness varies with formulation - Not as effective at low temp. as some - May be unsuitable for CIP due to foaming
Acid-Anionic	Combination of certain surfactants and acids	- Sanitize and acid rinse in one step - Very stable - Less affected by organic matter than some - Can be applied at high temperature - Not affected by hard water	- Effectiveness varies with microorganism - More expensive than some - pH sensitive (use below pH 3.0) - Corrode some metals - May be unsuitable for CIP due to foaming
Peroxy Compounds	Acetic acid and hydrogen peroxide combined to form peroxyacetic acid	- Best against bacteria in biofilms - Kills most types of microorganisms - Relatively stable in use - Effective at low temperatures - Meets most discharge requirements - Low foaming; suitable for CIP	More expensive than some - Inactivated by some metals/organics - May corrode some metals - Not as effective as some against yeasts and moulds

Disinfectant	Forms/ Description	Advantages	Disadvantages
Carboxylic Acid	Fatty acids combined with other acids; sometimes called fatty acid sanitizers	- Kills most types of bacteria - Sanitize and acid rinse in one step - Low foaming, suitable for CIP - Stable in presence of organic matter - Less affected by hard water than some	- Inactivated by some detergents - pH sensitive (use below pH 3.5) - Less effective than chlorine at low temp. - May damage non-stainless steel materials - Less effective against yeasts and moulds than some
Chlorine Dioxide	Á gas formed onsite and dissolved in solution or by acidification of chlorite and chlorate salts	- Kills most type of microorganisms - Stronger oxidiser (sanitizer) than chlorine - Less affected by organic matter than some - Less corrosive than chlorine - Less pH sensitive than some	- Unstable and cannot be stored - Potentially explosive and toxic - Relatively high initial equipment cost
Ozone	A gas formed onsite and dissolved in solution	- Kills most type of microorganisms - Stronger oxidiser (sanitizer) than chlorine and chlorine dioxide	- Unstable and cannot be stored - May corrode metals and weaken rubber - Potentially toxic - Inactivated by organic matter (similar to chlorine)
Hot Water / Heated Solutions	Water at 77-88°C	- Kills most types of microorganisms - Penetrates irregular surfaces - Suitable for CIP - Relatively inexpensive	- May form films or scale on equipment - Burn hazard - Contact time sensitive

1. CIP = cleaning in place

Iodophors contain iodine, bound to a carrier, usually a non-ionic compound, from which the iodine is released for sterilisation. Normally the pH is brought down to 2-4 by means of phosphoric acid. Iodine has its maximum effect at this pH range.

Iodophors are active disinfectants with a broad antimicrobial spectrum like chlorine. They are inactivated by organic material. Concentrations corresponding to approximately 25 ppm free iodine will be effective.

Commercial formulations are often acidic making them able to dissolve scales. They can be corrosive depending on the formulation and they should not be used above 45°C as free iodine may be liberated. If residues of product and caustic cleaning agents are left in dead ends and similar places, this may, in combination with iodophores, cause very unpleasant "phenolic" off-flavours.

Hydrogen peroxide and **peracetic acid** are effective disinfectants acting by oxidation and with a broad antimicrobial spectrum. Diluted solutions may be used alone or in combination for disinfection of clean surfaces. They lose their activity more readily than other disinfectants in the presence of organic substances and they rapidly lose their activity with time. They should be used in concentration of 200-300 ppm.

Quaternary ammonium compounds are cationic surfactants. They are effective fungicides and bactericides but are often less effective against Gram negative bacteria. To avoid development of resistant strains of microorganisms, these compounds should only be used by alternating with the use of other types of disinfectants.

Due to their low surface tension, they have good penetrating properties and for the same reason, they can be difficult to rinse off. If quaternary ammonium compounds come into contact with anion-active detergents, they will precipitate and become inactivated. Mixing or successive use of these two types of chemicals must therefore be avoided. They can be used in concentrations of 200 ppm on food contact surfaces. Table 7.6 summarizes the concentrations of commonly used disinfectants.

Table 7.6 Disinfectant concentrations commonly used in food plants (anon., 2000).

	Concentrations of disinfectants commonly used in food plants		
Disinfectant	**Food contact surface**	**Non-food contact surfaces**	**Plant water**
Chlorine	100-200[1] ppm	400 ppm	3-10 ppm
Iodine	25[1] ppm	25 ppm	
Quats	200[1] ppm	400-800 ppm	
Chlorine dioxide	100-200[1,2] ppm	100-200[2] ppm	1-3[2] ppm
Peroxyacetic acid	200-315[1] ppm	200-315 ppm	

1. *The higher end of the listed range indicates the maximum concentration permitted without a required rinse (surfaces must drain)*
2. *Includes mix of oxychloro compounds*

Monitoring of cleaning and disinfection

Effective cleaning is a prerequisite for an efficient disinfection. This indicates the importance of controlling cleaning. The most important control is sensory (visual, touch, smell) inspection to demonstrate:

- that all cleaned surfaces are visibly clean
- that all surfaces, by feeling, are free from food residues, scales and other materials and, by smelling, free from undesirable odours

Further, the concentrations and pH-values of cleaning agents, the temperatures, if hot cleaning is used, and the contact times should be monitored and registered. pH measurements, or similar testing, of rinse water may be used to ensure that the cleaning agent is removed so that it will not interfere with the disinfectant. These controls are all rapid and allow immediate decisions to be made as to whether cleaning should be repeated, partly or completely, or to proceed to the process of disinfection. All actions shall be registered as part of the Quality System. At this stage, microbiological control serves no real purpose. Firstly biofilms and surviving microorganisms are likely to be present and secondly, reliable rapid methods are not available.

Control of disinfection will be the final control of the complete cycle of cleaning and disinfection. Provided cleaning has been controlled effectively as described above, control of disinfection will be effective when the following conditions are met:

- control of time and temperature conditions for disinfection by heat
- control of active concentrations of chemical disinfectant
- control that all surfaces to be disinfected are covered by the disinfectant
- control of contact time.

The above controls should be documented and the observations reported and registered as required in standard Quality Systems.

Microbiological testing and control serve the purpose of verification. Various techniques are available, but none are ideal and they are not "real time" methods. "Real time" methods are highly desirable for control of cleaning and disinfection. Methods (bacterial counting) that require overnight incubation are too late to correct critical situations. However, if conducted at regular intervals and planned to cover all critical points, useful information from microbiological control can be accumulated with time. Various methods are used and shall be mentioned briefly.

- swab testing. This is the most usual technique and one of the better ones. By use of a sterile swab of cotton-wool, part of the disinfected surface is swabbed, and the bacteria now on the swab are transferred to a diluent for determination of colony forming units in standard agar substrates. Swabs are especially useful in places where other control methods can only be used with difficulty i.e. pockets, valves, etc.
- final rinse water. Membrane filtration of rinse water and incubation on agar substrate is a very sensitive technique for control of CIP systems as well as other cleaning and disinfection systems, where a rinse can be applied
- direct surface plates. In these methods petri dishes or contact slides with selective or general purpose agar media are applied to the surface to be examined, followed by incubation and counting of colony forming units. These techniques can only be applied to flat surfaces, which is a limiting factor
- bioluminometric assay of ATP. This is almost a "real time" method giving the answer within minutes. It is very sensitive and can be combined with swabbing for collection of microorganisms from surfaces. The method is rather non-specific, and it may not be able to distinguish between microorganisms and food residues. However, if applied under defined conditions it may prove useful and superior to the conventional methods because it provides the answer in minutes.

Regardless of the technique used, it is valuable to know from the verification analyses that the system was working when it was established. There is also a value in knowing trends as expressed in the verification results recorded. The objective of studying trends and conducting the microbiological control of cleaning and disinfection will be to take corrective action before loss of control of products or processes occur.

Model prerequisite programme: Cleanliness of food contact surfaces

Criteria:	A permanent cleaning and disinfection schedule must be drawn up specifying the frequency of cleaning and disinfection at each location. Food contact surfaces are most important, but non-food contact surface must also be kept clean. In addition, good housekeeping of all areas including employee restrooms and locker rooms is necessary. The following procedure should be followed in cleaning and disinfection procedures: - pre-cleaning, preparation of area for cleaning. - pre-rinse or soak in tanks. - cleaning – with appropriate detergent (type of detergent, concentration, contact time must be specified). - rinse - disinfection – application of approved chemical (name disinfectant, concentration, contact time). - post rinse. A full cleaning schedule must be applied at the end of a working day on all locations, but part of the schedule can be omitted in a "clean as you go" policy.
Monitoring:	What: Cleanliness of food contact surfaces, concentrations of cleaning and disinfection agents, cleaning operation, contact time for sanitation chemicals. How: Visual inspection, smelling for offensive odours, feeling for greasy surfaces. Check labels. When: Daily. Who: Foreman.
Corrective action:	Repeat operation
Records:	All observations and actions. Daily sanitation control records.
Verification:	Microbiological testing of food contact surfaces, review of records and procedures.

7.2.3 Prevention of cross-contamination

A key element in any hygiene programme is the prevention of cross-contamination, i.e. contamination of final product with any hazards originating in the raw material or the processing environment. This is of particular concern if the final product is a ready-to-eat product that is not usually cooked before being eaten. There are many possible routes of contamination of the final product as shown in Figure 7.5. It is not always possible to identify the most important routes and all of them must be included in a preventive programme.

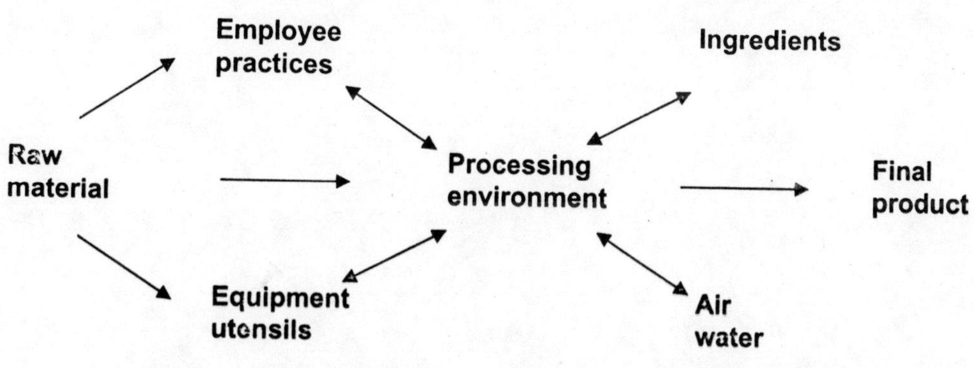

Figure 7.5 Routes of contamination in a seafood processing plant.

The main preventive measures to avoid cross-contamination are:

- a clear and effective separation of raw material and cooked or ready-to-eat products during processing, handling and storage (see section 7.1)
- proper employee hygiene, clothing and handling practices
- restricted and controlled traffic or movement about the plant (employees, product, equipment)
- food handling and processing areas and equipment adequately cleaned and disinfected (see section 7.2.2)
- use of potable water (see section 7.2.1).

Personnel can contaminate the final product directly with pathogens from their skin or hands, digestive system or respiratory tract. They can also function as an intermediary vector carrying bacteria, virus, etc. from raw material or the environment to the product. For this reason, employee hygiene and food handling practices are very important – particularly when ready-to-eat products are handled. Below some points on personal hygiene to consider in this part of the prerequisite programme:

- clean protective clothing, footwear, hair- and beardnets, caps or other effective hair restraints must be issued by the company and should be worn in the processing area only
- nail varnish, false nails and eyelashes, watches and jewellery should not be worn in processing area
- personal items (handbags, shopping bags, etc.) must not be taken into processing area
- eating food or sweets, chewing gum, drinking beverages or using tobacco should not occur in any processing area and spitting should be forbidden
- an effective hand washing program should be implemented, including:
    - how to wash hands:
        - wet hands with warm water
        - lather and rub using warm water
        - rinse
        - dry with disposable towels or
        - disinfect by dipping in sanitizing solution (iodine or 100 ppm chlorine).
    - when to wash hands:
        - before starting work – in the mornings and after breaks
        - after visiting the toilet
        - after coughing and sneezing
        - after handling soiled equipment

Model prerequisite programme: Prevention of cross-contamination	
Criteria:	Cooked, ready-to-eat products must be physically separated from raw materials during processing and storage Waste must be removed by the most direct route or at least downstream out of the processing-area. Care must be taken to avoid any possible contact with food products No traffic of employees, products or utensils between clean and less clean areas is permitted Food handling and processing areas must be clean and orderly at start-up Description of dress-code Description of hand-washing requirements
Monitoring:	Adequate separation of raw and cooked or ready-to-eat products and processing activities Cleanliness of food handling areas Employee hygiene, handling practices and traffic in the plant The monitoring should be carried out continuously by all supervisors in their areas of responsibility
Corrective action:	Stop all activities until areas or utensils are cleaned and disinfected or faulty procedures are corrected Further training of personnel If contamination of cooked or ready-to-eat products is likely to have happened, these products must be identified and segregated until a decision is made on their safety
Records:	Daily sanitation records – including specified time for checks on cleaning and disinfection procedures All observations and actions

7.2.4 Maintenance of facilities for personal hygiene

According to the US Federal Seafood HACCP regulations (FDA, 1995) the condition of the personal hygiene facilities should be monitored separately.

The number and location of toilets and hand-washing facilities needs consideration. An adequate number of readily accessible toilet facilities must be available and maintained in a hygienic condition and good repair. Hand-washing facilities must be strategically and conveniently located near toilets and at entrances to the processing areas. Wash basin taps must not be hand-operated.

Hand-washing facilities should be dedicated to hand-washing only and never be used for washing dishes, utensils or equipment. Similarly, hand-washing should never take place in sinks or tanks used for food preparation. Hand-washing facilities should include:

- liquid soap in a dispenser
- hot water (~40-43°C)
- disposable paper towels or air blowers (- refuse receptacles if needed)
- hand disinfection facilities (bowls for hand dip).

Typically hand disinfectants are composed of chlorine compounds (100-200 ppm chlorine) or iodine compounds (20-25 ppm iodine).

Model prerequisite programme: Maintenance of facilities for personal hygiene	
Criteria:	Toilets and hygiene areas kept cleaned and in good repair Hand-washing and disinfection facilities must be located at toilets and at the entrance to all processing areas and maintained in a good condition The facilities must be equipped with liquid soap, disposable towels and effective disinfectant dips
Monitoring:	Daily check of facilities for cleanliness and good repair. More than one daily check for concentration of disinfectant dip One person (e.g. the Q.A. supervisor) should be designated to carry out this monitoring
Corrective action:	Immediate repair if facilities are broken down or not functioning properly Replenishing of supplies if lacking or concentration is inadequate
Records:	The daily Hygiene Record form should include all observations made and actions carried out

7.2.5 Protection of food from adulterants

Food, food contact surfaces and food packaging material must be protected from adulteration with filth, lubricants, fuel, pesticides, cleaning compounds, disinfection agents, condensates, floor splash and other chemical, physical and biological agents. Thus it is clear, that this part of the programme goes beyond safety aspects addressing also contamination with filth.

Model prerequisite programme: Protection of foods from adulteration	
Criteria:	Food, food contact surfaces and food packaging material must be protected from adulteration with lubricants fuel, pesticides, cleaning compounds, disinfection agents, condensate and other chemical, physical and biological contaminants. Specify chemicals to be used in the facility and the requirements to handling and storage (refer to section 7.2.6)
Monitoring:	Daily check at start-up and every four hours during work hours by supervisor to observe on conditions
Corrective action:	Any unsatisfactory activity must be corrected. Possible correction could be to erect a screen to protect a product, correct air flow and ventilation to prevent condensation on the food or to reinforce training of employee
Records:	Must be kept on all actions. A daily hygiene record is kept

Processors need to be aware of all avenues that could cause the food to be adulterated. The maintenance department needs to establish a regular maintenance programme for the facility's ventilation system to avoid formation of condensation. Also floors must be maintained in good order to avoid formation of pools of water and supervisors must ensure that no floor splash occurs during processing or when food is exposed.

Only food grade lubricants should be used on all moving machinery parts that come into direct contact with food. Only approved chemicals for cleaning, disinfection, pesticides and rodenticides should be uses in the processing plant.

7.2.6 Proper labelling, safe storage and use of toxic compounds

All food processing plants use chemicals such as cleaning agents, disinfectants, rodenticides, insecticides, machine lubricants and various additives. These chemicals must always be used according to the manufacturer's instructions, have proper labelling and be stored in a safe manner that protects against contamination of food or food contact surfaces. Original containers (stock solutions) must be kept in a separate room for this purpose only. Working solutions of cleaning and/or disinfection compounds should be in the processing area only when in use – and when no food products are handled.

Model prerequisite programme: Safe storage and use of toxic compounds	
Criteria:	List all chemicals used in the plant, manufacturer's instruction must be followed when used. Specify storage conditions (separate room with limited access)
Monitoring:	Check labels Storage conditions and check if manufacturer's instructions are followed. Monitoring daily and visual by supervisor
Corrective action:	Toxic compounds without proper identification or documentation are discarded (or returned to supplier) Improperly placed or stored toxic compounds are removed to correct area Retraining of employee in case of misuse of toxic compounds
Records:	Daily hygiene control records

7.2.7 Control of employee health conditions

It is well known that poor personal hygiene has been implicated in a number of food-borne disease outbreaks. Even apparently healthy persons may carry pathogens, which can spread and contaminate food. However, persons showing symptoms such as: diarrhoea, vomiting, open skin sores, boils, fever, jaundice or discharge from ear, eye or nose, are likely to be infected with pathogens that can be transmitted to food. A food worker displaying any of these symptoms should therefore be excluded or restricted from food handling areas.

Model prerequisite programme: Control of employee health conditions	
Criteria:	No person suffering from any communicable disease should be engaged in handling of fish or fish products Before starting to work at the factory, for the first time, the employee should produce a medical certificate The new employee should be trained on GHP
Monitoring:	Supervisors check daily for infected lesions or signs of any communicable disease
Corrective action:	Workers who represent a potential risk are re-assigned to non-food contact jobs
Records:	Daily hygiene control records

7.2.8 Pest control

This programme relates to pests such as rodents, birds and insects as well as dogs and cats. These pests can carry a variety of human disease agents, which can be introduced into the processing environment. For this reason, the presence of pests in a processing plant is unacceptable.

A pest control programme should be based on three principles:

- exclusion or preventing access
- restriction by avoiding to create an environment conducive to pests
- destruction and eradication. This part of the programme must be carried out by qualified personnel as strong poison may be handled. An outside, specialist company is often contracted to carry out this part of the programme.

Model prerequisite programme: Pest control	
Criteria:	Presence of rodents, insects and other animals on the premises <u>is not</u> allowed in any area of the processing plant An effective plan for pest control will be in place and includes: - elimination of harbourage and attractant areas (Rapid removal of waste see section 7.2.9) - exclusion. All openings (doors, windows, ventilators) must be filled with fly protection - extermination. Company XX is hired for extermination of rodents
Monitoring:	What: Inspection of plant for presence or trace of pests (droppings), attractant areas, exclusion arrangements (screening of openings, windows etc.) and of rodent traps How: Visual When: Daily Who: Q.A. manager
Corrective action:	Immediate repair of defect screenings, removal of attractant areas
Records:	All actions and observations

7.2.9 Waste management

All offals and other waste materials must be removed from the processing area and premises on a regular basis. Separate facilities for containment of offal and waste material must be provided for this purpose only and those facilities should be properly maintained. A hygienic waste water disposal system must be in operation. Sewage disposal shall be made into an adequate sewerage system or disposed of through other adequate means.

Model prerequisite programme: Waste management	
Criteria:	Offal, waste and sewerage will be contained in closed containers, separate rooms or connected directly to a public septic system and be removed from the premises on a regular basis Any container, room etc. used for waste will be marked accordingly
Monitoring:	What: Inspection of waste management utensils and procedures How: Visual When: Daily Who: Processing manager
Corrective action:	Repair of system
Records:	Daily hygiene report

7.2.10 Storage and transportation

The conditions for storage and transportation must be as such to minimise contamination and damage of the fish. Storage areas and vehicles used for the transportation of fish and fish products must be clean. They must provide the fish with protection against contamination from dust and exposure to higher temperatures. Where appropriate, vehicles must be fitted with refrigeration and equipment to maintain fish at 0°C (chilling) or ≤-18°C (freezing). Below is an example of this part in a prerequisite programme.

Model prerequisite programme: Storage and transportation	
Criteria:	Storage rooms must be kept clean and orderly and equipped to maintain products at chilled (<+5°C) or frozen temperature (<-18°C) Vehicles for transportation of fish and fish products should be designed and constructed so the fish is protected against contamination and exposure to higher temperatures. Where appropriate vehicles must be equipped to maintain chilled (≤5°C) or freezer temperature (≤-18°C)
Monitoring:	What: Inspection of rooms and vehicles, recording of temperature How: Visual When: Daily (store-rooms) and all shipments Who: Loading foreman
Corrective action:	Correct room temperatures or remove products Replacement of vehicle
Records:	All actions and observations Documented cleaning and disinfection procedures

7.2.11 Traceability and recall procedures

A system for tracing all raw materials and finished products is a necessary component in a prerequisite programme. No process is fail-safe and traceability that includes lot identification is essential to an effective recall procedure. A crisis response plan should be in place to handle any incidents.

Appropriate records of processing, production and distribution should be kept and retained for a period that exceeds the shelf life of the product. Where there is a health hazard, products produced under similar conditions may be withdrawn. The need for public warning should be considered. Once retrieved, products must be held under supervision until the manner of product disposition e.g. rework or destruction has been determined.

Model prerequisite programme: Traceability and recall procedures

Criteria:	Each container of fish and fish product will be clearly marked to identify producer/processor and lot. Written procedures for recall of products and possible information to the public are laid down
Monitoring:	What: Inspection of packaging material and identification labels How: Visual When: Daily Who: Processing supervisor
Corrective action:	When there is a health hazard, products produced under similar conditions may be withdrawn. The need for public warnings should be considered. Recalled products to be held under supervision until decision on further action (destroyed, processed, used for other purposes)
Records:	Records of processing and production must be kept and retained for a period that exceeds the shelf life of the products All other actions and observations must be recorded
Verification:	Checks of final products in storage for proper labelling

7.2.12 Training

All employees should receive documented training on personal hygiene, GHP, cleaning and disinfection procedures, product handling and protection, the HACCP-system and process control. Periodic refresher training should be part of the overall training programme. Training in basic food hygiene is fundamentally important. All personnel should be aware of their roles and responsibilities in protecting fish and the fish products from contamination and deterioration.

An example of a checklist to be used in assessing the prerequisite programme is shown in Appendix 1.

Model prerequisite programme: Training

Criteria:	All fish handlers must have participated in a training course in personal hygiene, GHP, cleaning and disinfection procedures before starting to work in the plant Those who handle strong chemicals must be instructed in safe handling techniques Appropriate training in application of HACCP-system and process control to key personnel Periodic training of all employees so they understand the principles in the HACCP-system
Monitoring:	What: Skill, knowledge and code of conduct of employees How: Visual observation, occasional interviews When: Continuously Who: Supervisors
Corrective action:	Re-training
Records:	Number and type of training sessions/courses for personnel Interviews with personnel

References

Anonymous 2000. *Sanitation control procedures for processing fish and fishery products.* Manual available from Florida Sea Grant College Program. PO Box 110409 Gainesville, FL

CAC (Codex Alimentarius Commission) 2000. *Proposed Draft. Code of Practice for Fish and Fishery Products.* Alinorm 01/18. Food and Agriculture Organization / World Health Organization, Rome, Italy.

CAC (Codex Alimentarius Commission) 2001. *Food Hygiene Basic texts.* 2nd ed. Food and Agriculture Organization / World Health Organization, Rome, Italy.

EC (European Commission) 1980. Council Directive 80/778/EEC of 15 July 1980 relating to the quality of water intended for human consumption. *Official Journal of the European Communities* L 229, 30/08/1980 pp. 11-26.

EC (European Commission) 1991. Council Directive 91/493/EEC of 22 July 1991 laying down the health conditions for the production and the placing on the market of fishery products. *Official Journal of the European Communities* L 268 , 24/09/1991 pp. 0015 – 0034.

EC (European Commission) 1992. Proposal for a council directive on the hygiene of foodstuffs. *Official Journal of the European Communities* C 24/11, 31/01/1992 pp. 11-16.

EC (European Commission) 1993. Council Directive 93/43/EEC of 14 June 1993 on the hygiene of foodstuffs. *Official Journal of the European Communities* L 175 , 19/07/1993 pp. 0001 – 0011.

EC (European Commission) 1998. Council directive 98/83/EC of 3 November 1998 on the quality of water intended for human consumption. *Official Journal of the European Communities* L330, 05/12/1998. pp 0032-0054.

FDA (US Food and Drug Administration) 1995. Procedures for the Safe and Sanitary Processing and Importing of Fish and Fishery Products; Final Rule. Code of Federal Regulations, Parts 123 and 1240. Volume 60, No 242, 65095-65202.

FDA (US Food and Drug Administration) 2001. Current Good Manufacturing Practices. 21 CFR Part 110. http://seafood.ucdavis.edu/GUIDELINES/gmps.htm

FMF/FMA (Food Manufacturers Federation/Food Machinery Association) 1967. Joint Technical Committee. *Hygienic Design of Food Plant.* London, UK

Gould, W.A. 1994. *Current Good Manufacturing Practices. Food Plant Sanitation* 2nd ed. CTI Publications Inc., Baltimore, MD, USA.

Hayes, P.R. 1992. *Food Microbiology and Hygiene.* 2nd ed. Elsevier Applied Science. London and New York.

ICMSF (International Commission on Microbiological Specifications for Foods) 1988. *Microorganisms in Foods 4. Application of the Hazard Ananlysis Critical Control Point (HACCP) system to ensure microbiological safety and quality.* Blackwell Scientific Publications.

Imholte, T.J. 1984. *Engeneering for Food Safety and Sanitation.* Crystal, MINN: The Technical Institute for Food Safety, Medfield, MA, USA.

Jouve, J.L. 1998. Principles of food safety legislation. *Food Control* 9, 75-81.

Knøchel, S. 1990. *Microbiology and Groundwater: Aesthetic and Hygienic Problems.* Water Quality Institute, Hørsholm, Denmark.

Milledge, J.J. 1981. The hygienic design of food plant. Institute of Food Science and Technology (UK). *Proceedings* 14, 74-86.

NACMCF (National Advisory Committee on Microbiological Criteria for Foods) 1998. Hazard analysis and critical control point principles and application guidelines. *Journal of Food Protection* 61, 762-775.

Poretti, M. 1990. Quality control of water as raw material in the food industry. *Food Control* 1, 79-83.

Prasad, V.S. and M. Chaudhuri 1989. Development of filtration/adsorption media for removal of bacteria and turbidity from water. *Water Science Technology* 21, 67-71.

Reilly, A. 2000. *Discussion paper on the use of chlorinated water*. Prepared for Proposed Draft. Code of Practice for Fish and Fishery Products. CX/FFP/00/13. Food and Agriculture Organization / World Health Organization, Rome, Italy.

Shapton, D.A. and N.F. Shapton 1991. *Principles and Practices for the Safe Processing of Food*. Butterwood & Heinemann.

Sobsey, M.D. 1989. Inactivation of health-related microorganisms in water by disinfection processes. *Water Science Technology* 21, 179-195.

Troller, J.A. 1993. *Sanitation in Food Processing*. Academic Press.

Watson, P. and P. Prout 1996. *Technical development to improve hygiene in the inshore shrimp industry*. Seafish rcport No. SR 466. The Seafish Industry Authority, UK.

WHO (World Health Organization) 1993. *Guidelines for drinking water quality*. 2nd ed. Vol 1. World Health Organization, Geneva, Switzerland.

WHO (World Health Organization) 1996. *Guidelines for drinking water quality*. 2nd ed. Vol 2. Health criteria and other supporting information. World Health Organization, Geneva, Switzerland.

WHO (World Health Organization) 1999. *Strategies for implementing HACCP in small and/or less developed businesses*. Report on at WHO Consultation. WHO/SDE/PHE/FOS/99.7. World Health Organization, Geneva, Switzerland.

8 THE HACCP SYSTEM

8.1 Development and adoption of the HACCP principles (Hans Henrik Huss)

The traditional approach to food safety assurance was based on applying codes of Good Hygiene Practices (GHP) and Good Manufacturing Practices (GMP) in food processing. Confirmation of safety and identification of potential problems were obtained by end-product testing. Inspectors checked for compliance with the codes and sampled the foods for laboratory analysis. Although these actions are still essential parts of any foods control programme, they have certain limitations and shortcomings as pointed out in section 3.1.

In contrast, the HACCP system clearly identifies food safety problems and also where and how they can be controlled or prevented. To assure that these actions are executed regularly and consistently, they have to be described and people who are responsible for their execution have to be trained. A record-keeping system has to be developed to provide documentation for all actions and measurements.

> **HACCP**
> is a system which identifies, evaluates and controls hazards which are significant for food safety (CAC, 2001)

Originally, HACCP was developed and used by the private food industry. The concept was used by the Pillsbury Company in the late 60ies for the safety of food intended for the US Space Program. However, it took many years and endless discussions between regulatory agencies and the food industry on the value of end-product testing and microbiological standards for the food before the HACCP concept was generally accepted as the primary means to assure food safety. A few milestones in this development are shown below:

1971: The HACCP concept presented at the US National Conference on Food Protection

1973: Comprehensive treatise on HACCP published by the Pillsbury Co. HACCP – with only three principles

1980: WHO/ICMSF report on HACCP

1983: WHO EUROPE recommends HACCP

1985: National Academy of Sciences (NAS) (USA) recommends HACCP (Anon., 1985)

1988: Book on HACCP by International Commission on Microbiological Specifications for Foods (ICMSF, 1988)

1989: The National Advisory Committee on Microbiological Criteria for Foods (NACMCF), USA, approved the first major document on HACCP

1992: NACMCF issues a revised document on HACCP (NACMCF, 1992). HACCP now has seven principles

1993: Codex issues the first HACCP Guidelines which were adopted by the FAO/WHO Codex Alimentarius Commission

1997: Based on a number of FAO/WHO Consultations, Codex issues a revised document (CAC, 2001). NACMCF issues the third revised document (NACMCF, 1997). The two revised documents from Codex and NACMCF are very similar.

Integration of HACCP into the official regulations in the European Union (EU) and the United States (US) took place as follows:

1991: Council Directive no. 91/493/EEC (EC, 1991) which places the responsibility of product safety on the industry and introduces the concept of 'own checks' and Critical Control Points during processing

1993: Council Directive no. 93/43/EEC (EC, 1993) on the hygiene of foodstuffs

1994: Commission Decision 94/356/EEC (EC, 1994) detailing the rules for the application of the HACCP system

1995: US-Food and Drug Administration (FDA, 1995) issues the Code of Federal Regulations on safe and sanitary processing and importing of fish and fishery products

1996: US Department of Agriculture, Food Safety and Inspection Service adopts the final rule on the HACCP system (USDA, 1996).

Although the HACCP system both in EU and US is based on the same seven principles, there are some differences between the two systems. These differences are mainly related to the prerequisite programmes, the way they are documented and verified, and the scope and content of the identification of hazards.

Until April 1995, acceptance of the work of Codex by the member governments was voluntary. However, with the establishment of the World Trade Organization (WTO) in April 1995 the situation has changed. According to two of the Agreements of the WTO (the Agreement on Sanitary and Phytosanitary measures (SPS) and the Agreement on Technical Barrier to Trade (TBT)), the work of Codex is recognised as the reference for international food safety requirement. This implies that in the future member states of WTO cannot reject food, which meets Codex recommendations and standards without providing justification based on risk assessment. Since the application of HACCP is recommended by Codex, this means that HACCP has become the international reference system for food safety assurance.

Many excellent books and articles on the principles and the application of HACCP have been published in recent years. Examples are: ILSI (1997), Mortimore and Wallace (1998), Corlett (1998), Dillon and Griffith (2001), Motarjemi and van Schothorst (1999), and National Seafood HACCP Alliance (1997).

These publications should be consulted for detailed information. The present Chapter is intended as a general introduction to HACCP giving sufficient information to the reader to understand the system and to enable him/her to apply or assess the system in practical food safety assurance programmes.

8.2 The basic seven principles of HACCP (Hans Henrik Huss)

The HACCP system is science-based and uses a systematic approach to the identification of specific hazards and measures for their control or prevention to ensure the safety of food. The preventive measures must be described in detail and people who have to execute them must be trained. HACCP involves careful recording of all details and actions in order to provide documentation that the system is in operation and in full control of all hazards in food processing. The HACCP system consists of seven basic principles as outlined by CAC (1997) and NACMCF (1997):

Principle 1: Conduct a hazard analysis
Principle 2: Determine the critical control points (CCPs)
Principle 3: Establish critical limits
Principle 4: Establish monitoring procedures
Principle 5: Establish corrective actions
Principle 6: Establish verification procedures
Principle 7: Establish record-keeping and documentation procedures.

8.3 Application of the HACCP principles (Hans Henrik Huss)

Guidelines for the application of the HACCP system have been presented by CAC (1997). In these guidelines it is pointed out that, prior to application of HACCP to any food operation, this sector should be operating on the basis of a prerequisite programme as outlined in Chapter 7. Furthermore, it is essential that top-management is firmly committed to introduce the system. Many departments and different personnel from chiefs to line operators will be involved and responsible for part of the system, and their full support and cooperation will be needed.

The Codex guidelines suggest that the introduction and application of the HACCP principles should follow a series of 12 steps in a logic sequence as described below:

Step 1: Assemble the HACCP team

Introduction of a HACCP system in large food factories is a complex process and requires a multidisciplinary approach by a team of specialists. The microbiologist is of paramount importance, and must advise the team on all matters related to microbiology, safety and risks. He must have an updated knowledge on these matters and also access to technical literature on the most recent developments in his field. In many cases, he will also need access to the use of a well-equipped laboratory if specific questions and problems cannot be solved by studying the technical literature. Examples are investigations of the microbial ecology of specific products, challenge tests and inoculation studies for evaluation of safety aspects.

Another important member of the HACCP team is the processing specialist. He must advise on production procedures and constraints, prepare the initial process-flow diagram, advise on technological objectives at various points in the process and on technical limitations of equipment.

Other technical specialists such as a food chemist, a food engineer as well as packaging technologists, sales staff, training and personnel managers can provide valuable information to the HACCP team and they should attend some of the meetings.

Key-members of the HACCP team (including the leader) must have an intimate knowledge of the HACCP system. Small and medium size industries are not likely to have qualified personnel on the payroll and must therefore buy assistance form outside consultants in order to implement the system. One person should be appointed as leader of the team.

When the HACCP team is assembled, the scope of the HACCP plan should be identified, describing which segment of the food claim is involved and addressed in the work.

Step 2: Describe product

A full and detailed description of the final production must be drawn up. The raw materials and ingredients used must be specified including the market name or Latin name of the fishery component. Details regarding hazards in the raw material will be included in the HACCP plan. All factors which influence safety such as composition, physical/chemical structure including water activity (a_w) and pH must be described, and any microbiocidal/-static treatment such as heating, freezing, brining and smoking must be specified as well as packaging type, storage conditions and methods of distribution. The normal shelf life under specified condition should also be recorded as shown below.

Elements of the product description

1 Product name
2 Raw material and ingredients used
3 Parameters influencing safety (a_w, pH, salt%, etc.)
4 Processing
5 Packaging and packaging material
6 Storage conditions and shelf life
7 Conditions during distribution
8 Intended use and consumer
9 Labelling instructions

Step 3: Identify intended use and consumer

The HACCP team will need to identify the intended use and consumer of the product. The intended use should be based on expected use by the consumer. The use and preparation before use greatly influence the safety of the product. Certain products may be contaminated or carry pathogenic organisms as a part of the natural flora. If the processing does not include a killing step the only critical control point (CCP) which can render the product safe is adequate heat treatment during preparation.

The intended consumer may be the general public or a particular segment of the population such as infants or elderly. If the product is to be sold to hospitals or groups of the population with high susceptibility, more safety is required and critical limits need to be more strict.

Step 4: Construct flow diagram

The purpose of the flow diagram is to provide a clear simple description of all steps involved in the processing. Receiving and storage steps for raw materials and ingredients should be included. Time and temperature conditions during processing should be mentioned whenever there is a holding step e.g. in holding vats, buffer tanks or other areas, where this could be a potential delay in processing.

Step 5: On-site confirmation of flow diagram

The constructed flow diagram should be verified on-site for accuracy. The site should be inspected during all hours (night shifts, weekends) of operation to check for correctness and ensure that nothing crucial was overlooked.

Step 6: List all potential hazards associated with each step in the operation, conduct a hazard analysis and consider any measure to control identified hazards (Principle 1)

The words "hazard" and "hazard analysis" have been defined by Codex (CAC, 2001):

Hazard

A biological, chemical or physical agent in, or a condition of, food with the potential to cause an adverse health effect (CAC, 2001)

Hazard Analysis

The process of collecting and evaluating information on hazards and conditions leading to their presence to decide which are significant for food safety and therefore should be addressed in the HACCP plan (CAC, 2001)

Thus, the word hazard has a particular meaning. It refers to both a specific agent and/or a condition (e.g. elevated temperature) with the potential to cause harm. After having identified all potential hazards all the information available must be evaluated in order to decide, which ones of the hazards are significant and reasonably likely to cause illness if not effectively controlled.

The hazard analysis is the key to preparing an effective HACCP plan and serves three purposes (NACMCF 1997):

- The hazards and associated control measures are identified,
- Needed modifications to a process or product is identified,
- Providing a basis for determining CCPs (principle 2).

Examples of questions to be considered, when conducting a hazard analysis has been listed by NACMCF (1997) and includes[1]:

- Raw materials and ingredients – do they contain any hazardous agents?
- Intrinsic factors – will the food permit survival, multiplication of pathogens or toxin formation?
- Processing conditions – are any pathogens destroyed, are there any possibilities for recontamination?
- Packaging – does the packaging affect the microbial population?
- Preparation and intended use – will the food be heated by the consumer?
- Intended consumer – is the product for the general public or for consumption by a population with high susceptibility to illness?

A decision tree with a number of questions can be used to determine if potential hazards are "real" as demonstrated in Figure 8.1.

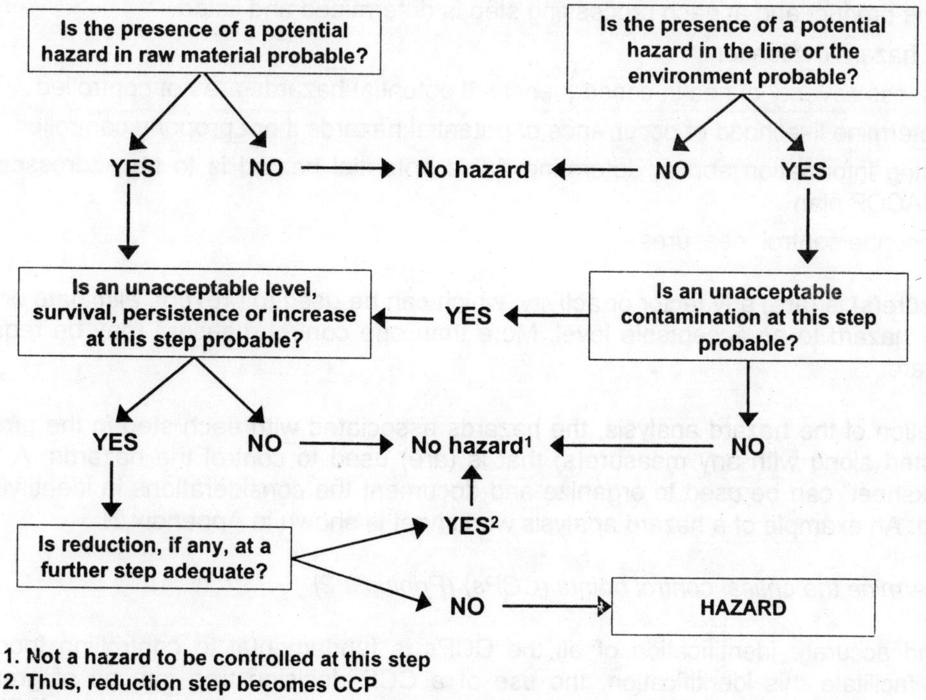

Figure 8.1 Hazard determination - Questions to be answered for each potential hazard at each step (based on ILSI, 1997).

1 *Conditions covered by the prerequisite programme have been excluded from the list*

The questions in Figure 8.1 have to be asked at each step of the processing chain and all hazards must be considered.

An element of risk assessment is involved in the evaluation of potential hazards. Only these hazards which are likely to occur and which will cause a reasonably serious adverse health affect are regarded as significant as shown in Figure 8.2.

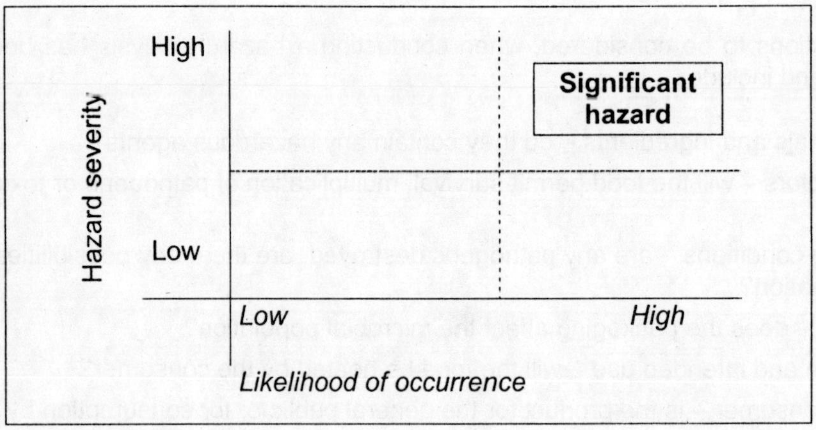

Figure 8.2 Determination of hazard significance (after Mortimore and Wallace, 1998).

Thus, the basic procedures to use in conducting the hazard analysis are as follows:

- based on the product description and the flow diagram, all the potential hazards associated with the product and at each processing step is determined and listed
- Make a hazard evaluation:
    - assess severity of health consequences if potential hazards are not controlled
    - determine likelihood of occurrence of potential hazards if not properly controlled
    - using information above, determine if this potential hazard is to be addressed in the HACCP plan
    - describe control measures.

Control measure(s) is (are) any factor or activity, which can be used to prevent, eliminate or reduce a food safety hazard to an acceptable level. More than one control measure may be required to control a hazard.

Upon completion of the hazard analysis, the hazards associated with each step in the production should be listed along with any measure(s) that is (are) used to control the hazards. A "hazard analysis worksheet" can be used to organize and document the considerations in identifying food safety hazard. An example of a hazard analysis worksheet is shown in Appendix 2.

Step 7: Determine the critical control points (CCPs) (Principle 2)

Complete and accurate identification of all the CCPs is fundamental to controlling food safety hazards. To facilitate this identification, the use of a CCP decision tree can be of great help. Example of decision trees are found in NACMCF (1997), CAC (1997) and in the ILSI (1997) document. The latter is shown in Figure 8.3.

Critical Control Point (CCP)
Is a step at which control can be applied and is essential to prevent or eliminate a food safety hazard or reduce it to an acceptable level (CAC, 2001)

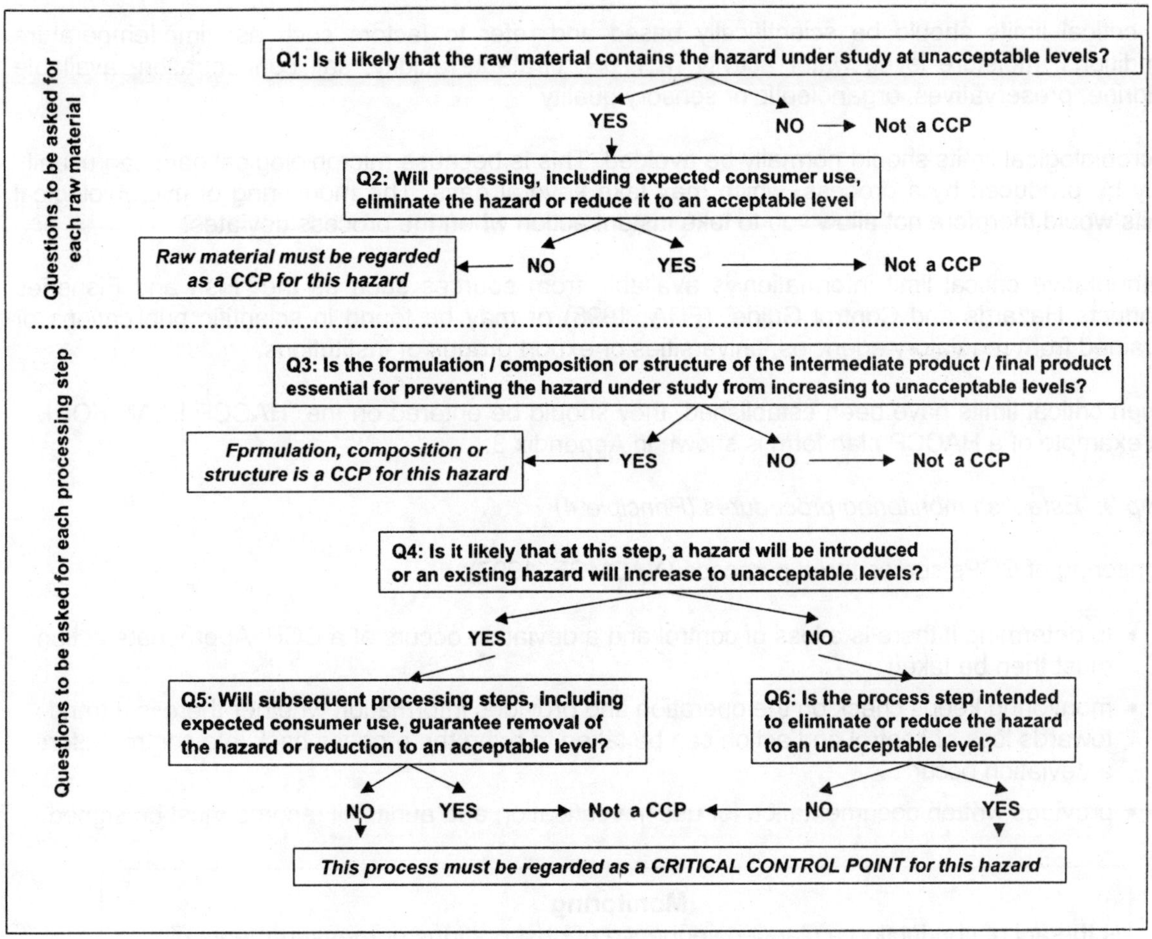

Figure 8.3 Critical control point decision tree (ILSI, 1997).

The first two questions in Figure 8.3 deal with the raw material. It is important to note, that if an identified hazard is eliminated or reduced at a later process step or by normal consumer use, the raw material is not a CCP. Question 3 deals with formulation or composition of the product. In Chapter 5 of this publication it has been pointed out, that in preventing multiplication of pathogens the pH or a_w or presence of specific antibacterial compounds may be extremely important. Question 4 asks, if contamination, recontamination or even multiplication of pathogens can take place at this step. If the answer is 'No', question 6 thus has to be answered, but if the answer is 'Yes', the answer to question 5 will decide whether this step is a CCP or not.

Only points where truly significant hazards can be controlled should be designated CCPs. A tendency exists to control too much and to designate too many CCPs. This should be avoided as it will create confusion and divert attention from the true CCP.

Step 8 Establish critical limits (Principle 3)

The third HACCP principle deals with establishing one or more maximum or minimum critical limits that must be controlled at each CCP.

Critical limit
is a criterion which separates acceptability from unacceptability (CAC, 2001)

All critical limits should be scientifically based and refer to factors such as: time/temperature conditions, moisture level, water activity (a_w), pH, titratable acidity, salt concentration, available chlorine, preservatives, organoleptic or sensory quality.

Microbiological limits should normally be avoided. This is because microbiological data can usually only be produced by a process, which may take several days. The monitoring of microbiological limits would therefore not allow you to take instant action when the process deviates.

Authoritative critical limit information is available from sources such as the "Fish and Fisheries Products Hazards and Control Guide" (FDA, 1998) or may be found in scientific publications or obtained from regulatory agencies, universities or export groups or institutions.

When critical limits have been established, they should be entered on the "HACCP PLAN FORM". An example of a HACCP plan form is shown in Appendix 3.

Step 9: Establish monitoring procedures (Principle 4)

Monitoring of CCPs serves three purposes (NACMCF, 1997):

- to determine if there is a loss of control and a deviation occurs at a CCP. Appropriate action must then be taken
- monitoring keeps check on the operation and provides information whether there is a trend towards loss of control and action can be taken to bring the process back into control before a deviation occur
- provides written documentation for use in verification and audit. All records must be signed.

Monitoring
is the act of conducting a planned sequence of observations or measurements of control parameters to assess whether a CCP is under control (CAC, 2001)

To be effective, all monitoring must be done rapidly and results must be evaluated by a designated person with knowledge and authority to carry out corrective actions. Typically, monitoring methods are:

- time/temperature recording
- pH and a_w measurements
- sensory quality.

Thus, in planning the monitoring procedures there are typically four questions to be answered (CAC, 2001):

Planning monitoring procedures

- What – usually a measurement or observation
- How – by observation and/or use of instruments
- When (frequency) – continuous or intermittent – but in real time
- Who – someone who is qualified and with authority

As already stated, the main purpose of monitoring is to determine if there is loss of control or deviation.

Deviation is failure to meet a critical limit (CAC, 2001)

An example of a process being in control and out of control (deviation) has been illustrated by Motarjemi and van Schothorst (1999) as shown in Figure 8.4.

Step 10: Establish corrective actions (Principle 5)

Corrective Action is any action to be taken when the results of monitoring at the CCP indicate a loss of control (CAC, 2001)

Whenever there is a deviation from established critical limits a corrective action must be instituted to ensure that defective products do not reach the consumer. These actions should include the following (NACMCF, 1997):

- determine and correct the cause of deviation
- determine the disposition of products that were produced during the process deviation
- record the corrective action taken.

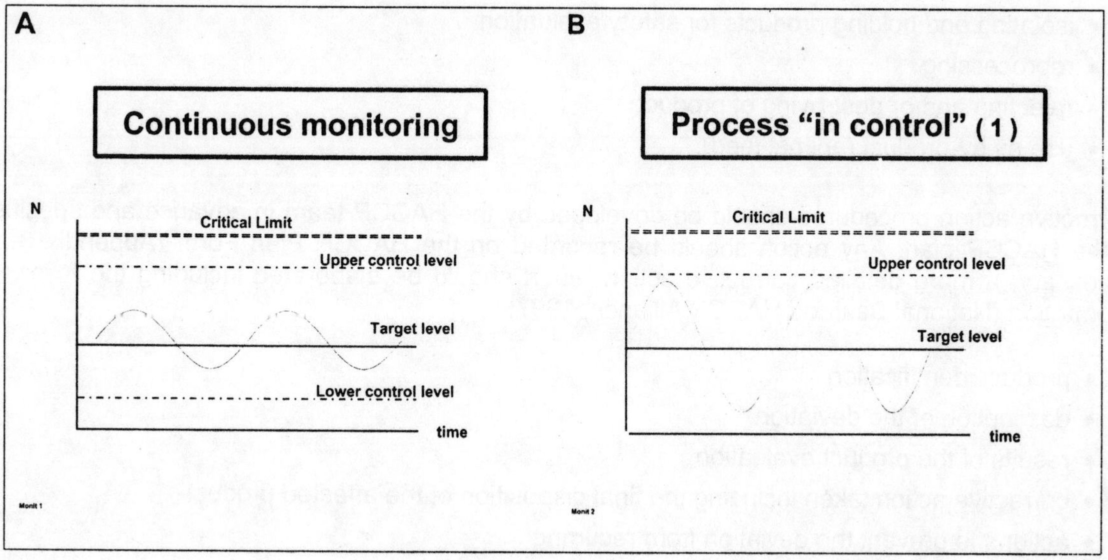

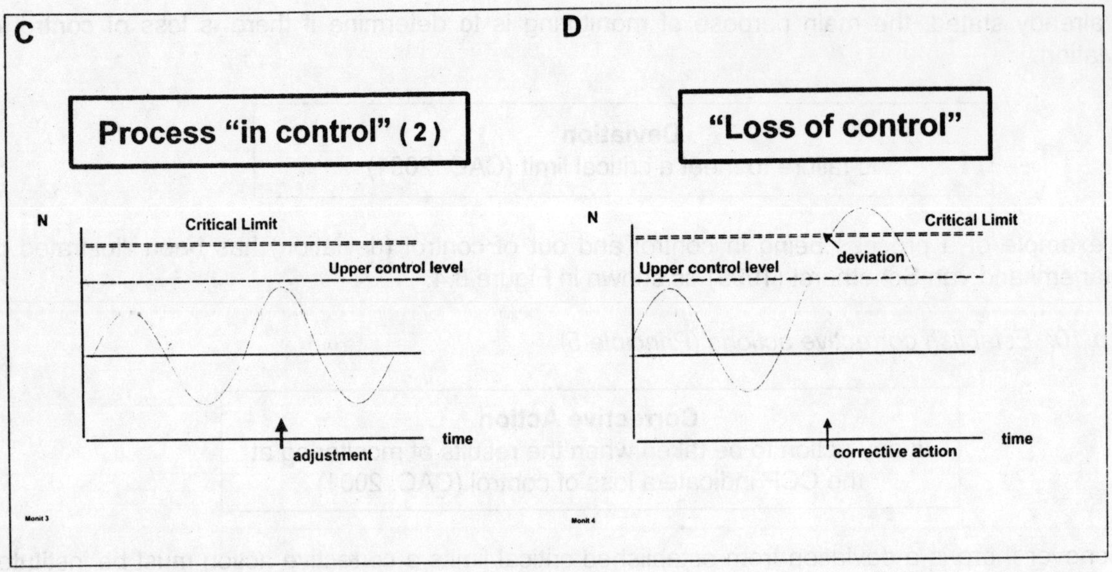

Figure 8.4 Monitoring: A: small fluctuations always occur around a target level, B and C: the process is under control but adjustment is needed in situation C as abnormal fluctuations are noted, D: a deviation occurs and corrective action is needed (from Motarjemi and van Schothorst ,1999).

Options for disposition of products placed on hold include:

- isolating and holding products for safety evaluation
- reprocessing
- rejecting and/or destroying of product
- use as by-product (animal feed).

Corrective action procedures should be developed by the HACCP team in advance and specified in the HACCP plan. Any action should be recorded on the HACCP Plan Form (Appendix 3). If necessary, a more detailed corrective action report should be elaborated including the following information (National Seafood HACCP Alliance, 1997):

- product identification
- description of the deviation
- results of the product evaluation
- corrective action taken including the final disposition of the affected product
- actions to prevent the deviation from recurring
- name of the individual responsible for taking action.

Step 11: Establish verification procedures (Principle 6)

> **Verification**
> is the application of methods, procedures, tests and other evaluations, in addition to monitoring to determine compliance with the HACCP plan (CAC, 2001)

The purpose of the HACCP plan is to prevent food safety hazards from occurring. Verification activities must provide a level of confidence that the HACCP plan is working properly and is adequate to control hazards. The NACMCF (1997) document is providing guidance on what elements should be included in the verification activities:

- Validation – initial and subsequent validation of the HACCP plan
- Verification of the CCP-monitoring
  - o CCP-record review
  - o calibration of instruments
  - o targeted sampling and testing
  - o microbiological testing
- Review of monitoring, corrective action records
- Comprehensive HACCP system verification.

Thus, the verification procedures include verification of both the individual CCP and the overall HACCP plan. An essential component of verification is validation.

> **Validation**
> is obtaining evidence that the elements of the HACCP plan are effective (CAC, 2001)

In validation of the HACCP plan it needs to be established that the plan is scientifically and technically sound. This means that scientific validation includes review of each part of the HACCP plan from the hazard analysis through to each CCP. The needed information can be obtained from expert advice, scientific studies and literature, in-plant observations and measurements.

Validation	• are the right things done? • will the system work when put into practice?
Verification	• are the things done right? • are they done as they were planned to be done?

Apart from the initial validation, subsequent validation as well as verification must take place whenever there is a change in raw materials, product formulation, processing procedures, consumer and handling practices, new information on hazards and their control, consumer complaints, recurring deviations or any other indication, that the system is not working. Figure 8.5 shows where validation fits into the process of HACCP implementation.

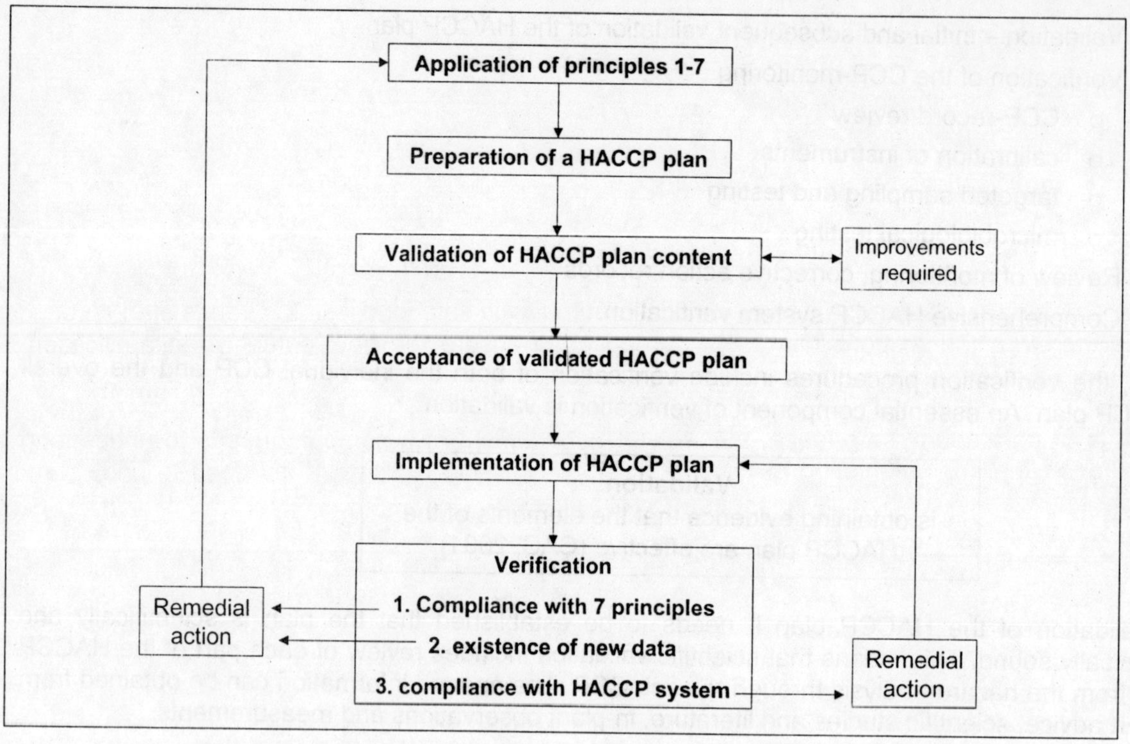

Figure 8.5 HACCP validation and verification (based on ILSI, 1999).

A periodic comprehensive verification of the HACCP system should be conducted yearly by an unbiased, independent authority. This should include a review of the HACCP plan for completeness, confirmation of the flow diagram, review of all records and validations, sampling and testing to verify CCPs (NACMCF, 1997).

Verification is the responsibility of the producer or food handler. However, where regulatory agencies are conducting audits or sampling end-products the results can be used by industry as part of the verification programme.

Verification procedures should be entered on the HACCP Plan Form (Appendix 3) and results into special verification records.

Step 12: Establish record-keeping and documentation procedures (Principle 7)

> **Record keeping**
> ensures that the information resulting from the HACCP study and implementation of the resulting HACCP plan is available for validation, verification, review, auditing and other purposes (ILSI, 1997)

Records and documentation are vital for the verification and auditing to determine, if the HACCP system in operation is in compliance with the HACCP plan and operating correctly. Also records of support documents must be kept such as data used to establish critical limits, reports from consultants or experts, a list of the HACCP team and their responsibilities and the preliminary steps taken before development and implementation of the HACCP plan. Examples of HACCP records are shown in NACMSF (1997). The CAC (1997) publication mentions the following examples of documentation:

- hazard analysis worksheet
- CCP determination
- critical limit determination

and as examples of records:

- CCP monitoring activities
- deviations and associated corrective actions
- modifications of the HACCP system.

8.4 HACCP implementation in the fish industry (Hans Henrik Huss)

It is generally accepted that responsibility for producing safe food is in the hands of the producer. It is therefore the responsibility of the producer to ensure the development and application of a proper HACCP plan.

It is of paramount importance, that senior management of a company needs to understand and support the implementation of HACCP in the processing facilities. They need to understand the benefits as well as the cost and the resources needed.

While the HACCP team is conducting the HACCP study, it is advisable to initiate training of key-personnel. No plan will work if the people who have to implement it are not trained. People who have to develop the plan as well as people responsible for implementation and maintenance may all need training.

When the HACCP plan has been developed, it needs to be approved by senior management. During the development of the HACCP plan including the prerequisite programme, it often becomes clear that improvements may be needed in construction or layout of facilities, or utensils need to be replaced. This could involve considerable costs and run into budgetary constraints. However, modifications, which are essential to food safety, should always be executed immediately, while a timetable for less necessary modifications should be made.

Although implementation of HACCP is the responsibility of the industry, government (that is regulatory fish safety and quality control authorities) also have a role to play. Government authorities can play three roles: they can act as facilitators, enforcers or trainers (Motarjemi and van Schothorst, 1999):

- as facilitators they can help industries understand the goals and scope of HACCP and provide expertise during the establishment of a HACCP plan or its verification
- as enforcers their task is to assess the correct application and implementation of the seven HACCP principles
- they can provide training courses and also participate in training courses organized by or for the industry.

Thus, it is a key role of government agencies to show leadership by promoting and facilitating the implementation of HACCP. However, the government has also a strategic role (i.e. a plan how to achieve a pre-set goal) as well as an ongoing role in assessing the HACCP systems applied in the industry.

With regard to the actual assessment of HACCP, government agencies also play an important role in providing guidance on the assessment process needed to be developed and provided to officials for its uniform and acceptable application. This guidance should be developed by government agencies in collaboration with, when possible, food control officials and industry (see also section 8.5).

Proper implementation of HACCP may also need the support of other institutions such as academia and research, trade associations, private sector etc. A consequence of the WTO/SPS agreement is that food safety criteria such as FSOs, performance criteria and microbiological end product criteria have to be based on scientific evidence, and where appropriate on a risk assessment. Scientific results produced *lege artis* and published in international literature is therefore the background for the HACCP plan and provides the transparency required by WTO/SPS.

Finally, consumers and consumer advocate groups have a counter-balancing role to ensure that safety and quality are not undermined by political and socio-economical considerations when drafting legislation or implementing safety and quality policies.

8.5 HACCP audit (Lahsen Ababouch)

Many fish producing, exporting and/or importing countries have undertaken a thorough evaluation and reorganization of fish inspection and control systems with the aim to improve efficiency, rationalize human resources and introduce risk analysis-based approaches. The HACCP principles play a pivotal role in these preventive approaches. Their application is the responsibility of the fish industry, whereas government control agencies are responsible for monitoring and assessing their proper implementation.

Many inspection agencies have developed approaches and procedures for carrying out HACCP compliance auditing. These approaches and modalities have used the terminology and basic requirements of the ISO 10011 standards (ISO, 1993a,b) that were adapted to the specificities of HACCP and to the countries regulations. Information regarding these procedures will not be reviewed here in details as it is widely accessible, especially via internet. This Chapter will rather attempt to demystify the issues and advise on how to achieve practical HACCP auditing.

8.5.1 Planning and conducting an HACCP audit

Audit is a systematic and independent examination to determine whether activities and results comply with the documented procedures; also whether these procedures are implemented effectively and are suitable to achieve the objectives (ISO, 1993a,b). In HACCP terms, achieving the objectives means managing the production and distribution of safe fish products through the use of an HACCP based approach.

The outcome of the audit is to have established whether the manufacturer has

- implemented a sound HACCP system
- the knowledge and experience needed to maintain it
- the necessary support (or prerequisite) programmes in place to assess adherence to Good Hygienic and Good Manufacturing Practices (GHP/GMP).

The audit will encompass assessment of the management commitment to support the system and assessment of the knowledge, competency and decision-making capabilities of the HACCP team members to apply the system and maintain it. Four types of HACCP audits can be envisaged:

- An internal HACCP audit to establish the effectiveness of the HACCP system using the company's own human resources or by bringing in an external HACCP assessor.
- An external HACCP audit of suppliers of critical raw materials or of packed finished products to establish whether they have robust HACCP systems in place. This includes regulatory HACCP auditing
- Audit of the customers HACCP system. This may be important where the customer is responsible for the distribution and sale of a high risk (e.g. a chilled ready meal) product which bears the brand of the manufacturing company
- An investigative audit can also be conducted to analyse a specific problem area. This may be used for example when a CCP regularly goes out of control and more studies are needed to investigate the real cause in order to take corrective action, or where a previously unknown problem has arisen.

An HACCP audit needs to be properly prepared. Figure 8.6 describes the steps generally required in a HACCP audit. This guidance is useful for independent (third-party) audits as well as for internal or compliance audits. It should be adapted to the particular circumstances of the firm being audited.

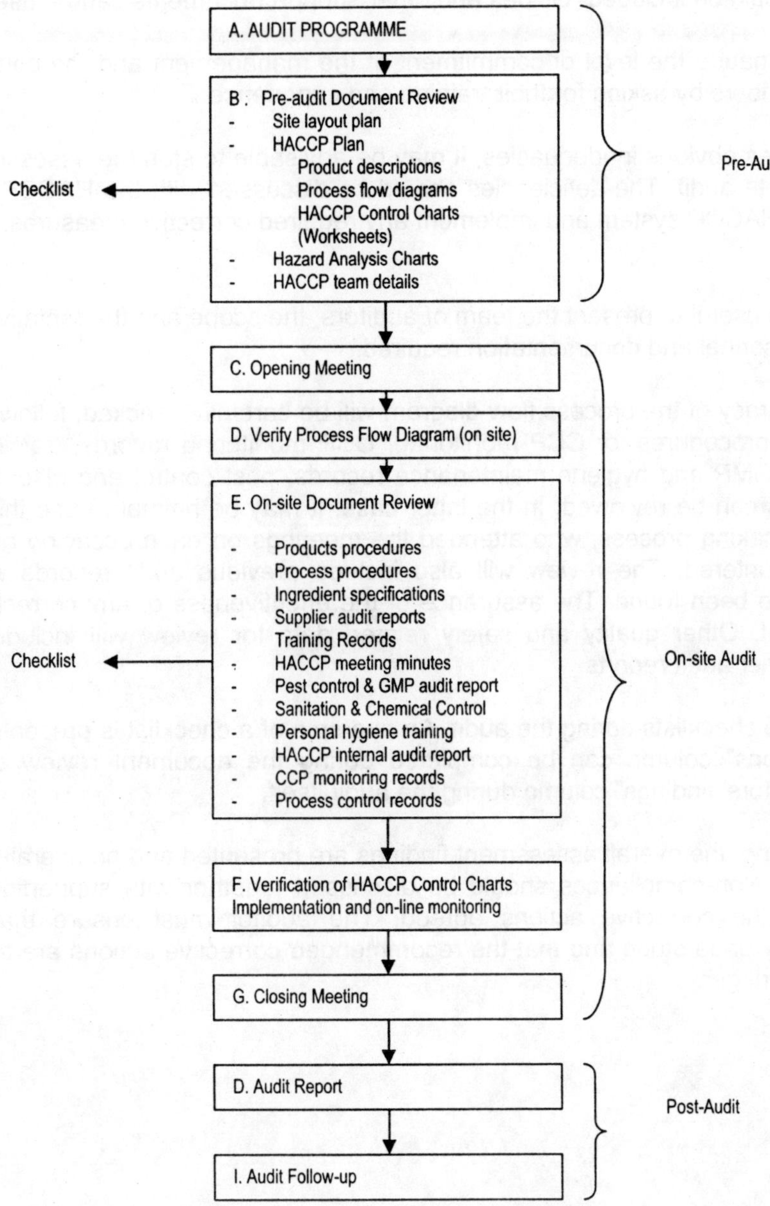

Figure 8.6 Steps in HACCP auditing (Mortimore and Wallace, 1998).

Pre- audit

A preparatory phase is necessary to elaborate the schedule and the definition of the scope of the audit. All the personnel required during the audit should be notified to ensure that they are available. Also the necessary documentation should be made available for the audit.

This starts with a "desktop assessment" of the HACCP system, to review all of the documentation relating to the scope of the audit such as the flow diagram layout, the time/temperature and other technological information, the hazard analysis, etc.

The pre-audit document review can be done as an initial scan to get a feel for who carried out the HACCP study, its style, its completeness, and also familiarisation with the site being audited and the products and process itself. It will give an opportunity for the auditor to carry out some research before the assessment. At this stage, it is important to build up knowledge of the product/process technology concerned. Literature searches of the technology, fish contamination outbreaks and legislative controls should be included. Guides and other support documents can be useful.

It is also important to gauge the level of commitment of the management and the competency of the HACCP team members by asking for their training and experience.

If the pre-audit indicates obvious inadequacies, it may be advisable to stop the assessment at this point prior to the on-site audit. The deficiencies should be discussed with the HACCP team, who can then review their HACCP system and implement any required corrective measures.

On-site audit

An opening meeting is useful to present the team of auditors, the scope and the tentative timetable and to identify the personnel and documentation required.

At this stage, the accuracy of the process flow diagram will be carefully checked, followed by a full review of operational procedures for CCP monitoring, CCP monitoring records, training records, etc. The prerequisite GMP and hygiene maintenance records, pest control and also the HACCP team meeting minutes can be reviewed. In the latter case, it may be helpful to use this to get an idea of the decision making process, who attended the meetings on each occasion and whether difficulties were encountered. The review will also include previous audit records where non-compliances may have been found. The assurance of the effectiveness of any corrective actions taken must be sought. Other quality and safety related data for review will include customer complaints and customer audit reports.

It is often useful to use checklists during the audit. An example of a checklist is presented in Table 8.1. The "considerations" column can be completed during the document review step of the process, and the "auditors' findings" column during the audit itself.

During a closing meeting, the overall assessment findings are presented and an overall view of the proceedings is given. Non-compliances should be discussed together with supporting evidence and a schedule for the corrective actions agreed. The auditor must ensure that identified deficiencies are clearly understood and that the recommended corrective actions are feasible and agreed by a senior manager.

Table 8.1 Example of a checklist for assessing HACCP implementation (Ababouch, 2000).

Component to assess	Compliance, considerations, points to raise on site	Findings of the auditor
(1) *Commitment of the management*		
Financial commitment		
Awareness/support		
(2) *HACCP team*		
The HACCP team leader has effective power of decision		
The HACCP team members are qualified		
(3) *Composition of products*		
Fish composition is properly described		
Any modification is recorded and taken into account for HACCP revision		
(4) *Intended use*		
Valid description of the intended use		
Any modification is recorded and taken into account for HACCP revision		
(5) *Process flow diagram(s)*		
The flow diagram is correct		
Any modification is recorded and taken into account for HACCP revision		
(6) *Hazard analysis*		
All control measures are correctly implemented, eventually validated		
Personnel in charge of control measures are identified and qualified		
New hazards, introduced because of changes in product, process,... were taken into consideration		
Control measures have been identified for these new hazards		
(7) *Critical control points (CCPs)*		
CCPs are properly identified (e.g. using the decision tree)		
Introduction of new hazards has resulted in CCP analysis to implement proper control measures		
(8) *Critical limits*		
Critical limits are properly identified and eventually validated		
Introduction of new hazard has resulted in the revision of the critical limits		
(9) *Monitoring procedures*		
Monitoring procedures are properly identified		
The reliability of the monitoring procedures has been validated		
Personnel in charge of monitoring is well identified and trained		
All necessary modifications have been made to take into account the introduction of new control measures		
(10) *Corrective actions*		
Corrective actions are properly identified and eventually validated		
Personnel in charge of corrective actions has been identified and trained		
All necessary modifications have been made to take into account the introduction of new control measures		
(11) *Verification of the HACCP system*		
The method and frequency of verification are appropriate		
The validity of the verification method has been confirmed		
Personnel in charge of verification is identified		
Changes of products, processes, standards, regulations, ... were taken into consideration		
(12) *Record-Keeping System*		
Forms are appropriate and complete		
Forms are up to date for recording the following:		
• Monitoring results,		
• Corrective actions,		
• Modifications of the HACCP system		
• HACCP Verification/revision results		
Some records have been tampered with		

Post- audit

Audit reports should provide evidence of the findings of the assessment - primarily what deficiencies have been found in the HACCP system, the non-compliance notes, the recommended corrective measures and the timetable to implement them.

During the audit follow-up, the auditor should ensure that the non-compliances are closed off. The effectiveness of corrected non-compliances should be verified as soon as the corrective action has been taken and reviewed during subsequent audit to ensure that the corrective actions taken have been effective on an ongoing basis

8.5.2 Frequency of audit

The frequency of HACCP audit should be based on:

- the risk category of the fish product being processed
- the level of commitment of management and the decision-making leverage of the HACCP team
- the reputation of the fish company: previous safety and quality records, HACCP manual and implementation classification, training and qualification.

8.5.3 Qualifications of HACCP auditors

An HACCP audit exercise should lead to an audit report which should state whether the system provides enough assurance to control fish safety and quality. However, fish processors look for a formal recognition (validation, certification). It should be stressed that although this is legitimate, an HACCP audit is a snapshot punctual evaluation and any recognition should not lead to false assurance. It is a temporary recognition and audit should be as frequent as seen fit.

In international fish trade, there is a danger of duplication of HACCP audit efforts. This can be alleviated by the development of an internationally recognized equivalency system, for example through the Codex Committee on import/export inspection and certification systems.

Furthermore, third party certification can complement the work of government inspectors in assessing HACCP. However, certifying bodies should demonstrate proper qualifications and integrity in HACCP development and verification. This may require the establishment of a certification system for third party HACCP assessors.

8.5.4 Qualifications of HACCP auditors

Proper assessment of HACCP requires demonstrated knowledge and qualifications in different areas of science and technology pertinent to the products and processes of interest, in addition to confidentiality, objectivity and experience and skills in auditing and communication (ISO, 1993b). These qualifications are acquired through training and experience. It should be stressed that any training activity should provide evidence of satisfactory completion through examination. Also, the training programs and examinations should be harmonized to allow for easy recognition and equivalency between countries.

References

Ababouch., L. 2000. The role of government agencies in assessing HACCP. *Food Control* 11, 137-142.

Anonymous 1985. An Evaluation of the Role of Microbiological Criteria for Foods and Food Ingredients. National Research Council, National Academy Press. Washington, DC, USA.

CAC (Codex Alimentarius Commission) 2001. *Food Hygiene Basic Texts.* 2nd ed. Food and Agriculture Organization / World Health Organization, Rome, Italy.

Corlett, D.A. 1998. HACCP Users Manual. A Chapman and Hall Food Science Title. Aspen Publishers Inc., Gaithersberg, Maryland, USA.

Dillon, M. and C. Griffith 2001. How to HACCP. 3rd ed. M.D. Associates, 32a Hainton Avenue, Grimsby, North East Lincolnshire DN 329 BB, UK.

EC (European Commission) 1991. Council Directive 91/493/EEC of 22 July 1991 laying down the health conditions for the production and the placing on the market of fishery products. *Official Journal of the European Community* L268, pp.15-34.

EC (European Commission) 1993. Council Directive 94/43/EEC of 14 June 1993 on the hygiene of foodstuffs. *Official Journal of the European Communities* L175, pp. 1-112.

EC (European Commission) 1994. Commission Decision 94/356//EC of 20 May 1994 laying down detailed rules for the application of Council Directive 91/493/EEC, as regards own health checks on fishery products. *Official Journal of the European Communities* L156, pp. 50-57.

FDA (US Food and Drug Administration) 1995. *Procedures for the Safe and Sanitary Processing and Importing of Fish and Fishery Products*; Final Rule. Code of Federal Regulations, Parts 123 and 1240. Volume 60, No 242, 65095-65202.

FDA (US Food and Drug Administration) 1998. *Fish and Fisheries Products Hazards and Controls Guide*. 2nd ed. Washington, USA.

ICMSF (International Commission on Microbiological Safety of Foods) 1988. *Microorganisms in Foods 4: Application of the Hazard Analysis Critical Control Point (HACCP) to ensure microbiological safety and quality*. Blackwell Scientific Publications, London, UK.

ILSI (International Life Sciences Institute) 1997. A simple Guide to understanding and applying the Hazard Analysis Critical Control Point Concept ILSI Europe, Brussels, Belgium.

ILSI (International Life Sciences) 1999. Validation and verification of HACCP. ILSI Europe, Brussels, Belgium.

ISO (International Standards Organization) 1993a. ISO 10011-1. Guidelines for auditing quality systems. Part 1: auditing. 8 pages. Geneva. Switzerland.

ISO (International Standards Organization) 1993b. ISO 10011-1. Guidelines for auditing quality systems. Part 2: Qualification criteria for quality systems auditors. 6 pages. Geneva. Switzerland.

Mortimore, S. and C. Wallace 1998. *HACCP, A practical approach*. A Chapman and Hall Food Science Book. Aspen Publishers Inc., Gaithersberg, Maryland, USA.

Motarjemi, Y. and M. van Schothorst 1999. HACCP, Principles and Practice. In Jongeneerl, S. (ed) *Teacher's Handbook*. A WHO/ICD Training Manual in Collaboration with FAO. World Health Organization, Geneva, Switzerland.

NACMCF (National Advisory Committee on Microbiological Criteria for Foods) 1992. HAZARD Analysis and Critial Control Point System. *International Journal of Food Microbiology* 16, 1-23.

NACMCF (National Advisory Committee on Microbiological Criteria for Foods) 1997. HAZARD Analysis and Critial Control Point Principles and Application Guidelines. *Journal of Food Protection* 61, 762-775.

National Seafood HACCP Alliance 1997. HACCP: Hazard Analysis and Critical Control Point Training Curriculum. 2nd ed. (Chairman editorial committee: Donn Ward). Publication UNC-SG-96-02, North Carolina State University, Raleigh, North Carolina.

USDA (US Department of Agriculture, Food Safety and Inspection Service) 1996. 9 CFR Pathogen reduction; hazard analysis and critical control point (HACCP) systems: final rule. *US Federal Register*, 61, 38806-38989, 25 July.

Web Sites relevant to seafood HACCP

FDA-Center for Food Safety & Applied Nutrition-Seafood
http://vm.cfsan.fda.gov/seafoo1.html

HACCP Manual – Food Safety Canada
http://www.haccp-seafood.com/

NOAA Fisheries-National Marine Fisheries Service
http://www.nmfs.gov/

SeafoodNIC Home Page
http://www-seafood.ucdavis.edu/

Seafood NIC Home Page – Compendium of Fish and Fishery Products Processing Methods, Hazards and Controls
http://seafood.ucdavis.edu/haccp/compendium/compend.htm

Seafood NIC Home Page – HACCP Plans
http://www-seafood.ucdavis.edu/hacp/Plans.htm

9 CONSIDERATIONS IN THE APPLICATION OF THE HACCP PRINCIPLES TO SEAFOOD PRODUCTION (Hans Henrik Huss)

The safety of seafood products varies considerably and is influenced by a number of factors such as origin of the fish, microbiological ecology of the product, handling and processing practices and preparations before consumption. Taking most of these aspects into consideration, seafood can conveniently be grouped as shown below (modified from Huss (1994))

- Molluscan shellfish
- Raw fish to be eaten without any cooking
- Fresh or frozen fish and crustaceans – to be fully cooked before consumption.
- Lightly preserved fish products i.e. NaCl <6% in water phase, pH >5.0. The prescribed storage temperature is <5°C. This group includes salted, marinated, cold smoked and gravad fish
- Fermented fish, i.e. NaCl <8% NaCl, pH changing from neutral to acid. Typically, the products are stored at ambient temperature
- Semi-preserved fish i.e. NaCl >6% in water phase, or pH < 5, preservatives (sorbate, benzoate, nitrite) may be added. The prescribed storage temperature is <10°C. This group includes salted and/or marinated fish or caviar, fermented fish (after completion of fermentation)
- Mildly heat-processed (pasteurised, cooked, hot smoked) fish products and crustaceans (including pre-cooked, breaded fillets). The prescribed storage temperature is <5°C
- Heat-processed (sterilised, packed in sealed containers)
- Dried, smoke-dried fish, heavily salted fish. Can be stored at ambient temperatures.

However, the safety of seafood products and –processing cannot be studied in isolation. A large number of hazards are related to the pre-harvest situation or the raw material handling and must be under control, when the raw material is received at the processing factory.

9.1 Hazard analysis of raw material

Most fish and shellfish are still extracted form a wild population, but aquaculture is a very fast growing food production system as outlined in Chapter 2. While there are specific safety aspects associated with wild fish caught in the high sea, the intensive husbandry in aquaculture pose new and increased risks. It is imperative that the HACCP principles are extended beyond the factory-gate and applied throughout the total food production chain from harvest to the consumers' plate.

In a general hazard analysis of the pre-harvest conditions for fish and shellfish and the procedures for handling the raw material before being received at the processing plant a number of significant hazards can be identified:

Pathogenic bacteria
Pathogenic bacteria from the aquatic or general environment may be present in low numbers in all fish and shellfish at the time of harvest (see section 5.1.1.1). This is not a significant hazard as it is unlikely that these pathogens will be there in sufficient numbers to cause disease – even if the fish are eaten raw. However, if growth and toxin production of these organisms is taking place as a result of time/temperature abuse, it is reasonably likely that these pathogens and their toxins could reach unsafe levels. For fish to be eaten raw or used as raw material in products that are not heat-treated, this situation is a significant hazard that must be controlled. High numbers of e.g. pathogenic *Vibrio* spp. may accumulate in bivalves, but it is unlikely that pathogenic levels will be reached (see section 5.1.1.1.).

Pathogenic bacteria from animal/human reservoir may be present in fish and shellfish harvested in contaminated waters. This is a significant hazard for fish and shellfish to be eaten raw due to the low MID (Minimum Infective Dose) for some of these organisms.

The preventive measures for these hazards are control and monitoring of harvest areas for faecal pollution (see section 11.2) and placing a limit on the time between harvest and refrigeration to prevent growth and toxin production.

Viruses
The presence of viruses in the harvest area is of particular concern in molluscan shellfish because:

- environments where molluscan shellfish grow are often subject to contamination from sewage which may contain pathogens (bacteria, viruses)
- molluscan shellfish filter and concentrate pathogens that may be present in the water
- molluscan shellfish are often consumed raw or only partially cooked.

Thus, the presence of virus is a significant hazard in molluscan shellfish and fish to be eaten raw. The preventive measure is control and monitoring of harvesting areas for faecal pollution (section 11.2).

Biotoxins
Contamination of fish and shellfish with natural toxins from the harvest area can cause serious consumer illness. The toxins accumulate in fish when they feed on marine algae, where the toxins are produced. They occur in fish from the tropical and subtropical area (ciguatera) and in shellfish worldwide (see section 5.1.5). In order to determine if ciguatera fish poisoning (CFP) is a significant hazard, some guidance can be provided by the historical occurrence of the toxin and knowledge about the safety of the reefs from which the fish has been obtained.

The preventive measures for the presence of toxins in shellfish are control and classification of shellfish harvesting areas (section 11.1). As a result, shellfish harvesting is only allowed from "safe" waters. Significant elements in this system is the requirement, that all shellfish containers bear a tag that identifies the type and quantity of shellfish, the harvester, harvest location and date of harvest.

The preventive measure for CFP is to ensure that incoming fish have not been caught in an area for which there is a CFP advisory or for which there is knowledge that CFP is a problem.

Biogenic amines
These amines are produced as a result of time/temperature abuse of certain fish species and they can cause illness in consumers. It is therefore a post-harvest hazard, but very often a pre-receiving hazard introduced during handling on board the fishing vessel or during transportation to the plant after landing.

The preventive measure is rapid chilling of fish immediately after capture. Generally, fish should be packed in ice or chilled sea water in less than 12 h after catch or – in case of large fish such as tuna – chilled to an internal temperature of 10°C or less within 6 h after capture.

Parasites
It is reasonably likely that parasites will be present in significant numbers of wild caught fish species – and certain aquaculture fish if they are fed on an unheated processing waste or by-catch fish. Thus, parasites should be considered a significant hazard and a preventive measure to eliminate parasites must be identified during processing of any particular fish products.

Chemicals
Concern for this hazard primarily focus on fish harvested from fresh water, estuaries and near shore coastal waters and on fish from aquaculture. Without proper control it would be reasonably likely to expect that unsafe levels of chemicals could be present in the fish, thus representing a significant hazard. Apart from a few acutely toxic chemicals such as mercury, most chemicals are of medium severity from a health perspective.

The preventive measure is the presence of government controlled monitoring programme (see section 11.3) and ensuring that fish have not been harvested from waters that are closed to commercial fishing. For aquaculture fish the preventive measures are full controls of chemical contamination of the environment (soil/water) surrounding the aquaculture site, control of water quality and of the feed supply. Only approved agrochemicals and veterinary drugs should be used and only according to manufacturers' instructions. Correct withdrawal times must be observed.

Table 9.1 summarizes the hazard analysis of the pre-harvest/pre-receiving situation.

One of the great problems in ensuring the safety of seafood products is that processors often have no control and no information about the history of the raw material. This is a serious weakness and every effort to overcome this problem must be carried out. The significant hazards associated with the raw material must be identified and controlled before the raw material is received at the factory. The receiving step is the first CCP in any seafood processing, and the monitoring procedures will mainly be to check documents (certificates of origin, harvester, date and location of harvesting, copies and results of government monitoring programs, etc.).

Table 9.1 Hazard analysis of pre-harvest conditions and raw material handling.

Organism/ component of concern	Potential hazard		Analysis of hazard			Control		
	Contamination	Growth	Severity	Likely occurrence	Significant	Govt. monitoring programme	PP[1]	Incl. in HACCP plan
Pathogenic bacteria								
indigenous	-	+	high	high	+	-	-	+
non-indigenous	+	+	high	high	+	+	+	+
Viruses	+	-	high	high/low[2]	+/-	+	+	+
Biotoxins	+	-	high	high/low[2]	+/-	+	-	+
Biogenic amines	-	+	low	high/low[2]	+/-	-	-	+
Parasites	+	-	low	high	+	-	-	+
Chemicals	+	-	medium	high/low[2]	+/-	+	-	+

1. *PP = Prerequisite Programme*
2. *depending on fish/bivalve shellfish species, geographical position and season, the likely occurrence may be high or low*

Table 9.2 Hazard analysis of processing of bivalve shellfish.

Organism/ component of concern	Potential hazard		Analysis of hazard			Control		
	Contamination	Growth	Severity	Likely occurrence	Significant	Govt. monitoring programme	PP[1]	Incl. in HACCP plan
Pathogenic bacteria								
indigenous	+	+	high	high	+	-	-	+
non-indigenous	+	+	high	high	+	+	+	+
Viruses	+	-	high	high	+	+	+	+
Biotoxins	+	-	high	high	+	+	-	+
Biogenic amines	-	-						
Parasites	-	-						
Chemicals	+	-	medium	high	+	+	-	+

1. *PP = Prerequisite Programme*

9.2 Molluscan shellfish

The molluscan shellfish are harvested by being raked or trawled from the bottom (oysters, mussels) or dug from the sand at low tide (clams and cockles). After harvesting, the shellfish are sorted (size), washed and packed in bags or crates or just left in a pile on deck. The shellfish may be transported and sold live to the consumer or they may be processed (shucked) raw or by use of heat. The heat applied in processing is only enough to facilitate shucking by causing the animal to relax the adductor muscle, and has no effect on the microbial contamination of the animals. The shucked meat is washed, packed and sold fresh, frozen or further processed and canned.

Most molluscs (oysters, mussels, clams, cockles) grow and are harvested in shallow, near-shore estuarine waters. Thus there is a strong possibility that the live animals may be contaminated with sewage-derived pathogens (pathogenic bacteria, viruses) as well as those from the general environment. Also biotoxins and chemicals can be present. Due to the filter feeding of molluscs, a high concentration of disease agents may be present in the animals and therefore constitutes a serious hazard. During processing further contamination with pathogens (bacteria, virus) may take place including growth of bacteria if time and temperature conditions are favourable. As most molluscs are traditionally eaten raw or very lightly cooked, this will further increase the risk. This is confirmed by the epidemiological evidence presented by Garret and Hudak-Roos (1991), who reported that 7% of all outbreaks of seafood-borne diseases (20% of all cases) in the USA in the period 1982-87 were caused by molluscan shellfish.

Although molluscan shellfish constitutes less than 0.1% of the seafood consumed in the USA, they are responsible for a great number of disease outbreaks caused by pathogenic bacteria, toxic marine algae or viruses. Available surveillance data suggests that seafood-borne diseases due to unknown aetiologies, such as unspecified hepatitis and certain *Vibrio* species (*V. parahaemolyticus*, *V. vulnificus*, non 01 *V. cholera*) represent the greatest risk for persons consuming raw molluscan shellfish (Ahmed, 1992). In England and Wales, 17 general outbreaks of gastroenteritis in 1996 and 1997 were associated with consumption of shellfish (Anon., 1998) where a total of 232 people became ill. Five outbreaks were associated with small round structured viruses (SRSV). Astrovirus, diarrhetic shellfish poisoning (DSP) and salmonellae were each associated with one outbreak. In another five outbreaks, a viral aetiology was suspected and in four outbreaks no pathogen was identified.

Viruses were also the most significant cause of shellfish-associated diseases in New York State (Lipp and Rose 1997). A total of 339 seafood-associated outbreaks were reported in the period 1980-94 and shellfish accounted for 216 (64%) outbreaks. Norwalk virus and gastrointestinal virus (small round structured virus) were the most common cause of disease. Thus a number of significant hazards can be identified as shown in Table 9.2 above:

It follows that the significant hazards to be controlled in molluscs processing are:

a. Contamination with pathogens (bacteria, viruses, biotoxins, chemicals) from the harvesting area
b. Further contamination with pathogens (bacteria, virus) during processing
c. Growth of pathogens during processing and storage

The following *preventive measures* can be applied to minimise the risk outlined above:

re a:
- Control and monitoring of harvesting areas (see Chapter 11). Check for tags and ensure that incoming raw material is from licensed harvesters or certified dealers
- Depuration (see section 5.1.3)

It is well known that none of these measures are 100% effective, but unfortunately no other CCP can be identified for this hazard (contamination). For this reason, molluscs to be eaten raw should be provided with a warning label to inform consumers of the risk.

re b:
- Further contamination during processing is a hazard, which will be controlled by the pre-requisite programme

re c:
- limit the time from harvest to refrigeration
- proper chilling (<5°C) at all times during storage (raw material and final product). This aspect is included in the prerequisite programme.

Therefore, the only two critical control points to be identified and included in the HACCP plan ar 1) the receiving step where it is possible to exercise control of the source of the molluscs, and 2 the labelling step, where it can be checked that the raw consumption warning is on the label. Th following details could be entered in the HACCP plan for the receiving step:

Critical limits
- All shell stock containers must bear a tag that discloses the date and place where harvested, the quantity and name and license number of harvester. No molluscs from closed areas must enter the plant

Monitoring program
- What: tags, labels, licence of fisherman
- How: visual check
- When: all containers
- Who: receiving employee, supervisor or QC-staff

Corrective actions
- reject if untagged or from closed areas

Record keeping
- Receiving records on all shellfish (quantity, harvesting details)

Verification
- Daily review of records

A generic HACCP plan for production and processing of oysters to be consumed raw is shown in Appendix 4.

9.3 Raw fish – to be consumed raw

The hazards related to these products are primarily associated with the pre-harvest / pre-receiving situation (section 9.1). However, in the hazard analysis some of these hazards can be excluded. As already stated, contamination of raw fish with indigenous pathogenic bacteria is unlikely to be high enough to provoke disease and therefore not a significant hazard. Growth of these bacteria and of histamine producing bacteria is a potential hazard, but it is very unlikely in a product to be eaten raw. For this to happen the fish must be kept for some time at elevated temperatures and in this case also spoilage organism will grow. Since the latter will grow much faster than the pathogens the fish is likely to spoil or be unfit for raw consumption before sufficient growth of pathogens and histamine producing bacteria has taken place. The results of a general hazard analysis are shown in Table 9.3.

The significant hazards are:

a. Contamination of fish with non-indigenous bacteria, viruses, biotoxins or environmental chemical contaminants (heavy metals, pesticides, drugs in aquaculture)

b. Presence of parasites.

The following preventive measures can be applied:

re a:
- Control and monitoring of harvesting areas (see Chapter 11) including control of the use of drugs in aquaculture
- Contamination (bacteria, viruses) during processing is controlled by the pre-

requisite programme
- Prohibition of the use of puffer fish for human consumption
- Avoidance (sorting) of fish with a record of causing ciguatera

re b: • Introduction of a freezing step to eliminate the risk from parasites.

While the preventive measure for control of parasites is 100% effective, this is not the case for control of the pre-harvest contamination of fish with pathogenic organisms or compounds. There are serious weaknesses in a monitoring program as outlined in Chapter 11, and no effective CCP can be identified for the control of ciguatera.

Only two CCPs are identified in the processing of raw fish to be eaten raw:

- the receiving step
- the freezing step

Critical limits
- in situations where contamination with non-indigenous pathogens from the harvest area as well as contamination with any chemical is a possibility, a source control or certificate must accompany all lots of fish. This certificate must ensure that the fish were not harvested in waters that are closed to fishing or in any way contaminated with unwanted compounds (i.e. drugs in aquaculture fish)
- A list of tolerances for environmental chemical contaminants is show in section 5.2
- Critical limits for the freezing step are show in section 5.1.4

Monitoring program
- What: time and temperature at freezing step. Tags, labels, licence of fisherman
- How: visual check
- When: all containers. Continuous recording of freezing temperature
- Who: receiving employee, supervisor or QC-staff

Corrective actions
- reject if untagged or from closed areas
- adjust freezer. Refreeze material not properly frozen

Record keeping
- Receiving records on all fish raw material (quantity, harvesting details)
- Temperature records

Verification
- Daily review of records

9.4 Fresh/frozen fish and crustaceans – to be fully cooked before consumption

The hazard analysis of these products is fairly straightforward and uncomplicated. The animals are in most cases caught in the sea or freshwater, handled and processed without any use of additives or chemical preservatives and finally distributed with chilling or freezing as the only means of preservation.

The epidemiological evidence has shown that the presence of histamine or biotoxins accounts for nearly 80% of all disease outbreaks caused by "fish". Low levels of pathogenic bacteria and viruses may be present on raw fish as part of the natural flora and/or as a result of contamination during handling and processing. As the product will be cooked before consumption, it is very unlikely that this low level of pathogens will cause any disease. Even if any growth has taken place in the raw fish to be cooked, it is unlikely to produce any disease. Pathogenic bacteria and viruses are therefore not significant hazards, which need to be controlled.

In contrast the biotoxin (ciguatoxin and tetrodotoxin) are heat stable and cooking the fish before consumption is not likely to eliminate this hazard. In areas where this hazard is likely to occur (see section 5.1.5) it must be noted as a significant hazard.

Similarly the biogenic amines (histamine) are resistant to heat, and if present in the raw fish it is likely to cause disease. Production of histamine in raw fish is therefore a significant hazard that must be controlled (see also section 5.1.2).

Parasites are common in fish, but normal household cooking will kill the parasites, and their possible presence is therefore not a significant hazard.

Chemical contamination of fish is unlikely and not a significant hazard except for aquaculture fish and fish from coastal areas subject to industrial pollution (see section 5.2).

Table 9.3 Hazard analysis of raw fish to be consumed raw.

Organism/ component of concern	Potential hazard		Analysis of hazard			Control		
	Contamination	Growth	Severity	Likely occurrence	Significant	Govt. monitoring programme	PP[1]	Incl. in HACCP plan
Pathogenic bacteria								
indigenous	-	+	high	low	-			
non-indigenous	+	-	high	high	+	+	+	+
Viruses	+	-	high	high	+	+	+	+
Biotoxins	+	-	high	high/low[2]	+/-	(+)	-	+
Biogenic amines	-	+	low	low	-			
Parasites	+	-	low	high	+	-	-	+
Chemicals	+	-	medium	high/low[2]	+/-	+	-	+

1. *PP = Pre-requisite Programme*
2. *depending on fish/bivalve shellfish species, geographical position and season, the likely occurrence may be high or low*

Table 9.4 Hazard analysis of fresh/frozen fish and crustaceans to be cooked before consumption.

Organism/ component of concern	Potential hazard		Analysis of hazard			Control		
	Contamination	Growth	Severity	Likely occurrence	Significant	Govt. monitoring programme	PP[1]	Incl. in HACCP plan
Pathogenic bacteria								
indigenous	-	+	high	low	-			
non-indigenous	+	+	high	low	-			
Viruses	+	-	high	low	-			
Biotoxins	+	-	high	high/low[2]	+/-	+	-	+
Biogenic amines	-	+	low	high/low[2]	+/-	-	+	+
Parasites	+	-	low	low	-			
Chemicals	+	-	medium	high/low[2]	+/-	+	-	+

1. *PP = Pre-requisite Programme*
2. *depending on fish/bivalve shellfish species, geographical position and season, the likely occurrence may be high or low*

Table 9.4 summarize the hazard analysis for this product. Thus, the significant safety hazards are:

- Presence of biotoxins. This hazard only applies to fish from warm waters with a history of causing ciguatera (Ciguatera fish poisoning, CFP) and to puffer fish
- Formation of histamine. This hazard only applies to scombroid fishes (see section 5.1.2)
- Presence of chemicals. This hazard only applies to fish from aquaculture or coastal areas.

For all other fish (~ the large majority of marine fish) there are no safety hazards and no HACCP plan is required, only a Hazard Analysis Worksheet needs to be elaborated.

The preventive measures that can be applied to the significant hazards are:

- Sorting of the catch to exclude puffer fish. Making sure that the fish have not been caught in an area for which there is a CFP advisory or for which there is knowledge of a CFP-problem. It is clear that the latter preventive measure is not 100% effective, but no other means are available
- Rapid chilling of fish immediately after catch to temperatures <10°C is the most important element in any strategy for preventing the formation of histamine. Further chilling towards the freezing point is desirable to prevent long-term low-temperature development of histamine. Control of temperature is part of the prerequisite programme
- The preventive measure for chemical contamination of fish is to compare information on capture area with government ban on fishing.

Based on the above, the only CCP for raw fish to be cooked before consumption is the receiving step [possible histamine formation during processing and storage of scombroid fish is taken care of by the pre-requisite programme]. The following details can be entered in the HACCP plan:

Critical limits	• No puffer fish allowed in processing. No fish from an area where there is an CFP advisory is allowed in processing • No fish harvested in an area closed for fishing is allowed in processing • For histamine the critical limit is <50 ppm
Monitoring program	• What: sorting procedures, tags, labels, harvesting vessels record decomposition of lot. Temperature records • How: Visual check • When: All lots • Who: Receiving employee
Corrective action	• Reject lots with no information on catching area, or if from closed area • Reject the lot or perform histamine analysis on lots of poor sensory quality • Inform harvester, adjust cooling procedures
Record keeping	• Receiving records, all lots, temperature records
Verification	• Records review, calibration of thermo-recorders, histamine analysis of selected samples

9.5 Lightly-preserved fish products

This group includes fish products with low salt content (Water Phase Salt (WPS) <6%) and low acid content (pH >5.0). Preservatives (sorbate, benzoate, NO_2, smoke) may or may not bee added. The products may be prepared from raw or cooked raw material, but are normally consumed without any prior heating. Product examples are salted, marinated, cold smoked or gravad fish. These products have a limited shelf life and are typically stored at temperature ≤ 5°C. The presence in these products of low numbers of pathogenic bacteria normally found in the aquatic and the general environment (*Clostridiums botulinum*, pathogenic *Vibrio* sp., *Listeria monocytogenes*) is a potential hazard. Due to their low numbers, the mere presence is not a significant hazard. However, if these organisms are allowed to grow to high numbers, they are very likely to cause a serious disease, and are therefore representing a significant hazard. It should be remembered, that growth and toxin production can take place in the raw material as well as in the final product.

Contaminations of products during processing with viruses and non-indigenous pathogenic bacteria as well as possible growth of the latter are also potential hazards. However, these hazards are prevented by the prerequisite programme and therefore not likely to occur.

The presence of biotoxins (Ciguatera Fish Poison, CFP) is a potential hazard if the raw material is a fish specie with a history of causing CFP and originating in an area where CFP is known to occur.

Production of biogenic amines is a significant hazard in all products based on scombroid fish or all fish containing large amounts of free histidine in the flesh. The production requires growth of histamine-decarboxylating bacteria. A number of different bacteria are able to produce histamine at various conditions (as discussed in section 5.1.2). It should be remembered that biogenic amines may be produced in the raw material as well as in final products.

Parasites are common in many fish species in all parts of the world, and the processing conditions and preservative parameters for lightly preserved fish products are not sufficient to kill the parasites. Thus, a "processing for safety" step must be included in the process of this type of products to control this significant hazard.

Chemical contamination of raw material is a potential hazard if it originates in aquaculture or certain coastal fisheries. Only if this is the case, should chemical contamination be regarded as a significant hazard.

The hazard analysis is summarized in Table 9.5. The significant hazards are the result of:

a. Growth of pathogenic bacteria from the aquatic or the general environment
b. Production of biogenic amines (scombroid fish)
c. Presence of parasites
d. Chemical contamination (depending on geographical area).

The following preventive measures can be applied.

re a:
- Growth of *C. botulinum* can be prevented by WPS $\geq$ 3.5% and a storage temperature $\leq$5°C (see also section 5.1.1.1.)
- Growth of *L. monocytogenes* cannot with certainty be prevented by the parameters used in the preservation of this category of products
- An alternative solution is to reduce shelf life of the products to a period of no growth of *L. monocytogenes*. The length of this period needs to be established by experimentation

re b:
- Storage at low temperature (<5°C) will prevent the growth of a number but not all of histamine producing bacteria. There are no experimental data to demonstrate complete control of this hazard

re c:
- Introduction of a freezing step (-20°C for at least 24 h, see also section 5.1.4)

re d:
- Securing raw material from areas with no chemical contamination.

Based on the considerations above, the following CCPs can be identified: Receiving step, salting step and freezing step. The following details can be entered in the HACCP plan:

Critical limits

- Receiving step: only raw material of good sensory quality will be used. No fish from an area where there is a CFP advisory must be used. No fish harvested in area closed for fishing is allowed
- Salting: WPS ≥ 3.5% NaCl
- Freezing step: -20°C for at least 24 hours
- Storage temperature ≤ 5°C

Monitoring program

- What: sensory quality of raw material. Certificate of origin of fish. Salting procedures. Temperatures and times of freezing
- How: visual
- When: all lots. Continuous recording of temperature
- Who: receiving employee. QC staff

Corrective action

- Reject lots of poor quality or with no certificate of origin
- Adjust salting process
- Check WPS in lots produced when process is out of control
- Adjust freezing procedures.

9.6 Fermented fish

Traditionally the term "fermented fish" covers both enzyme hydrolysed and microbial fermented fish products. However, a clear distinction should be made between these products. Thus, Paludan-Müller (2002) suggests to define fermented fish as "products which contain a carbohydrate source and in which the level of salt is less than 8% water phase salt (WPS)". This level of salt (≤8%) allows the fermentative growth of lactic acid bacteria and a concomitant decrease in pH to <4.5. In contrast enzyme hydrolysed fish has a WPS >8% and a final pH between 5-7. A large number of different fermented fish products are found in South-East Asia. The products are traditionally stored at ambient temperatures and consumed without any cooking. Fermented fish products have been associated with a number of outbreaks of food-borne diseases such as botulism, trematodiosis, salmonellosis and vibriosis.

The natural presence of pathogenic bacteria from the aquatic and general environment is not considered a significant hazard in this product due to the low numbers. However, conditions for growth of some of these organisms (*C. botulinum* type A and B, *Listeria monocytogenes*, *Vibrio sp.*) are good until the pH decreases to near 4.5. This takes about 1-2 days at 30°C in a natural fermentation. Rapid and adequate acidification is therefore the preventive measure for this significant hazard. For complete safety, temperatures during fermentation should be kept at <10°C until final pH has been reached.

Contamination of fermented fish products with pathogenic bacteria from the animal/human reservoir and with pathogenic virus are potential hazards, which will be controlled by the prerequisite programme.

Most fermented fish products are based on freshwater fish as raw material. However, if marine fish are used, the presence of biotoxin (CFP) should be considered a potential hazard as discussed in section 9.1.

Formation of biogenic amines (histamine) is a health hazard primarily related to marine, scombroid fish species and is not a potential hazard when freshwater fish are used as raw material.

Parasites, particularly trematodes are very common in fish used as raw material for fermented fish. As there is no killing step for these parasites in the normal processing they are very likely to cause disease and must be regarded as a significant hazard. The preventive measures are food safety education and to bring about changes in the traditional consumption practices of eating non-cooked fermented fish. Until then fermented fish to be eaten without any cooking must have a freezing step included (see section 5.1.4). The concern for chemical hazards are related to the raw material and described in section 9.1.

Table 9.5 Hazard analysis of lightly preserved fish products.

Organism/ component of concern	Potential hazard		Analysis of hazard			Control		
	Contamination	Growth	Severity	Likely occurrence	Significant	Govt. monitoring programme	PP[1]	Incl. in HACCP plan
Pathogenic bacteria								
indigenous	-	+	high	high	+	-	-	+
non-indigenous	+	+	high	high	+	-	+	-
Viruses	+	-	high	high	+	-	+	-
Biotoxins	+	-	high	high/low[2]	+/-	+	-	+
Biogenic amines	-	+	low	high/low[2]	+/-	-	-	+
Parasites	+	-	low	high	+	-	-	+
Chemicals	+	-	medium	high/low[2]	+/-	+	-	+

1. *PP = Prerequisite Programme*
2. *depending on fish/bivalve shellfish species, geographical position and season, the likely occurrence may be high or low*

Table 9.6 Hazard analysis of fermented fish.

Organism/ component of concern	Potential hazard		Analysis of hazard			Control		
	Contamination	Growth	Severity	Likely occurrence	Significant	Govt. monitoring programme	PP[1]	Incl. in HACCP plan
Pathogenic bacteria								
indigenous	-	+	high	high	+	-	-	+
non-indigenous	+	+	high	high	+	-	+	-
Viruses	+	-	high	high	+	-	+	-
Biotoxins	+	-	high	high/low[2]	+/-	(+)	-	+
Biogenic amines	-	+	low	high/low[2]	+/-	-	-	+
Parasites	+	-	low	high	+	-	-	+
Chemicals	+	-	medium	high/low[2]	+/-	+	-	+

1. *PP = Prerequisite Programme*
2. *depending on fish/bivalve shellfish species, geographical position and season, the likely occurrence may be high or low*

The hazard analysis for fermented fish products is summarized in Table 9.6. The CCPs in production of fermented fish are:

Receiving step:	Check on raw materials as described in section 9.1
Time/temperature conditions during fermentation:	Inhibition of growth of indigenous pathogens
Freezing step:	Control of parasites.

9.7 Semi-preserved fish

These are fish products with >6% water phase salt (WPS) or a pH <5.0. Preservatives (sorbate, benzoate, nitrate) may or may not be added. These products require chill storage (< 10°C) and may have a shelf life of 6 months or more. Normally, there is no heat-treatment applied neither during processing nor in the preparation before consumption. Traditional production often includes a long ripening period (several months) of the raw material before final processing. Product examples are salted and marinated fish, fermented fish and caviar products.

There is epidemiological evidence that this type of products has been the cause of illness related to the presence of bacterial toxins (botulism), parasites, biotoxins and histamine.

The presence of low numbers of pathogenic bacteria normally found in the environment is not a significant hazard in these products (not likely to cause disease). Contamination with non-indigenous pathogens (bacteria and viruses) is a potential hazard to be prevented by the prerequisite programme.

Growth and possible toxin production of pathogenic bacteria is not possible in these products if correctly processed and storage temperature is kept at ≤10°C. As for lightly preserved fish products it must be pointed out that growth and toxin production may take place in the raw material. Bacterial toxins, incl. botulinum toxins are very stable at high salt and low pH (Huss and Rye Petersen, 1980). Any toxin present or preformed in the raw material will be carried over to the final product, and this hazard can only be controlled by having full control over the complete handling and processing steps from harvesting to consumption.

Biotoxins (ciguatera) is a potential hazard only if the raw material used is a fish specie with a history of causing CFP and originating in an area where CFP is known to occur. This is not very likely to happen, and therefore biotoxins are not a significant hazard for this product.

Production of biogenic amines may take place both in the raw material and in the final product. It is a significant hazard as it is very likely to occur in scombroid fish if there is a loss of control.

Parasites are very common in fish species used as raw material for semi-preserved products. This hazard is therefore significant (likely to occur) and must be prevented.

Chemical contamination of raw material is a potential hazard if it originates from aquaculture or certain coastal fisheries. Table 9.7 summarizes the hazard analysis of these products. The CCPs in production of semi-preserved fish products are:

Receiving step:	Check on raw material as described in section 9.1
Time-temperature conditions:	Chilled storage for prevention of growth of pathogens. Critical limits are: < 5°C for raw materials < 10°C for final products
Salting step:	Critical limit is WPS ≥ 6%

	Critical limits for killing parasites: see section 5.1.4
Addition of acids and/or preservatives:	Critical pH limit ≤ 5
Freezing step:	Killing of parasites. Critical limits, see section 5.1.4.

Monitoring procedures, corrective action programme and verification procedures must be set up and records kept of all actions

9.8 Mildly heat-processed fish products

A number of fish products receive a heat treatment during processing. Examples are: pasteurised or cooked and breaded fish fillets, cooked shrimp and crabmeat, cook-chill products and hot smoked fish. After the heat-treatment the various products may pass through further processing steps before being packed and stored/distributed as chilled or frozen products. Some of these products may receive additional heat treatment before consumption (cooked and breaded fillets, cook-chill products) or they may be eaten without further treatment (hot smoked fish, cooked shrimp). Thus, some of these products are ready-to-eat and extremely sensitive to contamination after the heat treatment.

To further illustrate the safety aspects, there is ample epidemiological evidence that this type of product has been the cause of food poisoning due to growth of coagulase-positive *Staphylococcus aureus* and enteropathogenic organisms among the Enterobacteriaceae and Vibrionaceae. Marine crustaceans, usually shrimp, crab or dishes made from them, accounted for 25 outbreaks of food-borne diseases reported in the USA during the period 1977-84 (Bryan, 1988).

In the application of the HACCP system to these types of products, the heat-treatment is a very critical processing step. Hazards identified before this step may or may not be eliminated depending on the degree of heat being applied. Most criteria for heat-treatments have been laid down as a consequence of economical and technological considerations and not for hygienic or public health reasons. Increased safety will be obtained if the cooking/heating procedures could be designed to eliminate vegetative cells of pathogens and spores of the most sensitive species. Generally, a reduction of six orders of magnitude (six logarithms) in the level of contamination is recommended. This performance criterion is the so-called 6D process ("D" stands for "decimal reduction") as described in section 13.2.

Listeria monocytogenes is normally used as a target organism for measuring the heat treatment and is regarded as the most heat-resistant food-borne pathogen that does not form spores.

Most products in this group are depending entirely on the heating process and chilled storage for safety and shelf life as they do not contain any bacteria controlling ingredients. It is very likely that pathogens will cause disease if these factors are out of control. Pathogen survival during the cooking/heating procedure and pathogen growth during storage are significant hazards that must be included in the HACCP plan. In contrast, it is very unlikely that viruses, parasites and histamine producing bacteria will survive the heat treatment.

Recontamination of products after the heat-treatment and before packaging can also cause consumer illness. In many productions this hazard will be controlled by the prerequisite programme. In others, where e.g. the recontamination is caused by faulty container sealing or incorrect hot-filling procedures, recontamination is a significant hazard that needs to be included in the HACCP plan.

Considerations to the possible presence of biotoxin and chemical contamination should be as outlined in section 9.1. Table 9.8 summarizes the hazard analysis of these products.

In a simple production (e.g. cooked shrimp vacuum-packed in plastic bags) the significant hazards are:

a. Survival of pathogens
b. Recontamination after cooking
c. Growth of pathogens
d. Raw material quality (chemical hazards).

The CCPs during production will be:

Receiving step: Control of raw materials

Cooking step: Control of survival of pathogens

Recontamination and growth of pathogens will be taken care of by the prerequisite programme. The critical limits for the cooking step (time/temperature conditions) should be set at a point that if not met the safety of the product may be questionable. If a more restrictive limit is set, the result will be a loss of product.

Table 9.7 Hazard analysis of semi-preserved fish.

Organism/ component of concern	Potential hazard		Analysis of hazard			Control		
	Contamination	**Growth**	**Severity**	**Likely occurrence**	**Significant**	**Govt. monitoring programme**	**PP[1]**	**Incl. in HACCP plan**
Pathogenic bacteria								
indigenous	-	+	high	high	+	-	-	+
non-indigenous	+	+	high	high	+	-	+	-
Viruses	+	-	high	high	+	-	+	-
Biotoxins	-	-						
Biogenic amines	-	+	low	high/low[2]	+/-	-	-	+
Parasites	+	-	low	high	+	-	-	+
Chemicals	+	-	medium	high/low[2]	+/-	+	-	+

1. *PP = Prerequisite Programme*
2. *depending on fish/bivalve shellfish species, geographical position and season, the likely occurrence may be high or low*

Table 9.8 Hazard analysis of mildly heat-processed fish.

Organism/ component of concern	Potential hazard		Analysis of hazard			Control		
	Survival or re-contamination	**Growth**	**Severity**	**Likely occurrence**	**Significant**	**Govt. monitoring programme**	**PP[1]**	**Incl. in HACCP plan**
Pathogenic bacteria								
indigenous	+	+	high	high	+	-	+	+
non-indigenous	+	+	high	high	+	-	+	+
Viruses	+	-	high	high	+	-	+	+
Biotoxins	+	-	high	high/low[2]	+/-	+	-	+
Biogenic amines	-	+	low	high/low[2]	+/-	-	-	+
Parasites	+	-	low	low	-			
Chemicals	+	-	medium	high/low[2]	+/-	+	-	+

1. *PP = Pre-requisite Programme*
2. *depending on fish/bivalve shellfish species, geographical position and season, the likely occurrence may be high or low*

9.9 Heat-sterilized fish products packed in sealed containers (canned fish)

The basis for canning is the use of thermal processing to achieve sterility of the final product. The containers are distributed at ambient temperatures and often stored for months even years under these conditions. The contents of the cans are normally eaten without any heating immediately before consumption.

Canned fish has been the cause of outbreaks of botulism and cases of histamine and staphylococcal enterotoxin poisoning (Ababouch, 2002). The general hazard analysis is shown in Table 9.9.

The significant hazards related to this type of products are:

- Quality of raw material (biotoxins, chemicals)
- Survival of pathogens (*C. botulinum*) during heat processing
- Presence of heat-stable toxins (biotoxins, histamine, *S. aureus* ET)
- Recontamination of product after heat processing (faulty containers, poor sealing, contaminated cooling water, faulty container handling).

The CCPs for these hazards are:

Receiving step: Hazards are raw material quality as described in section 9.1
Quality of cans
Critical limit: Cans must meet container specifications for safety.
Monitoring: Letter of guarantee from supplier. Visual examination of all lots of empty cans
Corrective action: Reject defect cans. Contact supplier

Filling: Corrective filling is important for proper heat-penetration
Visual check regularly (every half hour) by floor supervisor

Sealing: Faulty sealing may result in recontamination
Can closures must be checked at regular intervals (every half hour) visually and always when setting up a new machine or adjusting an old one. Tear down measurements must be done at the beginning of the shift and every 2 hours thereafter by Q.C.
Corrective actions: Shut down of processing line and inform plant manager. All products produced since last good check is put on hold. The cause of the problem must be identified before start up again
Any actions and measurements are recorded

Retorting: The hazard is survival of pathogens
Critical limit is the botulinum cook or 12-D process (see section 5.1.1.1.)
If time/temperature requirements are violated, products must be put on hold for reprocessing and the cause must be identified. Records on all actions and measurements must be kept
The verification programme should include a review of all operations and monitoring procedures and calibration of thermometers and automatic recorders

Cooling: Recontamination is possible if minute quantities of water enter the can. Use of chlorinated cooling water is a safe precaution. There must be measurable residual chlorine in the water (critical limit) and samples should be tested at least two times per day by a designated person (monitoring).

Post-process handling: Contamination of hot and wet cans with *S. aureus* is prevented by isolation of the storage area of hot and wet cans and application of GHP by personnel.

Additional verification procedures are common practice and in some cases a legal requirement (EC 1991). This includes checks carried out at random to ensure that products have undergone appropriate heat treatment. This requirement involves taking samples of the final product for:

- incubation tests. Incubation of samples must be carried out at 37°C for seven days or at 35°C for ten days or any other equivalent combination
- microbiological examination of contents of containers in the establishments laboratory or in any other approved laboratory.

9.10 Dried, smoke-dried, heavily-salted fish

These are products with a very high salt content (>10% WPS) and/or a very low water activity ($a_w \leq$ 0.85). Dried or salted fish are usually considered stable at high temperatures and therefore stored and distributed at ambient temperatures.

No growth of pathogens is possible in these products if correctly processed, not even at ambient temperatures. The most salt-tolerant pathogenic organism is *Staphylococcus aureus* (which can grow at $a_w \geq 0.83$ and produce toxin at Aw $\geq$ 0.85, see also section 5.1.1.2), and this organism should therefore be considered as target pathogen for drying.

A critical phase in processing is the time until salt has penetrated and the WPS reaches 10% or the a_w is below 0.85 in the thickest part of the fish. For this reason larger fish (>15 cm in length) should be eviscerated prior to processing.

Contamination of dried or salted fish with enteropathogenic bacteria and viruses is a potential hazard, which will be prevented by the prerequisite programme.

The presence of toxic fish and chemical contamination of raw material are potential hazards as discussed in section 9.1.

The possible presence of parasites is not a significant hazard in these products. It is very unlikely they will cause a disease due to the rapid killing of the parasites in an environment with very high salt content (see section 5.1.4).

Table 9.9 Hazard analysis of heat sterilised products packed in sealed containers (canned fish).

Organism/ component of concern	Potential hazard		Analysis of hazard			Control		
	Survival and/or re-contamination	Growth	Severity	Likely occurrence	Significant	Govt. monitoring programme	PP[1]	Incl. in HACCP plan
Pathogenic bacteria								
indigenous	+	+	high	high	+	-	+	+
non-indigenous	+	+	high	high	+	-	+	+
Viruses	+	-	high	low	-			
Biotoxins	+	-	high	high/low[2]	+/-	+	-	+
Biogenic amines	+	+	low	high/low[2]	+/-	-	-	+
Parasites	+	-	low	low	-			
Chemicals	+	-	medium	high/low[2]	+/-	+	-	+

1. *PP = Prerequisite Program me*
2. *depending on fish/bivalve shellfish species, geographical position and season, the likely occurrence may be high or low*

Table 9.10 Hazard analysis of dried, smoke-dried or heavily salted fish.

Organism/ component of concern	Potential hazard		Analysis of hazard			Control		
	Re-Contamination	Growth	Severity	Likely occurrence	Significant	Govt. monitoring programme	PP[1]	Incl. in HACCP plan
Pathogenic bacteria								
indigenous	-	-						
non-indigenous	+	-	high	high	+	-	+	-
Viruses	+	-	high	high	+	-	+	-
Biotoxins	+	-	high	high/low[2]	+/-	+	-	+
Biogenic amines	-	+	low	high/low[2]	+/-	-	-	+
Parasites	+	-	low	low	-			
Chemicals	+	-	medium	high/low[2]	+/-	+	-	+

1. *PP = Pre-requisite Programme*
2. *depending on fish/bivalve shellfish species, geographical position and season, the likely occurrence may be high or low*

When scombroid fish are used as raw material, formation of histamine is a significant hazard. Histamine may be formed in the raw material before processing (see section 9.1.) but also in the final product as some halophilic bacteria are able to produce this compound (Kimma *et al.*, 2001). However, there is some uncertainty if this is a theoretical risk only. There are no reported cases of histamine poisoning from these products and there are no experimental data to demonstrate the possible risk.

The CCPs in the production of dried or salted fish are:

Receiving step:	Hazard to be controlled is the raw material quality (presence of biotoxin, chemical contamination and histamine)
Salting/drying step:	The hazard is growth of pathogens Critical limit is time to reach 10% WPS or a_w 0.85 in fish flesh.

9.11 Seafood risk categories

In ranking seafood into risk categories, the method of NACMCF (1992) with some modifications has been applied. The following six hazard characteristics and risk factors have been considered:

1. No terminal heat treatment. Apart from raw fish to be eaten cooked or fried, all other fish products are ready-to-eat
2. The safety record. Is there any evidence, that this particular product has been associated with food borne disease many times – or with very serious diseases? With reference to tables in section 4.1 it can be stated, that the safety record is poor for:
   - molluscan shellfish and fish to be eaten raw due to the presence of (accumulated) biological hazards (viruses, pathogenic bacteria, parasites, biotoxins)
   - molluscan shellfish, tropical reef fish and scombroid fish to be cooked before consumption due to the presence of heat stable aquatic toxins or scombrotoxin
   - presence of heat stable biogenic amines in canned sterilised products and few outbreaks of botulism caused by the same type of product
   - some fermented fish; e.g. salted fish from the Middle East or products from Alaska
3. The production/processing does not include a Critical Control Point for at least one identified hazard. This situation applies to the:
   - accumulation of biological hazards in shellfish (see section 5.13)
   - presence of biotoxins (ciguatera) in fish from tropical reefs (see section 5.13).
4. The product is subject to potentially harmful contamination or recontamination after processing and before packaging. All raw fish and fish product, which has not been subject to any bactericidal treatment, are likely to harbour pathogenic organisms as part of their natural flora (see section 5.1.1.). Potentially harmful recontamination is possible and reasonably likely to occur for products being mildly heat-treated before being placed in the final container (cooked shrimp, hot smoked fish). However, also the risk associated with lightly preserved fish and fish and shellfish to be eaten raw may increase due to this factor (e.g. contamination of cold smoked fish with *L. monocytogenes*).

5. Products with a potential for abusive handling. This hazard refers mainly to handling and storing the fish product at abuse (elevated) temperatures. With the exception of sterilised, canned or fully preserved products, there is a potential for this hazard for all other types of fish products. However, this is not likely to occur for fish to be consumed raw, as spoilage will be very fast at elevated temperatures

6. Growth of pathogens. The growth of pathogens, particularly in ready-to-eat products is a serious hazard. Two potential hazards of this nature are known and likely to occur: the possible growth of *L. monocytogenes* in lightly preserved fish products and the growth of *C. botulinum* in some types of fermented seafoods. Growth of other pathogens in preserved

or heat-processed products is possible only if the preserving parameters are not applied as specified (see text) and other potential hazards are in fact occurring (temperature abuse, recontamination of heat processed fish). Spoilage bacteria will grow in all types of fish products (except sterilised products) and in most cases they will grow faster than any pathogen. This is particularly the case in raw, unprocessed or unpreserved fish, and for this reason growth of pathogens it is not considered an additional hazard likely to occur and influence the safety of this product.

The above considerations above are summarized in Tables 9.11 and 9.12. The various seafoods are assigned to a risk category in terms of health hazards by using a "+" (plus) to indicate a potential risk related to the hazard characteristics. The number of plusses will then determinate the risk category of the seafood concerned.

Table 9.11 Risk categories for fresh seafood products (modified after Huss *et al.*, 2000).

Seafood product	Characteristic that increases risk			Events that are reasonably likely to occur and which will increase risk			Risk Category
	No terminal heat application	Bad safety record	No CCP for identified Hazard	Harmful recontamination	Abusive handling	Growth or accumulation of hazard	
Molluscan shellfish							
Live, raw	+	+	+	+	+	+	High[1]
Cooked	-	+	+	-	-	+	Medium
Raw Fresh / frozen fish and crustacean							
Tropical reef	+	+	+	+	-	+	High
Scombroid	+	+	-	+	-	-	Medium
Other	+	-	-	+	-	-	Low
Fresh / frozen fish and crustacean to be cooked							
Tropical reef	-	+	+	-	-	+	Medium
Scombroid	-	+	-	-	+	+	Medium
Other	-	-	-	-	-	-	Low

1. *High risk products have 4 or more plusses. Medium risk products have 3 plusses. Low risk products have 2 plusses or less.*

Table 9.12 Risk categories for processed seafood products (modified after Huss *et al.*, 2000).

Seafood product	Characteristic that increases risk			Events that are reasonably likely to occur and which will increase risk			Risk Category
	No terminal heat application	Bad safety record	No CCP for identified Hazard	Harmful recontamination	Abusive handling	Growth or accumulation of hazard	
Lightly preserved NaCl < 6%, pH > 5.0; e.g. cold-smoked	+	-	(-)	+	+	+	High[1]
Fermented NaCl < 8%, pH changing	+	+	(+)	+	-	+	High
Semipreserved NaCl > 6%, pH < 5.0; e.g. marinated	+	-	-	-	+	+	Medium
Heat processed Hot smoked, pasteurised	+	-	-	+	+	+	High
Heat processed Canned, sterilised	+	+	-	-	-	-	Low
Dried, smoke dried, heavily salted	+/-	-	-	-	-	-	Low

1. *High risk products have 4 or more plusses. Medium risk products have 3 plusses. Low risk products have 2 plusses or les*

References

Ababouch, L. 2002. HACCP in the fish canning industry. In: Bremner, H.A. (ed) *Safety and quality issues in fish processing.* Woodhead Publishing Limited, Cambridge, UK. pp. 31-53.

Ahmed, F.E. 1992. Review: Assessing and managing risk due to consumption of seafood contaminated with microorganisms, parasites and natural toxins in the U.S. *International Journal of Food Science and Technology* 27, 243-260.

Anonymous 1998. Communicable Disease Report, vol 8, No 3, PHLS Public Health Laboratory Service, UK.

Bryan, F.L. 1988. Risks associated with vehicles of foodborne pathogens and toxins. *Journal of Food Protection* 51, 498-508.

EC (European Commission) 1991. Council Directive 91/493/EEC of 22 July 1991 laying down the health conditions for the production and the placing on the market of fishery products *Official Journal of the European Communities* L 268 , 24/09/1991 p. 0015 – 0034.

Huss, H.H. 1994. *Assurance of Seafood Quality.* FAO Fisheries Technical Paper No. 334., FAO, Rome, Italy.

Huss, H.H. and E. Rye Petersen 1980. The stability of *Clostridium botulinum* Type E toxin in a salty and/or acid environment. *Journal of Food Technology* 15, 619-627.

Huss, H.H., P.K. Ben Embarek and A. Reilly 2000. Prevention and control of hazards in seafood. *Food Control* 11, 149-156

Garrett, E.S. and M. Hudak-Ross 1991. Development of an HACCP based inspection system for the seafood industry. *Food Technology* 45, 53-57.

Kimma, B., Y. Konagaya and T. Fujii 2001. Histamine formation by *Tetragenococcus muriaticus* a halophilic lactic acid bacterium isolated from fish sauce. *International Journal of Food Microbiology* 70, 71-77.

Lipp, E.K. and J.B. Rose 1997. The role of seafood in foodborne diseases in the United States of America. *Revue Scientifique et Technique Office International des Epizooties* 16, 620-640.

NACMCF (National Advisory Committee on Microbiological Criteria for Foods) 1992. *Hazard Analysis Critical Control Point System.* FSIS Information Office, Washington DC, USA.

Paludan-Müller, C. 2002. Microbiology of fermented fish products. Ph.D. thesis. Danish Institute for Fisheries Research, Department of Seafood Research, Lyngby, and The Royal Veterinary and Agricultural University, Copenhagen.

10 APPLICATION OF HACCP PRINCIPLES IN THE MANAGEMENT OF OTHER QUALITY ASPECTS (Lone Gram)

Whilst the HACCP principles and concepts of farm-to-fork in risk assessments are clearly developed to ensure food safety, the approach and thinking can easily be applied to cover other quality aspects, such as sensory quality, composition or labeling, as well. Instead of identifying the hazards of the process / product, potential defects are considered. The steps or points at which control of the defects are to be controlled are called defect action points (DAPs) (CAC, 2002) as a parallel to the critical control points (CCPs) where hazards can be controlled. Similar to the procedures for CCPs, limits, monitoring procedures, corrective actions and verification procedures must be established at the DAPs.

Defect	**Defect Action Point (DAP)**
A condition found in a product which fails to meet essential quality, composition and/or labelling provisions of the appropriate standards or specifications (NOAA, 2000)	A point, step or procedure at which control can be applied and a defect can be prevented, eliminated or reduced to acceptable level, or a fraud risk eliminated (NOAA, 2000)

The analysis of potential defects and identification of DAPs follows the same procedures as when conducting a hazard analysis. For instance, the decision tree used to determine if a point is really a critical control point, can be used equally well to decide if a given point is a DAP.

Defects may, as hazards, be of (micro) biological, chemical or physical nature. The substitution of one (lower value) fish species for another (high value) is an example of a biological defect, fraud. Similarly, raw materials for production of semi-preserved herring must have specific lipid content for the right ripening and texture to develop. Therefore lower or higher lipid content is a biological defect. This should be monitored on the incoming raw material and batches with wrong lipid content should be used for other products.

Other kinds of defects include incorrect weight or incorrect labelling.

10.1 Microbiological aspects

This book has so far focused on the risk to consumer health arising from the presence and growth of microorganisms. However, microorganisms may have other adverse effects on the quality of fish and fish products. Thus growth and activity of microorganisms is the major cause of decomposition (spoilage) of all types of products where microorganisms have not been completely eliminated (such as in canned foods) or where growth of microorganisms has not been completely arrested (such as in frozen foods). A description of the spoilage patterns of different fish products and the microorganisms involved can be found in Huss (1995), Gram and Huss (2000) and Gram *et al.* (2002).

It has been estimated that between 10 and 50% of all foods produced are lost *post harvest* or *post slaughter* due to microbial activity (Kaferstein and Moy, 1993; cf Baird-Parker, 2000; WHO, 1995). Decomposition or presence of filth is the most common cause of detention of fish products imported into the US (FDA, 2002). Thus, out of 4,527 detentions in April, May and June 2002, 443 of the detained products were fish or seafood products. Of the 443 detentions, half (213) were detained because of filth and/or spoilage (FDA, 2002).

In principle control of decomposition of fish and fish products is simple since low temperature will retard all spoilage processes. In contrast, just a few hours exposure to high temperatures may accelerate spoilage. In some tropical countries, icing is not done on board the fishing boats and this leads to rapid reduction in eating quality (Figure 10.1). It also follows indirectly from the figure that temperature during storage is critical. Loss of quality occurs rapidly.

Figure 10.1
Quality changes in iced Nile perch, iced immediately after trawl-catch (v) or with 3, 6, 9 or 12 hours delay in icing (Gram, 1989).

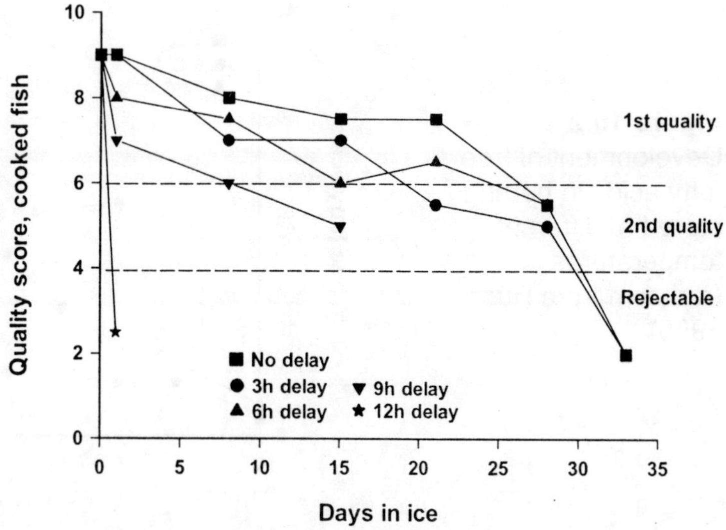

Therefore control of the time x temperature chain is critical. This DAP applies to all steps from catch, through processing and distribution to the consumer. Several initiatives are on the way, where different tags will allow monitoring of the accumulated time x temperature, however, none are used commercially in the fish industry. To date, the most efficient and reliable way of determining whether or not this DAP is under control is sensory evaluation.

Monitoring of time x temperature during handling and processing can be done by date marking of boxes and containers and by visual inspection of icing and chilling conditions. Time and temperature recording at specific points and during processing should preferably be controlled automatically. Process flow must be designed to avoid stops and interruptions, and chill rooms must be supplied with thermometers. Visual inspection (e.g. quantity of ice) and control checks of temperature must be done in a daily routine. A log of temperature recordings (manually or automatically read) must be kept and be available at all times.

Off-flavour may also arise in fish due to microbial growth that is not related to spoilage aspects. The muddy flavour often detected in fresh water fish such as trout is caused by the compound geosmin. Blue-green-algae, actinomycetes and cyanobacteria are capable of producing geosmin. The compound accumulates in the fish flesh and is not toxic to fish nor humans. Again, sensory evaluation is the most reliable detection technique. Allowing the fish to swim in clean water for 4-7 days can reduce (purge) the off-flavour.

10.2 Chemical aspects

Chemical defects refer to quality deterioration due to chemical reactions. Very common are the changes which may occur in the fish lipid fraction. This may be either oxidation or hydrolysis. Both reactions result in the production of substances with unpleasant – rancid – off-flavours. Other changes such as dehydration and autolysis may lead to poor texture and freeze burns. During frozen storage, especially of gadoid fish species, trimethylamine oxide (TMAO) is reduced to dimethylamine (DMA) and formaldehyde (FA). This adds to the changes in texture and flavour occurring during frozen storage.

Availability of oxygen (or other oxidizing compounds) is required for oxidative rancidity to develop and non-oxygen containing packaging of fatty fish species will control this defect. As with microbial reactions, temperature is important. Thus, the development of free fatty acids in herring is greatly accelerated at 12°C as compared to 0°C (Figure 10.2)

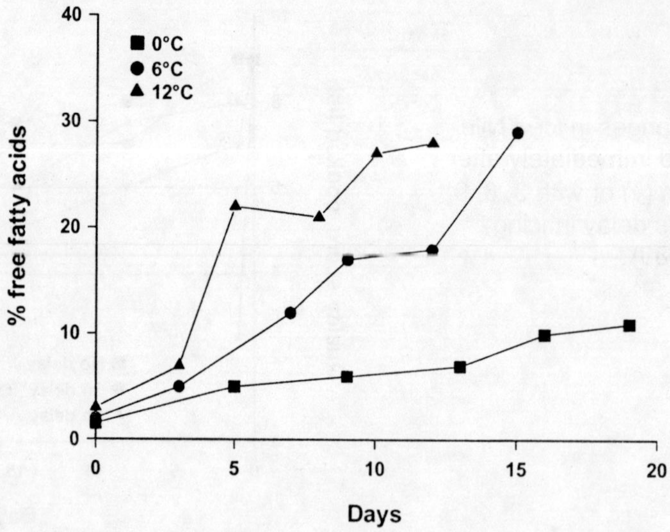

Figure 10.2
Development of free fatty acids in herring stored at different temperatures (redrawn from Huss 1995).

Any contamination occurring during processing – which is not included as a hazard in the HACCP plan – will also constitute a defect. This could be (re)contamination by cleaning agents, by mechanical grease or by using wrong ingredients. During canning of foods, metals may leak from the cans and contaminate the product.

10.3 Physical aspects

Defects of physical nature cover a range of aspects such as the presence of small bones, foreign matter (e.g. hairs, straw) or material which should not be there (scales, pieces of skin etc.). Other physical defects can damage the packaging causing bruising or change of carton shape.

10.4 Example

CAC (2002) provides a good example of the use of defect analysis and identification of DAPs (Tables 10.1, 10.2 and 10.3). As with the hazard-analysis, the production flow must first be outlined (Figure 10.3).

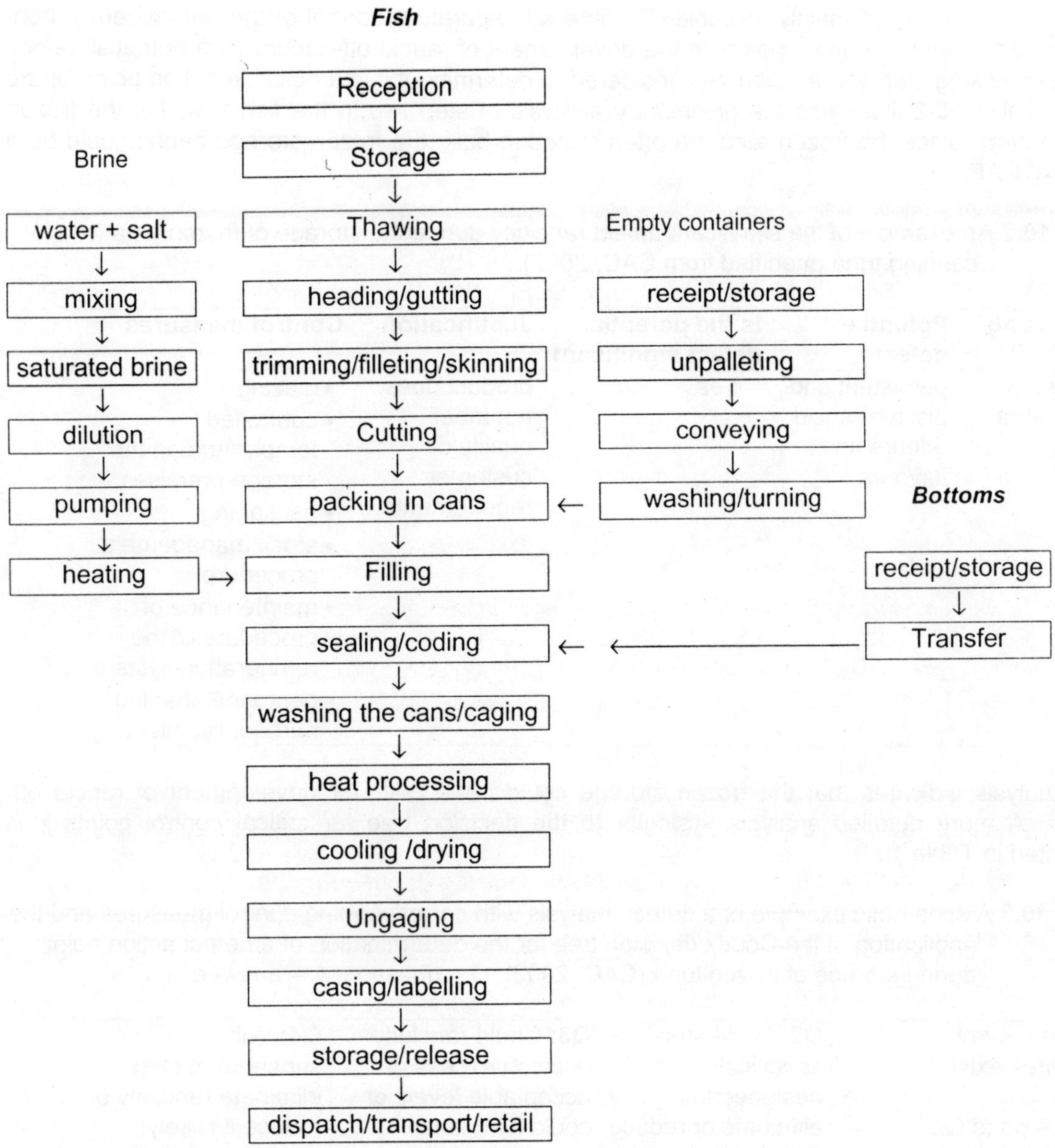

Figure 10.3 Example of a flow diagram for a processing line of canned tuna fish in brine (CAC, 2002).

The defect analysis identifies several possible defects (Table 10.1).

Table 10.1 An example of potential defects of canned tuna (modified from CAC, 2002).

Defect type	In raw tuna	During processing, storage or transportation
Biological	spoilage	spoilage, survival and growth of spoilage microorganisms
Chemical	oxidation	Oxidation
Physical		objectional matter (viscera, scales, skin...), formation of struvite crystals, container defects
Other	species substitution	abnormal flavours, incorrect weight, incorrect coding, incorrect labelling

Spoilage is as outlined mainly a problem of time x temperature control of the non-frozen or non-canned fish. Further analysis points to the development of rancid off-odours as a potential defect. Each processing step should then be considered to determine if it is a possible action point for the defect. Table 10.2 illustrates the preliminary analysis of step two in the fish flow, i.e. the frozen storage step. Since the frozen tuna are often stored in bulk, the frozen storage period could be a potential DAP.

Table 10.2 An example of the significant defect rancidity during the storage of frozen tuna for canning tuna (modified from CAC, 2002).

Processing step	**Pótential defect**	**Is the potential defect significant**	**Justification**	**Control measures**
Storage of frozen tuna	persistent and distinct rancid odours and flavours	Yes	product does not meet quality or customer requirements	• glazing • controlled temperature in the storage premises • packaging • stock management procedure • maintenance of procedure of the refrigeration system • personnel training and qualifications

The analysis indicates that the frozen storage could be a DAP for development of rancid off-odours. A more detailed analysis – similar to the decision tree for critical control points – is presented in Table 10.3.

Table 10.3 A schematic example of a defect analysis with corresponding control measures and the application of the Codex decision tree for the determination of a defect action point during storage of frozen tuna (CAC, 2002). Q = question; A = answer.

Q1: Do control measures exist? **If yes** – go to Q2 **If no** – consider whether control measures are available or necessary within the process proceed to next identified defect	**Q2:** Is the step specifically designed to eliminate or reduce the likely occurrence of rancidity to an acceptable level? **If yes** – this step is a DAP **If no** – go to Q3	**Q3:** Could rancidity occur in excess of acceptable levels or could it increase to unacceptable levels **If yes** – go to Q4 **If no** – not a DAP	**Q4:** Will a subsequent step eliminate rancidity or reduce its likely occurrence to an acceptable level? **If yes** – not a DAP **If no** – DAP
A: Yes, the storage temperature is controlled, procedures exist	**A:** No	**A:** Yes, if the storage time is too long and/or the storage temperature is too high or if packaging is broken or unsuitable, or if glacing is inadequate	**A:** No
Decision: storage of frozen tuna is a defect action point			

References

Baird-Parker, T.C. 2000. The production of microbiologically safe and stable foods. In: Lund, B.M., T.C. Baird-Parker and G.W. Gould (eds.) *The Microbiological Safety and Quality of Foods.* Aspen Publishers Inc., Gaitherburg, Maryland, USA. pp.3-18.

CAC (Codex Alimentarius Commission) 2002. *Draft Code of Practice for Fish and Fishery Products.* Alinorm 03/18. Food and Agriculture Organization / World Health Organization, Rome, Italy.

FDA (Food and Drug Administration) 2002. Import refusal reports for OASIS http://www.fda.gov/ora/oasis/ora_oasis_ref.html

Gram, L. 1989. Isolation, identification and characterization of bacteria isolated from tropical fish. Ph.D. thesis. The Technological Laboratory of the Danish Ministry for Fisheries and The Royal Veterinary and Agricultural University, Denmark.

Gram, L. and H.H. Huss 2000. Fresh and processed fish and shellfish. In: Lund, B.M., T.C. Baird-Parker and G.W. Gould (eds.) *The Microbiological Safety and Quality of Foods.* Aspen Publishers Inc., Gaitherburg, Maryland, USA. pp. 472-506.

Gram, L., L. Ravn, M. Rasch, J. B. Bruhn, A.B. Christensen and M. Givskov 2002. Food spoilage – interactions between food spoilage bacteria. *International Journal of Food Microbiology* 78, 79-97.

Huss, H.H. (eds) 1995. *Quality and Quality Changes in Fresh Fish.* FAO Fisheries technical paper No. 348., FAO, Rome, Italy.

Kaferstein, F.K. and G. Moy 1993. Public health aspects of food irradiation. *Journal of Public Health Policy* 3, 502-510.

NOAA (National Oceanic and Atmospheric Administration) 2000. *NOAA HACCP Quality Management Program. Program Requirements.* National Marine Fisheries Service, Seafood Inspection Program, Maryland, USA.

WHO (World Health Organization) 1995. *Food Safety Issues: Food Technologies and Public Health.* WHO/FNA/FOS 95.13. WHO, Geneva.

11 MONITORING PROGRAMMES (Hans Henrik Huss)

11.1 Toxic algae

The goal of a monitoring programme is to protect public health by providing information on toxic algae sufficiently early to take management action. The basic elements of monitoring and management programmes are the following (Anderson *et al,*. 2001):

- environmental observations including plankton observations, fish kills and anomalous animal behaviour
- sampling of plankton, shellfish or fish
- analysis of samples (identification of harmful algae, quantification of harmful algae and measurement of toxicity in shellfish)
- evaluation of results
- dissemination of information and implementation of regulatory action
- action plans/mitigation measures

The complete monitoring and management programme can be the responsibility of one agency, or it can be split between a government agency, industry/fishermen and private consultancy as shown in Figure 11.1.

Figure 11.1
Monitoring and management of toxic algae in Denmark.

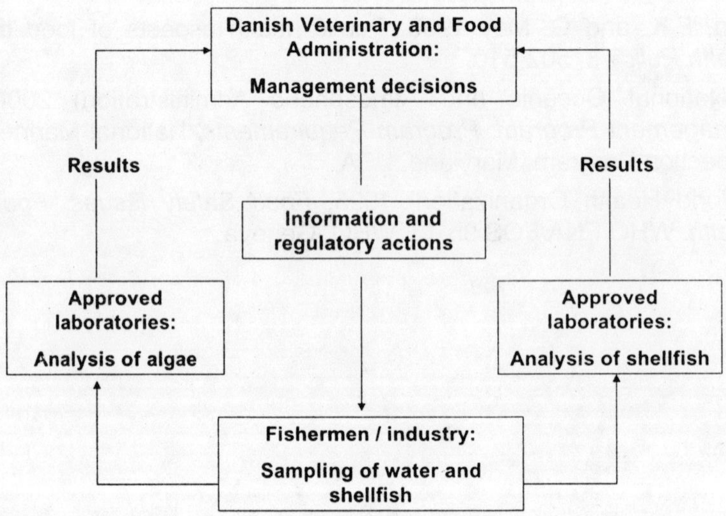

The structure of a monitoring programme can be complex and vary according to the local situation, but it should preferably be kept as simple as possible to facilitate fast and uncomplicated flow of information. The operational structure should be well documented and it should be clear to everyone involved who is responsible for different parts of the programme.

Environmental observations, including plankton observations, fish kills and anomalous animal behaviour are most often done by local residents or field officers on patrol. Aircraft Visual Operation, underway ferry monitoring and moored sensors can be applied in remote sensing for bloom detection and tracking.

Sampling of water, plankton and shellfish are most easily done by fishermen and industry or by inspection officers. The frequency of sampling and the number of sampling stations depends on the local situation and historical data. Routine sampling every week may be increased to daily sampling when low levels of toxic phytoplankton are observed.

Analysis of samples must be done at a certified laboratory and only approved and official methods of analysis should be applied. In the EU, a national reference laboratory must be designated to coordinate the analysis of biotoxins (EC, 1993). The national reference laboratories shall collaborate with the Community reference laboratory in Vigo, Spain (Laboratorio de biotoxinos marinos del Area de Sanidad).

Results of analysis should immediately be forwarded to the competent authority for evaluation and possible action. An effective communication system is important for rapid action and possible closure of fisheries. Results can be distributed instantly to the users of the monitoring system by telephone, automatic telephone answering machine, fax, e-mail and Internet. The use of Internet is quite common in many countries, although in some cases restricted access websites or list servers available only to governmental officials are used to control sensitive information.

Information and education of the public should be an integral part of the communication programme. It is recommended that booklets and pamphlets about health problems associated with algal blooms and toxic algae, the diagnosis and treatment of poisonings be prepared and published. Using the Internet is also an obvious way of distributing general information. Local web-pages can be linked to other general web-pages such as http:/www.redtide.whoi.edu/hab/.

The action or regulatory limits for toxins are shown in section 5.1.5. For cell concentration in the water the action level varies from presence (some *Alexandrium* spp. and *Prorocentrum* spp.) to several thousands cells/L of other algae (see Anderson *et al.*, 2001). In the USA a closed status shall be established when the cell count of *Gymnodium breve* exceeds 5 000/L (NSSP, 1999).

When toxin levels in bivalve or cell numbers of toxic algae exceeds the accepted limit, harvesting areas are closed or some sort of restriction of harvesting is imposed. A toxic bloom may vary, being extensive or sporadic only, thus affecting large areas or only spotty locations. The intensity of a bloom may also vary resulting in significant differences in toxicity levels among bivalves of the same species. The decision to close an area should therefore be affected by the dynamics of the bloom, but it is always advisable to include a safety zone in the closure of an affected area.

Procedures to re-open closed areas include increased sampling from the area and adjacent open areas. Samples should be free of toxin for at least two weeks before re-opening is considered. Species with long retention time should, however, remain on the closure list. An example of an action plan for a shellfish-monitoring program is shown in Figure 11.2.

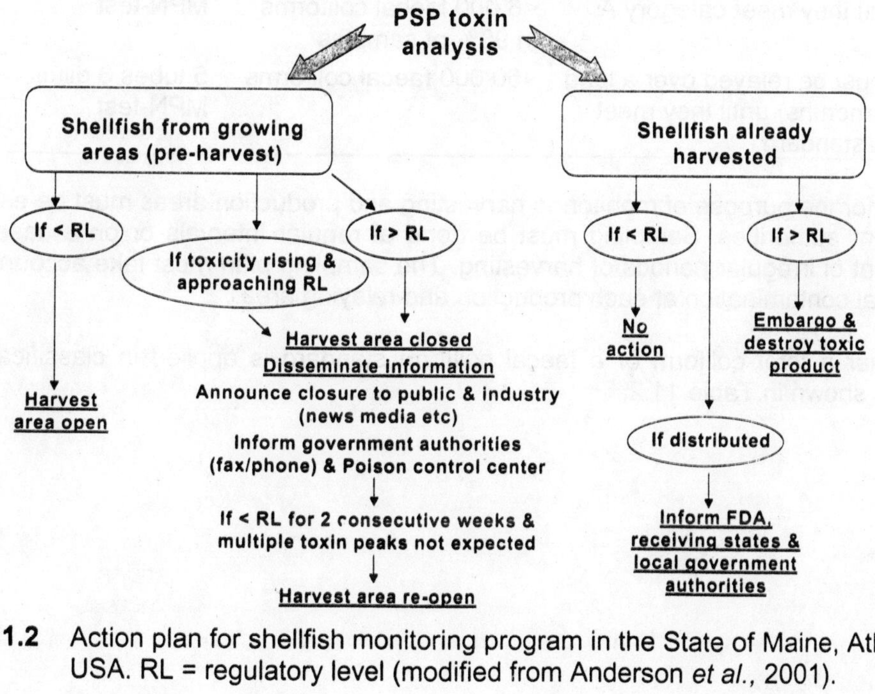

Figure 11.2 Action plan for shellfish monitoring program in the State of Maine, Atlantic, USA. RL = regulatory level (modified from Anderson *et al.*, 2001).

In the USA as well as in the EU, all containers and all consignments of shellfish must be accompanied by a tag and a health certificate that identifies the production area of origin, the harvester and the date of harvesting. This information must follow the shellfish during transport, processing, distribution until retail sales allowing tracing of the product should a health problem arise.

11.2 Pathogenic bacteria and viruses

Pathogenic bacteria and virus may be present in water from which shellfish are harvested. Of particular concern is the situation, when the environment where shellfish grow is contaminated from sewage. Molluscan shellfish filter and concentrate these pathogens from the surrounding water, and high numbers sufficient to cause disease may be reached. As shellfish are often consumed raw or only partially cooked, these pathogens (bacteria or viruses) will not be eliminated, and the risk of causing disease will be high.

To minimize this risk, Government authorities must have a monitoring programme for classifying the waters where shellfish are harvested. This monitoring programme can be based on examination of samples of shellfish or in part on an assessment of water quality. The programme must then be managed so that harvesting only takes place when the area is free of contamination. This programme also requires that all consignments and containers of shellfish are tagged as described above and that shell-fish harvesters and processes are licensed.

The EU requirements and conditions for productions areas are shown in Table 11.1.

Table 11.1 Classification of harvesting areas for shellfish in the EU. Microbiological examination of shellfish samples (EC, 1991).

Classification		Microbiological criteria (cfu /100 g shellfish)	Method
A	No restriction. Shellfish acceptable for immediate consumption	<230 *E. coli* or <300 faecal coliforms no *Salmonella* in 25g	5 tubes 3 dilutions MPN-test
B	Shellfish must be depurated or relayed until they meet category A standard	<4,600 *E. coli* or <6,000 faecal coliforms in 90% of samples	5 tubes 3 dilutions MPN-test
C	Shellfish must be relayed over a long period (>2 months) until they meet category A standard	<60 000 faecal coliforms	5 tubes 3 dilutions MPN-test

Sampling plans for the purpose of monitoring harvesting and production areas must be established by the competent authorities. Sampling must be done at regular intervals or on a case-by-case basis in the event of irregular periods of harvesting. The sampling plan must take account of likely variation in faecal contamination at each production and relaying area.

In the USA either a total coliform or a faecal coliform standard is applied in classification of a growing area as shown in Table 11.2.

Table 11.2 Classification of shellfish growing areas. Microbiological examination of water samples (NSSP, 1999).

	Faecal coliform		
Classification	**Geometric mean**	**<10% of samples**	**Method**
Approved	MPN <14/100 ml	MPN <43/100 ml	5 tube dec. dilution
		MPN <49/100 ml	3 tube dec. dilution
Restricted	MPN <88/100 ml	MPN <260/100 ml	5 tube
		MPN <300/100 ml	3 tube

It will be noted that both the EU and the USA classification programmes are relying heavily on conventional bacterial pollution indicators for measuring water quality. Although it has been generally accepted that it is better to monitor for the indicators of faecal pollution than for specific bacterial pathogens this is not the case for pathogenic viruses. There is ample evidence that viral pathogens are more resistant to environmental conditions, sewage and water treatment processes compared to coliform organisms (review by Leclerc *et al.,* 2000). Enteric viruses can survive for months in the marine environment, which is far longer than any bacterial indicator (Lees, 2000). New viral test methods are needed and under development as reliable faecal pollution indicators, but a number of critical issues must be addressed before their use.

11.3 Chemical contaminants

Chemical contaminants (heavy metals, persistent organic pollutants) may pose a potential human health hazard (section 5.2). Concern for these contaminants are mainly related to fish harvested in fresh water, estuaries and coastal waters where shore-side industries are located or intensive agriculture are using large amounts of pesticides or other agro-chemicals. In such areas, a government programme for monitoring all possible chemical contaminants in the harvesting area for fish and shellfish should be implemented and in place. The council directive (EC, 1991) makes reference to the compounds listed in the annex of directive 79/923/EEC (EC, 1979) and specify that these substances must no occur on shellfish in quantities that the calculated dietary intake exceeds the permissible daily intake (PDI). The directive (EC, 1979) states sampling frequency of several chemical contaminants, such as organohalogenated substances and metals which must be measured half-yearly. Tolerances, action levels and guidance levels for the more toxic chemical contaminants are discussed in section 5.2.

References

Anderson, D.M., P. Andersen, V.M. Bricelig, J.C. Cullen and J.E.J. Rensel 2001. *Monitoring and Management Strategies for Harmful Algal Blooms in Coastal Waters*, APEC # 201-MR-01.1. Asia Pacific Economic Program, Singapore and Intergovernmental Oceanographic Commission, Technical Series No. 59, Paris.

EC (European Commission) 1979. Council Directive 79/923/EEC of 30 October 1979 on the quality required of shellfish waters. *Official Journal of the European Communities* No.L 281, 10/11/1979. pp. 0047-0055.

EC (European Commission) 1991. Council Directive 91/492/EEC of 15 July 1991 laying down the health conditions for the production and placing on the market of live bivalve molluscs. *Official Journal of the European Communities* No.L 268, 24/09/1991. pp. 001-0014.

EC (European Commission) 1993. Council Decision 93/383/EEC of 14 June 1993 on reference laboratories for the monitoring of marine biotoxins. *Official Journal of the European Communities* L116, 08/07/1993. pp. 0031-0033.

Leclerc, H., S. Edberg, V. Pierzo and J.M. Deláthe 2000. A review. Bacteriophages as indicators of enteric viruses and public health risk in groundwaters *Journal of Applied Microbiology* 88, 5-21.

Lees, D. 2000. Viruses and bivalve shellfish. *International Journal of Food Microbiology* 59, 81-116.

NSSP (National Shellfish Sanitation Program) 1999. *Guide for the Control of Molluscan Shellfish, Model Ordinance*, Chapter IV. U.S. Department of Health and Human Services, Food and Drug Administration, Center for Food Safety and Applied Nutrition, Washington, DC, USA.

12 EXAMPLES OF FSOs FOR BACTERIA OR TOXINS IN SEAFOOD PRODUCTS (Lone Gram)

12.1 *Listeria monocytogenes* in RTE seafoods[1]

Both FAO/WHO (2001) and FDA/FSIS (2001) are currently in the process of carrying out quantitative risk assessments on *Listeria monocytogenes* in ready-to-eat foods. This section relies heavily on these documents. *L. monocytogenes* is a ubiquitous bacterium typical of decaying plant material and it is also associated with several animals. *L. monocytogenes* can cause listeriosis in humans. The main form of listeriosis is a food-borne infection which affects particular risk groups such as immuno-compromised, elderly and neonates. Recently, a milder form of gastro-enteritis affecting otherwise healthy people was reported. Many ready-to-eat (RTE) food products have been linked to listeriosis which typically occurs in sporadic, small outbreaks. *L. monocytogenes* is halo- and psychrotolerant and capable of multiplying in RTE foods, especially with extended shelf lives. Whilst dairy and meat products seem to be the most common causes of listeriosis, the disease has also been traced to lightly preserved fish products such as smoked mussels or cold-smoked fish (trout).

L. monocytogenes can easily be isolated from RTE food products in low concentrations. Thus between 0 and 80% of samples of cold-smoked fish are positive for the organism. It typically occurs in levels of < 10 /gram but is sporadically isolated at higher levels. Inoculated trials have shown that rapid growth may occur in the vacuum-packed chill-stored product. Based on German data on prevalence and levels of *L. monocytogenes*, Buchanan *et al.* (1997) developed a dose-response curve for the organism. The study used cold-smoked salmon as the food case. This study, as well as the very thorough studies by FAO/WHO and US FDA conclude that although one cannot define a threshold concentration, i.e. a minimal infectious dose, low levels of the organism (< 100 cfu/g) are very unlikely to cause the disease. The WHO/FAO team concluded as part of an expert consultation in May 2001 that if levels of *L. monocytogenes* were kept below 1000 cfu/g at point of consumption, then 99% of all listeriosis cases would be eliminated.

Due to the widespread occurrence of *L. monocytogenes* it will be extremely difficult (and expensive) to produce all RTE foods without sporadic occurrence of the organism in low levels. The dose-response relationships (and resulting Risk Estimate) indicates that such low levels constitute a very low risk. In the terminology introduced above, an "appropriate level of protection" / "tolerable level of risk" (ALOP/TLR) could be 100 cfu/g (assuming serving sizes of ≤ 100 gram). Following this line of thought, a Food Safety Objective is derived directly from the ALOP and could be 100 *L. monocytogenes* per gram at point of consumption.

Risk management options

In principle, two interlinked options exist for the management of microbial risks: the implementation of GHP and of HACCP. A HACCP analysis of *L. monocytogenes* in cold-smoked salmon reveals that with current processing and storage practices, no critical control point exists for the hazard which is growth of *L. monocytogenes*. The organism survives the processing steps (no listericidal step) and the typical product and storage conditions (vacuum-packed, chill-stored (5°C), NaCl at 3-6% (water phase salt) and pH of approximately 6.2) does not guarantee against growth to hazardous levels. It must be emphasised that CCPs that guarantee that counts do not increase to hazardous levels can be introduced, e.g. by frozen storage or by limiting shelf life. *L. monocytogenes* is capable of colonizing food processing environments and product contamination typically is caused by contamination during processing rather than by survivors from the raw material. *L. monocytogenes* may hide in brines, colonise slicers and have its harbouring niches in drains and on floors. Therefore the GHP programme of a food processing plant with *L. monocytogenes* as an identified hazard, must focus specific actions on eliminating and surveying this bacterium.

---

[1] *The text in this Listeria section has been prepared and modified from text prepared for an FAO/WHO Expert Consultation in Kiel, March 2002. The concepts of this Chapter are based on ICMSF 2002.*

Performance standards

The performance standard (PS) is the level of the hazard (here *L. monocytogenes*) that the processor must meet. In several RTE products, *L. monocytogenes* will not grow during storage and the PS for instance at the end of processing can then equal the FSO. However, if growth of the organism is possible/likely during storage and distribution, the FSO must be translated to PS depending on the amount of growth expected between sampling and consumption. It has been demonstrated that in naturally contaminated cold-smoked salmon stored at 5°C, approximately 1 log increase occurs during a 3 week storage period (Jørgensen and Huss, 1998). Thus, using a shelf life limit of 3 weeks or shorter at chill temperatures, a PS of 10 *Listeria* per gram off processing line will allow the FSO to be met. Most processors will set a PS of <10 *Listeria* per gram to built in safety margins.

Process and Product Criteria

Process or product criteria are levels of e.g. a heat treatment or a salting concentration that ensures that the hazard is under control. The preservation and safety of cold-smoked salmon depends on use of appropriate raw materials and combinations of salt and low temperature after processing. Since no listericidal step is included in the processing and neither of the food preservation parameters will control growth of *L. monocytogenes*, process or product criteria cannot be identified.

Microbiological criteria

It is possible, when appropriate, to develop microbiological criteria using an FSO of 100/g or PS of lower values. Such criteria may be used as acceptance criteria in situations where the pre-history of the product is not known, such as at port-of-entry or at certain retail outlets. Clearly, such criteria should only be used where other acceptance criteria, such as product criteria, cannot be developed. Also, the product should be epidemiologically linked to the hazard – or a hazard analysis should indicate reason for concern (van Schothorst, 1996). This is the case with cold-smoked salmon since listeriosis has been linked to cold-smoked trout (Swedish outbreak with 9 infected people and 2 fatalities), and several inoculated food trials have demonstrated growth in the product (Table 12.1).

Table 12.1 Questions evaluating the use of MC for *Listeria monocytogenes* in cold-smoked salmon (based on CAC, 2001)

Questions	Answers	Action
1) Has the food received a listericidal treatment	No, the cold-smoking process although sometimes reducing numbers of *L. monocytogenes* cannot guarantee that the organism is removed	
2) Is (re)-contamination likely	Yes. Several studies have documented that the main source of *Listeria* contamination is the process environment (slicers, brine) itself	
3) Is the presence of *Listeria monocytogenes* likely?	Yes. Although plant contamination can be minimized, its presence in the product is not un-expected.	If no: Do not test
4) Will the food receive a listericidal treatment prior to consumption?	No, Cold-smoked salmon is typically eaten without heat processing	If yes, Do not test
5) Is it likely that multiplication to levels of > 100/g or ml at the moment of consumption will take place during the intended conditions of storage, distribution and use?	Yes	Examine 20 samples c=0 and m=100 c=0 and m= N – where N is a product specific level that is set (a PS) so that the level does not increase above the FSO of 100/g at point of consumption absence in 25 g samples if no data on the product are available.
	No	Examine 10 samples Reject if any sample contains > 100 *L.m.* per gram

As with other microbiological criteria, careful consideration must be given to the choice of sampling plans and the degree of assurance it provides. Currently spreadsheet systems are available that allows one to determine the performance of a particular sampling plan (http://www.foodscience.afisc.csiro.au/icmsf/samplingplans. htm). For instance, if a sampling plan with 20 samples are used and c= 0 and m=100, then there is a 95% (or higher) probability of rejecting lots if the mean concentration of *Listeria* in the lot is ≥ 15 cfu/g. It therefore follows that even with 20 samples, the probability of accepting a lot which actually contains *L. monocytogenes* increases rapidly if the mean concentrations drops below 15 cfu/g.

Similarly, a sampling plan with 10 samples and c=0 and m=100 has a 95% (or higher) probability of rejecting the lot if the mean concentration is ≥ 30 cfu/g. If a sampling plan uses only 5 samples and c=0 and m=100, then there is a 95% probability of rejecting the lot if the mean concentration is ≥ 80 cfu/g. These figures emphasise the well-known fact, that low levels of pathogens are difficult to control using product sampling and testing.

If products are inspected just before consumption or the products do not support growth, the MC can equal the FSO. Depending on the assurance required from the sampling, i.e. the probability of only accepting acceptable lots, the number of samples is decided upon. If growth is supported, a PS and a MC of "not detectable" in 25 g may be opted for.

12.2 Staphyloccocal enterotoxin in cooked crustaceans

Staphylococcus aureus is, as described in Chapter 5, a mesophilic, Gram-positive bacterium associated with warm-blooded animals. It is a common member of the skin and nasal microflora of humans. Many strains of *S. aureus* may produce enterotoxins which upon ingestion causes a sudden reaction in terms of cramps, abdominal pain and vomiting. Several different enterotoxins may be produced and they have, based on antigenic properties been divided into sero-types A to J. Enterotoxin A is assumed to be the most commonly involved in food-poisoning outbreaks, however, recently type C has become prevalent (Jablonski and Bohack, 1997).

S. aureus is commonly detected from foods, either raw foods from warm-blooded animals or foods that have been manually handled. *S. aureus* can be detected sporadically on raw fish but is clearly more typical of seafood products that have been heat treated and manually handled, such as crustacean products (Table 12.2).

Table 12.2 Prevalence of *S. aureus* in seafood commodities (modified from Jablonsky and Bohach, 1997).

Product	No of samples tested	% positive for *S. aureus*	No. *S. aureus* per gram
Salmon steaks	86	2	>3.6
Oysters	59	10	>3.6
Blue crabmeat	896	52	> 3
Peeled shrimp	1,468	27	> 3
Lobster tail	1,315	24	> 3

The enterotoxins are part of a larger family of toxins produced by *S. aureus* (and *Streptococcus pyogenes*), the pyrogenic toxin family that can act as so-called super-antigens. These toxins can provoke a very strong response from the host immune defence system.

Disease symptoms may occur with ng levels of enterotoxin per gram, however, in most disease outbreaks, an estimated 1 to 5 µg has been ingested. The dose depends on the food matrix and the consumer – thus several children became ill after eating chocolate containing 100-200 ng enterotoxin. The enterotoxins are small molecules that are not degraded by gut proteases and that are relatively heat-stable and require prolonged boiling to inactivate.

Enterotoxins are produced in extremely low amounts during exponential growth but production increases markedly in the late exponential phase and stationary phase. It therefore follows that marked growth of *S. aureus* has to take place before toxic levels of enterotoxin are formed. Thus, it is the growth and toxin-production of the organism that is the hazard – not its mere presence. Stewart *et al.* (2002) when assaying 94 samples detected toxin in all samples with a positive OD-reading (i.e. cfu $\geq 10^7$ /ml) and not in any samples with a negative OD-reading. In a range in inoculated foods, Notermans and Otterdijk (1985) found that enterotoxin was not detected in any sample with less than 10^7 cfu/g. Many samples with higher *S. aureus* counts were positive (>0.1 µg enterotoxin/100g) but also several samples with counts of 10^9-10^{10} were negative. Hence, it can be concluded that $\geq 10^6$ cfu/g food are required to produce toxin at hazardous levels (Adams and Moss, 2000).

S. aureus is a poor competitor with respect to other microorganisms and outbreaks have mostly been associated with cooked foods, that have been manually handled and temperature abused. Thus cooked, hand-peeled crustaceans which may be temperature abused are high-risk products.

Quantitative risk assessments using mathematical representations of all steps from farm-to-fork have not been conducted on staphyloccocal enterotoxins. However, based on evaluations of dose-response, an FSO of 1 µg per gram (of cheese) has been suggested as an example of an FSO (van Schothorst, 1998). However, as indicated above lower levels have been causing disease when ingested in a protective (fatty) food matrix and when consumed by children. Therefore an FSO of 50 ng may be a safer option.

Risk management options

The presence of *S. aureus* in cooked seafoods is clearly a result of cross-contamination from people handling the product. Therefore the GHP procedures must specify the hygienic level during handling of cooked foods. Obviously people with sores or infected scratches must not handle such foods. Also, sneezing and coughing which will spread *S. aureus* from the nasal reservoir must be avoided. Gloves and mouth protection ware may, if used appropriately, minimise the spread. However, control of the hazard (growth and toxin production) is, in principle straight forward. Clearly, all storage/processing conditions that prevent growth (see tables in Chapter 5) will control the hazard. Proper cooling is essential to prevent growth. Also, staphylococcal enterotoxins are formed under a more limited range of conditions compared with growth (ICMSF, 1996). Whilst *S. aureus* may grow down to 7°C, toxin is not formed below 10°C and only very limited amounts are produced between 10 and 20°C. Growth occurs down to a_w values of 0.83 but toxin production stops at 0.87 (Table 12.3).

Performance Standards

Although the FSO is based on the agent, the toxin, it is not likely that producers of foods in which *S. aureus* growth is a risk will measure toxin on a regular basis. Therefore most criteria and standards "translate" the toxin levels to levels of *S. aureus*. As mentioned, significant growth is required for toxin to be produced.

Table 12.3 Limits for growth and enterotoxin production (from ICMSF, 1996)

Parameter	Temperature, °C	pH	Water activity	NaCl[1]
Growth, optimum	37	6-7	0.98	3.5
Growth, range	7-48	4-10	0.83 – >0.99	25 – >1.7
Toxin production, optimum	40-45	7-8	0.98	3.5
Toxin production, range	10-48	4.5-9.6	0.87->0.99	17 – >1.7

1. *NaCl % (water phase salt) calculated based on water activity values. Note that some studies report 20% as maximum for growth and 10-15% as maximum for toxin production.*

Therefore the FSO of 50 ng toxin/gram could theoretically be translated to 10^5-10^6 cfu/g. This requires that the number is reached by growing, toxin producing bacteria and not a result of massive recontamination. However, the producer is unlikely to set e.g. 10^5 *S. aureus* per gram but will target a much lower level to incorporate extra safety. In most foods, a PS of 100 *S. aureus* per gram will ensure that the FSO is met – assuming that the appropriate controls are in place.

Process and Product Criteria

In cooked crustaceans, the most important criteria ensuring control of the hazard is keeping the temperature low (< 10°C). The products do not *per se* include other preservation parameters that can be relied upon for growth control. However, if the cooked crustaceans are used for brined foods, the combination of low pH, salt and preservation compounds such as sorbate or benzoate can guarantee that growth does not occur.

Microbiological Criteria

The EU (EC, 1991) has set a microbiological standard for *S. aureus* in cooked crustaceans with a 5 sample sampling plan and c = 2, m= 100 cfu/g and M=1000 cfu/g. Such standards are widely used at port-of-entry where there is no knowledge of the GHP or HACCP programmes of the producer.

References

Adams, M.R. and M.O. Moss 2000. *Food Microbiology*. 2nd ed. Royal Society of Chemistry, Cambridge, UK.

Buchanan R.L., W.G. Damert, R.C. Whiting & M. van Schothorst 1997. Use of epidemiologic and food survey data to estimate a purposefully conservative dose-response relationship for *Listeria monocytogenes* levels and incidence of listeriosis. *Journal of Food Protection* 60, 918-922.

CAC (Codex Alimentarius Commission) 2001. Report on the thirty-fourth session of the Codex Committee on food hygiene. Alinorm 03/13. Food and Agriculture Organization / World Health Organization, Rome, Italy.

EC (European Commission) 1991. Council Directive 91/493/EEC of 22 July laying down the health conditions for the production and placing on the market of fishery products. *Official Journal of the European Communities*. No. L268. pp.15-34.

FAO/WHO (Food and Agriculture Organization/World Health Organization) 2001. *Joint FAO/WHO Expert Consultation on Risk Assessment of Microbiological Hazards in Foods. Risk characterization of Salmonella spp. in eggs and broilers and Listeria monocytogenes in ready-to-eat foods.* FAO Food and Nutrition Paper No. 72.

FDA/FSIS (US Food and Drug Administration/Food Safety Inspection Service) 2001. *Draft Assessment of the Relative Risk to Public Health from Foodborne Listeria monocytogenes among Selected Categories of Ready-to-Eat Foods*. FDA Center for Food Safety and Applied Nutrition.

ICMSF (International Commission on Microbiological Specifications for Foods) 1996. *Microorganisms in Foods 5. Characteristics of Microbial Pathogens.* Blackie Academic & Professionals.

ICMSF (International Commission on Microbiological Specifications for Foods) 2002. *Microorganisms in Foods 7. Microbiological Testing in Food Safety Management.* Aspen Publishers Inc.

Jablonsky, L.M. and G.A. Bohach 1997. *Staphylococcus aureus*. In Doyle, M.P., L.R. Beauchat and T.J. Montville (eds.) *Food Microbiology. Fundamentals and Frontiers*. ASM Press, Washington, USA. pp.353-375.

Jørgensen, L.V. and H.H. Huss 1998 Prevalence and growth of *Listeria monocytogenes* in Danish Seafood. *International Journal of Food Microbiology* 42, 127-131.

Notermans, S. and R.L.M. van Otterdijk 1985. Production of enterotoxin A by *Staphylococcus aureus* in food. International *Journal of Food Microbology* 2, 145-149.

Stewart, C.M., M.B. Cole, J.D. Legan, L. Slade, M.H. Vandeven and D.W. Schaffner 2002. *Staphylococcus aureus* growth boundaries: Moving towards mechanistic predictive models based on solute-spectific effects. *Applied and Environmental Microbiology* 68, 1864-1871.

van Schothorst, M. 1996. Sampling plans for *Listeria monocytogenes*. *Food Control* 7, 203-208.

van Schothorst, M. (International Commission on Microbiological Specifications for Foods) 1998. Principles for the establishment of microbiological food safety objectives and related control measures. *Food Control* 9, 379-384.

13 USE OF CRITERIA (Hans Henrik Huss)

Control measures to ensure safety and hygienic processing of food have traditionally included the use of criteria. Two types of criteria will be discussed in this Chapter:

- Microbiological criteria
- Performance- and process criteria

13.1 Microbiological criteria (MC) and testing

Traditionally, control of microorganisms in food was demonstrated by microbiological testing of samples at various stages of production and the final product. Results were compared with criteria developed to give some degree of assurance that the food was safe and of good quality. It is now fully recognized that this type of activity can never give an absolute assurance of product quality and safety. A much higher degree of assurance can be provided by a preventative approach based on the application of the Hazard Analysis Critical Control Point (HACCP) principles at all steps in the food supply and processing system.

Nevertheless it is recognised that MC are widely used in the food industry and by government authorities. For this reason, the basic requirements of MC will be discussed below. As outlined by the Codex Alimentarius Commission (CAC, 2001) and in published opinion papers and recommendations by scientific bodies such as EU Scientific Committee for Food (EU, 1997) and the Institute of Food Science and Technology (Stannard, 1997). A part of this section (13.1) has already been published in Huss, 2001.

13.1.1 Definitions and components of MC

Three types of MC are generally recognized according to their use:

- standards
- guidelines
- specifications

These terms have been defined and redefined a number of times, but it is generally recognised that the term "standard" is a MC contained in a law or regulation with mandatory compliance. In case of non-compliance some (specified) action is required by the regulatory agency. A microbiological "guideline" is a MC applied at any stage in food processing and aids in identifying situations requiring actions for food safety or quality reasons. Results obtained from testing assist in trend analysis and situations (products, processes) not complying with guidelines should result in investigative action to identify and rectify the cause. A "specification" is a MC used for contractual purposes by food business as part of their own safety management system and should not be confused with legal requirements. Codex Alimentarius and EU now operate with only one definition:

Microbiological Criteria
Microbiological criteria for food defines the acceptability of a product or a food lot based on the absence or presence or number of microorganisms, including parasites and/or quantity of their toxins / metabolites per unit of mass, volume, area or lot (CAC,1997; EC, 1997)

It is recommended in the documents (CAC, 2001; EC, 1997) that the components of MC for foods should consist of:

- a statement of the microorganisms of concern and/or their toxins/metabolites and the reason for that concern
- the analytical method for their detection

- a sampling plan and the size of the analytical units
- the microbiological limits (ML) considered appropriate for the food at the specified points(s) of the food chain
- the number and size of analytical units that should be tested and conform to these limits
- the food to which and where in the food chain MC applies
- actions to be taken when the criterion is not met, (non-compliance).

The analysis of foods for compliance with mandatory microbiological criteria must be undertaken in an official laboratory in compliance with the Official Control of Foodstuffs Directive (EC, 1989).

Both the Codex- and the EU document specify that in situations of non-compliance with a mandatory MC some regulatory control actions are required such as sorting, reprocessing, rejection or destruction of product or further investigations into the situation. The decision on control action depends on an assessment of the possible risk to the consumer, the point in the food chain and the type of product. This means that non-compliance is not automatically followed by destruction of products. The decision on possible action depends on a carefully scientific evaluation of the whole situation and the stated microbiological limits in the MC are in reality guidelines to assist the authorities in choosing the correct control action.

In the EU directives applicable to fish (see Table 13.2) it is specified that if the products do not comply with the mandatory criteria set out in the Directives, the products cannot be placed on the market. This applies both to the criteria for pathogens and for organisms that are "indicators of poor hygiene" (*Staphylococcus aureus*, thermotolerant coli (44°C) and *E. coli*).

In contrast, it is stated that the "guidelines" used for indicator organisms (Standard Plate counts) are meant to help manufacturers decide whether their plants are operating satisfactorily and to assist them in implementing the production monitoring procedures.

Thus the EU Directives for fish have:

- mandatory criteria for specified pathogens (*Salmonella*) and for "unspecified pathogens"
- criteria for specific organisms as indication of poor hygiene and for the checking of GMP and HACCP (also mandatory criteria)
- and use of other parameters ("coliforms" and "plate count") in guidelines to be used solely by the manufacturers.

13.1.2 Purpose and application of MC

MC should only be applied to products or processes when no other means of securing safety and shelf life are available and when the use of a MC enhances food safety. Thus, there must be scientific evidence that a MC is effective, practical and meaningful in terms of consumer protection.

MC may be useful in the following situations:

- to indicate the microbiological status of raw materials, ingredients and final products of unknown origin (e.g. at port-of-entry)
- as validation and verification of HACCP-based control systems, Good Manufacturing Practices (GMP) and Good Hygienic Practices (GHP)
- to assess whether the prevalence of a pathogen in specific foods is increasing/decreasing relative to a target level (e.g. a FSO)
- for contractual purposes by food business.

MC cannot stand in isolation, but should only be established and used within the framework of a general risk management programme. They should be based on scientific analysis and advice together with an assessment of the risk appropriate to the foodstuff and its use. Furthermore they should be developed in a transparent fashion and meet the requirements of fair trade.

13.1.3 Principles for establishing MC

When establishing MC, consideration must be given to the following (CAC, 2001):

- evidence of actual or potential hazards to health
- possibility of controlling the hazard by other means (e.g. at a CCP in a HACCP-programme or by use of process criteria)
- likelihood of improved safety to consumers by applying a MC
- microbiological status of the raw material. A number of potential pathogenic organisms are present as part of the normal microflora on the raw material and are therefore likely to be present on raw, non-heat treated final products. This is a potential hazard which need to be controlled by controlling the growth conditions for the pathogen (e.g. by salt, temperature control etc.)
- effect of processing on the microbiological status of the food
- likelihood and consequences of microbial contamination and/or growth during subsequent handling, storage and use
- category of consumers concerned
- intended use of the food. It must be included into the evaluation of a possible need for a MC if the risk will be eliminated by normal preparation before consumption
- cost/benefit ratio associated with application of a criterion. It must be taken into consideration, if the microbiological examination can be carried out for a reasonable price
- when establishing MC they must be based on a thoroughly well-documented examination of the particular product produced when GMP and GHP have been applied. The MC should be technically attainable and realistic in terms of achievability.

Based on these principles a number of situations can immediately be excluded as suitable for application of mandatory MC for pathogens:

- raw products (intended to be cooked before consumption)
- ready-to-eat products where a Critical Control Point or a process criteria can be identified for growth/elimination of relevant pathogens.

13.1.4 Sampling and microbiological testing

According to the principal documents on MC (CAC, 2001; EC, 1997) the choice of a sampling plan should take into account:

- consideration of severity of the hazard and assessment of the risk to public health
- susceptibility of the target group of consumers
- heterogeneity of distribution of microorganisms
- statistical probability of detecting unacceptable food lots.

A sampling plan should include the sampling procedure and the decision criteria to be applied to a food lot based on the examination of a prescribed number of sample units by defined methods. A sampling plan should further be administratively and economically feasible. Statistically based, 2- or 3 class sampling plans are defined by ICMSF (1986).

A 2-class plan is used essentially for pathogens and/or where a presence/absence test is to be performed, while a 3-class plan is mainly used for hygiene indicators.

Microorganisms are not distributed homogeneously in fish and fish products and pathogens, if present, are usually at low levels. For these reasons, no practical sampling plan can ensure complete absence of a target microorganism, nor can it ensure that the concentration of a microorganism measured may be exceeded in a part of the fish product that was not sampled.

A 2-class sampling plan will mainly detect gross defects. Table 13.1 shows the calculated acceptance probabilities for 2-class sampling plans with different numbers of samples and percentages of defective lots. Application of a sampling plan with five samples of which none should contain pathogens (n = 5, c = 0) would lead to acceptance of a lot that contains 10% defective samples with a probability of 59.1%. When it comes to food safety, food processors would aim at much lower rate of defective samples in a lot.

Table 13.1 Effect of lot quality (% defective in a lot) on the probability of acceptance (%) for different 2-class sampling plans (EC, 1998).

% defective samples in lot	probability of acceptance (%) given sampling plans with a total of n samples and allowance of "c" defect samples			
	n = 1; c = 0	n = 5; c = 0	n = 10; c = 0	n = 60; c = 0
1	99.0	95.1	90.4	54.7
2	98.0	90.4	81.7	30
5	95.0	77.4	59.9	4.6
10	90.0	59.1	34.9	0.18
20	80.0	32.8	10.7	0.00015

The most stringent sampling plan proposed by ICMSF (1986) is the sampling plan for *Salmonella* in baby food. In this plan 60 samples are analysed (n = 60) and none are allowed to contain *Salmonella* (c = 0) Even in this case there is a 30% chance of accepting products with 2% of sample units contaminated with *Salmonella*.

If the level of contamination in a lot is 0.5% it can be estimated that examination of 600 samples would be necessary for a 95% probability of detecting the contaminated lot. This probability would decrease to 45%, if the level of contamination is 0.1%. It can be concluded that if the level of contamination is not at least in the order of 5% or more, there is very little chance of detecting contaminated lots, and sampling and testing would therefore not improve the safety or decrease the risk. Sampling and microbiological testing is in this situation not suitable means for defining the acceptability of food lots and a MC is meaningless.

When evaluating the need for MC, the principle discussed above can be applied in a decision tree as shown in Figure 13.1.

13.1.5 MC applied by the EU and others

Food safety and hygienic practices throughout the EU is controlled by a multitude of "Vertical Directives" dealing with specific products of animal origin (meat, milk, eggs, fish) or the so-called "Horizontal Directives" covering all foodstuffs entering the market. Directives that include MC for fish are:

- Live Bivalve Molluscs Directive (91/492/EEC) (EC, 1991a)
- Fishery Products Directive (91/493/EEC) (EC, 1991b)
- Commission Decision on the microbiological criteria applicable to the production of cooked crustaceans and molluscan shellfish (93/51/EEC) (EC, 1993)

In addition a number of Directives have provision for MC to be added in the future (e.g. Council Directive 93/43/EEC on the hygiene of foodstuff).

The ML listed in the Directives above are shown in Table 13.2.

Table 13.2 Microbiological limits for fish and fish products laid down in EU Directives (EC, 1991a,b, 1993).

Products	Microorganisms	Microbiological standard	Status/action
Live bivalve molluscs	*Salmonella* spp.	absent in 25 g	w
"	*Escherichia coli*	< 230/100g	w
"	Faecal coliforms	< 300/100g	w
"	Paralytic shellfish poison (PSP)	≤ 80μg/100g	w
"	Diarrhetic shellfish poison (DSP)	Negative in bioassay	a
Cooked crustaceans and molluscan shellfish	*Salmonella* spp.	Absent in 25g, n=5, c=0	w, n, r
"	Other pathogens and toxins thereof	Not present in quantities such as to affect health	w, n, r
Whole products	Mesophilic aerobic bacteria (30°C)	m=10 000, M=100 000, n=5, c=2	r
Shelled or shucked products	*Staphylococcus aureus*	m=100, M=1000, n=5, c=2	w, n, r
"	*Escherichia coli* (on solid medium)	m=10, M=100, n=5, c=1	n, r
"	Thermotolerant coliforms (44°C on solid medium)	m=10, M=100, n=5, c=2	n, r
Shelled or shucked products except crabmeat	Mesophilic aerobic bacteria (30°C)	m=50 000, M=500 000, n=5, c=2	r
Crabmeat	Mesophilic aerobic bacteria (30°C)	m=100 000, M=1 000 000, n=5, c=2	r

w = withhold from market
n = notify the competent authorities of findings and action taken
r = review the methods and checking at CCPs.

The criteria listed in the EU Directives were developed 5-10 years ago, and there is a wide diversity and complexity in some of the MC selected. None of the MC is based on current Codex Alimentarius principles as outlined in this paper and many of the MC applied does not appear to be meaningful in terms of consumer health protection (e.g. aerobic plate counts, coliform counts in certain foods). The terminology used is not harmonised as MC is named as: MC, obligatory criteria, analytical criteria, guidelines, or standard without any clear definition of the meaning of these designations. Thus in the MC for cooked shellfish and molluscs the microbiological limit for aerobic mesophilic bacteria is called a "standard", while it is specified in the heading of the table to be a "guideline". None of the current MC is based on a formal risk assessment and sampling plans and detection methods to be used are not prescribed either.

The number of non-harmonised microbiological criteria in EU member states varies considerably. Thus France have more that 80 MC for foods while in Germany no microbiological criteria exist in the German Federal Legislation except those laid down by EC Directives. Countries which have non-harmonised, national microbiological criteria for fish and fish products are France, Norway, Spain, Denmark and Belgium (EC, 1998).

Some of the microbiological limits specified in the national non-harmonised MC mentioned above are given in Table 13.3. Other figures are from industry specification. However, it is claimed by Stannard (1997) that figures in Table 13.3 are considered to be practical, realistic and relevant.

Table 13.3 Microbiological limits for fish and fish products considered to be practical and relevant (extracted from Stannard, 1997).

Product	Organism/Toxin	GMP[1]	Maximum
Raw fish/shellfish to be cooked	Bacterial pathogens	Criteria for absence not applicable	
	Histamine	< 50 ppm	50 ppm
	PSP (bivalves)	ND/l00 g	80 μg/100g
	DSP (bivalves)	ND in bioassay	ND in bioassay
	ASP (edible parts of molluscs)	< 20 mg domoic acid/g by HPLC	< 20 mg domoic acid/g by HPLC
Non-heated, ready-to-eat products (e.g. cold smoked, salted, marinated or fermented fish)	*Salmonella* spp.	ND in 25 g	ND in 25 g
	V. parahaemolyticus	ND in 25 g	10^2/g
	L. monocytogenes	ND in 25 g	10^3/g
	S. aureus	< 10^2/g	10^3/g
	Histamine	< 50 ppm	50 ppm
	PSP (bivalves)		
	DSP (bivalves)	as above	
	ASP (edible parts of molluscs)		
Cooked, ready-to-eat products (e.g. cooked shrimp)	*Salmonella* spp.	ND in 25 g	ND in 25 g
	L. monocytogenes	ND in 25 g	10^3/g
	V. parahaemolyticus	ND in 25 g	10^2/g
	S. aureus	< 20 /g	10^3/g
	Histamine	< 50 ppm	50 ppm
	PSP (bivalves)		
	DSP (bivalves)	as above	
	ASP (edible parts of molluscs)		

1. see text

It must be emphasised that the figures in Table 13.3 are microbiological limits which may be included in MC. GMP-values are those expected immediately following production of food under good manufacturing conditions. Maximum values are those regarded as the maximum acceptable at any point in the shelf life of a product.

In the table it is pointed out that criteria requiring the absence of pathogens in raw foods are generally not practical. Absence of pathogens in raw food which are eaten raw is desirable but can never be guaranteed. In contrast, it is stated that pathogens (*Salmonella, V. parahaemolyticus, L. monocytogenes*) should be non-detectable in 25 g immediately following production of ready-to-eat products. This is clearly unrealistic for *V. parahaemolyticus* and *L. monocytogenes* in non-heated ready-to-eat products. The figures quoted under maximum values are more realistic and could be used as guidelines for microbiological testing also during and immediately after processing.

However, in many countries 10^2/g of *Listeria monocytogenes* is regarded as maximum.

S. aureus is a toxin-producing organism and growth in the fish product is required before there is any risk to the consumer. Since *S. aureus* competes very poorly with a large associate microflora, it is unlikely to grow in non-heated ready-to-eat products like cold smoked salmon. Thus the authors cannot agree that a MC for this organism in this type of products is relevant. In contrast, cooked peeled shrimp, which may have been recontaminated with *S. aureus* after cooking can be of risk and a MC for *S. aureus* may be very useful in this situation.

13.1.6 Concluding remarks

Many of the microbiological examinations of foods both by industry and regulatory agencies are meaningless and a waste of time and resources. Indiscriminate application of microbiological testing and criteria should be avoided. As the existence of a MC always requires some degree of microbiological testing, it needs very careful consideration, before any MC is established.

Testing foods for pathogens is not very effective as a tool to protect health of the consumer. Safety is obtained by the application of GMP, GHP and HACCP as safety management tools throughout the food chain. Microbiological analysis and MC can be used to support and to verify the effective application of these management tools. Any MC introduced for this purpose should not be used as rejection criteria but as guidelines taking into consideration all other factors of importance. In most cases the corrective action will be a re-evaluation of the processing- and HACCP procedures.

The real problem is how to control the food in international trade. At the port-of-entry the regulatory agency may not always know whether the incoming food was produced under hygienic conditions and application of the HACCP-principles. In this situation some MC will be needed, but then they should be established according to the principles described in the Codex documents. However, a much better and more modern approach would be to let control of foodstuffs in international trade be based on signed agreements between internationally recognised and competent authorities or business partners approved by such authorities (e.g. Memoranda of understanding, purchasing agreements). Alternatively, food may be passed without testing, but with some restrictions on storage condition (e.g. keep frozen until use), limitation on shelf life after thawing or some degree of warning to the consumer (see Figure 13.1).

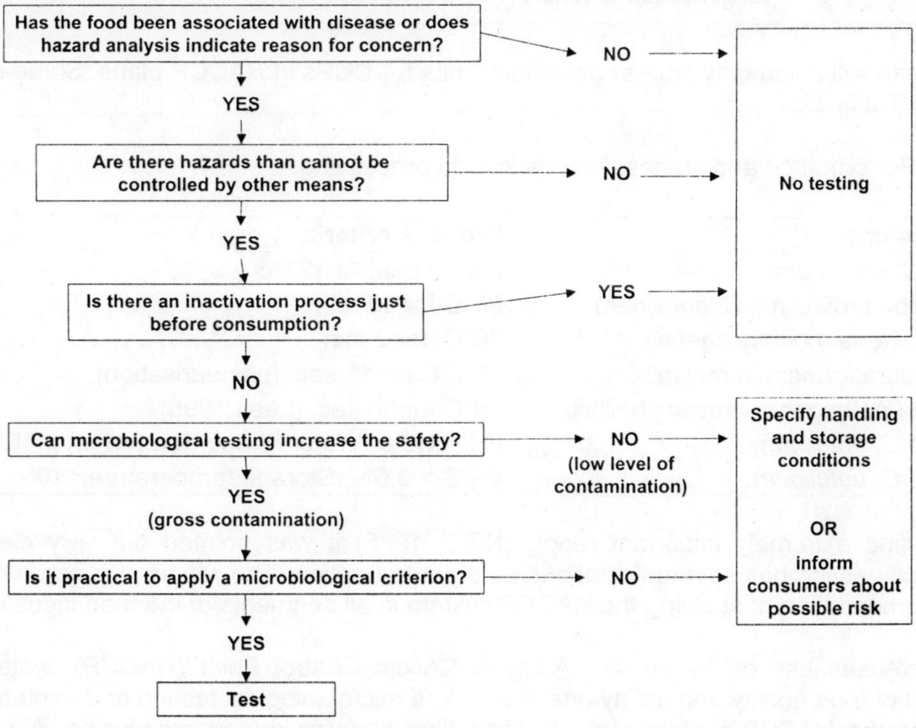

Figure 13.1 Establishment of MC for pathogens (Modified after ICMSF, 2002).

13.2 Performance and process criteria

Performance Criterion
A performance criterion is the required outcome of one or more control measures at a step or combinations of steps which will assume the safety of a food (van Schothorst, 1998)

Examples of performance criteria are:

- the requirement of a 12 D-reduction in the number of *Clostridium botulinum* spores in sterilized canned food
- the prevention of any growth of a given pathogen
- a 6 D-reduction in number of *Listeria monocytogenes*
- destruction of non spore forming pathogens that are known to occur in raw milk.

Process criteria are applied during the production of food, with the aim of building into the manufacturing process effective measures to control the risk of identified microbiological hazards.

Process Criteria
Process criteria are the control parameters (e.g. time, temperature, pH, a_w) at a step or combinations of steps, that can be applied to achieve a performance criterion (van Schothorst, 1998)

Process criteria will commonly appear as critical limits for CCPs in HACCP plans. Some examples are shown in Table 13.4.

Table 13.4 Performance and process criteria in food processing.

Performance criteria	Process criteria
12 D Kill of *C. botulinum*	2.4 - 3 min. At 121°c
6 D Kill of non proteolytic *C. botulinum*	90°C for 10 min
6 D Kill of *Listeria monocytogenes*	70°C for 2 min
Kill of non spore formers in raw milk	71,7°C for 15 sec. (pasteurisation)
Destruction of pathogenic virus in shellfish	90°C for 90 sec. (Lees 1995)
No growth of *C. botulinum*	pH < 4.6 or Water Phase Salt (WPS) > 10%
No growth of *C. botulinum*	WPS > 3.5%, Storage temperature <10°c

In an early and extremely important report (NRC, 1985) it was pointed out very clearly, that microbiological testing has severe limitations as a control option. The report also came out with a strong recommendation of applying the HACCP system in all segments of the food industry.

With the increased use of the Hazard Analysis Critical Control Point (HACCP) system in the management of food quality and safety one may ask, if microbiological testing and –criteria are still necessary as the HACCP system aims at controlling hazards during processing. A number of microbiological criteria (MC) are still required by both national and international legislation, but there is a considerable debate whether MC are needed or necessary in all instance to increase food safety.

Already in 1970, Sir Grahame Wilson when summarizing a meeting on the use of microbiological, criteria, stated: "Bacteriologists are better employed in devising means to prevent or overcome contamination than in examining more and more samples". Processing concerns the whole volume of food; samples' only a minute fraction of it. Thirty years later two other distinguished and eminent microbiologists further pointed out that "It is an historical fact that the major advances in public health have been made by applying interventions, such as the use of milk pasteurisation or water chlorination to control specific microbiological hazards, i.e., application of performance and process criterion. We are not aware where significant food borne hazards to health have been reduced through the application of a microbiological criterion of a foodstuff as the primary means of control" (Baird Parker and Tompkin, 2000).

Thus it can be concluded, that while process criteria can be extremely effective in control of microbiological hazards and should be build into the HACCP system, microbiological testing and the use of microbiological criteria should never be carried out at the expense of a HACCP based system of control.

References

Baird -Parker, T.C. and R. Bruce Tompkin 2000. Risk and Microbiological criteria. In Lund, B., T.C. Baird-Parker and G.W. Gould (eds) *The Microbiological Safety and Quality of Foods* Vol II Aspen Publishers, Inc. Gaithensbury, Maryland, USA. pp.1852-1885.

CAC (Codex Alimentarius Commission) 1997. *Principles for the Establishment and Application of Microbiological Criteria for Foods*. Alinorm 97/13A, Supplement to Volume 1B, Appendix III CAC/GL, 21. Food and Agriculture Organization / World Health Organization, Rome, Italy.

EC (European Commission)1989. Council Directive 89/397/EEC of 14 June 1989 on the official control of foodstuffs. *Official Journal of the European Communities* L 186, 30/06/1989

EC (European Commission) 1991a. Council Directive 91/492/EEC of 15 July 1991 laying down the health conditions for the production and the placing on the market of live bivalve molluscs *Official Journal of the European Communitites* L 268, 24/09/1991 pp. 0001 - 0014

EC (European Commission) 1991b. Council Directive 91/493/EEC of 22 July 1991 laying down the health conditions for the production and the placing on the market of fishery products *Official Journal of the European Communities* L 268, 24/09/1991 pp. 0015 - 0034

EC (European Commission) 1993. Commission Decision 93/51/EEC of 15 December 1992 on the microbiological criteria applicable to the production of cooked crustaceans and molluscan shellfish. *Official Journal of the European Communities* L 013, 21/01/1993 p. 0011 - 0013

EC (European Commission) 1997. *Report of the Scientific Committee for Food (39th series).* Luxembourg: Office for Official Publications of the European Communies.

EC (European Commission) 1998. *Report on tasks for scientific cooperation. Report of experts participating in Task 2.1.* Luxembourg: Office for Official Publications of the European Communities.

ICMSF (International Commission on Microbiological Specifications for Food) 1986. *Microorganisms in Food 2. Sampling for microbiological analysis: Principles and specific applications.* 2nd ed. Blackwell Scientific Publications, UK.

ICMSF (International Commission on Microbiological Specifications for Food) 2002. *Microorganisms in Foods 7. Microbiological testing in food safety management*. Aspen Publishers.

Huss, H.H. 2001. Use and misuse of microbiological criteria for seafood. In Gudjonsson and O. Niclasen (eds) Proceedings of the 30th WEFTA Plenary Meeting. June 2000. Thorshavn, the Faroe Islands. *Annales Societatis Scientiarrum Færoensis Supplementum* XXV??? pp.63-73.

Lees, D. 1995. Control measures in seafood. In *Workshop on Foodborne Vital Infections* Advisory Committee on the Microbiological Safety of Food, pp. HMSO, London, UK.

NRC (US – National Research Council) 1985. An evalution of the Role of Microbiological Criteria for Foods and Food Ingredients. National Academy Press. Washington DC, USA.

Stannard, C. 1997. Development and use of microbiological criteria for foods. *Food Science and Technology Today* 11, 137-177.

van Schothorst, M. 1998. Principles for the establishment of microbiological food safety objectives and related control measures. *Food Control* 9, 379-384.

14 PREDICTIVE MICROBIOLOGY (Paw Dalgaard)

Growth and/or inactivation of pathogenic and spoilage microorganisms are very important factors determining safety and shelf-life of seafood. Clearly, assessment and management of safety and quality is facilitated when microbial growth and inactivation can be quantitatively related to characteristics of products and processes like temperature, atmosphere, pH and NaCl %. Predictive microbiology is the area of food microbiology where such relations between controlling factors in foods and responses of pathogenic and spoilage microorganisms are quantified and modelled by mathematical equations. Predictive microbiology has numerous practical applications and is an active area of research.

14.1 Development and validation of predictive models

Large amounts of experimental data are required to predict the effect of controlling factors on growth, probability of growth, survival or inactivation of microorganisms (Table 14.1). Such data have often been generated using liquid laboratory media as levels of controlling factors (pH, NaCl %, etc.) are easy to adjust. In addition, automated methods for measuring microbial growth such as absorbance or conductance measurements can be used to facilitate the generation of data in liquid media. However, to accurately predict microbial growth in seafoods, liquid media cannot be used uncritically. With apparently similar levels of controlling factors, growth rates in seafood and standard liquid media like Brain Heart Infusion or Tryptone Soya Broth may differ by a factor of two. Therefore generation of data in product storage trials can be required for development of accurate predictive models (Dalgaard *et al.,* 2002). Knowledge about controlling factors is a prerequisite for development of accurate predictive models. In fact, major controlling factors and even the microorganisms responsible for seafood spoilage have in some cases remained unknown until mathematical modelling studies was initiated.

Table 14.1 Summary of general methodology for development of predictive growth models.

Data generation	Primary modelling	Secondary modelling	Product validation
Generate growth curves for combinations of controlling factors (temp., atmosphere, pH, etc.). Often liquid laboratory media are used.	Estimate kinetic parameters, primarily lag time and maximum specific growth rate, by fitting of growth curves with appropriate model	Model the effect of controlling factors on lag phase and growth rates	Evaluate the performance of a model by comparison of predictions and kinetic parameter values determined in product studies

To estimate lag times, maximum specific rates of growth (μ_{max}) or rates of inactivation, simple primary models are available and include:

(i) the exponential model, with or without a lag phase (Lodge and Hinshelwood 1943)
(ii) the three parameter Logistic model (Eqn. 14.1; solid line in Figure 14.1) or
(iii) four parameter versions of the Logistic model (Eqn. 14.2).

Numerous more flexible and complex primary models have been suggested but in most cases they have no advantage over the simpler primary growth models (Dalgaard, 2002). Nevertheless, the practical usefulness of at least one of the more complicated primary growth models has been increased by including it in the *MicroFit* software which is available free of charge (www.ifr.bbsrc.ac.uk/MicroFit/).

$$Log(N_t) = Log\left[\frac{N_{max}}{1+\exp[-\mu_{max}(t-t_i)]}\right] = Log\left[N_{max} \quad (1+\left[\frac{N_{max}}{N_0} - 1\right] \times \exp(-\mu_{max} \times t))\right] \quad 14.1$$

$$Log(N_t) = Log\left[N_{min} + \frac{N_{max} - N_{min}}{1+\exp[-\mu_{max}(t-t_i)]}\right] \quad 14.2$$

In eqn. 14.1 and 14.2 N_t is the cell concentrations (cfu g^{-1}) at the time t, N_{max} and N_{min}, respectively, are the maximum and minimum cell concentrations (cfu g^{-1}), μ_{max} the maximum specific growth rate (h^{-1}) and t_i the time when $N_t = N_{max}/2$ i.e. the inflection point.

Microbial interactions can be an important factor controlling growth of pathogenic microorganisms in seafood. E.g. for sliced and vacuum packed cold-smoked salmon, growth of *Listeria monocytogenes* has been found to cease when lactic acid bacteria reach their maximum cell concentration (Figure 14.1). This so-called Jameson effect can be modelled by a simple expansion of the differential form of the Logistic model (Eqn. 14.3, Jørgensen, 2000; Ross *et al.*, 2000a; Dalgaard, 2002).

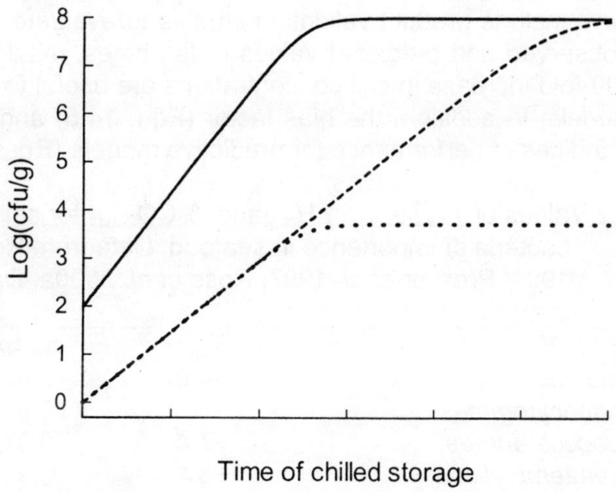

Figure 14.1
Predicted growth of *Listeria monocytogenes* (Lm) and lactic acid bacteria (LAB) during chilled storage of cold-smoked salmon. LAB (solid lines), Lm growing alone (dashed lines) and Lm growing together with LAB (dotted line).

$$\frac{dLm}{dt} = Lm_t \times \mu_{max}^{Lm} \times \left(1 - \frac{Lm_t}{Lm_{max}}\right) \times \left(1 - \frac{LAB_t}{LAB_{max}}\right) \quad 14.3$$

In eqn. 14.3 *Lm* and *LAB* signifies lactic acid bacteria and *L. monocytogenes*, respectively. *dLm*/*dt* is the absolute growth rates, Lm_t *and* LAB_t cell concentrations (cfu g^{-1}) at the time *t*, Lm_{max} and LAB_{max} the maximum cell contrations (cfu g^{-1}) and μ_{max}^{Lm} the maximum specific growth rate (h^{-1}).

Polynomial equations have been used extensively as secondary models for estimating the combined effect of several controlling factors on values of lag time and maximum specific growth rates (McClure *et al.* 1994). The polynomial models include a relatively large number of parameters and this makes it difficult to compare values from different studies particularly as the parameters have no biological interpretation. In contrast, square root type models like eqn. 14.4 include parameters with some biological meaning. The parameters T_{min}, $a_{w\ min}$, pH_{min} and $\%CO_{2\ max}$ correspond to theoretical growth limits for temperature, water activity, pH and CO_2. Rather than corresponding to the lowest temperature, water activity, pH or the highest CO_2 level where growth is actually observed T_{min}, $a_{w\ min}$, pH_{min} or $\%CO_{2\ max}$ are determined mathematically as the extrapolated values where the growth rate as a function of these controlling factors theoretically becomes zero. Thus, T_{min} –values of –5°C to –10°C are common for psychrotolerant Gram-negative bacteria although these microorganisms are typically inactivated at –5°C to –10°C. Nevertheless, T_{min}, $a_{w\ min}$, pH_{min} or $\%CO_{2\ max}$ each seems little influenced by other controlling factors. Therefore, when reliable estimates of these parameters are available, only few data are required to develop new models for specific pathogen/product combinations. As an example a model for growth of *L. monocytogenes* in a specific seafood may be developed from values of existing parameters and storage trials required to estimate the value of '*b*' in eqn. 13.4 (Ross *et al.*, 2000a). This approach has not yet been extensively used and deserves further study. Table 14.2 shows values of T_{min}, $a_{w\ min}$, pH_{min} or $\%CO_{2\ max}$ for selected pathogenic and spoilage bacteria of importance in seafood.

$$\begin{aligned}\sqrt{\mu_{\max}} &= b \\ &\times (T - T_{\min}) \\ &\times \sqrt{(a_w - a_{w\min})} \\ &\times \sqrt{(pH - pH_{\min})} \\ &\times (\%CO_{2\max} - \%CO_2)/\%CO_{2\max}\end{aligned} \qquad 14.4$$

Irrespective of the approach and the type of equations applied, development of a predictive model must always include product validation studies to evaluate the performance of the model. Graphs showing observed and predicted values of lag times, maximum specific growth rates or times for e.g. a 1000-fold increase in cell concentrations are useful to evaluate the performance of predictive growth models. In addition, the bias factor (Eqn. 14.5) and accuracy factor (Eqn. 14.6) are most important indices of performance for predictive models (Ross, 1996).

Table 14.2 Values of T_{min}, $a_{w\ min}$, pH_{min} and $\%CO_{2\ max}$ for selected pathogenic and spoilage bacteria of importance in seafood. Data from Ross and McMeekin 1991, Miles *et al.* 1997, Presser *et al.* 1997, Ross *et al.* 2000a, Dalgaard 2002.

	T_{min}	$a_{w\ min}$	pH_{min}	$\%\ CO_{2\ max}$
Escherichia coli	+4.0	0.93	3.9	-
Listeria monocytogenes	0	0.92	4.2	-
Staphylococcus aureus	+7.4	0.87	-	-
Vibrio parahaemolyticus	+5.4	0.92	-	-
Brochothrix thermosphacta	-10.9	-	-	187*
Lactobacillus curvatus	-3.3	0.93	4.2	-
Photobacterium phosphoreum	-9.0	0.95	4.3	376
Shewanella putrefaciens	-8.0 to –9.9	0.95	-	150-156

* *Values of CO_2 above 100% correspond to partial pressures above atmospheric pressure.*

$$\text{Bias factor } (\mu_{\max}) = 10^{(\Sigma \log(\mu_{\max\ predicted} / \mu_{\max\ observed})/n)} \qquad 14.5$$

$$\text{Accuracy factor } (\mu_{\max}) = 10^{(\Sigma |\log(\mu_{\max\ predicted} / \mu_{\max\ observed})| / n)} \qquad 14.6$$

The bias factor indicates systematic over- or under prediction and a value of 1.0 shows predicted and observed values to be equal on average. A bias factor value between 0.75 and 1.25 has been suggested as a criterion for successful validation of microbial models to predict shelf-life of seafood. For pathogenic microorganisms limits for bias factors has been suggested to be slightly closer to 1.0 (Dalgaard, 2000; Ross *et al.*, 2000a).

Bias factor

Index of performance to compare predicted growth and values observed in product studies. Successful validation of a predictive model requires a bias factor value between 0.75 and 1.25 for a specific seafood

Predictive models developed in liquid laboratory media may not include all major factors actually limiting microbial growth in seafood. Predictions from such incomplete models can be strongly biased and if used uncritically predictions can be misleading. As an example, models including the effect of temperature, NaCl/a_w, pH and lactate were unable to accurately predict growth of *L. monocytogenes* in naturally contaminated cold-smoked salmon. In fact, the bias factor was above 5 and it was pointed out that the effect of microbial interactions and smoke components was missing in the existing models (Dalgaard and Jørgensen, 1998; Ross *et al.*, 2000a). Recent studies confirmed that predictions could be substantially improved when the effect of interaction between *L. monocytogenes* and lactic acid bacteria (Eqn. 14.3) was added to a model already including the effect of temperature, NaCl/a_w, pH and lactate (Ross *et al.*, 2000b; Dalgaard, 2002).

Experimental data continuously indicate that the major factors controlling microbial growth in seafood are not all identified. Clearly, predictive models may be incomplete and should never be used uncritically. Users of a model must verify that a bias factor between 0.75 and 1.25 has been obtained in product validation studies before predictions are applied for assessment or management of seafood safety. Most important, the validation studies need to be carried out with seafood having microbial ecology similar to the product of interest. Furthermore, if a bias factor is e.g. 1.4 and a single controlling factor like smoke components in cold-smoked salmon is lacking in the model, then predictions can be corrected by the value of bias factor. In this way, a corrected model can be used (with caution) to predict the effect of the factors actually included in the model.

14.2 Practical use of models and application software

Successfully validated predictive models have numerous applications in assessment and management of seafood safety and quality, particularly when models are included in application softwares. Application software does not improve the models but they allow users, including people without interest in the mathematics of microbial kinetics, to obtain prediction rapidly and conveniently.

Seafood is never distributed at a constant temperature and in practice fresh and lightly preserved products that are supposed to be chilled can be exposed to between ~ 0°C and ~ 15°C. In tropical regions the temperature of fish raw material may be in the range of 25-30°C. Thus, the rate of chilling is a very critical parameter for both shelf-life and safety of products. The Seafood Spoilage Predictor (SSP) software has been developed specifically to predict the effect of constant and fluctuating temperature conditions on shelf-life of products from temperate and tropical waters as well as on growth of the spoilage bacteria *Photobacterium phosphoreum* and *Shewanella puftefaciens*. SSP is available free of charge at www.dfu.min.dk/micro/ssp/ (Dalgaard *et al.*, 2002). The Food Spoilage Predictor (FSP) software (www.geminidataloggers.com) and several predictive models are available (Koutsoumanis 2001, Rasmussen *et al.* 2002) for prediction of growth of psychrotolerant pseudomonads in fresh aerobically stored fish.

Pathogen Modeling Programme (PMP, www.arserrc.gov/mfs/PATHOGEN.HTM) includes 13 models for growth and survival and 9 models for inactivation of pathogenic bacteria. Food MicroModel (Anon., 1997) includes 23 growth and survival models and 7 models for heat inactivation of primarily pathogenic microorganisms. These software packages do not yet allow models to be used for time-temperature integration as described above. Models in PMP and Food MicroModel include the effect of wide ranges of several controlling factors. Thus, the models may be used to determine how one controlling factors e.g. NaCl % can be substituted by other factors such as a reduction of temperature or a change in packaging from aerobic to vacuum or modified atmosphere. Models in PMP and Food MicroModel may also be used to establish limits for critical control point as part of HACCP plans. Unfortunately, successful validation of the growth, survival and inactivation models in PMP and Food MicroModel remain to be documented for most types of seafood.

For *L. monocytogenes* in cold-smoked salmon and *Vibrio parahaemolyticus* and *V. vulnificus* in raw oysters predictive models have recently been included in exposure assessment models. By using the predictive models together with Monte Carlo simulation software the effect of initial product contamination, product temperature and product characteristics on levels of the pathogens can be predicted at the time product are consumed. Used in this way predictive models become a key component in quantitative risk assessments (Ross *et al.,* 2000b; FAO/WHO, 2002).

In the future, the use of predictive models in the assessment and management of seafood safety and quality will most likely increase substantially. New software to predict safety and shelf-life is likely to appear and predictive models may be combined with seafood traceability systems.

References

Anonymous 1997. *Food MicroModel - User Manual v. 2.5.* Food Micromodel Ltd., Surrey, UK.

Dalgaard, P. 2000. Fresh and lightly preserved seafood. In: Man,C.M.D. and A.A. Jones (eds) *Shelf-Life Evaluation of Foods.* Aspen Publishers Inc., London, UK. pp. 110-139.

Dalgaard, P. 2002. Modelling and prediction the shelf-life of seafood. In: Bremner, H.A. (ed.) *Safety and quality issues in fish processing.* Woodhead Publishing Ltd. pp. 191-219.

Dalgaard, P. and L.V. Jørgensen 1998. Predicted and observed growth of *Listeria monocytogenes* in seafood challenge tests and in naturally contaminated cold smoked salmon. *International Journal of Food Microbiology* 40, 105-115.

Dalgaard, P., P. Buch and S. Silberberg 2002. Seafood Spoilage Predictor - development and distribution of a product specific application software. *International Journal of Food Microbiology* 73, 227-233.

FAO/WHO (Food and Agriculture Organization/World Health Organization) 2002. Joint FAO/WHO Activity on Risk Assessment of Microbiological Hazards in Foods. Hazard identification, exposure assessment and hazard characterizatrion of *Vibrio* spp. in seafood. Preliminary document.

Jørgensen, L. V. 2000. *Spoilage and safety of cold-smoked salmon.* Ph.D. thesis. Danish Institute for Fisheries Research, Lyngby, and the Royal Veterinary and Agricultural University, Frederiksberg, Denmark.

Koutsoumanis, K. 2001. Predictive modeling of the shelf life of fish under nonisothermal conditions. *Applied and Environmental Microbiology* 67, 1821-1829.

Lodge, R.M. and C.N. Hinshelwood 1943. Physiological aspects of bacterial growth. Part IX. The lag phase of *Bact. Lactis Aerogenes. Journal of the Chemical Society* 288, 213-219.

McClure, P.J., C.D. Blackburn, M.B. Cole, P.S. Curtis, J.E. Jones, J.D. Legan, I.D. Ogden and M.W. Peck 1994. Modelling the growth, survival and death of microorganisms in foods: the UK Food Micromodel approach. *International Journal of Food Microbiology* 23, 265-275.

Miles, D.W., T. Ross, J. Olley and T.A. McMeekin 1997. Development and evaluation of a predictive model for the effect of temperature and water activity on the growth rate of *Vibrio parahaemolyticus. International Journal of Food Microbiology* 38, 133-142.

Presser, K.A., D.A. Ratkowsky and T. Ross 1997. Modelling the growth rate of *Escherichia coli* as a function of pH and lactic acid concentration. *Applied and Environmental Microbiology* 63, 2355-2360.

Rasmussen, S.K.J., T. Ross, J. Olley and T.A. McMeekin 2002. A process risk model for the shelf-life of Atlantic salmon fillets. *International Journal of Food Microbiology* 73, 47-60.

Ross, T. 1996. Indices for performance evaluation of predictive models in food microbiology. *Journal of Applied Bacteriology* 81, 501-508.

Ross, T.A. and T.A. McMeekin 1991. Predictive microbiology: Application of a square root model. *Food Australia* 43, 202-207.

Ross, T., P. Dalgaard and S. Tienungoon 2000a. Predictive modelling of the growth and survival of *Listeria* in fishery products. *International Journal of Food Microbiology* 62, 231-245.

Ross, T., E. Todd and M. Smith 2000b. Exposure assessment of *L. monocytogenes* in ready-to-eat foods. World Health Organization, Geneva, and Food and Agriculture Organization of the United Nations, Rome, Italy.

15 TRACEABILITY (Marco Frederiksen/Lone Gram)

An important aspect of quality and safety assurance is to be able to trace products, ingredients, suppliers, retailer, processing operations or storage procedures through the food production chain. This is especially relevant when failures occur. The term "traceability" has been introduced to describe systems in which information about a particular attribute of a food product is systematically recorded from creation through marketing (Golan *et al.,* 2002). For instance if a particular batch of cold-smoked fish has caused an outbreak of listeriosis, authorities will want to trace the product in question to the producer to establish re-call procedures. Similarly, the producer will want to determine if contamination with *L. monocytogenes* occurred in the plant and/or if temperature abuse occurred during distribution or during storage at the retailer or at the consumer. One may regard an epidemiological investigation as part of a traceability study, e.g. determining the sources of an agent involved in an outbreak of food-borne disease.

Traceability systems have been used for many years in several other sectors such as the aviation, automobile and pharmaceutical industry. As the food chain has lengthened from local production, processing and consumption to more global commercial opportunities, the need to transfer information related to production and public health and the complexity of these transfer vehicles have expanded (McKean, 2001). With the increase in complexity, the consumer wishes to know the origin (species, place, condition of rearing or catch.....), the transformations and the distribution of their food products (Pascal and Mahé, 2001).

Quantitative risk assessments typically aim at covering the whole "farm-to-fork" chain and at any point in time, one must therefore be able to trace an event or a product. ISO 9000 (ISO, 2000) defines traceability as the ability to trace the history, application or location of that which is under consideration. When considering a product, traceability can relate to

- the origin of materials and parts
- the processing history
- the distribution and location of the product after delivery.

In general the term "trace" is used when the history of product origin is searched and the term "track" is used for searching its history after delivery. Moe (1998) described the terms used in traceability studies as

- a step is referring to a discrete operation or location at which some task or process is performed on the product
- a chain is composed of the sequence of these steps, and
- a product can be any material at any stage of processing, e.g. a live fish, a whole fish, or a processed fish product.

Interest in traceability in food processing has been increasing in recent years, primarily because of the different crisis in the food sector such as the mad cow disease (BSE) in 1996 in the UK and the dioxin contamination in Belgium in 1999. Authorities have focused on traceability to assure consumer safety to be able to re-call defective/hazardous products and to identify the source of the problem.

Also, traceability may be advantageous within a company allowing different raw materials to be directed to production of different categories of product – and subsequently allowing the company to determine if yield, quality, or safety of a particular category was related to a particular raw material – or a particular ingredient. Since traceability systems basically are record-keeping systems, these are in some form required for a HACCP system to be implemented. However, the record keeping step of the HACCP system aims at documenting that the system is under control, that corrective actions are taken when pre-defined critical limits are exceeded, and that re-call of unsafe products is undertaken when required (Caporale *et al.,* 2001). A fully implemented traceability system is broader and covers also a range of aspects not related to safety.

Finally, implementation of traceability systems, although costly to implement, can also be an economic benefit to the producer. The whole chain from vessel to retailer can be managed in a more effective way, when the traceable information is used actively to enhance mutual trust and cooperation between steps in the chain. Significantly less time (and money) can be spent on quality checks and storage, and when recalls are to be carried out traceability is an insurance that the company limits the loss, and protect its brand on the market (Frederiksen, 2002).

15.1 Internal versus external (chain) traceability

The widespread acceptance of hazard analysis and critical control point (HACCP) systems for safety management has increased the need for product chain information throughout the chain (McKean, 2001). Many food (fish) processing companies already have effective internal traceability systems as part of their HACCP based quality assurance systems. In many cases, however, traceability is lost before and after the company deals with the raw materials and the final products. Much effort is spent on quality and safety grading of in-coming raw material. This effort can be minimised if the external traceability, the so-called chain traceability, and the attached information on quality is established. The traceable information must be reliable and this is substantiated by open access from other chain members to audit the quality assurance systems in the chain. Chain traceability is the key to cooperation and mutual trust between independent companies in a chain. More developed industries as for instance the automotive industry focus on auditing their sub-suppliers quality assurance systems today and makes less inspection of incoming products and the same already happens in some food industries.

15.2 Traceability systems

Traceability in its simplest form is in the form of a paper trail. This implies that every relevant piece of information is written on paper that follows the raw material through the processing line to retail. This method can be used for products of high value that are only produced in small quantities, but for basic commodity fish products the costs are too high for manual tracking (Frederiksen and Bremner, 2001). Despite the costs, analysis of three different fish chains in Denmark, Iceland and Norway (fresh whole fish, frozen fish and fresh farmed salmon) have shown that the paper-based systems (faxes, notes, postal letters) are widely used (Palsson *et al.,* 2000).

With the explosive development in electronic data analysis, traceability systems based on information technology must be developed (Frederiksen *et al.*, 2002). Several e-business companies produce software allowing integration of financial and production data in one program package, and most of these have traceability capabilities components implemented (e.g. i2 technologies Inc., Dallas, USA; SAP AG, Walldorf, Germany). However, such systems are typically too costly for the small business units in the fish industry. In an EU concerted action project (Tracefish) - an open and voluntary industry standard for how traceability may be implemented electronically is now being developed (Tracefish, 2002). The work will be transferred to a CEN (Comité Européen Normalisation) standard in early 2003.

The EDIFACT (electronic data interchange for administration, commerce and transport) standard is currently the standard most used for transferring data between steps in the chain. Transfer costs are high and the standard is mostly used by supermarkets at the retail end of the chain. Clearly the Internet is the future as transfer medium and XML (extensible mark-up language) is the new Internet standard allowing transfer of information in a readable, easy, and cheap way (W3C, 2002).

15.3 Labelling products

The minimum requirement for traceability is that each traceable unit has been uniquely labelled to allow identification. The most common labelling method is to label products with barcodes of which the EAN-13 and UCC-12 codes (European Article Number and Uniform Code Council) are the most used. However, these codes, which can be read by retail units, do not allow inclusion of a unique identifier, which is crucial for traceability. Other bar codes (EAN/UCC-128) include the identifier but cannot be read by the retail bar code scanner.

The newest development is the use of RFID (radio frequency identification) tags, but the price is too high to justify their use in the consumer end of the chain. However it is today used for some reusable fish tubs and as internal traceability keeper in the meat industry (Rowan, 2002). The advantage of these tags is that they are fast and easy to read. It must be anticipated that the price of the RFID tags will decrease to a level allowing them to be introduced more widely in the food chain.

15.4 Fresh fish quality traceability

Traceability is important in the fresh fish chain where it may allow tracing of fish from tropical reef waters (potentially containing marine toxins) or tracing of fish from waters polluted with e.g. heavy metals. However, the most important issue in fresh fish trading is the assurance of freshness. Freshness is – for all species – almost exclusively a function of time and temperature. In principle, each fish should be continuously monitored with a time-temperature recording device; however, this is not technically or economically feasible. Therefore these two aspects are dealt with separately. In a well-functioning distribution chain where each step can be relied upon in terms of temperature control, the quality traceability can be implemented by a time recording. Clearly, spot checks of quality must be carried out using standardised fresh fish quality inspection methods such as the Quality Index Method (QIM) (Bremner, 1985; Jónsdóttir *et al.*, 1991).

A traceability system has been developed for fresh fish supply chains in the Danish domestic market and initial studies determined that temperature could be appropriately controlled in this particular chain (Figure 15.1, Frederiksen *et al.*, 2002).

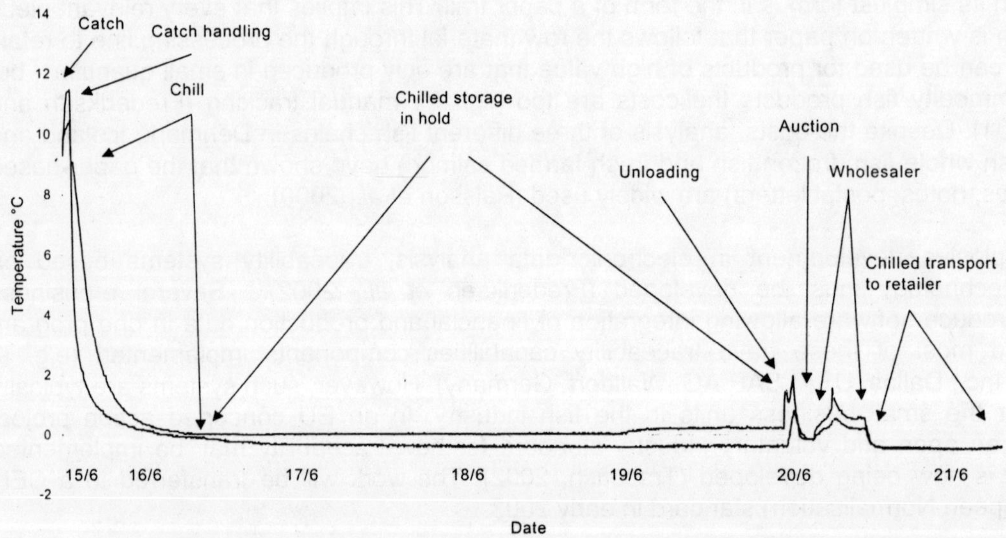

Figure 15.1 Time-temperature measurements of two fish in two different boxes (positions) trough the whole chain from vessel to retailer (modified from Frederiksen *et al.*, 2002).

Internet technology (XML) has been used to transfer data from five steps in the chain from fisherman to retailer (Figure 15.2).

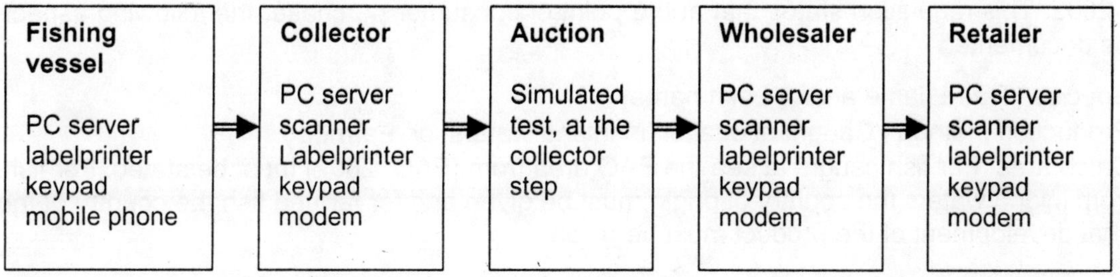

Figure 15.2 The complete test chain and the equipment installed in each step of the chain. Modified from Frederiksen *et al.* (2002).

Fish are sorted on-board according to species and iced in boxes. Each box is labelled with information on fish species, catch date, vessel name/number, and a unique box number, readable as ordinary numbers and in the form of a barcode. The information is registered in a computer onboard the vessel, and the data are transmitted via a mobile phone to a computer at the next step in the chain, the collector. The collector receives all information from the vessel before it enters the harbour. At the collector, each species is sorted according to size, keeping fish from each catch date separate (the traceable unit is fish from the same vessel with the same catch date). The fish is ice-packed in boxes, with new labels attached, and information about collector name, fish size/weight and a new box number registered at the computer adding this new information to the database.

The boxes were distributed through a wholesaler and further on to a retailer and same procedures were used in all steps to retrieve and add new information to existing product data. At the wholesaler information on wholesaler name, new fish weight and new box number was added. At the retailer information on retailer name, new fish weight, process type and customer number was added.

All information was available at the retailer step. An example on a possible customer label is shown in Figure 15.3.

Retailer name
This Cod size 3 was caught June 30 2002 by the vessel: 'AB123'

Filleted weight: 600 g
Internet number: 1234567

Bar-code: EAN/UCC 128 (01)(11)(21)
(01)057 12345 00001 4(11)010615(21)00001

Figure 15.3 An example of a possible customer label. Modified from Frederiksen *et al.* (2002).

15.5 EU legislation on traceability of fish and fish products

There is a great international awareness with respect to the need for traceability. Recent international working documents, e.g., The European White Paper on Food Safety (EC, 2000) and the Bangkok Declaration and Strategy on Aquaculture Development (NACA/FAO, 2000), both include statements encouraging the development of traceability to be applied throughout the supply chain.

The general EU principles and requirements of food law including traceability definition and requirements are contained in EU commission regulations 178/2002 (EC, 2002). The present legislation for traceability of fish and fish products is described in EU council regulation 104/2000 (EC, 2000a) and commission regulation 2065/2001 (EC, 2001) that has been in action since

January 2002. This regulation states that at the point of consumer purchase, the following aspects should be documented

- Species (Trade name and/or Latin name)
- Production method ('Caught at sea' or 'in inland waters' or 'Farmed')
- Catch area. For fish caught at sea the FAO area from (FAO, 2002) must be stated. For fish from inland waters the country of origin must be given and for farmed fish the country of the final development of the product must be given.

These are the first implemented demands for traceability for fish products in the EU system and more demands will follow in the years to come. For instance, the catch area demand is very broad and currently only requires a distinction between fish from the whole North Sea and the Baltic Sea for catches from the North of Europe. This has far reaching consequences if, for example, pollution is detected in a small sea area in the North Sea, then all fish caught from the North Sea must be recalled.

Recently, the European Union proposed government-mandated traceability for genetically engineered crops and foods to help distinguish them from their conventional counterparts (Golan *et al.*, 2002).

References

Bremner, H.A. 1985. Estimating time-temperature effects by a rapid systematic sensory method. In: Kramer, D.E. and J. Liston (eds) *Seafood quality determination.* Elsevier, Amsterdam, The Netherlands. pp. 59-70.

Caporale, V., A. Giovannini, C. Di Francesco and P. Calistri 2001. Importance of the traceability of animals and animal products in epidemiology. *Revue Scientifique et technique de l'Office International des Epizooties* 20, 372-378.

EC (European Commission) 2000. *White Paper on Food Safety*. Office for Official Publications of the European Communities, Brussels, Belgium (www.cordis.org 05/06/2002).

EC (European Commission) 2000a. Commission Regulation (EC) No 104/2000 of 17 December 1999 on the common organization of the markets in fishery and aquaculture products. *Official Journal of the European Communities* No. L 17, 21.01.2000, 22-52.

EC (European Commission) 2001. Commission Regulation 2065/2001 22 October 2001 laying down detailed rules for the application of Council Regulation (EC) no 104/2000 as regards informing consumers about fishery and aquaculture products. *Official Journal of the European Communities* No. L 278, 23.10.2001, 6-8.

EC (European Commission) 2002. Regulation No 178/2002 of the European parliament and of the council of 28 January 2002 laying down the general principles and requirements of food law, establishing the European food safety and laying down procedures in matter of food safety. *Official Journal of the European Communities* No. L 31, 01.02.2002, 1-24.

FAO (Food and Agriculture Organization) 2002. Public server of FAO (ftp://ftp.fao.org/fi/maps/world_2001.gif 05/06/2002).

Frederiksen, M. (2002). Quality chain management in fish processing. In: Bremner, H.A. (ed) *Safety and Quality in Fish processing*. Cambridge: Woodhead Publishing Ltd, pp. 289-307.

Frederiksen, M. and H.A. Bremner 2001. Fresh fish distribution chains. An analysis of three Danish and three Australian chains. *Food Australia* 54, 117-123.

Frederiksen, M., C. Østerberg, S. Silberg, E. Larsen, and H.A. Bremner 2002. Info-fisk. Development and validation of an Internet based traceability system in a Danish domestic fresh fish chain. *Journal of Aquatic Food Product Technology* 11, 13-34.

Golan, E., B. Krissoff and F. Kuchler 2002. Traceability for food marketing & food safety: what's the next step?. *Agricultural Outlook*, January-February, 21-25.

ISO (International Organization for Standardization) 2000. *Quality management systems – Fundamentals and vocabulary*. European Standard (EN ISO 9000:2000, Point 3.5.4). Committee for Standardisation, Brussels, Belgium.

Jónsdóttir, S., Larsen, E., Martinsdóttir, E., Brattår, R. and Gudjónsson, A. (1991). *'Kvalitetsnormer på fisk'*, A report and manual (sensory evaluation of fish) to the Nordic Industry Foundation.

McKean, J.D. 2001. The importance of traceability for public health and consumer protection. *Revue Scientifique et technique de l'Office International des Epizooties* 20, 363-371.

Moe, T. 1998. Perspectives on traceability in food manufacture. *Trends in Food Science and Technology* 9, 211-214.

NACA/FAO (Network of Aquaculture Centres in Asia-Pacific /Food and Agriculture Organization) 2000. *Aquaculture development Beyond 2000*. The Bangkok Declaration and Strategy. Conference on Aquaculture development in the Third Millennium, Bangkok, Thailand. (www.fao.org 05/06/2002).

Palsson, P.G., Storøy, J., Frederiksen, M. and Olsen, P. (2000). Nordic Ministry Council. Project 66031400: *Traceability and electronic transmission of qualitative data for fish products*, status report no. 3 June 2000, Lyngby, Denmark: Danish Institute for Fisheries Research, Department of Seafood Research.

Pascal, G. and S. Mahé 2001. Identity, traceability, acceptability and substantial equivalence of food. *Cellular and Molecular Biology* 47, 1329-1342.

Rowan, C. 2002. Traceability: Integration is key. *Food Engineering and Ingredients* February, 14-19.

Tracefish (2002). Homepage of Tracefish (www.tracefish.org 05.06.2002).

W3C 2001. The World Wide Web Consortium consists of more than 500 organizations. The current work and the latest version of XML and SOAP are available from: www.w3.org.

APPENDIX 1 ASSESSMENT OF FOOD SAFETY PROGRAMMES (Hans Henrik Huss)

The assessment process covers the following 7 steps:

1. Pre-assessment document review

   - process flow diagram with location of CCPs
   - product specifications
   - HACCP plan including worksheets and records
   - Prerequisite plans including worksheet and records

2. Opening meeting

   - scope
   - process
   - schedule
   - amenities needed

3. On-site verification of process flow diagram

4. On-site document review and observations

   - product and ingredients specifications
   - previous audit reports and minutes of HACCP meetings
   - assessment of prerequisite programmes and functions (form attached)
   - assessment of HACCP programmes and functions (form attached)

5. Closing meeting

6. Assessment report

7. Assessment follow-up

The following five pages give examples of forms that can be used for on-site evaluation of the HACCP and prerequisite programmes.

ON-SITE DOCUMENT REVIEW AND OBSERVATIONS

Assessment of HACCP Programme

Name and address of establishment audited	*Phone/fax/email*
Facility Owner (company or person)	*Date of audit*
Products Concerned	*Products - High or low risk*
Name and Number of Inspector	
Name and Title of Accompanying Individual	

HACCP	A	B	C	Note
HACCP team used was appropriate				
Raw materials specifications defined and written down				
Product and ingredient specifications are defined and written down				
Product end use is defined and recorded (high or low risk product)				
Flow diagram is written down and is accurate and complete				
Hazard analysis is written down and is accurate and complete (evidence of Hazard Worksheets)				
Identification of CCPs is documented and CCPs are appropriate for product and end use of product				
Critical limits have been established, documented and are appropriate for the CCP				
Monitoring procedures for each CCP are documented, are followed and records are kept				
Corrective actions identified, written down and are followed when critical limits exceeded. Records exist				
Verification procedures are documented and are followed. Records exist				
All necessary documentation exists and are available for inspection				

A = excellent, good or only minor deficiencies (no safety risk)
B = major or serious deficiencies, which could lead to a safety risk if not controlled. Any condition or situation rated as a B requires a plan or programme for rapid improvement. Repetitive or cumulative B-ratings can lead to a critical situation.
C = an unacceptable or critical situation representing a safety risk. Any C-rating requires immediate response and corrective action.

FACTORY CHECK

Processing Plant		A	B	C	Note
Outside					
Condition of grounds outside the factory					
Condition of the factory outside wall - especially holes through to inside					
Inside					
Rooms	- layout and flow of goods and people allows easy cleaning and prevents cross contamination				
Rooms	- for clean and unclean areas are separated (including waste areas)				
Rooms	- for non food items are separated e.g. packaging, chemicals, etc.				
Ceilings, walls, floors, doors and windows are well designed and maintained in good repair -					
	- for areas directly affecting food product or primary packaging material				
	- for other areas				
Drains	- are well designed, sufficient and maintained in good repair				
Drains	- there is protection against back-flow, back-siphoning, or other sources of contamination				
Lighting	- is sufficient and lights are covered				
Pest control	- exclusion devices (screens, mesh, etc.) are present at all openings to outside and maintained in good repair				
Pest control	- No areas present to harbour or attract pests				
Ventilation	- is sufficient, well designed and there is no condensation evident				
Facilities in Processing Plant		**A**	**B**	**C**	**Note**
Water	- sufficient quantity of cold water available, clear marking and separation of potable and non-potable water				
Water	- sufficient quantity of hot water/steam available				
Ice	- sufficient quantity available and storage facility well designed and kept in good order and repair				
Chilling and freezing facilities – sufficient capacity					
Waste-water	- leaves the property in a condition that meets environmental laws				
Hygiene	- changing rooms are sensibly located, are well designed and are kept in good repair				
Hygiene	- toilets are sensibly located and in sufficient numbers and kept in good repair				
Hygiene	- Hand-washing and sanitizing stations are in sufficient numbers, well designed, well located and kept in good repair				
Equipment	- containers made of appropriate materials, in proper repair and removed when necessary				
Equipment	- machinery designed well, easy to clean and kept in good repair - Food contact surfaces				
Equipment	- machinery designed well, easy to clean and kept in good repair - Non-food contact surfaces				

PROCEDURES

Safety of water and ice	A	B	C	Note
Criteria are written down and are appropriate				
Monitoring procedure is written down, is followed and records are kept				
Corrective actions identified, written down and are followed when critical limits exceeded. Records exist.				
Cleaning and disinfection	**A**	**B**	**C**	**Note**
Cleaning and disinfection methods (food contact and non-contact surfaces) are written down and are appropriate				
Monitoring procedure for cleanliness is written down, is followed and records are kept				
Corrective actions identified, written down and are followed when critical limits exceeded. Records exist.				
Personal observations in factory by auditor				
Personnel hygiene and health	**A**	**B**	**C**	**Note**
Personnel hygiene criteria (cleanliness, dress code) are written down and are appropriate				
Procedures to handle illness are written down and are appropriate				
Monitoring procedure for personnel hygiene and health is written down, is followed and records are kept				
Corrective actions identified, written down and are followed when critical limits exceeded. Records exist.				
Personal observations of personnel by auditor				
Prevention of cross contamination	**A**	**B**	**C**	**Note**
Criteria to prevent cross contamination are written down and are appropriate				
Monitoring procedure is written down, is followed and records are kept				
Corrective actions identified, written down and are followed when critical limits exceeded. Records exist.				
Personal observations in factory by auditor				
Maintenance of facilities for personal hygiene				
Methods to maintain personal hygiene facilities are written down and are appropriate				
Monitoring procedure is written down, is followed and records are kept				
Corrective actions identified, written down and are followed when critical limits exceeded. Records exist.				
Personal observations in factory by auditor				
Protection of food from adulterants	**A**	**B**	**C**	**Note**
Criteria to protect food from adulteration are written down and are appropriate				
Monitoring procedure is written down, is followed and records are kept				
Corrective actions identified, written down and are followed when critical limits exceeded. Records exist.				
Personal observations in factory by auditor				

Waste management	A	B	C	Note
Methods to handle sewage and processing waste are written down and are appropriate				
Monitoring procedure is written down, is followed and records are kept				
Corrective actions identified, written down and are followed when critical limits exceeded. Records exist.				
Personal observations in factory by auditor				
Recalls and traceability	**A**	**B**	**C**	**Note**
Methods to allow full traceability and recall of product are written down and are appropriate				
Monitoring procedure is written down, is followed and records are kept				
Corrective actions identified, written down and are followed when critical limits exceeded. Records exist.				
Personal observations in factory by auditor				
Training	**A**	**B**	**C**	**Note**
Training policy and programme are written down, are appropriate and followed				
Monitoring procedure is written down, is followed and records are kept				
Corrective actions identified, written down and are followed when critical limits exceeded. Records exist.				
Personal observations of training in factory by auditor, if possible				
Pest Control	**A**	**B**	**C**	**Note**
Pest control procedures are written down and are appropriate				
Monitoring procedure is written down, is followed and records are kept				
Corrective actions identified, written down and are followed when critical limits exceeded. Records exist.				
Personal observations in factory by auditor				
Labeling and safe storage and use of toxic chemicals	**A**	**B**	**C**	**Note**
Toxic chemical handling, use and storage procedures are written down and are appropriate				
Monitoring procedure is written down, is followed and records are kept				
Corrective actions identified, written down and are followed when critical limits exceeded. Records exist.				
Personal observations in factory by auditor				
Transport and storage	**A**	**B**	**C**	**Note**
Temperature and cleanliness criteria for transport and storage are written down and are appropriate				
Monitoring procedure is written down, is followed and records are kept				
Corrective actions identified, written down and are followed when critical limits exceeded. Records exist.				
Personal observations in factory by auditor				

NOTES

Note number from form	Comment

SUMMARY

Totals numbers of each category				

General comments from auditor
General comments from establishment representative

SIGNATURES

Signature of auditor	*Date*
Signature of establishment representative	*Date*

APPENDIX 2 HAZARD ANALYSIS WORKSHEET (based on National Seafood HACCP Alliance, 1997)

(1) Ingredient/ processing step	(2) Identify potential hazards introduced, controlled or enhanced at this step	(3) Are any potential food-safety hazards significant? (Yes/No)	(4) Justify your decision for column 3	(5) What preventative measure(s) can be applied to prevent the significant hazards?	(3) Is this step a critical control point? (Yes/No)
	BIOLOGICAL CHEMICAL PHYSICAL				
	BIOLOGICAL CHEMICAL PHYSICAL				
	BIOLOGICAL CHEMICAL PHYSICAL				
	BIOLOGICAL CHEMICAL PHYSICAL				
	BIOLOGICAL CHEMICAL PHYSICAL				
	BIOLOGICAL CHEMICAL PHYSICAL				

APPENDIX 3 HACCP PLAN FORM (based on National Seafood HACCP Alliance, 1997)

(1) Critical Control Point (CCP)	(2) Significant Hazards	(3) Critical Limits for each Preventive Measure	(4) Monitoring	(5)	(6)	(7)	(8) Corrective Action(s)	(9) Records	(10) Verification
			What	How	Frequency	Who			

APPENDIX 4 GENERIC HACCP PLAN FOR THE PRODUCTION AND PROCESSING OF OYSTERS

Product description:

Name:	Shucked raw oysters
Raw material:	Live oysters from: (specification of harvesting area) No ingredients used
Parameters influencing safety:	None
Processing:	Manually shucked, washed and packed
Packaging:	In buckets
Storage conditions and shelf life	5 days at temperatures < 2°C
Intended use and consumer:	To be eaten raw by the general public
Labelling instructions:	Storage and distribution at temperatures < 2°C

The process flow chart and hazard analysis is shown in the following table:

Hazard analysis – Raw, shucked oysters

(1) Ingredient/ processing step	(2) Identify potential hazards introduced, controlled or enhanced at this step	(3) Are any potential food-safety hazards significant? (Yes/No)	(4) Justify your decision for column 3	(5) What preventative measure(s) can be applied to prevent the significant hazards?	(3) Is this step a critical control point? (Yes/No)
Harvesting	Contamination with pathogenic bacteria, virus Biotoxins Chemical	Yes Yes Yes	Water filtration and accumulation of pathogenic compounds from harvesting area	Monitoring of harvesting area. Licensing of harvester. Tagging of all lots	Yes
Cooling / transport	Growth of pathogenic bacteria	Yes	Pathogenic bacteria will increase in numbers at high temperatures	Limit the time from harvesting to refrigeration	Yes
Receiving	As above	Yes	As above	Check labels, certificates, tags	Yes
Storage	Growth of pathogens	Yes	Prevented by PP[1]		No
Shucking	Contamination	No	Prevented by PP[1]		No
Washing / draining	Contamination	No	Prevented by PP[1]		No
Packing	*None*				
Labelling	*Failure in applying warning label*	Yes	All hazards are not fully controlled	Check labelling procedure	Yes
Storage / distribution	*Growth of pathogens*	No		Prevented by PP[1]	No

1. PP = prerequisite programme

HACCP Plan Form – Raw, shucked oysters

(1) Critical Control Point (CCP)	(2) Significant Hazards	(3) Critical Limits for each Preventive Measure	(4) Monitoring	(5)	(6)	(7)	(8) Corrective Action(s)	(9) Records	(10) Verification
			What	How	Frequency	Who			
Harvesting	Contamination with pathogenic bacteria, virus, biotoxins, chemicals	Harvesting area must be monitored and open for fishing	Check with monitoring programme	Phone Fax Internet	Before harvesting	Fishermen	Do not harvest Reject harvest if area is closed	Copies of permits	Record review
Cooling / transport	Growth of pathogens	Oysters should be cooled to 10°C in less than 24 h	Time / temperature conditions	Visual check Thermometer	After 24 h and every 2 h	Fishermen, transporter	Adjust cooling system, Evaluate based on exposure	Temperature records Capture time	Record review
Receiving	Unsafe products As above	Must bear a tag from a certified harvester	Identification tag and harvester licence	Visual	Every container	QC person	Reject untagged containers or from unlicensed harvester	Receiving records	Record review
Labelling	Failure in applying warning label	All final product containers must carry label	The presence of label	Visual	Every container	QC person	Apply label	Statement of actions and observations	Record review

INDEX

A

Aerobic Plate Count · 114, 199
Aeromonas sp. · 27, 45, 83
Aeromonodaceae · 45
Agmatine · 53
Alexandrium · 71, 185
Amino acid precursor · 53
Amnesic Shellfish Poisoning · *See* ASP
Angiostrongylus sp. · See Nematodes
Anionic acid · 119
Anisakis simplex · 62
Anisakis sp · See Nematodes
Anserine · 53, 82
Antibiotic · 80–84
  antimicrobial resistance · 82
  prevention · 84
  residues · 80–82
  vaccines · 79, 82
Aquaculture · 3–6, 68–166
  antibiotics · 77–83
  antimicrobial agents · 79, 82
  chemicals · 154
  drugs · 79
  feeds · 81, 83
  organisms · 77, 82, 110
  risks · 78, 83, 153
Arsenic · See Chemicals (inorganic chemicals)
ASP symptoms · 74
Audit · 146–150
  definition · 147
  procedures · 146
  qualifications · 150
Autolysis · *See* Spoilage (chemical)

B

Benzoate · 153, 162, 193
Bias factor · 206
Bioaccumulation · 77
Biogenic amines · 52–56
  Enterobacteriaceae · 22, 46, 49, 54, 167
  hazard analysis · 154–173
  preventive measures · 124, 154·173
  production · 52
Bioluminometric assay · 122
Biomagnification · 77
Biotoxins · *See* Toxins
Black spots · 73
Botulinum · 27–34, 162, 202
  cook · 29–34, 162
  toxins · 27–34, 163
Botulism · 20, 31, 164–173
  outbreaks · 20, 164, 170, 173
  symptoms · 31
Brevetoxins · 72
  stability · 73
Brining · 135
BSE crisis · 1, 210

C

Cadaverine · 53
Cadmium · See Chemicals (inorganic chemicals)
Campylobacteriaceae · 50
Canning · 34, 59, 75, 170, 180
  canned fish · 5, 170, 182
  Industry · 34
Capillaria philippensis · See Nematodes
Capillaria sp. · See Nematodes
CCPs · 105, 134, 137–144, 159–189, *See* HACCP
  definition · 136
  hazards · 136, 170
  monitoring · 140
Cestodes · 61, 65
  diphyllobothrium sp · 61, 65
  life cycles · 61, 66
CFP · 74, 76, 154, 162–166
  symptoms · 74
Chemicals · 22, 24, 77–105, 123, 154
  inorganic chemicals · 77
  organic compounds · 77, 118
  processing related compounds · 77
  recommendations · 78
  residues · 23, 77, 112
  see also disinfectants · 60, 105–125
Chill storage · 34, 166
Chilling · 46, 52–56, 129, 154, 159, 162, 179
Chloramines · 111, 118
Chlordane · *See* Chemicals
Chlorine · 111–115, 118–121, 125
  chlorination · 114
  cleaning · 111, 114–118, 121, 125
  disinfection · 110, 117–123
  inactivation · 112
  residual level · 111
Chlorine dioxide · 111, 118, 120
Cholera · 20, 27, 35, 38–40, 83
Ciguatera fish poisoning · *See* CFP
Ciguatoxins · 74
CIP · *See* Cleaning
Clams · *See* Molluscs
Cleaning · 75, 105–108, 114, 117, 121
  CIP (cleaning in place) · 119–122
  steps · 115
  water · 75, 102, 109–118, 124
Cleaning agents · 111, 115, 120, 126, 180
  properties · 116–118, 121
Clonorchiasis · 68
Clonorchis sp. · See Trematodes
Clostridium botulinum · 31–34, 202
Clostridium perfringens · 28–31, 44
Clupeidae · 56
Code of Practice · *See Codex Alimentarius* Commission
Codex Alimentarius Commission (CAC) · 96, 133, 195
Cold chain · 24
Corrective actions · 103, 109, 134, 141, 145, 148, 158, 170, 178
  definition · 141
Coryphaenidae · 56
Crabmeat · 167, 192, 199
Criteria · *See* Microbiological criteria
Critical Control Point · *See* CCPs
Critical limit · 26, 79, 103, 134, 139–144, 149, 158
  definition · 140

D

DAPs (Defect Action Points) · 178
DDT · 77, 79
Decarboxylase · 53–56
Decarboxylation · 53, 56
Defect · 9, 56, 77, 128, 170, 178, 198
  definition · 178–182
Detergents · 116, 119–121
Diamine oxidase (DAO) · 53
Diarrhetic Shellfish Poisoning · *See* DSP
Dieldrine · 77

Dimethylamine · 179
Dinoflagellates · 70–74
  bloom · 70–73
Dinophysis · 72
Dioxins · *See* Chemicals (organic compounds)
Diphyllobothrium sp. · See Cestodes
Disease control · 26–84
  Aeromonas sp. · 46
  antibiotic · 83
  campylobacter sp. · 51
  CDC · 46
  Clostridium botulinum · 34
  enterobacteriaceae · 50
  histamine · 55
  Listeria sp. · 43
  other clostridia and bacilli · 45
  parasites · 63
  physical hazards · 84
  Staphylococcus sp. · 52
  toxins ·
  Vibrio sp. · 36
  viruses · 59
Disinfectants · 117–123
  carboxylic acid · 120
  chemicals · 117, 121, 123
  chlorine dioxide · 111, 118, 120
  hot water · 115, 117, 120
  ozone · 111, 120
  UV · 111
Disinfection · *See* Disinfectants
DMA · *See* Dimethylamine
Domoic acid · 72, 74, 76, 200
Drinking water · *See* Water quality
DSP · 21, 70, 73, 157, 199
  symptoms · 73

E

E. coli · See Escherichia coli
Echinostomatidae · *See Trematodes*
EDIFACT · 211
Engraulidae · 56
Enterobacteriaceae · 22, 46–50, 54, 167
  Yersinia enterocolitica · 46, 50
Enterotoxins · 51, 192
Escherichia coli · 28, 46, 48, 60, 199, 206

F

FA · *See* Formaldehyde
FDA (Food and Drug Administration) · 14, 22, 48, 78, 84, 152, 189
  Health Hazard Board · 84
  regulations · 63, 78, 101, 125, 133
  seafood import refusals · 22
Fish utilization · 5, 99
Flow diagram · 136, 144, 147–149, 181, 216
Flukes · See Trematodes
Food contact surfaces · 102, 107, 114, 121–123, 126
  definition · 114
Food-borne diseases · 19–25, 35, 46, 51, 57, 127, 157, 164, 167, 210
  cost · 1
  outbreaks · 19–21, 36, 47–59, 127, 157–159, 164, 167
  seafood · 19, 26, 35, 46, 57, 157
  statistics · 19
Formaldehyde · 179
Freezing · 43, 45, 56, 63, 69, 129, 159, 162–168
FSO (Food Safety Objectives) · 13, 15, 145, 189–194

G

GHP · 7–16, 101–106, 130, 133, 189, 201
GMP · 7–11, 101, 133, 146–148, 196, 200
Gnathostoma sp. · See Nematodes
Good Hygiene Practices · *See* GHP
Good Manufacturing Practices · *See* GMP
Gymnodinium · 73

H

HACCP · 11–14, 43, 68, 98, 101–109, 133–153, 158, 161, 178, 201, 217
  audit · 146
  corrective actions · 109
  definition · 101, 147
  documentation · 133, 140, 144, 147
  fish industry · 145
  guidelines · 99, 101, 133, 135
  introduction · 149
  plan · 11, 102, 135–145, 152, 158, 162–169, 216
  preventive measures · 43, 68
  principles · 133–135
  problems · 133
  regulatory agencies · 133, 140, 144. 201
  validation · 143
  verification · 140, 142
HACCP, application of · 153–183
  canned fish · 170
  crustaceans · 153, 159, 161, 167
  dried fish · 153, 171
  fermented fish · 153, 164–166
  frozen fish · 159–161, 175
  lightly-preserved fish · 153, 162–166, 173
  mildly heat-processed fish · 153, 167–169
  molluscan shellfish · 153, 157
  other quality aspects · 178–183
  raw fish · 153, 158–162
  raw materials · 153–156, 166–168, 178
  semi-preserved fish · 153, 166–169
Hard water · 116, 120
Hazard · 7, 26–84
  definition · 26
  preventive measures · 34, 36, 38, 39, 43–46, 50, 52, 55, 59, 63, 75
Hazard analysis · 135–144
  definition · 136
Heat processed products · 42
Helminths · 61
  life cycles · 61
Hepatitis · 24, 37, 57–59, 157
  type A · 57–59
  type non-B · 58, 157
Heterophyes sp. · See Trematodes
Histamine · 22–24, 52–56, 158–170
  control · 55
  formation · 54
  guidelines levels · 56
  heat resistance · 55
  poisoning · 52–55
Histamine N-methyltransferase (HMT) · 53
Histidine · 53–56, 163
Hydrogen peroxide · 119

I

Ice · 56, 102, 109
  safety · 109, 114
Indicator organisms · 23, 113, 196
Indigenous bacteria · 54

Insecticides · 77, 105, 126 *See* Chemicals (organic compounds)
International standards · 12. 96
International Standards Organization · *See* ISO
Intestinal flukes · *See Trematodes*
Iodine · 40, 60, 119–121
Iodophors · 119
ISO · 10, 12, 110, 146, 150, 210
  10011 · 146
  14000 · 12
  9000 · 12
  mission · 12

K

Kanagawa reaction · 35
kepone · 77

L

LAB · *See* Lactic acid bacteria
Lactic acid bacteria · 40–43, 55, 164, 205–207
Lag time · 204–206
Lead · *See* Chemicals (inorganic chemicals)
Lightly preserved products · 207
Listeria monocytogenes · 14, 22, 27–31, 40–43, 119, 162, 167, 189–193, 200, 205
Listeriosis · 40–43, 189
  control · 43
  symptoms · 41
Liver flukes · *See Trematodes*
Logistic model · 204
Low acid canned food · 34
Lung flukes · *See Trematodes*

M

Mackerel · 4, 53
Mahi-mahi · 54
Mercury · 23, 77–79, 154
Metagonimus yokagawai · See Trematodes
Microbiological criteria (MC) · 16, 44, 52, 109, 133, 186, 190, 194–203
  definition · 195
Microbiological limits · 140, 196, 199
  fish · 199
  guideline · 199
Molluscan shellfish · 19–21, 28, 36, 57–59, 70, 76, 153, 157, 173, 186
Molluscs · 21, 27, 36, 57, 65, 75, 79, 157, 198–200
Monitoring Programmes · 184
Morganella morganii · 54
Muscle · 37, 54, 72, 157
Mussels · 41, 70, 83, 157, 189

N

Nematodes · 61–64, 69
  angiostrongylus sp. · 61, 64
  anisakis sp. · 61–63
  capillaria philippensis · 61
  capillaria sp. · 64
  control · 63
  gnathostoma sp. · 61, 64
  life cycles · 61, 64–68
Neurotoxic shellfish poisoning · *See* NSP
Nitrosamines · 77
NLV gastroenteritis · 58
Non-indigenous bacteria · 158
Norwalk virus · 20, 57, 157
NSP · 70, 73
  symptoms · 73

O

Off-flavours · *See* Spoilage (control)
Off-odours · *See* Spoilage (control)
Opisthorchiasis · 68
Opisthorchis sp. · See Trematodes
Oxidation · *See* Spoilage (Chemical)
Oysters · *See* Molluscs
Ozone · *See* Disinfectants

P

Paragonimus sp. · See Trematodes
Paralytic shellfish poisoning · *See* PSP
Parasites · 23, 60, 154, 163–173
  prevention · 63, 159, 163
Peroxy Compounds · 119
PFP · *See* Tetrodotoxin
Photobacterium phosphoreum · 54, 206
Phycotoxins · 70
Physical hazards · 84
Plant · 103–109, 121–130, 218
  building requirements · 104
  disinfectants · 117, 121
  equipment · 107
  location · 104
Plesiomonas shigelloides · 27, 30, 45
Polychlorinated biphenyls · *See* Chemicals (organic compounds)
Potentiator · 53
Prawn · 4, 39
Preservative parameters · 69
Preservatives · 33, 140, 153, 162, 166
Preventive measure · 28, 124, 134, 154, 157–159, 162–164
Process criteria · 202
Prorocentrum sp. · 185
Protozoans · 69
  prevention · 70
Pseudoterranova dicipiens · 62
PSP · 21, 71, 76, 199
  bloom · 72
  stability · 72
  symptoms · 72
Puffer fish · 70, 74, 162
Puffer fish poisoning · *See* PFP
Putrescine · 53
Pyrodinium · 71

Q

Quality assurance (QA) · 10–12, 21, 96, 99, 103, 211
Quality control (QC) · 7, 10, 40, 145
  definition · 11
  traditional program · 7
Quality Management (QM) · 10, 12
Quality Systems · 7, 10, 13, 121
Quantitative risk assessment · 14, 26, 78, 189, 193, 208, 210
Quaternary ammonium compounds · 60, 119–121

R

Raw fish · 29, 42, 68, 153, 158–162, 192, 200
  consumption · 158–162
  hazard · 158
  preventive measures · 158
Risk analysis · 13–17, 146
  definition · 13

objectives · 15
steps · 13
Risk assessment · 1, 13–17, 19–84
Risk communication · 17
Risk management · 13, 16, 189, 193

S

S. aureus gastroenteritis · 44
Salmonella · 20–24, 27–29, 46–50, 198–200
Salt · 33, 63, 116, 120, 153, 162–164, 171–176, 181
salting · 45, 56, 69, 173, 190
Sanitation · 10, 39, 102–115, 123
definition · 102, 115
Saxitoxin · 53, 71
Scombridae · 56
Selenium · *See* Chemicals (inorganic chemicals)
shelf-life · 56, 204–208
products · 204
Shelf-life · 204–208
seafood · 204
Shellfish · 19–21, 36–38, 46, 57–60, 70–79, 153–157, 173, 185, 200
molluscan shellfish · 153, 157, 173
outbreaks · 19, 21, 73
pathogenic bacteria · 26, 28, 153, 156, 186
toxins · 70, 153
viruses · 57, 186
Shigella · 20, 27–29, 46, 48–50
Shrimp · 4, 22, 27, 42, 81–83, 167, 200
vaccines · 82
Spermidine · 53
Spermine · 53
Spoilage · 29, 33, 46, 99, 174, 178–182, 204–207
chemical · 179
control · 173
FSP (Food Spoilge Predictor · 207
microorganisms · 178, 181, 204–206
off-flavour · 29, 179
predective growth models · 204
SSP (Seafood Spoilage Predictor) · 207
SPS · 13, 96–98, 145
agreement · 13, 96–98, 145
Storage · 26, 33–40, 45, 50, 59, 69, 84, 102–104, 109, 126–130, 136, 153, 163, 166, 181, 189–191, 205
Storage trials · 204, 206
Sulphites · *See* Chemicals (inorganic chemicals)

T

TBT · 96, 134
agreement · 97–99
Tetrodotoxin · 16, 20, 72, 74
PFP · 74–76
symptoms · 74
Total Quality Management (TQM) · 10, 13
Toxins · 26, 31, 45, 49, 70–77, 154–172, 185, 189–199
biotoxins · 70, 154–173, 185
biotoxins (control) · 154
bloom · 70–73, 184
diseases · 19, 77, 192
monitoring · 70, 76
prevention · 75–77, 154
stability · 72
Transport · 129, 181, 186
Trematodes · 61, 65-69
intestinal flukes · 66–68
Clonorchis sp. · 61
control · 68
Echinostomatidae · 67
flukes · 61, 66–68
Heterophyes sp. · 61, 67
intestinal flukes · 66–68
Metagonimus yokagawai · 61, 67
life cycles · 61, 66
liver flukes · 66
Opisthorchis. · 61, 67
lung flukes · 66
Paragonimus sp. · 61, 67
Metagonimus yokagawai · 61, 67
Trimethylamine · *See* Potentiator
Trimethylamine oxide (TMAO) · 53, 179
TTX · *See* Tetrodotoxin
Tuna · 23, 54–56, 154, 181
chilling · 55, 154
histamine · 23, 54
pathogenic bacteria · 23
processing line · 181

U

UV · *See* Disinfectants

V

V. parahaemolyticus gastroenteritis · 37
Vibrio sp. · 20–23, 27, 30, 35–44, 153, 157
V. cholerae · 38–40
symptoms · 39
Vibrio parahaemolyticus · 35–37
symptoms · 35
Vibrio vulnificus · 37
symptoms · 37
Vibrionaceae · 35, 45, 167
Viruses · 57–60, 186
fish · 58

W

Water quality · 109–114, 186
control · 40, 114
criteria · 109, 114
drinking water · 39, 58, 109–111
model prerequisite programme · 114
monitoring · 113
residual levels · 111
treatment · 110, 114, 117
WTO · 96–99

Z

Zoonotic · 46, 50